Bantam Books by Daniel Keyes

FLOWERS FOR ALGERNON (CHARLY)
THE MINDS OF BILLY MILLIGAN

THE MINDS OF BILLY MILLIGAN

DANIEL KEYES

BANTAM BOOKS
TORONTO · NEW YORK · LONDON · SYDNEY

To the victims of child abuse,
especially those in hiding . . .

This low-priced Bantam Book
has been completely reset in a type face
designed for easy reading, and was printed
from new plates.

THE MINDS OF BILLY MILLIGAN
A Bantam Book

PRINTING HISTORY
Random House edition published October 1981

A Selection of Bertelsmann Book Club, Preferred Choice Book Plan, Quality
Paperback Book Club, September 1981 and Book-of-the-Month Club.
Serialized in Penthouse magazine.

"Adalana," "Christine," "The Rag Doll" and "The Bitch: Portrait
of April," courtesy of William and Lola Sowry.
"Dr. David Caul," courtesy of Dr. David Caul.
"The Grace of Cathleen," courtesy of Sammi George, the Barefoot
Gallery, Photographs taken by Daniel Keyes.

Bantam edition / December 1982

ISBN 0-553-22585-5

Published simultaneously in the United States and Canada

Bantam Books are published by Bantam Books, Inc. Its trademark, consisting of the words "Bantam Books" and the por-
trayal of a rooster, is Registered in U.S. Patent and Trademark
Office and in other countries. Marca Registrada. Bantam
Books, Inc., 666 Fifth Avenue, New York, New York 10103.

PRINTED IN THE UNITED STATES OF AMERICA

H   0 9 8 7 6 5 4 3 2 1

ACKNOWLEDGMENTS

In addition to the hundreds of meetings and conversations with William Stanley Milligan, this book was developed from interviews with sixty-two people whose lives touched his. Although most of these people are clearly identified as they appear in the story, I would like to express my gratitude for their help.

I would like, also, to thank personally the following, whose cooperation played an important part in my research and investigations, and in the beginning, development and publication of this book:

Dr. David Caul, clinical director of the Athens Mental Health Center; Dr. George Harding, Jr., director of Harding Hospital; Dr. Cornelia Wilbur; Gary Schweickart and Judy Stevenson, public defenders; L. Alan Goldsberry and Steve Thompson, attorneys-at-law; Dorothy Moore and Del Moore, Milligan's mother and present stepfather; Kathy Morrison, Milligan's sister; and Milligan's close friend Mary.

I am grateful for the cooperation of the staffs of the following institutions: the Athens Mental Health Center, Harding Hospital (especially Ellie Jones, public relations), the Ohio State University police department, the Ohio prosecutor's office, the Columbus police department, the Lancaster police department.

My thanks and respect to two of the Ohio State University rape victims (portrayed by the pseudonyms Carrie Dryer and Donna West), who volunteered to give, in detail, the victims' point of view.

I should like to thank my agent-attorney, Donald Engel, for his confidence and support in launching the project, and to my editor, Peter Gethers, whose unflagging enthusiasm and critical eye helped me get the material under control.

Although most people were eager to cooperate, several preferred not to talk to me, and I want to make clear the source of my material about them:

Dr. Harold T. Brown of the Fairfield Mental Health Clinic, who treated Milligan when he was fifteen, is represented in his comments, thoughts and insights by quotations and paraphrases from his case notes. Dorothy Turner and Dr. Stella Karolin of the Southwest Community Mental Health Center, who discovered and first diagnosed Milligan's multiple personalities, are described through his clear memory of meetings with them, corroborated by their written reports, their sworn court testimony and descriptions of other psychiatrists and attorneys who knew and spoke with them at the time.

Chalmer Milligan, William's adoptive father (identified at the trial and by the media as his "stepfather") refused to discuss the allegations against him, and refused my offer to tell his side of the story. In statements he sent to newspapers and magazines and in publicized interviews, he denied William's accusations of "threatening, abusing and sodomizing him." Chalmer Milligan's alleged actions are, therefore, derived from trial transcripts, which were supported by depositions from relatives and neighbors and corroborated in my taped interviews with his daughter, Challa; his adopted daughter, Kathy; his adopted son, Jim; his former wife, Dorothy; and, of course, William Milligan.

I would like to give special recognition and express my appreciation to my daughters, Hillary and Leslie, for their help and understanding during the difficult days of researching this material, and to my wife, Aurea, who in addition to making her usual helpful editorial suggestions listened to hundreds of hours of interview tapes and logged them into a retrieval system so that I could find and cross-check conversations and information. Without her encouragement and help, this book would have taken many more years to write.

PREFACE

This book is the factual account of the life, up to now, of William Stanley Milligan, the first person in U.S. history to be found not guilty of major crimes, by reason of insanity, because he possessed multiple personalities.

Unlike other multiple personalities in psychiatric and popular literature who were kept anonymous at the outset by the use of fictional names, Milligan became a controversial public figure from the moment he was arrested and indicted. His face appeared on the front pages of newspapers and on the covers of magazines. Results of his mental examinations made evening television news programs and newspaper headlines around the world. He is also the first multiple personality patient to have been carefully examined around the clock as an inpatient in a hospital setting, with findings of multiplicity attested to in sworn testimony by four psychiatrists and a psychologist.

I first met the twenty-three-year-old man at the Athens Mental Health Center in Athens, Ohio, shortly after he had been sent there by the courts. When he asked me to write his story, I told him it would depend on whether or not there was more to it than had been reported extensively in the media. He assured me that the deeper secrets of his inner people had never been revealed to anyone, including his attorneys and the psychiatrists who had examined him. Now he wanted the world to understand his mental illness. I was skeptical but interested.

Several days after I met him, my curiosity was further aroused by the last paragraph of a *Newsweek* article entitled "The Ten Faces of Billy":

There remain, however, unanswered questions: How did Milligan learn the Houdini-like escape skill demonstrated by Tommy [one of his personalities]? What about his conversations with his rape victims in which he claimed to be a "guerrilla" and a "hit man"? Doctors think that Milligan may have personalities yet unfathomed—and that some of them may have committed undiscovered crimes.

When I talked with him alone during visiting hours in his room at the mental hospital, I discovered that Billy, as he came to be called, was very different from the poised young man I'd first met. He now spoke hesitantly, his knees jiggling nervously. His memory was poor, with long periods blanked out by amnesia. He could generalize about those portions of his past that he vaguely recalled, his voice often quavering at painful memories, but he could not provide many details. After trying, vainly, to draw out his experiences, I was ready to give it up.

Then one day something startling happened.

Billy Milligan fused completely for the first time, revealing a new individual, an amalgam of all his personalities. The fused Milligan had a clear, almost total recall of all the personalities from their creation—all their thoughts, actions, relationships, tragic experiences and comic adventures.

I mention this at the outset so that the reader will understand how I was able to record Milligan's past events, private feelings and solitary conversations. All the material in this book was given to me by the fused Milligan, his other personalities and sixty-two people whose paths crossed his at different stages in his life. Scenes and dialogue are re-created from Milligan's recollections. Therapy sessions are taken directly from videotapes. I have invented nothing.

One serious problem we faced as I began to write was developing a chronology. Because Milligan had "lost time" frequently since early childhood, he rarely paid attention to clocks or calendars and was often too embarrassed to admit not knowing the day or month. I was able, finally, to arrange events in time by using bills, receipts, insurance reports, school records, employment records and the many other documents turned over to me by his mother, sister, employers, attorneys and physicians. Though Milligan rarely dated his correspondence, his former girl friend had kept the hundreds of letters he wrote to her during his two years in prison, and I was able to date them by the postmarks on the envelopes.

As we worked, Milligan and I agreed on two basic ground rules:

First, all people, places and institutions would be identified by their real names, except for three groups of individuals whose privacy had to be protected by pseudonyms: other mental patients; unindicted criminals with whom Milligan had been involved, both as a juvenile and as an adult, and whom I was not able to interview directly; and the three Ohio State University rape victims, including the two who agreed to be interviewed by me.

Second, to assure Milligan that he would not incriminate himself in the event some of his personalities revealed crimes for which he might still be indicted, we agreed that I would use "poetic license" in dramatizing these scenes. On the other hand, those crimes for which Milligan has already stood trial are reported in hitherto unrevealed detail.

Of those who have met, worked with or been victimized by Billy Milligan, most have come to accept the diagnosis of his having multiple personalities. Many of these people remembered the thing Milligan said or did that made them finally admit, "He just can't be faking this." Others still feel he is a fraud, a brilliant con man using the plea of not guilty by reason of insanity to avoid prison. I sought out as many people in both groups as would talk to me. They gave me their reactions and their reasons.

I, too, maintained an attitude of skepticism. Hardly a day went by when I wasn't pulled one way and then the other. But during the two years I worked with Milligan on this book, the doubt I felt when his recalled acts and experiences seemed incredible turned to belief when my investigation showed them to be accurate.

That the controversy still absorbs Ohio newspapers can be seen from an article in the *Dayton Daily News* of January 2, 1981—three years and two months after the last crimes were committed:

FAKE OR VICTIM? EITHER WAY, MILLIGAN CASE ILLUMINATING
by Joe Fenley

William Stanley Milligan is a troubled man living a troubled existence.

He is either a con man who has duped society and beaten the rap for violent crimes or he is an authentic victim of a multiple personality disorder. Either way it's a bad scene . . .

Only time will tell whether Milligan has played the world for a fool or is one of its saddest victims . . .

Perhaps the time is now.

D.K.
Athens, Ohio
January 3, 1981

THE PEOPLE INSIDE

The Ten

The only ones known to psychiatrists, attorneys, police and the media at the time of the trial.

1. *William Stanley Milligan ("Billy")*, 26. The original, or core, personality, later referred to as "the unfused Billy," or "Billy-U." High school dropout. Six feet tall, 190 pounds. Blue eyes, brown hair.

2. *Arthur*, 22. The Englishman. Rational, emotionless, he speaks with a British accent. Self-taught in physics and chemistry, he studies medical books. Reads and writes fluent Arabic. Though he is staunchly conservative and considers himself a capitalist, he is an avowed atheist. The first to discover the existence of all the others, he dominates in safe places, deciding who in the "family" will come out and hold the consciousness. Wears glasses.

3. *Ragen Vadascovinich*, 23. The keeper of hate. His name is derived from "rage-again." Yugoslavian, he speaks English with a noticeable Slavic accent, and reads, writes and speaks Serbo-Croatian. A weapons and munitions authority as well as a karate expert, he displays extraordinary strength, stemming from the ability to control his adrenaline flow. He is a communist and atheist. His charge is to be the protector of the family, and of women and children in general. He dominates the consciousness in dangerous places. Has associated with criminals and drug addicts, and admits to criminal, sometimes violent behavior. Weighs 210 pounds, has enormous arms, black hair and a long, drooping mustache. He sketches in black and white because he is color-blind.

4. *Allen*, 18. The con man. A manipulator, he is the one who most often deals with outsiders. He is an agnostic, and his

attitude is, "Make the best of life on earth." He plays the drums, paints portraits and is the only one of the personalities who smokes cigarettes. Has a close relationship with Billy's mother. Same height as William, though he weighs less (165). Hair parted on right, he is the only one who is right-handed.

5. *Tommy*, 16. The escape artist. Often mistaken for Allen, he is generally belligerent and antisocial. Plays the saxophone and is an electronics specialist and a painter of landscapes. Muddy-blond hair and amber-brown eyes.

6. *Danny*, 14. The frightened one. Afraid of people, especially men. He was forced to dig his own grave and was then buried alive. Thus he paints only still lifes. Shoulder-length blond hair, blue eyes, short and slender.

7. *David*, 8. The keeper of pain, or the empath. Absorbs all the hurt and suffering of the other personalities. Highly sensitive and perceptive, but has a short attention span. Confused most of the time. Dark reddish-brown hair, blue eyes, physically small.

8. *Christene*, 3. The corner child, so called because she was the one to stand in the corner in school. A bright little English girl, she can read and print, but has dyslexia. Likes to draw and color pictures of flowers and butterflies. Blond shoulder-length hair, blue eyes.

9. *Christopher*, 13. Christene's brother. Speaks with a British accent. Obedient but troubled. Plays the harmonica. Hair brownish-blond like Christene's, but his bangs are shorter.

10. *Adalana*, 19. The lesbian. Shy, lonely and introverted, she writes poetry, cooks and keeps house for the others. Adalana has long, stringy black hair, and since her brown eyes occasionally drift from side to side with nystagmus, she is said to have "dancing eyes."

The Undesirables
Suppressed by Arthur because they possessed undesirable traits. Revealed, for the first time, at the Athens Mental Health Center to Dr. David Caul.

11. *Philip*, 20. The thug. New Yorker, has a strong Brooklyn accent, uses vulgar language. References to "Phil" gave police and media the clue that there were more personalities than the ten known ones. Has committed minor crimes. Curly brown hair, hazel eyes, beak nose.

12. *Kevin*, 20. The planner. A small-time criminal, he planned the Gray Drug Store robbery. Likes to write. Blond hair, green eyes.

13. *Walter*, 22. The Australian. Fancies himself a big-game hunter. Has an excellent sense of direction and is often used as a "spotter." Suppressed emotions. Eccentric. Has a mustache.

14. *April*, 19. The bitch. Boston accent. She is filled with thoughts and plans of diabolical revenge against Billy's stepfather. The others say she is insane. Does the sewing and helps with the housekeeping. Black hair, brown eyes.

15. *Samuel*, 18. The wandering Jew. Orthodox in his religion, he is the only one who believes in God. Sculptor and woodcarver. Black curly hair and beard, brown eyes.

16. *Mark*, 16. The workhorse. No initiative. Does nothing unless he's told by the others. Takes care of monotonous labor. If there is nothing to do, he will stare at the wall. Sometimes referred to as "the zombie."

17. *Steve*, 21. The perpetual impostor. Laughs at people as he imitates them. An egomaniac, he is the only one of the inner selves who has never accepted the diagnosis of multiple personality. His mocking imitations often cause trouble for the others.

18. *Lee*, 20. The comedian. Prankster, clown, wit, his practical jokes get the others into fights, and causes them to be thrown into solitary confinement in prison. Doesn't care about life or the consequences of his actions. Dark-brown hair, hazel eyes.

19. *Jason*, 13. The pressure valve. With his hysterial reactions and temper tantrums, which often result in punishment, he releases the built-up pressures. Carries off bad memories so

the others can forget them, causing amnesia. Brown hair, brown eyes.

20. *Robert (Bobby)*, 17. The daydreamer. Constantly fantasizes of travel and adventure. Though he dreams of making the world a better place, he has no ambition or intellectual interests.

21. *Shawn*, 4. The deaf one. Short attention span and is often assumed to be retarded. Makes buzzing sounds to feel the vibrations in his head.

22. *Martin*, 19. The snob. A New Yorker and flashy show-off. Boasts and puts on airs. Wants things without earning them. Blond hair, gray eyes.

23. *Timothy (Timmy)*, 15. Worked in a florist shop, where he had an encounter with a homosexual who made advances that frightened him. Went into his own world.

The Teacher

24. *The Teacher*, 26. The sum of all twenty-three alter egos fused into one. Taught the others everything they've learned. Brilliant, sensitive, with a fine sense of humor. He says, "I am Billy all in one piece," and refers to the others as "the androids I made." The Teacher has almost total recall, and his emergence and cooperation made this book possible.

CONTENTS

CONTENTS

BOOK ONE
THE MIX-UP TIME

CHAPTER ONE

(1)

On Saturday, October 22, 1977, University Police Chief John Kleberg placed the area of Ohio State University's medical school under heavy police security. Armed officers patrolled the campus in cruisers and on foot, and armed observers watched from rooftops. Women were warned not to walk alone, and to be cautious of men when entering their cars.

For the second time in eight days, a young woman had been kidnapped from the campus, at gunpoint, between seven and eight o'clock in the morning. The first was a twenty-five-year-old optometry student, the second a twenty-four-year-old nurse. Each had been driven into the countryside, raped, made to cash checks and then robbed.

The newspapers published police photographic composites, and the public responded with hundreds of phone calls, names and descriptions—all worthless. There were no significant leads and no suspects. Tension in the university community mounted. Pressure on Chief Kleberg grew more intense as student organizations and community groups demanded the capture of the man Ohio newspapers and TV broadcasters had begun to refer to as "the Campus Rapist."

Kleberg put Eliot Boxerbaum, the young investigations supervisor, in charge of the manhunt. A self-styled liberal, Boxerbaum had become involved in police work while attending OSU following the student disturbances that closed the campus down in 1970. After his graduation that year, he was offered a job in the university police department if he would cut his long hair and shave off his mustache. He cut his hair, but he balked at shaving his mustache. They hired him anyway.

3

As Boxerbaum and Kleberg examined the photographic composites and the data provided by the two victims, everything seemed to point to a single assailant: a white American male, between twenty-three and twenty-seven, weighing between 175 and 185 pounds, with brown or reddish-brown hair. Both times the man had worn a brown jogging top, jeans and white sneakers.

Carrie Dryer, the first victim, remembered that the rapist wore gloves and carried a small revolver. Occasionally his eyes drifted from side to side—the symptom of an eye condition she recognized as nystagmus. He had handcuffed her to the inside door of her car and drove her to a desolate country area, where he raped her. After the rape he told her, "If you go to the police, don't give them my description. If I see anything in the newspaper, I'll send someone after you." As if to prove he meant business, he took names from her address book.

Donna West, a short, plump nurse, said her assailant carried an automatic pistol. There was something on his hands—not dirt or grease, but an oily stain of some kind. At one point he had said his name was Phil. He cursed a lot. He wore brown-tinted sunglasses, and she never saw his eyes. He took the names of relatives and warned her that if she identified him, she or someone in her family would be harmed by a "brotherhood" that would carry out his threats. She, and the police, assumed he was boasting about being part of a terrorist organization or the Mafia.

Kleberg and Boxerbaum were confused by only one significant difference in the two descriptions. The first man was described as having a full, neatly trimmed mustache. The second was described as having a three-day growth of beard but no mustache.

Boxerbaum smiled. "I guess between the first time and the second he shaved it off."

At the Central Police Station in downtown Columbus, Detective Nikki Miller, assigned to the Sexual Assault Squad, checked in for the second shift at three o'clock. Wednesday, October 26. She had just returned from a two-week vacation in Las Vegas, feeling and looking refreshed, her tan complementing her brown eyes and feathercut sandy hair. Detective Gramlich of the first shift told her he was transporting a young rape victim to University Hospital. Since it would be Miller's case, Gramlich gave her the few details he had.

Polly Newton, a twenty-one-year-old student at Ohio State, had been abducted behind her apartment near the university campus at about eight o'clock that morning. After she parked her boyfriend's blue Corvette, she was forced back inside and told to drive out to an isolated area in the countryside, where she was raped. Her assailant then made her drive back to Columbus to cash two checks, before having her drive him back to the campus area. Then he suggested that she cash another check, stop payment, and keep the money herself.

Because Nikki Miller had been on vacation, she hadn't read of the university Campus Rapist or seen the composites. Detectives on the first shift filled her in on the details.

"The facts of this case," Miller noted in her report, "are similar to those of two rape/abductions . . . being handled by the Ohio State University Police, that occurred in their jurisdiction."

Nikki Miller and her partner, Officer A. J. Bessell, drove to University Hospital to interview Polly Newton, an auburn-haired girl.

The man who abducted her, Polly said, had told her that he was a member of the Weathermen, but that he also had another identity—as a businessman—and drove a Maserati. After Polly was treated at the hospital, she agreed to accompany Miller and Bessell to search for the place she'd been forced to drive to. But it was getting dark and she was becoming confused. She agreed to try again the following morning.

The Crime Scene Search Unit dusted her car for fingerprints. They found three partial prints with sufficient ridge detail to be used for comparison with any future suspects.

Miller and Bessell drove Polly back to the Detective Bureau to work with the department artist at making a composite drawing. Then Miller asked Polly to look through photographs of white male sex offenders. She studied three trays of mug shots, a hundred to a tray, with no success. At ten that evening, exhausted after seven hours with the police, she stopped.

At ten-fifteen the next morning, detectives of the Assault Squad morning shift picked up Polly Newton and drove her to Delaware County. In the daylight she was able to lead them to the scene of the rape, where they found 9-millimeter bullet casings near the edge of the pond. That, she told one of the detectives, was where the man had fired his gun at some beer bottles he had tossed into the water.

When they returned to headquarters, Nikki Miller had just arrived on duty. She sat Polly in a small room directly opposite the receptionist's desk and brought in another tray of mug shots. She left Polly alone and shut the door.

A few minutes later, Eliot Boxerbaum arrived at the Detective Bureau with Donna West, the nurse who had been the second victim. He wanted her to go through the mug shots, too. He and Chief Kleberg had decided to keep the optometry student in reserve for a line-up identification in case the mug-shot evidence didn't hold up in court.

Nikki Miller sat Donna West at a table in the corridor alongside the filing cabinets and brought her three trays of mug shots. "My God," she said, "are there that many sex offenders walking the streets?" Boxerbaum and Miller waited nearby as Donna studied face after face. Looking angry and frustrated, she flipped through the photographs. She saw a face she recognized—not the man who'd raped her, but a former classmate, someone she'd seen on the street just the other day. She peeked at the back and saw he'd been arrested for indecent exposure. "Christ," she mumbled, "you never know."

Halfway through the tray, Donna hesitated at a picture of a handsome youth with muttonchop whiskers and dull, staring eyes. She jumped up, nearly knocking the chair over. "That's him! That's him! I'm positive!"

Miller had her sign her name on the back of the photograph, then got the I.D. number, checked it against the record and wrote down, "William S. Milligan." It was an old mug shot.

She then slipped the identified photograph three quarters of the way back in a tray Polly Newton had not yet looked through. She, Boxerbaum, a detective named Brush and Officer Bessell went into the room to join Polly.

Nikki Miller felt Polly must have known they were waiting for her to pick out one of the photographs in that tray. Polly fingered the cards, flipping them carefully, and when she reached the halfway point, Miller found herself growing tense. If Polly picked out the same mug shot, they had the Campus Rapist.

Polly stopped at Milligan's picture, then went past it. Miller felt the tension in her own shoulders and arms. Then Polly turned the photos back and looked again at the young man with the muttonchop whiskers. "Boy, that sure looks like him," she said, "but I can't say for sure."

Boxerbaum was hesitant about filing for a warrant for Milligan's arrest. Even though Donna West had made a positive identification, it bothered him that the picture was three years old. He wanted to wait for the fingerprint check. Detective Brush took Milligan's I.D. down to the first-floor Bureau of Criminal Identification to match his fingerprints against the ones lifted from Polly's car.

Nikki Miller was annoyed at the delay. She felt they had a good start on the man, and she wanted to go after him. But since her victim, Polly Newton, hadn't made a positive identification, she had no alternative but to wait. Two hours later the report came up. The print of the right index finger lifted from the outside glass of the Corvette's passenger door and the right ring finger and right palm were Milligan's. All fair-value prints. A ten-point match. Enough to take to court.

Boxerbaum and Kleberg still hesitated. They wanted to be absolutely sure before going after a suspect and asked that an expert be called in to evaluate the prints.

Since Milligan's prints matched those lifted from her victim's car, Nikki Miller decided to go ahead and file for kidnapping, robbery and rape. She would get a warrant for his arrest, bring him in, and then Polly would be able to look at him in a line-up.

Boxerbaum checked with his chief, Kleberg, who insisted the university police should wait for the expert. Shouldn't take more than another hour or two. Better to be certain. It was eight that evening when the outside expert agreed that the prints were Milligan's.

Boxerbaum said, "Okay, I'll file for kidnapping. That's the only crime actually committed on campus—our jurisdiction. The rape happened somewhere else." He checked out the information that had come in from the Bureau of Criminal Identification: William Stanley Milligan, a twenty-two-year-old ex-convict, had been paroled six months earlier from Ohio's Lebanon Correctional Institution. His last-known address was 933 Spring Street, Lancaster, Ohio.

Miller called for a SWAT team, and they assembled in the Assault Squad office to plan the approach. They had to find out how many people were in the apartment with Milligan. Two of the rape victims had reported him saying he was a terrorist and a hit man, and he had fired a gun in Polly's presence. They had to assume he was armed and dangerous.

Officer Craig of the SWAT team suggested a gimmick approach. He would use a dummy Domino's pizza box, pretending someone from that address had ordered it, and when Milligan opened the door, Craig would try to look inside. They agreed to the plan.

But ever since the address had come through, Boxerbaum had been puzzled. Why would an ex-convict come forty-five miles, all the way from Lancaster to Columbus, three times within two weeks to commit rape? Something wasn't right. As they were about to leave, he picked up the phone, dialed 411 and asked if there was a new listing on a William Milligan. He listened for a moment and then jotted down the address.

"He's moved, to 5673 Old Livingston Avenue, in Reynoldsburg," Boxerbaum announced. "Ten minutes away by car. On the east side. Now, that makes more sense."

Everyone looked relieved.

At nine o'clock Boxerbaum, Kleberg, Miller, Bessell and four officers from the Columbus SWAT team set out in three cars at twenty miles an hour on the freeway, their headlights bouncing back off the densest fog any of them had ever seen.

The SWAT team got there first. What should have been a fifteen-minute drive had taken an hour, and then it took another fifteen minutes to find the right address in the winding, newly laid-out street of the Channingway apartment complex. While they waited for the others to arrive, the SWAT officers spoke to some of the neighbors. There were lights on in the Milligan apartment.

When the detectives and university officers arrived, they all took positions. Nikki Miller hid out of sight on the right-hand side of the patio. Bessell went around the corner of the building. The remaining three SWAT officers took up positions on the other side. Boxerbaum and Kleberg ran around back and moved up to the double sliding glass doors.

Craig took the dummy Domino's pizza box out of the trunk of his car and scrawled on it, "Milligan—5673 Old Livingston," with a black marking pen. He pulled his shirttail out of his jeans to cover his revolver and walked casually to one of the four doors facing the patio. He rang the bell. No answer. He rang again and, hearing a noise inside, struck a bored pose, one hand holding up the pizza box and the other on his hip near his gun.

From his position behind the house, Boxerbaum saw a young man sitting in a brown easy chair in front of a large color TV set. To the left of the front door, he saw a red chair. An L-shaped living room/dining room. No one else in view. The TV watcher got up from the chair and went to answer the front doorbell.

When Craig rang the doorbell again, he saw someone peer at him through the glass panel beside the door. The door opened and a handsome young man stared at him.

"I got your pizza."

"I didn't order no pizza."

Craig tried to look past him into the apartment and could see Boxerbaum through the open drapes at the rear glass doors.

"It's the address I got. For William Milligan. That your name?"

"No."

"Somebody from here phoned the order," Craig said. "Who are you?"

"This is my friend's apartment."

"Where's your friend?"

"He ain't here right now." He spoke in a dull, halting voice.

"Well, where is he? Somebody ordered this pizza. Bill Milligan. This address."

"I don't know. The people next door know him. Maybe they can tell ya, or maybe they ordered it."

"Would you show me?"

The young man nodded, walked to the door a few steps across from his own, knocked, and waited a few seconds and knocked again. There was no answer.

Craig dropped the pizza box, pulled his gun and pressed it into the back of the suspect's head. "Freeze! I know you're Milligan!" He snapped handcuffs on him.

The young man looked dazed. "What's this for? I didn't do nothing."

Craig jabbed the gun between his shoulder blades, pulling Milligan's long hair as if yanking on reins. "Let's get back inside."

As Craig pushed him into the apartment, the other SWAT officers stormed in around him, guns leveled. Boxerbaum and Kleberg came around front to join them.

Nikki Miller had the I.D. picture out, showing a mole on Milligan's neck. "He's got the mole. Same face. It's him."

They put Milligan in the red chair, and she noticed he stared straight ahead with a dazed, trancelike expression. Sergeant Dempsey bent and looked under the chair. "Here's the gun," he said, sliding it out with a pencil. "Nine-millimeter magnum. Smith and Wesson."

A SWAT officer turned over the seat of the brown chair in front of the TV set and started to pick up a bullet clip and a plastic bag with ammunition, but Dempsey stopped him. "Hold it. We've got an arrest warrant, not a search warrant." He turned to Milligan. "You want to let us go ahead and search?"

Milligan just stared blankly.

Kleberg, knowing he didn't need a search warrant to check whether anyone else was in the other rooms, wandered into the bedroom and saw the brown jogging suit on the unmade bed. The place was a mess, laundry strewn all over the floor. He glanced inside the open walk-in closet, and there on the shelf, neatly stacked, were credit cards belonging to Donna West and Carrie Dryer. Even scraps of paper taken from the women. The brown-tinted sunglasses and a wallet lay on the dresser.

He went to tell Boxerbaum what he'd seen, and found him in a dinette that had been converted into an artist's studio.

"Look at this." Boxerbaum pointed to a large painting of what seemed to be a queen or an eighteenth-century aristocratic lady dressed in a blue gown with lace trim, sitting beside a piano and holding sheet music. The detail was amazing. it was signed "Milligan."

"Hey, that's beautiful," Kleberg said. He glanced at the other canvases lined up against the wall, the brushes, the tubes of paint.

Boxerbaum slapped his forehead. "The stains Donna West said he had on his hand. That's what they were. He'd been painting."

Nikki Miller, who had also seen the painting, came up to the suspect, still sitting in the chair. "You're Milligan, aren't you?"

He looked up at her, dazed. "No," he mumbled.

"That's a beautiful painting over there. Did you paint it?"

He nodded.

"Well," she said, smiling, "it's signed 'Milligan.'"

Boxerbaum walked up to Milligan. "Bill, I'm Eliot Boxerbaum of the OSU police. Will you talk to me?"

No response. There was no sign of the eye-drifting Carrie Dryer had noticed.

"Has anyone read him his rights?" No one answered, so Boxerbaum pulled out his rights card and read it aloud. He wanted to be sure. "You're accused of kidnapping those girls from the campus, Bill. Do you want to talk about it?"

Milligan looked up, shocked. "What's goin on? Did I hurt anybody?"

"You told them other people would come after them. Who are they?"

"I hope I didn't hurt anybody."

As an officer headed into the bedroom, Milligan glanced up. "Don't kick that box in there. You'll blow it up."

"A bomb?" Kleberg asked quickly.

"It's . . . in there . . ."

"Will you show me?" Boxerbaum asked.

Milligan got up slowly and walked to the bedroom. He stopped at the door and nodded in the direction of a small carton on the floor beside the dresser. Kleberg stayed with Milligan while Boxerbaum went inside to look. The other officers crowded behind Milligan in the doorway. Boxerbaum kneeled beside the box. Through the open top flap he could see wires and what looked like a clock.

He backed out of the room and said to Sergeant Dempsey, "You'd better call the fire department bomb squad. Kleberg and I are going back to the station. We'll take Milligan in."

Kleberg drove the university police car. Rockwell, from the SWAT team, sat beside him. Boxerbaum sat in back with Milligan, who didn't respond to questions about the rapes. He just leaned forward, awkward because of the handcuffs at his back, and mumbled disconnected remarks: "My brother Stuart is dead . . . Did I hurt anyone?"

"Did you know any of the girls?" Boxerbaum asked. "Did you know the nurse?"

"My mother's a nurse," Milligan mumbled.

"Tell me why you went to the OSU campus area for your victims."

"The Germans are going to come after me . . ."

"Let's talk about what happened, Bill. Was it the nurse's long black hair that attracted you?"

Milligan looked at him. "You're strange." Then, staring again, he said, "My sister's gonna hate me when she finds out."

Boxerbaum gave up.

They arrived at the Central Police Station and took their prisoner in through the back entrance up to the third-floor processing room. Boxerbaum and Kleberg went into another office to help Nikki Miller prepare the affidavits for the search warrants.

At eleven-thirty Officer Bessell read Milligan his rights again and asked if he would sign the waiver. Milligan just stared.

Nikki Miller heard Bessell say, "Listen, Bill, you raped three women and we want to know about it."

"Did I do that?" Milligan asked. "Did I hurt anyone? If I hurt someone, I'm sorry."

After that, Milligan sat mute.

Bessell took him to the fourth floor slating room to get him fingerprinted and photographed.

A uniformed policewoman looked up as they entered. Bessell grabbed Milligan's hand to begin the fingerprinting, but the prisoner jerked back suddenly, as if terrified to be touched by him, and moved behind the policewoman for protection.

"He's scared about something," she said. Turning to the white-faced, trembling youth, she spoke softly, as if to a child: "We've got to take your prints. Do you understand what I'm saying?"

"I—I don't want him to touch me."

"All right," she said. "I'll do it. Is that okay?"

Milligan nodded and let her fingerprint him. After the fingerprinting and photographing, an officer led him away to a holding cell.

When the search warrant forms were completed, Nikki Miller phoned Judge West. Hearing the evidence she had, and considering the urgency of the matter, he told her to come to his home, and at one-twenty that morning he signed the warrants.

Miller drove back to the Channingway apartment complex through the fog, which had gotten even worse.

Miller than phoned the mobile Crime Scene Search Unit. At two-fifteen, when they arrived at the apartment, she presented the warrants and they made the search. They listed the items removed from the suspect's apartment:

DRESSER—cash $343.00, sunglasses, handcuffs and key, wallet, I.D. for William Simms and William Milligan, charge slip to Donna West.

CLOSET—Master Charge cards to Donna West and Carrie Dryer, Clinic Card for Donna West, photograph of Polly Newton, .25 calibre [Tanfoglio Giuseppe] A.R.M.I. [sic] automatic pistol with five live rounds.

VANITY—3½ × 11 piece of paper with name and address of Polly Newton. Page from her address book.

HEADBOARD—Switchblade knife, two packets of powder.

CHEST OF DRAWERS—phone bill for Milligan, S & W holster.

UNDER RED CHAIR—Smith & Wesson 9mm with clip and six live rounds.

UNDER SEAT OF BROWN CHAIR—clip with fifteen live rounds and a plastic bag containing fifteen live rounds.

Back at the Central Police Station, Nikki Miller took the evidence to the clerk of courts, had it notarized and turned it over to the property room.

"There's enough here to go to trial with," she said.

Milligan cringed in the corner of the tiny cell, shaking violently. Suddenly, after a slight choking sound, he fainted. A minute later, he opened his eyes and stared around in astonishment at the walls, the toilet, the bunk.

"Oh God, no!" he shouted. "Not again!"

He sat on the floor, staring dully into space. Then he saw cockroaches in the corner and his expression blanked and changed. Crossing his legs, he hunched up close, his chin cupped in his hands, and smiled childishly as he studied them running in circles.

(2)

Milligan was awake a few hours later when they came to transfer him. He was handcuffed to a huge black man in a line of prisoners, which was led out of the lobby, down the stairs and out the back door to the parking area. They marched to the van bound for the Franklin County Jail.

The van drove to the center of the Columbus shopping area, to a futuristic fortress in the heart of the city. Its concrete walls jutted up two stories at an inward slope, massive and windowless. Above the second story, it loomed upward as a modern office building. The patio of the Franklin County Jail was presided over by a statue of Benjamin Franklin.

The van turned into an alleyway behind the jail and paused in front of the corrugated-steel garage door. From this angle, the jail stood in the shadow of the taller building it was attached to—the Franklin County Hall of Justice.

The steel door cranked upward. The van drove in and the door came down behind it. The handcuffed prisoners were led out of the van into the sally port, the area between the two steel drop doors beside the prison—that is, all except one. Milligan had slipped out of the handcuffs and was still in the van.

"Get down outta there, Milligan!" the officer shouted. "You goddamned sonofabitchin' rapist. What do you think is going on here?"

The black man to whom Milligan had been manacled said, "I didn't have nothin' to do with it. I swears to God he just flipped 'em off."

The jail door hissed open, and the six prisoners were herded into the passageway between the outer door and the barred area. Through the bars they could see the control center—TV monitors, computer terminals and dozens of officers, men and women in gray trousers or skirts and black shirts. When the outer door closed behind them, the inner barred gate opened and they were led inside.

The lobby was filled with black shirts moving around and the sound of computer terminal typewriters. At the entranceway, a woman officer held up a manila envelope. "Valuables," she said. "Rings, watches, jewelry, wallet." When Milligan emptied his pockets, she took his jacket, searching the lining before turning it over to the property room officer.

He was frisked again, more carefully, by the young officer, and then put into a holding cell with the other prisoners, waiting to be slated and booked. Eyes peered through the small square window. The black man nudged Milligan and said, "Ah guess you is the famous one. You got outta them cuffs. Now let's see y'all get us outta here."

Milligan looked at him blankly.

"You just keep messin' with these po-lice," he said, "they's gonna beat you to death. You c'n jus' take my word, 'cause I been in the joint many times. You evah been locked up?"

Milligan nodded. "That's why I don't like it. That's why I like to leave."

(3)

When the phone rang in the public defender's office, a block away from the jail, Gary Schweickart, the tall, bearded, thirty-three-year-old supervising attorney, was trying to light his pipe. The call was from Ron Redmond, one of the staff attorneys.

"I picked something up while I was in municipal court," Redmond said. "The police booked the Campus Rapist last night, and they've just moved him to the Franklin County Jail. They're holding him on half a million dollars' bond. You ought to get someone down there to do some first-aid counseling."

"There's no one else here right now, Ron. I'm holding the fort myself."

"Well, the word's out, and there'll be reporters from the *Citizen-Journal* and the *Dispatch* crawling all over the place. I've got a feeling the police are going to pressure the guy."

In major felony cases, in which it was likely the police might continue their investigation post-arrest, Gary Schweickart routinely chose an attorney at random to send down to the county jail. But this was no routine arrest. The wide media attention given the Campus Rapist made the breaking of this case a major coup for the Columbus police department, and Schweickart assumed they'd be hounding the prisoner for a statement or a confession. It was going to take a major effort to protect his rights.

Schweickart decided to slip over to the Franklin County Jail. Just a few words with the man to introduce himself as a public defender and to warn him not to talk to anyone but his attorney.

Schweickart was admitted to the county jail in time to see two police officers bring Milligan in through the sally port and turn him over to the sergeant in charge. Schweickart asked the officer to let him talk briefly with the prisoner.

"I don't know anything about what they say I did," Milligan whined. "I don't remember. They just came in and—"

"Look, I just wanted to introduce myself," Schweickart said. "A crowded hallway isn't the place to go into the facts of the case. We'll have a private conference in a day or so."

"But I don't remember. They found those things in my apartment and—"

"Hey, don't go into it! The walls around here have ears. And when they've got you upstairs, be careful. The police have lots of tricks. Don't talk to anyone. Even other prisoners. Some of them could be plants. There are always guys around waiting to pick up information to sell to somebody. If you want a fair trial, keep your mouth shut."

Milligan kept shaking his head and rubbing his cheek, trying to talk about the facts of the case. Then he mumbled, "Plead me not guilty. I think I may be crazy."

"We'll see," Schweickart said, "but we can't talk about it here."

"Is there a lady lawyer who could handle my case?"

"We've got a lady lawyer. I'll see what I can do."

Schweickart watched as the officer took Milligan to change from his street clothes to the blue jump suit worn by all felons in the county jail. It was going to be difficult to work with a panicky bundle of nerves like this guy. He wasn't really denying the crimes. All he was saying, over and over, was that he didn't remember. That was unusual. But the Campus Rapist pleading insanity? Schweickart could guess what a field day the newspapers would have with that.

Outside the Franklin County Jail, he bought a *Columbus Dispatch* and saw the front-page headline:

POLICE ARREST SUSPECT IN CAMPUS-AREA RAPES

The story reported that one of the victims, a twenty-six-year-old graduate student raped almost two weeks earlier, would be asked to view a police line-up to identify the suspect. And there at the top of the story was a mug shot labeled "Milligan."

Back in the public defender's office, Schweickart called the other area newspapers and asked them not to run the photograph because it might prejudice the line-up on Monday. They turned him down. If they got the picture, they said, they'd run it. Schweickart scratched his beard with the bit of his pipe, then started to phone his wife to say he'd be late for dinner.

"Hey," came a voice from the door of his office, "you look like a bear caught with his nose in a beehive."

He looked up and saw the smiling face of Judy Stevenson.

"Oh, yeah?" he growled, hanging up the receiver and smiling back. "Well, guess who asked for you?"

She brushed her long brunette hair back out of her face, revealing the beauty mark on her left cheekbone. Her hazel eyes questioned.

He pushed the newspaper toward her, pointed to the photograph and the headline, and his deep laugh filled the small office. "The line-up is Monday morning. Milligan asked for a lady lawyer. *You've* got the Campus Rapist."

(4)

Judy Stevenson arrived at the police line-up at a quarter to ten Monday morning, October 31, and when they brought Milligan to the holding cell, she saw how frightened and desperate he looked.

"I'm from the public defender's office," she said. "Gary Schweickart said you wanted a woman lawyer, so he and I will be working together. Now, just settle down. You look as if you're going to fall apart."

He handed her a folded paper. "My parole officer brought me this Friday."

She uncreased it and saw it was an "Order to Hold" from the Adult Parole Authority, to keep Milligan in custody and to inform him that a preliminary hearing on a parole violation would be held in the Franklin County Jail. Because the police had discovered weapons at his home during his arrest, she realized, his parole could be revoked and he could be immediately sent back to Lebanon prison near Cincinnati to await trial.

"The hearing is a week from this Wednesday. We'll see what we can do to keep you here. I'd rather have you in Columbus, where we can talk with you."

"I don't want to go back to Lebanon."

"Now, just take it easy."

"I don't remember doing any of the things they said I did."

"We'll have a conference later. Right now you've just got to go up on that platform and stand there. You think you can handle that?"

"I guess so."

"Brush your hair out of your face so they'll be able to see you clearly."

The police officer led him up the steps to join the others in the line, and he was placed in the number 2 position.

Four people were present at the line-up to make identification. Donna West, the nurse who had identified his mug shot, had been told she wasn't needed and had gone off to Cleveland with her fiancé. Cynthia Mendoza, a Kroger store clerk who cashed one of the checks, did not identify Milligan. She picked number 3 instead. A woman who had been sexually assaulted in August under very different circumstances said she thought it might be number 2 but she wasn't positive. Carrie Dryer said without the mustache she couldn't be sure, but number 2 did look familiar. Polly Newton made positive identification.

On November 3, the grand jury handed down an indictment on three counts of kidnapping, three counts of aggravated robbery and four counts of rape. All were first-degree felony charges, punishable by prison terms of four to twenty-five years on each count.

The prosecutor's office rarely got involved in assigning attorneys—even in major murder cases. The normal procedure was for the head of the Felony Division to assign one of the senior prosecutors two or three weeks in advance, by random selection. But County Prosecutor George Smith called in two of his top senior prosecutors and told them that the publicity surrounding the Campus Rapist case had stirred public outrage. He wanted them to handle the case and to prosecute vigorously.

Terry Sherman, thirty-two, with curly black hair and a fierce, guardman's mustache, had a reputation for coming down hard on sex offenders and boasted that he had never lost a rape case before a jury. When he looked at the file, he laughed. "It's a locked case. The warrants were good. We've got this guy. The public defenders have nothing."

Bernard Zalig Yavitch, a thirty-five-year-old member of the prosecutor's criminal-trial staff, had been two years ahead of Judy Stevenson and Gary Schweickart in law school and knew them well. Gary had been his law clerk. Yavitch had practiced law for four years as a public defender before coming to the prosecutor's office. He agreed with Sherman that it was as good a case for the prosecution as he had ever seen.

"As good?" said Sherman. "With all the physical evidence, the fingerprints, the identification, we've got it all. I tell you, they've got nothing."

Sherman talked to Judy a few days later and decided to set her straight. "There won't be any plea-bargaining on the Milligan case. We've got the guy and we're going for a conviction and the maximum sentence. You don't have anything."

But Bernie Yavitch was thoughtful. As a former public defender, he knew what he would do if he were in Judy and Gary's position. "There's still one thing they've got left—an insanity plea."

Sherman laughed.

The following day William Milligan tried to kill himself by smashing his head into his cell wall.

"He's not going to live long enough to stand trial," Gary Schweickart said to Judy Stevenson when he got the news.

"I don't think he's competent to stand trial," she said. "I think we should tell the judge we feel he is incapable of assisting in his own defense."

"You want him examined by a shrink?"

"We've got to."

"Oh my God," Gary said. "I can see the headlines now."

"The hell with the headlines. There's something wrong with this boy. I don't know what it is, but you've seen how different he appears at different times. And when he says he doesn't remember the rapes, I believe him. He should be examined."

"And who pays for it?"

"We've got funds," she said.

"Yeah, millions."

"Oh, come on, we can afford to have him tested by a psychologist."

"Tell it to the judge," Gary grumbled.

When the court agreed to a delay so that William Milligan could be examined by a psychologist, Gary Schweickart then turned his attention to the on-site hearing by the Adult Parole Authority at eight-thirty Wednesday morning.

"They're going to send me back to Lebanon," Milligan said.

"Not if we can help it," Gary said.

"They found guns in my apartment. And that was one of the conditions of my parole. 'Never purchase, own, possess, use or have under your control a deadly weapon or firearm.'"

"Well, maybe," Gary said. "But if we're going to defend you, we want you here in Columbus, where we can work with you, not off in Lebanon prison."

"What are you gonna do?"

"Just leave it to me."

Gary saw Milligan's smile, the excitement in his eyes he had not seen before. He was relaxed, easygoing, trading jokes in an almost light-hearted way. A very different person from that bundle of nerves he'd met the first day. It might be a lot easier to defend him than he'd thought.

"That's it," Gary told him. "Keep cool."

He led Milligan into the conference room, where members of the Adult Parole Authority were already passing around copies of a report by Milligan's parole officer and testimony of Sergeant Dempsey that during Milligan's arrest he had found a 9-millimeter Smith and Wesson and a .25-caliber semiautomatic with a clip of five bullets.

"Tell me, gentlemen," Schweickart asked, rubbing his beard with his knuckles, "have these weapons been test-fired?"

"No," said the chairman, "but they're genuine guns, with clips."

"If they have not been shown capable of propelling ballistics, what makes them guns?"

"Well, the test-firing won't be done until next week."

Gary slammed his open hand on the table. "But I insist you make your decision about his parole revocation today or else wait until *after* the court hearing. Now, is this a gun or is it a toy? You haven't proven to me that this thing is a gun." He looked around from one to the other.

The chairman nodded. "Gentlemen, I believe we have no alternative but to postpone the parole revocation until we determine whether or not this is a gun."

At ten-fifty the following morning, Milligan's parole officer delivered a notice that a parole revocation hearing would be held on December 12, 1977, at the Lebanon Correctional Institution. Milligan's presence was not required.

Judy went to see Milligan about the evidence the Crime Scene Search Unit had found in his apartment.

She saw the despair in his eyes when he said, "You think I did it. Don't you?"

"It's not what I think that counts, Billy. It's all this evidence we've got to deal with. We've got to review your explanation for having all this stuff in your possession."

She saw the glazed stare. He seemed to be retreating from her, drawing back into himself.

"It doesn't matter," he said. "Nothing matters anymore."

The next day she got a letter written on lined yellow legal paper:

Dear Miss Judy,

I am writing this letter because sometimes I can't say what I feel and I want you more than anything to understand.

First of all I want to thank you for everything you have done for me. You are a kind, sweet person and you did your best. That's all anyone can ask.

Now you will be able to forget about me with a clear conscience. Tell your office that I don't want *any* lawyers. I won't need one.

Now that *you* believe I am guilty, I must be. All I ever wanted to know, is for sure. All my life all I ever have done is cause pain and hurt the ones I love. The bad part is, I can't stop it because I can't help it. Locking me away in a prison will make me worse, like it did the last time. The shrinks don't know what to do because they can't figure out what is wrong.

I will now have to stop myself. I am giving up. I just don't care anymore. Would you do one last thing for me? Call Mom or Kathy and tell them not to come up here anymore. I don't want to see anyone again, so don't waste their gas. But I do love them and I am sorry. Your the best lawyer I know and I'll always remember you for being kind to me. Goodbye.

Billy

That evening the desk sergeant called Schweickart at home. "Your client tried to kill himself again."

"Oh my God! What'd he do?"

"Well, you're not going to believe this, but we've got to press charges against him for destroying county property. He shattered the toilet bowl in his cell and slashed his wrists with a sharp piece of porcelain."

"Holy shit!"

"I'll tell you something else, counselor. There's definitely something strange about your client. He smashed the bowl with his fist."

(5)

Schweickart and Stevenson ignored Milligan's letter firing them and visited him in prison daily. The public defender's office released funds to pay for a psychological evaluation, and on January 8 and 13, 1978, Dr. Willis C. Driscoll, a clinical psychologist, administered a battery of tests.

The intelligence tests showed Milligan's IQ to be 68, but Driscoll stated that Milligan's depression had lowered his score. His report diagnosed acute schizophrenia.

> He is suffering from a major loss of identity such that his ego boundaries are very poorly defined. He is experiencing schizophrenic loss of distance and has a very restricted capacity to differentiate between self and his environment. . . . He hears voices that tell him to do things and yell and scream at him when he does not comply. Milligan expresses his belief that these voices are from people who have come from hell to torment him. He also speaks of good people who periodically invade his body in order to combat the bad people. . . . In my opinion, Mr. Milligan is not capable at present, of counseling in his own behalf. He is not capable of establishing adequate contact with reality to understand events that are transpiring. I strongly urge this man to be hospitalized for further examination and possible treatment.

The first legal skirmish came on January 19, when Stevenson and Schweickart presented the report to Judge Jay C. Flowers as evidence that their client could not assist in his own defense. Flowers said he would issue an order for Southwest Community Mental Health Center in Columbus to assign its forensic psychiatry unit to examine the defendant. Gary and Judy were worried, since Southwest was usually on the side of the prosecution.

Gary insisted that whatever came out during the examination by Southwest be privileged information, not to be used against their client under any circumstances. Sherman and Yavitch disagreed. The public defenders threatened to tell Milligan not to speak with the psychologists and psychiatrists from Southwest. Judge Flowers came close to declaring them in contempt.

They came to a compromise when the prosecutors agreed that only if Milligan took the stand in his own defense would they question him about anything incriminating he might have said to the court-appointed psychologists. A partial victory was better than nothing. The public defenders finally decided to gamble and allow Southwest's forensic psychiatric unit to interview William Milligan on those terms.

"It's a good try," Sherman said, laughing, as they walked out of Judge Flowers' chambers. "Shows how desperate you guys are getting. But it's not going to do you any good. I still say this case is locked."

To prevent future suicide attempts, the sheriff's office moved Milligan to a single cell in the infirmary range and put him in a strait jacket. Later that afternoon, Russ Hill, the medic, checking on the prisoner, couldn't believe what he saw. He called Sergeant Willis, the officer in charge of the three-to-eleven shift, and pointed at Milligan through the bars. Willis' mouth gaped. Milligan had removed his strait jacket and, using it as a pillow, was fast asleep.

CHAPTER TWO

(1)

The first interview by Southwest was scheduled on January 31, 1978. Dorothy Turner, a slight, motherly psychologist with a shy, almost frightened expression, looked up when Sergeant Willis brought Milligan into the interview room.

She saw a handsome six-foot-tall young man in a blue jump suit. He had a full mustache and long sideburns, but his eyes held a childlike fear. He seemed surprised to see her, but by the time he sat in the chair opposite, he was smiling, hands folded in his lap.

"Mr. Milligan," she said, "I'm Dorothy Turner, from the Southwest Community Mental Health Center, and I'm here to ask you some questions. Where are you currently living?"

He glanced around. "Here."

"What is your social security number?"

He frowned and thought about it for a long time, gazing at the floor, the yellow cinder-block walls, the tin butt can on the table. He nibbled on his fingernail and studied the cuticle.

"Mr. Milligan," she said, "if I'm to help you, you'll have to cooperate. You have to answer my questions so I'll be able to understand what's going on. Now, what is your social security number?"

He shrugged. "I don't know."

She looked down at her notes and read off a number.

He shook his head. "That's not my number. That must be Billy's."

She glanced up sharply. "Well, aren't you Billy?"

"No," he said. "Not me."

She frowned. "Wait a minute. If you're not Billy, who are you?"

24

"I'm *David*."

"Well, where's Billy?"

"Billy's asleep."

"Asleep where?"

He pointed to his chest. "In here. He's asleep."

Dorothy Turner sighed and braced herself, nodding patiently. "I have to talk to Billy."

"Well, *Arthur* won't let you. Billy's asleep. Arthur won't wake him up, 'cause if he does, Billy'll kill himself."

She studied the young man for a long time, not sure how to proceed. His voice, his expression as he spoke, were childlike. "Now, wait a minute. I want you to explain this to me."

"I can't. I made a mistake. I wasn't even supposed to tell."

"Why not?"

"I'll get into trouble with the others." There was panic in the young voice.

"And your name is 'David'?"

He nodded.

"Who are the others?"

"I can't tell you."

She tapped the table gently. "Well, David, you've got to tell me about these things so I can help you."

"I can't," he said. "They'll get real mad at me and they won't let me on the spot anymore."

"Well, you've got to tell somebody. Because you're very scared, aren't you?"

"Yes," he said, tears forming in his eyes.

"It's important for you to trust me, David. You've got to let me know what's going on so I can help."

He thought about it long and hard, and finally he shrugged. "Well, I'll tell ya on one condition. You got to promise you won't never tell the secret to nobody in the whole world. Nobody. Never. Never. Never."

"Yes," she said. "I promise."

"In your whole life?"

She nodded.

"Say you promise."

"I promise."

"Okay," he said. "I'll tell ya. I don't know everything. Only Arthur does. Like you said, I'm scared, because a lot of times I don't know what's going on."

"How old are you, David?"

"Eight, going on nine."

"And why are you the one who came to talk to me?"

"I didn't even know I was coming on the spot. Somebody got hurt in the jail and I came to take the pain."

"Would you explain that?"

"Arthur says I'm the keeper of the pain. When there's hurt, I'm the one who takes the spot and feels it."

"That must be awful."

Tears brimmed in his eyes as he nodded. "It's not fair."

"What's 'the spot,' David?"

"That's what Arthur calls it. He explained to us how it works when one of the people has to come out. It's a big white spotlight. Everybody stands around it, watching or sleeping in their beds. And whoever steps on the spot is out in the world. Arthur says, 'Whoever is on the spot holds the consciousness.'"

"Who are the *other* people?"

"There are a lot. I don't know them all. I know some of them now, but not everyone. Oh, wow." He gasped.

"What's the matter?"

"I told you Arthur's name. Now for sure I'll get in trouble for telling the secret."

"It's all right, David. I promised I wouldn't tell."

He cringed in his chair. "I can't talk no more. I'm scared."

"All right, David. That's enough for today, but I'll come back tomorrow and talk to you some more."

Outside the Franklin County Jail, she stopped and pulled her coat tightly around her against the cold wind. She had come prepared to face down a young felon who might be feigning insanity to avoid prosecution, but she had never expected anything like this.

(2)

The next day Dorothy Turner noticed something different in Milligan's expression as he entered the interview room. He avoided her eyes and sat in the chair with his knees drawn up, playing with his shoes. She asked how he was feeling.

He didn't respond at first, looking around, glancing at her from time to time with no sign of recognition. Then he shook his head, and when he spoke it was as a boy with a cockney accent. "Everythin' is loud," he said. "You. All the sounds. Oye don't know what's goin' on."

"Your voice seems funny, David. Is that an accent?"

He peered up at her impishly. "Oy'm not David. Oy'm *Christopher.*"

"Well, where's David?"

"David's been naughty."

"What do you mean?"

"Oh, the others are awful mad at 'im 'cause 'e told."

"Will you explain that to me?"

"Oye can't. Oye don't want t'get inter trouble loike David."

"Well, why is he in trouble?" she asked, frowning.

" 'Cause 'e told."

"Told what?"

"You know. 'E told the secret."

"Well then, will you tell me some things about yourself, Christopher? How old are you?"

"Thirteen."

"And what do you like to do?"

"Oye play the drums a little, but Oy'm better on the 'armonica."

"And where are you from?"

"England."

"Do you have any brothers or sisters?"

"Just Christene. She's three years old."

She watched his face closely as he spoke in his crisp cockney accent. He was open, earnest, happy, so different from the person she had spoken to just the day before. Milligan had to be an incredibly good actor.

(3)

On February 4, her third visit, Dorothy Turner noticed that the young man who walked into the interview room had a different bearing than she had seen either of the other two times. He sat casually, slouched back in the chair, gazing at her arrogantly.

"How are you today?" she asked, almost afraid of what he might answer.

He shrugged. "Awright."

"Could you tell me how David and Christopher are doing?"

He frowned and glared at her. "Hey, lady, I don't even know you."

"Well, I've come here to help you. We have to talk about what's going on."

"Shit, I don't even know what's going on."

"Don't you remember talking to me the day before yesterday?"

"Hell, no. I ain't never seen you in my life."

"Could you tell me your name?"

"Tommy."

" 'Tommy' who?"

"Just Tommy."

"And your age?"

"Sixteen."

"And could you tell me a little bit about yourself?"

"Lady, I don't talk to strangers. So leave me alone."

For the next fifteen minutes she tried to draw him out, but "Tommy" remained sullen. When she left the Franklin County Jail, Dorothy Turner stood on Front Street for a while, dazed, thinking about "Christopher" and of her promise to "David" never to reveal the secret. Now she was torn between her promise and her realization that Milligan's attorneys had to be told about this. Later she phoned the public defender's office and asked for Judy Stevenson.

"Look," she said when Stevenson got on the line, "I can't really talk with you about it right now, but if you haven't read the book *Sybil*, get yourself a copy and read it."

Judy Stevenson, surprised by the call from Turner, bought a paperback copy of *Sybil* that evening and began to read it. Once she understood where it was going, she lay back in bed and stared at the ceiling, thinking: Oh, come on! A multiple personality? Is that what Turner was trying to tell her? She tried to visualize the Milligan who had trembled so badly at the line-up; she thought of the other times he'd been talkative and manipulative, trading jokes, quick-witted. She'd always attributed his changed behavior to depression. And then she thought of the stories Sergeant Willis told about the slippery character who could get out of any strait jacket, and medic Russ Hill's comments about the superhuman strength he showed at times. Milligan's words echoed in her mind: *I don't remember what they said I did. I don't know anything.*

She thought of waking her husband and talking to him about it, but she knew what Al would say. She knew what anyone would say if she tried to tell them what she was thinking now. In more than three years in the public defender's office, she'd

never come up against anyone like Milligan. She decided to
say nothing to Gary yet, either. She had to check it out for
herself.

The next morning she called Dorothy Turner. "Look," she
said, "the Milligan I've met and talked to for the past few
weeks has acted strange at times. There have been changes of
mood. He's temperamental. But I haven't seen the major
differences that would lead me to conclude it's like the *Sybil*
case."

"This is something I've been struggling with for days,"
Turner said. "I promised not to tell anyone and I've stuck to
that. All I told you was to read that book. But I am going to try
to get him to agree to let me tell you the secret."

Reminding herself that this was a psychologist from Southwest—from the prosecutor's side—Judy said, "You take the
lead. Let me know what you want me to do."

When Dorothy Turner came back to see Milligan for the fourth
time, she met the frightened little boy who had called himself
David that first day.

"I know I promised never to tell the secret," she said, "but
I've got to tell Judy Stevenson."

"No!" he shouted, jumping to his feet. "You promised! Miss
Judy won't like me anymore if you tell her."

"She will like you. She's your lawyer and she needs to know
so she can help you."

"You promised. If you break a promise, that's like a lie. You
can't tell. I got into trouble. Arthur and Ragen are mad at me
for letting the secret slip out, and—"

"Who's 'Ragen'?"

"You made a promise. And promises are the most important
things in the world."

"Don't you understand, David? If I don't tell Judy, she won't
be able to save you. You might even go to jail for a long time."

"I don't care. You promised."

"But . . ."

She saw his eyes glaze and his mouth begin to move as if he
were talking to himself. Then he sat erect, placed his fingertips
together and glared at her.

"Madam, you have no right," he said in a crisp, upper-class
British accent, his jaw barely moving, "to break your promise
to the lad."

"I don't believe we've met," she said, gripping the arms of the chair, trying desperately to hide her surprise.

"He told you about me."

"You're 'Arthur'?"

He acknowledged with a curt nod.

She took a deep breath. "Now, Arthur, it's essential that I tell the attorneys what's going on."

"No," he said. "They will not believe you."

"Why don't we see? I'll just bring Judy Stevenson over to meet you and—"

"No."

"It might save you from prison. I've got to let—"

He leaned forward and glared at her disdainfully. "I tell you this, Miss Turner. If you bring anyone along, the others will just remain silent, and you'll look like a fool."

After fifteen minutes of arguing with Arthur, she noticed the glazed look in his eyes. He leaned back in the chair. When he leaned forward, the voice was different, the expression casual and friendly.

"You can't tell," he said. "You made a promise, and that's a sacred thing."

"Who am I talking to now?" she whispered.

"Allen. I'm the one who talks to Judy and Gary most of the time."

"But they only know Billy Milligan."

"We all answer to Billy's name so the secret won't get out. But Billy's asleep. He's been asleep for a long time. Now, Mrs. Turner—You mind if I call you Dorothy? Billy's mother's name is Dorothy."

"You say *you* talk to Judy and Gary most of the time. Who else have they met?"

"Well, they don't know it, because Tommy sounds a lot like me. You met Tommy. He's the one they can't keep the strait jacket or the handcuffs on. We're a lot alike, except I do most of the talking. He gets kind of nasty and sarcastic. Doesn't get along with people like I do."

"Who else have they met?"

He shrugged. "The first one Gary saw when they booked us was Danny. He was scared and confused. He doesn't know much about what's going on. He's only fourteen."

"How old are you?"

"Eighteen."

She sighed and shook her head. "All right . . . 'Allen.' You seem like an intelligent young man. You understand that I've got to be released from my promise. Judy and Gary have to be told what's going on so they can defend you properly."

"Arthur and Ragen are against it," he said. "They say people will think we're crazy."

"But won't it be worthwhile if you can be kept from going back to prison?"

He shook his head. "It's not up to me. We've kept this secret all our lives."

"Who is it up to?"

"Well, everyone, really. Arthur is in charge, but the secret belongs to all of us. David told you, but it really shouldn't go any further."

She tried to explain to him that it was her job as a psychologist to make these things known to his attorney, but Allen pointed out that there was no guarantee it would help, and then with all the publicity and newspaper headlines, it would make life impossible in prison.

David, whom she had come to recognize by his little-boy demeanor, came out and begged her to keep her promise.

She asked to speak to Arthur again, and he came out frowning. "You are persistent," he said.

She argued with him, and finally she had the feeling that she was wearing him down. "I don't like arguing with a lady," he said. He leaned back with a sigh. "If you feel this is absolutely necessary, and if the others agree, I give *my* permission. But you must get the agreement of each one."

It took hours of arguing as she explained the situation to each one who came forward, never ceasing to be amazed when a transformation occurred. On the fifth day, she confronted Tommy, who was picking his nose: "So you do realize I have to tell Miss Judy."

"Lady, I don't give a damn what you do. Just get off my back."

Allen said, "Promise you won't tell anyone in the world except Judy. And you've got to make *her* promise she won't tell anyone else."

"I agree," she said. "And you won't be sorry."

That afternoon, Dorothy Turner went directly from the prison to the public defender's office down the street and talked with Judy Stevenson. She explained the conditions Milligan had set forth.

"You mean I can't tell Gary Schweickart?"

"I had to give my word. I was lucky to get him to agree to let you in on it."

"I'm skeptical," Judy said.

Turner nodded. "Good. So was I. But I promise you, when we see your client, you're in for a surprise."

(4)

As Sergeant Willis led Milligan into the conference room, Judy Stevenson noticed her client's manner was withdrawn, like a shy adolescent. He seemed frightened of the officer, as if he didn't know him, and ran quickly to the table to sit beside Dorothy Turner. He wouldn't speak until Willis left. He kept rubbing his wrists.

Turner said, "Would you tell Judy Stevenson who you are?"

He sank back in the chair and shook his head, looking toward the door as if to make sure the officer was gone.

"Judy," Turner said finally, "this is Danny. I've come to know him quite well."

"Hi, Danny." Stevenson tried to hide her bewilderment at the different voice and facial expression.

He looked up at Turner and whispered, "See? She's looking at me like she thinks I'm crazy."

"I don't," Judy said. "It's just that I'm confused. This is a very unusual situation. How old are you, Danny?"

He rubbed his wrists as if he'd just been untied and was trying to restore the circulation. But he didn't answer.

"Danny is fourteen," Turner said. "He's a fine artist."

"What kind of paintings do you do?" Stevenson asked.

"Still lifes mostly," Danny said.

"Did you also paint some of those landscapes the police found in your apartment?"

"I don't paint landscapes. I don't like the ground."

"Why is that?"

"I can't tell or he'll kill me."

"Who will kill you?" She was surprised to find herself cross-examining him, knowing she didn't believe any of it, determined she was not going to be taken in by a hoax, but amazed by what seemed to be a brilliant performance.

He closed his eyes and the tears ran down his cheeks.

Feeling herself more and more baffled by what was happening, Judy watched closely as he seemed to shrink back into himself. His lips moved silently, his eyes glazed and then drifted sideways. He looked around, startled, until he recognized both women and realized where he was. He settled back, crossed his legs and withdrew a cigarette from his right sock without removing the pack.

"Anybody got a light?"

Judy lit his cigarette. He took a deep drag, puffed the smoke upward. "So what's new?" he said.

"Would you tell Judy Stevenson who you are?"

He nodded, blowing a smoke ring. "I'm Allen."

"Have we met before?" Judy asked, hoping the trembling in her voice wasn't obvious.

"I've been here a few times when you or Gary came to talk about the case."

"But we've always talked to you as Billy Milligan."

He shrugged. "We all answer to Billy's name. Saves a lot of explaining. But I never *said* I was Billy. You just assumed it, and I didn't think it would do any good to tell you otherwise."

"Can I talk to Billy?" Judy asked.

"Oh, no. They keep him asleep. If they let him on the spot, he'd kill himself."

"Why?"

"He's still scared of being hurt. And he doesn't know about the rest of us. All he knows is that he loses time."

"What do you mean by 'loses time'?" Judy asked.

"It happens to all of us. You're someplace doing something. Then suddenly you're someplace else, and you can tell that time has passed, but you don't know what happened."

Judy shook her head. "That must be awful."

"You never get used to it," Allen said.

When Sergeant Willis came to take him back to his cell, Allen looked up and smiled at him. "That's Sergeant Willis," he said to the two women. "I like him."

Judy Stevenson left the Franklin County Jail with Turner.

"You see why I called you," Dorothy said.

Stevenson sighed. "I came here sure I'd be able to see through a phony act. But I'm convinced I've talked to two different people. Now I can understand why he seemed so different at times. I attributed it to changes of mood. We've got to tell Gary."

"It was difficult enough for me to get permission to tell you. I don't think Milligan will permit it."

"He has to," Judy said. "I can't carry the burden of this knowledge by myself."

When she left the jail, Judy Stevenson found herself in turmoil, awed, angry, confused. It was all incredible. Impossible. But somewhere in the back of her mind, she knew, she was beginning to believe it.

Later that day Gary phoned her at home to tell her the sheriff's office had called to inform him that Milligan had attempted suicide again by smashing his head against the wall of his cell.

"Funny thing," Gary said. "Looking through his records, I just realized today's February 14, his twenty-third birthday. You know something else . . . it's Valentine's Day."

(5)

The next day Dorothy and Judy told Allen it was important to let Gary Schweickart in on the secret.

"Absolutely not."

"But you've got to allow it," Judy said. "To save you from prison, other people have to be told."

"You promised. That was the agreement."

"I know," Judy said. "But it is essential."

"Arthur says no."

"Let me talk to Arthur," Dorothy said.

Arthur came out and glared at both of them. "This is getting very tiresome. I have a lot of thinking and studying to do, and I'm weary of all this badgering."

"You've got to give us permission to tell Gary," Judy said.

"Absolutely not. Two people too many already know."

"It's necessary if we're to help you," Turner said.

"I don't *need* help, madam. Danny and David may need help, but it's really none of my concern."

"Don't you care about keeping Billy alive?" Judy asked, infuriated by Arthur's superior attitude.

"Yes," he said, "but at what cost? They're going to say we're crazy. This is all getting quite out of hand. We've been keeping Billy alive ever since he tried to jump off the school roof."

"What do you mean?" Turner asked. "Keeping him alive how?"

"By keeping him asleep all this time."

"Don't you see how this can affect our case?" Judy said. "It can determine prison or freedom. Wouldn't you have more time and freedom to think and study outside the prison walls? Or do you want to go back to Lebanon?"

Arthur crossed his legs, looking from Judy to Dorothy and back again. "I don't like to argue with ladies. I'll agree only on the same condition as before—that you get all the others to agree as well."

Three days later Judy Stevenson got permission to tell Gary Schweickart.

She walked from the Franklin County Jail in the cold February morning back to the public defender's office. She poured herself a cup of coffee, went directly to Gary's cluttered office, sat down and braced herself.

"Okay," she said. "Have them hold all your calls. I've got something to tell you about Billy."

When she was done telling him about her meetings with Dorothy Turner and Milligan, he looked at her as if she were crazy.

"I've seen it with my own eyes," she insisted. "I've talked to them."

He stood up and lumbered back and forth behind his desk, his unbrushed hair hanging outside his collar, his baggy shirt half out of his belt. "Oh, come on," he protested. "No way. I mean, I know he's mentally disturbed, and I'm on your side. But this isn't going to work."

"You have to come and see it for yourself. You just don't know . . . I'm absolutely convinced."

"All right. But I'll tell you this—I don't believe it. The prosecutor's not going to believe it. And the judge isn't going to believe it. I've got great confidence in you, Judy. You're a fine lawyer and an excellent judge of people. But this is a con. I think you're being had."

The following day, Gary went with her to the Franklin County Jail at three o'clock, expecting to stay just half an hour. He had rejected the whole idea completely. It was impossible. But his skepticism turned to curiosity as he confronted one personality after another. He saw the frightened David turn into the shy Danny, who remembered meeting him that first terrifying day when they brought him in and booked him.

"I didn't have any idea what was going on when they busted into the apartment and arrested me," Danny said.

"What made you say that there was a bomb?"

"I didn't say there was a bomb."

"You told the officer, 'You'll blow it up.'"

"Well, Tommy is always saying, 'Keep away from my stuff or it might blow up.'"

"Why does he say that?"

"Ask him. He's the electronics expert, always fooling around with wires and stuff. It was his thing."

Schweickart pulled on his beard several times. "An escape artist *and* an electronics expert. All right, can we talk to 'Tommy'?"

"I don't know. Tommy only talks to people he wants to talk to."

"Can't you bring Tommy out?" Judy asked.

"I can't just *do* it. It has to happen. I guess I could ask him to talk to you."

"Try," Schweickart said, restraining a smile. "Do your best."

Milligan's body seemed to withdraw into itself. His face paled, eyes glazed as if turning inward. His lips moved as he talked to himself, and the intense concentration pervaded the small room. Schweickart's smirk faded as he held his own breath. Milligan's eyes drifted from side to side. He glanced around, like someone wakened from a deep sleep, and put his hand to his right cheek as if to feel its solidity. Then he leaned back arrogantly in his chair and glared at the two attorneys.

Gary let out his breath. He was impressed. "Are you Tommy?" he asked.

"Who wants to know?"

"I'm your lawyer."

"Not *my* lawyer."

"I'm the one who's going to help Judy Stevenson keep that body you're wearing out of jail, whoever you are."

"Shit. I don't need nobody to keep me out of anything. No jail in the world can hold me. I can bust out anytime I want to."

Gary stared him down. "So you're the one who keeps slipping out of the strait jacket. You must be Tommy."

He looked bored. "Yeah . . . yeah."

"Danny was telling us about that box of electronic stuff the police found in the apartment. He said it was yours."

"He always did have a big mouth."

"Why did you make a fake bomb?"

"Shit, it wasn't a fake bomb. Can I help it if the damned cops are too dumb to know a black box when they see one?"

"What do you mean?"

"Just what I said. It was a black box to override the telephone company system. I was just experimenting around with a new telephone for the car. I taped up those cylinders with red tape, and the dumb cops thought it was a bomb."

"You told Danny it might explode."

"Oh, for Chrissakes! I always tell the young ones that so they'll keep their hands off my stuff."

"Where did you learn about electronics, Tommy?" Judy asked.

He shrugged. "On my own. From books. Ever since I can remember, I wanted to know how things worked."

"And the escape-artist stuff?" asked Judy.

"Arthur encouraged me on that. Someone was needed to get out of the ropes when one of us was tied up in the barn. I learned how to control my hand muscles and bones. Then I got interested in all kinds of locks and bolts."

Schweickart thought for a moment. "Are the guns yours, too?"

Tommy shook his head. "Ragen is the only one allowed to handle guns."

"Allowed? Who does the allowing?" Judy asked.

"Well, that depends where we are . . . Look, I'm tired of being pumped for information. That's Arthur's job, or Allen's. Ask one of them, okay? I'm leaving."

"Wait . . ."

But Judy was too late. His eyes blanked and he shifted position. He placed his fingertips together, making his hands a pyramid. As his chin lifted, his face changed to the expression she had come to recognize as Arthur. She introduced him to Gary.

"You have to forgive Tommy," Arthur said coldly. "He is a rather antisocial youth. If he weren't so clever with electronic equipment and locks, I think I would have banished him long ago. But his are useful talents."

"What are your talents?" Gary asked.

Arthur waved his hand deprecatingly. "I'm just an amateur. I dabble in biology and medicine."

"Gary was asking Tommy about the guns," Judy said. "It's a parole violation, you know."

Arthur nodded. "The only one permitted to handle guns is Ragen, the keeper of rage. That is his specialty. But he may use them only for protection and survival. Just as he may use his great strength only for the common good, never to harm others. He has the ability to control and concentrate his adrenaline, you know."

"He used the guns when he kidnapped and raped those four women," Gary said.

Arthur's voice dropped to an icy calmness. "Ragen never raped anyone. I've spoken to him about this case. He started to commit robberies because he was worried about the unpaid bills. He admits robbing the three women in October, but he denies, absolutely, any involvement with that woman in August or with any sex crimes."

Gary leaned forward, watching Arthur's face closely, aware that his own skepticism was melting away. "But the evidence—"

"Evidence be damned! If Ragen says he didn't do it, there's no use in questioning it. He won't lie. Ragen is a thief, but he is no rapist."

"You say you've spoken to Ragen," Judy said. "How does that work? Do you talk to each other out loud or in your head? Is it speech or thought?"

Arthur clasped his hands. "It happens both ways. Sometimes it's internal, and in all probability no one else knows it's happening. At other times, usually when we're alone, it's definitely aloud. I imagine if someone was watching us, he or she would think we were quite mad."

Gary sat back, pulled out his handkerchief and wiped the perspiration from his brow. "Who's going to believe this?"

Arthur smiled condescendingly. "As I was saying, Ragen, like the rest of us, never lies. All our lives people have accused us of being liars. It has become a point of honor among us never to tell a falsehood. So we don't really care who believes."

"But you don't always volunteer the truth," Judy said.

"And that's lying by omission," Gary added.

"Oh, come now," Arthur said, making no effort to hide his disdain. "As an attorney, you know very well a witness is under no compulsion to volunteer information he hasn't been asked for. You would be the first to tell a client to stick to a yes or no answer and not elaborate unless it was in his interest. If you come out and ask one of us a direct question, you'll get a truthful answer or silence. Of course, there will be times when the truth may be taken several ways. The English language is by nature ambiguous."

Gary nodded thoughtfully. "I'll keep that in mind. But I think we've gotten off the track. About those guns . . ."

"Ragen knows, much more than anyone, what happened the mornings of the *three* crimes. Why don't you talk to him?"

"Not right now," Gary said. "Not yet."

"I sense you're afraid to meet him."

Gary looked up sharply. "Isn't that what you want? Isn't that part of your reason for telling us how evil and dangerous he is?"

"I never said he was evil."

"That's the effect," Gary said.

"I think it's important for you to know Ragen," Arthur said. "You've unlocked Pandora's box. I think you should open the lid all the way. But he won't come out unless you want him to."

"Does he want to talk to us?" Judy asked.

"The question is, Do you want to speak to him?"

Gary found that the thought of Ragen coming out did frighten him.

"I think we should," Judy said, looking at Gary.

"He won't hurt you," Arthur told them with a tight-lipped smile. "He knows you're both here to help Billy. We've talked about it, and now that the secret's out, we realize we have to be open with you. It's the last hope, as Mrs. Stevenson so forcefully put it, to keep us out of prison."

Gary sighed and put his head back. "All right, Arthur. I'd like to meet Ragen."

Arthur moved his chair to the far end of the small interview room, to put as much distance between them as possible. He sat down again, and his eyes grew distant, as if looking inward. His lips moved, his hand jerked up to touch his cheek. His jaw tightened. Then he shifted, the body dropping from a stiff-backed posture to the aggressive crouchlike position of a wary fighter. "Is not right. Vas not good to reveal secret."

They listened in astonishment as the voice dropped to a low, harsh tone with confident power and hostility. It boomed out in the small conference room with a deep, rich Slavic accent.

"I tell you now," Ragen said, glaring at them, the tension in his face muscles changing his appearance, eyes piercing, brows beetled. "Even after David tells secret by mistake, I vas against it."

It did not sound like an imitation of a Slavic accent. His voice now truly had the natural sibilant quality of someone who had been raised in Eastern Europe, had learned to speak English, but had never lost his accent.

"Why were you against letting the truth come out?" Judy asked.

"Who vill believe?" he said, clenching his fist. "They vill all say ve are crazy. It is do no good."

"It might keep you out of prison," Gary said.

"How is possible?" Ragen snapped. "I am not a fool, Mr. Schweickart. Police have evidence I commit robberies. I admit three robberies near university. Only three. But other things they say I do is lie. I am not rapist. I vill go into court and confess robberies. But if ve go to jail, I kill children. Is euthanasia. Jail is no place for little ones."

"But if you kill . . . the little ones . . . won't that also mean your own death?" asked Judy.

"Not necessary," Ragen said. "Ve are all different people."

Gary ran his fingers impatiently through his hair. "Look, when Billy—or whoever—smashed his head into the wall of his cell last week, didn't it damage the skull you're wearing?"

Ragen touched his forehead. "Is true. But vas not for me pain."

"Who felt the pain?" Judy asked.

"David is keeper of pain. Is one who accepts all suffering. David is empath."

Gary started out of his chair to pace, but when he saw Ragen tense, he thought better of it and sat back. "Is David the one who tried to bash his brains out?"

Ragen shook his head. "Vas Billy."

"Ah," said Gary, "I thought Billy has been asleep all this time."

"Is true. But it vas his birthday. Little Christene makes for him birthday card, and she vants give it to him. Arthur allows Billy to vake up for birthday and to take spot. I vas against it. I am protector. Is my responsibility. Maybe is true Arthur is more intelligent than I am, but he is human. Arthur makes mistakes."

"What happened when Billy woke up?" Gary asked.

"He looks around. He sees he is in prison cell. He thinks he is do something bad. So he smashes head into vall."

Judy winced.

"You see, Billy knows nothing about us," Ragen said. "He has—vat you call it?—amnesia. Let me put it this vay. Ven he is in school, losing so much time, he goes up to roof. He starts to jump. I remove him from spot to stop him. He is asleep ever since that day. Arthur and I keep him asleep to protect him."

"When was that?" Judy asked.

"Right after sixteenth birthday. I remember he vas depressed because his father makes him vork on his birthday."

"My God," Gary whispered. "Asleep for seven years?"

"Is still asleep. He vas only for few minutes avake. It vas mistake to let him on spot."

"Who's been doing things?" Gary asked. "Working? Talking to people ever since? No one we've spoken to has reported a British or Russian accent."

"Not Russian, Mr. Schweickart. Yugoslavian."

"Sorry."

"Is all right. Just to keep record straight. To answer question: Allen and Tommy are mostly on spot ven dealing vit other people."

"They just come and go as they please?" Judy asked.

"Let me put it this vay. In different circumstances, spot is ruled by me or by Arthur, depending on situation. In prison I control spot—decide who goes on, who stays off—because is dangerous place. As protector, I have full power and command. In situations vere is no danger and vere intelligence and logic are more important, then Arthur dominates spot."

"Who controls the spot now?" Gary asked, aware that he had lost all professional detachment and had become totally curious, totally involved in this incredible phenomenon.

Ragen shrugged and looked around. "Is prison."

The door to the interview room opened unexpectedly, and Ragen jumped up, catlike, quickly alert and defensive, his hands in karate position. When he saw it was only an attorney checking to see if the room was occupied, Ragen settled back.

Though Gary had expected to spend the usual fifteen minutes or half-hour with his client, positive he would debunk a total fraud, by the time he left five hours later, he was completely convinced that Billy Milligan was a multiple personality. As he walked out with Judy into the cold night, Gary found his mind racing with absurd notions of taking a trip to England or Yugoslavia to see if he could find records of Arthur's or Ragen's existence. It wasn't that he believed there was anything like reincarnation or possession by the devil, but walking along in a daze, he had to admit that he had met different people today in that little conference room.

He glanced at Judy, who was also walking in stunned silence. "Okay," he said. "I have to admit I'm in an intellectual and emotional state of shock. I believe. And I think I can convince Jo Anne when she asks why I missed dinner again. But how the hell are we ever going to convince the prosecutor and the judge?"

(6)

On February 21, Dr. Stella Karolin, a psychiatrist from the Southwest Community Mental Health Center and a colleague of Dr. Turner's, informed the public defenders that Dr. Cornelia Wilbur, world famous for having treated Sybil, the woman with sixteen personalities, had agreed to come from Kentucky to see Milligan on March 10.

Preparing for Dr. Wilbur's visit, Dorothy Turner and Judy Stevenson assumed the task of convincing Arthur, Ragen and the others to allow yet another person to be told the secret. Again they were forced to spend hours convincing each of the personalities one at a time. They had by now heard nine names—Arthur, Allen, Tommy, Ragen, David, Danny, Christopher, but they had not yet met Christene, Christopher's three-year-old sister, nor had they met the original or core person, Billy, whom the others were keeping asleep. When they finally received permission to let others in on the secret, they made arrangements for a group, including the prosecutor, to observe the meeting between Dr. Wilbur and Milligan at the Franklin County Jail.

Judy and Gary interviewed Milligan's mother, Dorothy, his younger sister, Kathy, and older brother, Jim, and though none of them could provide firsthand knowledge of the abuses alleged by Billy, the mother described her own experiences of being beaten by Chalmer Milligan. Teachers, friends and relatives described Billy Milligan's strange behavior, his attempts at suicide and his trancelike states.

Judy and Gary were certain they were building a convincing case of a defendant who—by all legal tests in Ohio—was incapable of standing trial. But they realized they faced another hurdle: If Judge Flowers accepted the report by Southwest, Billy Milligan would now have to be sent to a mental institution for evaluation and treatment. They didn't want him sent to the Lima State Hospital for the Criminally Insane. They knew its reputation from many of their former clients, and they felt certain he would never survive there.

Though Dr. Wilbur was to have seen Milligan on Friday, her plans were changed for personal reasons, and Judy called Gary from home to tell him.

"You coming into the office this afternoon?" he asked.

"I wasn't planning on it," she said.

"We've got to go through this thing," he said. "Southwest keeps saying there's no alternative to Lima, and something in the back of my head says there's got to be."

"Look, with the thermostat turned down, the office is damned cold," she said. "Al's out and I've got a fire going here. Come on over. I'll make you some Irish coffee and we can review it."

He laughed. "You twisted my arm."

A half-hour later, they were both sitting in front of the fire.

Gary warmed his hands on the steaming mug. "I'll tell you, I was really thrown for a loop when Ragen came out," he said. "What amazes me is how likable he is."

"Just what I was thinking," Judy said.

"I mean, Arthur calls him the 'keeper of hate.' I expected something with horns. But he's really a charming and interesting guy. I believe him completely when he denies the August rape of the woman assaulted at the Nationwide Plaza, and now I find myself wondering when he says he didn't rape the other three."

"I agree about the first. It's obviously a copy-cat accusation. Completely different pattern. But the last three were certainly abducted, robbed and raped," Judy said.

"All we get are bits and pieces of what he remembers of the crimes. It's damned odd, you know, Ragen saying he recognized his second victim, certain that one of them had met her before."

"And now we learn about Tommy remembering coming out and being on the spot at the Wendy's drive-in, having a hamburger with the third victim, figuring one of the others was out on a date with her."

"Polly Newton's story confirms the stop at the burger place. And she's the one who said he got the strange look and quit the sex after a couple of minutes, and said he couldn't do it, and said to himself, 'Bill, what's wrong with you? Get yourself together.' And then told her he needed a cold shower to cool off."

"But all that crazy talk about being from the Weathermen and driving a Maserati."

"One of them was boasting."

"Okay, let's just admit we don't know what happened, and neither do any of the personalities we've dealt with."

"Ragen admits the robberies," Judy said.

"Yeah, but denies the rapes. I mean, the whole thing is strange. Can you imagine, three different times within a two-week period Ragen drinks and takes amphetamines and then in the early hours of the morning jogs eleven miles across town to the Ohio State campus? And then after selecting a victim, he blacks out—"

"Leaves the spot," Judy corrected.

"That's what I mean." He held his cup out for a refill. "So in each case he leaves the spot, and the next thing he finds himself in downtown Columbus with the money in his pocket and figures he committed the robberies he set out to do. But he doesn't remember doing it. Any of the three. As he says, someone stole time in between."

"Well, there are pieces missing," Judy said. "Someone was tossing those bottles into the pond and taking target practice."

Gary nodded. "That proves it wasn't Ragen. According to the woman, he couldn't get the gun operating for a few seconds. I mean, fooling with it until he got the safety catch off. And then missing a couple of the bottles. An expert like Ragen wouldn't miss."

"But Arthur says the others are forbidden to handle Ragen's guns."

"I can just see us explaining that to Judge Flowers."

"Are we going to?"

"I don't know," he said. "It's dumb to use an insanity defense for a multiple personality, since it's classified officially as a neurosis and not a psychosis. I mean, the shrinks themselves say multiples are not insane."

"Okay," Judy said, "why not just a straight not guilty without calling it insanity? We attack the notion of purposefulness of the acts, like the multiple personality case in California."

"That was a minor offense," Gary said. "With a notorious case like ours, a multiple personality defense just won't fly. That's a fact of life."

She sighed and stared into the fire.

"And I'll tell you something else," Gary said, stroking his beard. "Even if Judge Flowers sees it the way we do, he's going to send him to Lima. Billy heard about the kind of place Lima is when he was in prison. You remember what Ragen said about euthanasia? About killing the children if he's sent there? I believe he would."

"Then we get him sent somewhere else!" said Judy.

"Southwest says Lima's the only place for treatment before trial."

"He goes to Lima over my dead body," she said.

"Correction," Gary said, raising his cup. "Over *our* dead bodies."

They clinked their cups and then Judy refilled them. "I can't accept that we don't have a choice."

"Let's find a choice," he said.

"Right you are," she said. "We'll find a choice."

"It's never been done before," he said, wiping the cream from his beard.

"So what? Ohio has never had a Billy Milligan before."

She pulled her well-thumbed copy of the *Ohio Criminal Law Handbook* from the shelf, and they both went over it, taking turns reading aloud.

"More Irish?" she asked.

He shook his head. "Just black, and make it strong."

Two hours later, he made her reread a passage from the handbook. She ran her finger down the page to Section 2945.38.

. . . if the court or jury finds him to be not sane he shall be forthwith committed by the court to a hospital for the mentally ill or mentally retarded within the jurisdiction of the court. If the court finds it advisable, it shall commit such person to the Lima State Hospital until he is restored to reason, and upon being restored to reason the accused shall be proceeded against as provided by the law.

"Yeah!" shouted Gary, jumping up. " 'A *hospital within the jurisdiction of the court*.' It doesn't say *only* Lima."

"We found it!"

"Jesus," he said, "and everybody's been saying there's never been an alternative to Lima for pretrial commitment."

"Now we've just got to find another mental hospital within the jurisdiction of the court."

Gary slapped his forehead. "Oh my God. This is incredible. I know one. I worked there as a psychiatric aide after I got out of the service. Harding Hospital."

"Harding? Is that in the court's jurisdiction?"

"Sure. Worthington, Ohio. And listen, it's one of most conservative, respectable psychiatric hospitals in the country. It's affiliated with the Seventh-Day Adventist Church. I've heard tough prosecutors say, 'If Dr. George Harding, Jr., says the man's insane, I'll buy it. He's not like some other doctor who will examine a patient for thirty minutes for the defense and say he's crazy.' "

"Prosecutors say that?"

He held up his right hand. "I heard it, so help me. I even think it was Terry Sherman. And, hey, I think I remember Dorothy Turner saying she often did testing for Harding Hospital."

"So we get him into Harding," she said.

Gary sat down quickly, dejected. "Just one thing. Harding Hospital is an exclusive, expensive private hospital, and Billy has no money."

"We're not going to let that stop us," she said.

"Yeah, how do we get him in?"

"We make them want to take Billy."

"And just how do we do that?" he asked.

A half-hour later, Gary wiped the snow off his boots and rang Harding's doorbell. He was suddenly very conscious of himself as a bearded, wacko public defender confronting the conservative, Establishment psychiatrist—the grandson of the brother of President Warren G. Harding, no less—in his luxurious home. Judy should have come. She'd have made a better impression. He tightened his loose tie and tucked his curled-up shirt collar into his jacket as the front door opened.

George Harding at forty-nine was an impeccable, lean, smooth-faced man with soft eyes and a soft voice. He struck Gary as quite handsome. "Come in, Mr. Schweickart."

Gary struggled to pull off his boots and left them in a puddle in the foyer. Then, shucking his coat and hanging it on the rack, he followed Dr. Harding into the living room.

"I thought your name was familiar," Harding said. "Then, after you phoned, I checked back in the newspapers. You're defending Milligan, the young man who attacked the four women on the Ohio State campus."

Gary shook his head. "Three. The August rape at the Nationwide Plaza was a very different kind of assault and will surely be thrown out. The case has taken a very unusual turn. I was hoping for your opinion in this matter."

Harding pointed to the soft couch for Gary to sit in but took a hardbacked chair himself. He placed the tips of his fingers together and listened closely as Gary explained in detail what he and Judy had learned about Milligan, and about the forthcoming meeting on Sunday at the Franklin County Jail.

Harding nodded thoughtfully, and when he spoke, he chose his words very carefully. "I certainly do respect Stella Karolin and Dorothy Turner." He mused and stared at the ceiling. "Turner does part-time testing for us, and she has already talked to me about the case. Now, since Dr. Wilbur will be there . . ." He stared at the floor between the steeple of his fingers. "I don't see any reason why I might not be able to attend. Sunday, you say?"

Gary nodded, not daring to speak.

"Well, I must tell you, Mr. Schweickart. I have grave reservations about the syndrome known as multiple personality. Although Dr. Cornelia Wilbur did give a lecture at Harding Hospital about Sybil in the summer of 1975, I'm not sure I really believe it. With all due respect to her and other psychiatrists who have worked with such people . . . Well, in a case like this, it's too obviously possible for the patient to feign amnesia. Still, if Turner and Karolin will be there . . . and if Dr. Wilbur is making the trip . . ."

He stood up. "I make no commitment for myself or on behalf of the hospital. But I shall be pleased to attend the meeting."

As soon as Gary got home, he called Judy. "Hey, Counselor," he said with a laugh. "Harding's involved."

On Saturday, March 11, Judy went to the Franklin County Jail to tell Milligan that the plans had been changed, and that Dr. Cornelia Wilbur wouldn't be there until the next day.

"I should have told you yesterday," she said. "I'm sorry."

He began to tremble violently. By his expression, she realized she was talking to Danny.

"Dorothy Turner isn't coming back, is she?"

"Of course she is, Danny. What makes you think such a thing?"

"People make promises and then they forget. Don't leave me alone."

"I won't. But you've got to get hold of yourself. Dr. Wilbur will be here tomorrow, and so will Stella Karolin and Dorothy Turner and me . . . and a few other people."

His eyes opened wide. "Other people?"

"There's another doctor—George Harding, from Harding Hospital. And the prosecutor, Bernie Yavitch."

"Men?" gasped Danny, shaking so hard his teeth began to chatter.

"It's essential for your defense," she said. "But Gary and I will be there too. Look, I think we should get you some medication to calm you down."

Danny nodded.

She called the guard and asked to have her client placed in a holding room while she went up for a medic. When they returned a few minutes later, Milligan was cowering in the far corner of the room, his face covered with blood, his nose bleeding. He had smashed his head against the wall.

He looked at her blankly, and she realized it was no longer Danny. It was the keeper of the pain. "David?" she asked.

He nodded. "It hurts, Miss Judy. It hurts bad. I don't want to live anymore."

She pulled him toward her and cradled him in her arms. "You mustn't say that, David. You have a lot to live for. A lot of people believe in you, and you're going to get help."

"I'm afraid of going to prison."

"They're not going to send you to prison. We're going to fight it, David."

"I didn't do nothing bad."

"I know, David. I believe you."

"When is Dorothy Turner coming back to see me?"

"I told . . ." And then she realized it was *Danny* she had told. "Tomorrow, David. With another psychiatrist by the name of Dr. Wilbur."

"You're not going to tell her the secret, are you?"

She shook her head. "No, David. In Dr. Wilbur's case, I'm sure we won't have to."

(7)

March 12 was a bright, cold Sunday morning. Bernie Yavitch stepped out of his car and went into the Franklin County Jail, feeling very strange about it all. It would be the first time, as a prosecutor, that he had ever been present while the defendant was being examined by psychiatrists. He had gone through the report from Southwest and over the police reports again and again, but he had no idea what to expect.

He just couldn't believe that all these eminent doctors were taking the multiple personality thing seriously. Cornelia Wilbur coming down to examine Milligan didn't impress him. She believed in it, and she'd be looking for it. It was Dr. George Harding's face he had to watch. As far as Yavitch was concerned, there was no more highly respected psychiatrist in the state of Ohio. He knew no one would pull anything on Dr. Harding. Many of the leading prosecutors, who had little or no respect for psychiatrists testifying in insanity cases, said the one exception would be George Harding, Jr.

After a while the others arrived, and they arranged to have the interview in the lower-level sheriff's squad room, a large room with folding chairs, blackboards and a desk where the officers gathered at shift change.

Yavitch greeted Dr. Stella Karolin and Sheila Karolin and Sheila Porter, the social worker from Southwest, and was introduced to Drs. Wilbur and Harding.

Then the door opened, and he saw Billy Milligan for the first time. Judy Stevenson walked beside him, holding his hand. Dorothy Turner walked in front, Gary walked behind. They entered the squad room, and Milligan, seeing the crowd of people, hesitated.

Dorothy Turner introduced them one by one and then led him to the seat closest to Cornelia Wilbur. "Dr. Wilbur," Dorothy said in a low voice, "this is Danny."

"Hello, Danny," Wilbur said. "I'm glad to meet you. How are you feeling?"

"All right," he said, clinging to Dorothy's arm.

"I know it must make you nervous to be in the room with a lot of strangers, but we're here to help you," Wilbur said.

They took their seats and Schweickart leaned over and whispered to Yavitch, "When you see this, if you still don't believe it, I'll turn my license in."

As Wilbur started to question Milligan, Yavitch relaxed. She looked to him like an attractive, energetic mother with bright-red hair and bright-red lipstick. Danny answered her questions and told her about Arthur and Ragen and Allen.

She turned to Yavitch. "You see? It's typical of multiple personalities that he's willing to speak of what happened to the others, but not about what happened to him."

After a few more questions and answers, she turned to Dr. George Harding. "This is a clear example of the dissociative state of the hysterical neurotic."

Danny looked at Judy and said, "She left her spot."

Judy smiled and whispered, "No, Danny. It's not like that with her."

"She must have a lot of people inside her," Danny insisted. "She talks to me one way, and then she changes and starts using all those big words like Arthur does."

"I wish Judge Flowers were here to see this," Wilbur said. "I know what's going on inside this young man. I know what he really needs."

Danny's head snapped around, glaring at Dorothy Turner accusingly. "You told her! You promised you wouldn't, but you told."

"No, Danny," Turner said. "I didn't. Dr. Wilbur knows what's wrong because she knows other people like you."

In a firm but soft voice, Cornelia Wilbur put Danny at ease. She looked into his eyes and told him to relax. She held her left hand up to her forehead, and her diamond ring glinted and reflected in his eyes.

"You are totally relaxed and feeling good now, Danny. Nothing is bothering you. Relax. Whatever you feel like doing or saying is all right. Anything you want."

"I want to leave," Danny said. "I want to get off the spot."

"Whatever you want to do is all right with us, Danny. I'll tell you what. When you leave, I'd like to talk to Billy. The Billy who was born with that name."

He shrugged. "I can't make Billy come. He's asleep. Arthur and Ragen are the only ones who can wake him up."

"Well, you tell Arthur and Ragen that I have to talk to Billy. It's very important."

Yavitch watched in growing astonishment as Danny's eyes went blank. His lips moved, his body jerked erect, and then he looked around, dazed. He said nothing at first and then asked for a cigarette.

Dr. Wilbur gave him one, and as he settled back, Judy Stevenson whispered to Yavitch that the only one who smoked cigarettes was Allen.

Wilbur once again introduced herself and the people in the room who hadn't met Allen before, and Yavitch marveled at how changed Milligan seemed, how relaxed and outgoing. He smiled and spoke earnestly and fluently, very different from the shy, boyish Danny. Allen answered her questions about his interests. He played the piano and the drums, he said, and painted—mostly portraits. He was eighteen and loved baseball, though Tommy hated the game.

"All right, Allen," Wilbur said, "I'd like to talk to Arthur now."

"Yeah, okay," Allen said. "Wait, I . . ."

Yavitch stared as Allen took a couple of quick, deep puffs of the cigarette before leaving. It seemed so spontaneous, such a small detail, to take those final drags before Arthur, who didn't smoke cigarettes, emerged.

Again, the eyes went blank, the lids fluttered. He opened them, leaned back, gazed around with a haughty expression and put his fingertips together, forming a pyramid. When he spoke, it was with an upper-class British accent.

Yavitch frowned as he listened. He found himself actually seeing and hearing a new person talking to Dr. Wilbur. Arthur's eye contact, his body language, were obviously different from Allen's. A friend of Yavitch's, an accountant in Cleveland, was British, and Yavitch was amazed at the resemblance—the authentic speech pattern.

"I don't believe I've met these people," Arthur said.

He was introduced around, and Yavitch felt silly greeting Arthur as if he had just walked into the room. When Wilbur asked Arthur about the others, he described their roles and explained who would or would not be allowed to come out. Finally Dr. Wilbur said, "We must speak with Billy."

"It is very dangerous to waken him," Arthur said. "He's quite suicidal, you know."

"It's very important that Dr. Harding get to meet him. The outcome of the trial could depend upon it. Freedom and treatment, or else prison."

Arthur thought about it, pursed his lips and said, "Well, really, I'm not the one to decide. Since we are in a prison—a hostile environment—Ragen is dominant, and only he makes the final decision about who does and does not come on the spot."

"What is Ragen's role in your lives?" she asked.

"Ragen is the protector and the keeper of hate."

"All right, then," Dr. Wilbur said sharply. "I must speak to Ragen."

"Madam, I suggest that—"

"Arthur, we don't have much time. A lot of busy people have given up their Sunday morning to come down here and help you. Ragen must agree to let Billy talk to us."

Again the face went blank, eyes staring, trancelike. Lips moved as if in an inner, unheard conversation. Then the jaw tightened and his brow furrowed deeply.

"*Is not possible,*" growled the deep Slavic voice.

"What do you mean?" Wilbur asked.

"Is not possible to speak vit Billy."

"Who are you?"

"I am Ragen Vadascovinich. Who are these people?"

Dr. Wilbur introduced everyone, and Yavitch wondered again at the change, at the striking Slavic accent. He wished he knew some phrases in Yugoslavian or Serbo-Croatian, to see if it was just the accent or if Ragen could understand the language. He wished Dr. Wilbur would probe into that. He wanted to mention it, but they had all been asked not to speak beyond the introduction.

Dr. Wilbur asked Ragen, "How did you know I wanted to speak to Billy?"

Ragen nodded with mild amusement. "Arthur asks my opinion. And I am opposed. Is my right as protector to decide who comes on spot. Not possible for Billy to come out."

"And why not?"

"You are doctor, no? Let me put it this vay. Is impossible because if Billy vakes, he vill kill himself."

"How can you be sure of that?"

He shrugged. "Each time Billy comes on spot, he thinks he is do something bad and he tries to kill himself. Is my responsibility. I say no."

"What are your responsibilities?"

"To protect all, especially the young ones."

"I see. And you have never failed in your duties? The young ones have never been hurt or felt pain, because you've protected them from it?"

"Not exactly true. David feels pain."

"And you *let* David take the pain?"

"Is his purpose."

"A big, strong man like you, letting a child bear all that pain and suffering?"

"Dr. Vilbur, I am not one to—"

"You ought to be ashamed of yourself, Ragen. Now, I don't think you should set yourself up as an authority. I am a medical doctor, and I have treated cases like this before. I think *I* should be the one to decide if Billy can come out—certainly not someone who lets a defenseless child bear the pain when he is around to take some of it on his own shoulders."

Ragen shifted in his seat, looking embarrassed and guilty. He mumbled that she didn't understand the situation at all, but her voice went on, softly but sharply persuasive.

"All right!" he said. "You are responsible. But all men must first leave room. Billy is afraid of men because of vat his father did to him."

Gary, Bernie Yavitch and Dr. Harding rose to leave the room, but Judy spoke up.

"Ragen, it's very important that Dr. Harding be allowed to stay and see Billy. You have to trust me. Dr. Harding is very interested in the medical aspects of this case, and he's got to be allowed to stay."

"We'll go out," Gary said, pointing to himself and Yavitch.

Ragen looked around the room, evaluating the situation. "I permit," he said, pointing to a chair in the far corner of the large room. "But he must sit back there. And stay."

George Harding, looking uncomfortable, smiled weakly. He nodded and sat down in the corner.

"And not move!" Ragen said.

"I won't."

Gary and Bernie Yavitch went out into the corridor, and Gary said, "I've never met the core personality, Billy. I don't know if he'll come out. But what's your reaction to what you've seen and heard?"

Yavitch sighed. "I started out very skeptical. Now I don't know what to think. But I don't think it's an act."

Those who remained in the room watched closely as Milligan's face paled. His gaze seemed to turn inward. His lips twitched as if he were talking in his sleep.

Suddenly his eyes opened wide.

"Oh my God!" he cried. "I thought I was dead!"

He jerked around in his seat. Seeing people looking at him, he jumped out of the chair onto the floor on all fours and scuttled crablike to the opposite wall, as far from them as he could get, squeezing between the writing arm rests of two chairs, cowering and sobbing.

"What'd I do now?"

With a gentle but firm voice, Cornelia Wilbur said, "You did nothing wrong, young man. There is nothing for you to be upset about."

He was quivering, pressing himself back into the wall as if trying to go through it. His hair had fallen into his eyes and he peered through it, making no attempt to brush it back.

"I realize you don't know it, Billy, but everyone in this room is here to help you. Now, I think you should get off the floor and sit in that chair so we can talk to you."

It became apparent to everyone in the room that Wilbur was in control and knew exactly what she was doing, touching the right mental buttons to make him respond.

He got up and sat in the chair, knees jiggling anxiously, body shaking. "I ain't dead?"

"You're very much alive, Billy, and we know you're having problems and you need help. You do need help, don't you?"

He nodded, wide-eyed.

"Tell me, Billy, why did you smash your head into the wall the other day?"

"I thought I was dead," he said, "and then I woke up and found myself in jail."

"What was the last thing you remember before that?"

"Going up to the school roof. I didn't want to see any more doctors. Dr. Brown at the Lancaster Mental Health Center couldn't cure me. I thought I jumped off. Why ain't I dead? Who are all of you? Why you lookin' at me like that?"

"We're doctors and lawyers, Billy. We're here to help you."

"Doctors? Daddy Chal will kill me if I talk to you."

"Why, Billy?"

"He doesn't want me to tell what he done to me."

Wilbur looked questioningly at Judy Stevenson.

"His adoptive father," Judy explained. "His mother divorced Chalmer Milligan six years ago."

Billy stared around him, dumfounded. "Divorced? Six years?" He touched his face as if to be sure it was real. "How's that possible?"

"We have a lot to talk about, Billy," said Wilbur. "A lot of missing pieces to put together."

He looked around wildly. "How'd I get here? What's going on?" He began to sob and rock back and forth.

"I know you're tired now, Billy," Wilbur said. "You can go back and rest now."

Suddenly the crying stopped. The expression on his face turned instantly into an alert but confused state. He touched the tears running down his face, and he frowned.

"What's going on here? Who was that? I heard someone crying, but I didn't know where it was coming from. Jesus, whoever he was, he was just about to run and crash himself into the wall. Who is he?"

"That was Billy," Wilbur said, "The original Billy, sometimes known as the host or core personality. Who are you?"

"I didn't know Billy was allowed out. No one told me. I'm Tommy."

Gary and Bernie Yavitch were permitted back into the room, and Tommy was introduced to everyone, asked a few questions and taken back to his cell. When Yavitch heard what had happened in their absence, he shook his head. It all seemed so unreal—like bodies possessed by spirits or demons. He said to Gary and Judy, "I don't know what it means, but I guess I'm with the rest of you. He doesn't seem to be faking."

Only Dr. George Harding was noncommital. He was reserving judgment, he said. He had to think about what he'd heard and seen. The next day he would write his opinion for Judge Flowers.

(8)

Russ Hill, the medic who had brought Tommy back upstairs, had no idea what was wrong with Milligan. All he knew was that there were a lot of doctors and lawyers coming and going to see this patient, and that he was a very changeable young man who could draw good pictures. A few days after the big Sunday meeting, he passed by the cell and saw Milligan drawing. He peeked through the bars and saw a very childish line drawing with some words printed on it.

A guard came up and started to laugh. "Hell, my two-year-old draws better 'n that goddamn rapist."

"Leave him alone," said Hill.

The guard had a glass of water in his hand, and he flung it through the bars, wetting the drawing.

"What'd you do that for?" Hill said. "What the hell is wrong with you?"

But the guard who had thrown the water drew away from the bars when he saw the expression on Milligan's face. The rage was unmistakable. He seemed to be looking around for something to throw. Suddenly, the prisoner grabbed the toilet bowl, ripped it out of the wall and threw it against the bars, shattering the porcelain.

The guard stumbled back and ran to hit the alarm button.

"Jesus, Milligan!" Hill said.

"He threw vater on Christene's drawing. Is not right to destroy the vork of children."

Six officers burst into the corridor, but by that time they found Milligan sitting on the floor with a dazed expression on his face.

"You're gonna pay for that, you sonofabitch!" the guard shouted. "That's county property."

Tommy sat back against the wall, put his hands behind his head arrogantly and said, "Fuck county property."

In a letter dated March 13, 1978, Dr. George Harding, Jr., wrote to Judge Flowers: "Based upon the interview, it is my opinion that William S. Milligan is not competent to stand trial due to his inability to cooperate with his attorney in his own defense, and that he lacks the emotional integration necessary to be able to testify in his own defense, to confront witnesses, and to maintain an effective psychological presence in court beyond his mere physical presence."

Dr. Harding now had to make another decision. Both Schweickart and Yavitch had asked him to go beyond the competency evaluation and request that Harding Hospital admit Milligan for evaluation and treatment.

George Harding struggled with his decision. He'd been impressed that Prosecutor Yavitch had been at that interview— a most unusual thing for a prosecutor to do, Harding thought. Schweickart and Yavitch had assured him that he would not be placed in an adversarial role "for the defense" or "for the prosecution," but that both sides would agree in advance that his report would go into the trial record "by stipulation." How could he resist when both sides were asking this of him?

As medical director of Harding Hospital, he presented the request to the hospital administrator and the finance officer. "We've never turned away from difficult problems," he told them. "Harding Hospital doesn't accept just the easy cases."

On the basis of George Harding's strong recommendation that this would be an opportunity for the staff to learn, as well as for the hospital to make a contribution to psychiatric knowledge, the committee agreed to admit William Milligan for the three months mandated by the court.

On March 14, Hill and another officer came to get Milligan. "They want you downstairs," the guard said, "but the sheriff says you got to go in straits."

Milligan put up no resistance while they fastened the jacket on him and led him from the cell to the elevator.

Downstairs, Gary and Judy were waiting in the corridor, eager to tell their client they had good news for him. When the elevator door opened, they saw Russ Hill and the guard looking on in open-mouthed amazement as Milligan stepped out of the strait jacket, almost freeing himself completely.

"It's impossible," the guard said.

"I told you it wouldn't hold me. And no jail or hospital can hold me, either."

"Tommy?" Judy asked.

"Damned right!" he snorted.

"Come on in here," said Gary, pulling him into the conference room. "We've got to talk."

Tommy shook his arm loose from Gary's grip. "What's the matter?"

"Good news," Judy said.

Gary said, "Dr. George Harding has offered to accept you at Harding Hospital for pretrial observation and treatment."

"What does that mean?"

"One of two things can happen," Judy explained. "Either at some future time you'll be declared competent, and a trial date will be set; or after a certain period you'll be ruled incompetent to stand trial, and the charges will be dismissed. The prosecution agreed to it, and Judge Flowers has ordered you removed from here and sent to Harding Hospital next week. On one condition."

Tommy said, "There's always a condition."

Gary leaned forward and jabbed at the table with his forefinger. "Dr. Wilbur told the judge that multiple personalities keep their promises. She knows how important promises are to all of you."

"So?"

"Judge Flowers says if you'll promise not to try to escape from Harding Hospital, you can be released and sent there right away."

Tommy crossed his arms. "Shit. I'm not promising that."

"You've got to!" Gary shouted. "Jesus, we've been working our tails off to keep you from being sent to Lima, and now you take this attitude?"

"Well, it's not right," Tommy said. "Escaping is the one thing I do best. That's one of the main reasons I'm here. I'm being denied the use of my talent."

Gary ran his fingers through his hair as if he wanted to pull it out.

Judy put her hand on Tommy's arm. "Tommy, you've got to give us your promise. If not for yourself, you've got to do it for the children. The little ones. You know this is a bad place for them. They'll be cared for at Harding Hospital."

He uncrossed his arms and stared at the table, and Judy knew she had touched the right nerve. She had come to understand that the other personalities had a deep love and a sense of responsibility for the younger ones.

"All right," he said reluctantly. "I promise."

What Tommy did not tell her was that when he first heard that he might be transferred to Lima, he had bought a razor blade from a trusty. Right now it was taped to the sole of his left foot. There was no reason to tell because no one had asked him. He had learned long ago that when you are transferred from one institution to another, you always bring along a weapon. He might not be able to break his promise by escaping, but at least he could defend himself if someone tried to rape him. Or else he could give it to Billy and let him cut his own throat.

Four days before the scheduled transfer to Harding Hospital, Sergeant Willis came down to the cell. He wanted Tommy to show him how he managed to get out of the strait jacket.

Tommy looked at the lean, balding officer with the fringes of gray hair framing his dark complexion and said with a frown, "Why should I?"

"You're leaving here anyway," Willis said. "I figure I'm not too old to learn something new."

"You been okay to me, Sergeant," Tommy said, "but I don't give up my secrets that easy."

"Look at it this way. You could help save someone's life."

Tommy had turned away, but now he looked up, curious. "How's that?"

"You're not sick, I know that. But we've got other people in here who are. We put them in straits to protect them. If they got out, they might kill themselves. If you show me how you do it, we could prevent other people from doing it. You'd be saving lives."

Tommy shrugged to show that didn't concern him.

But the next day he showed Sergeant Willis his trick of taking off the strait jacket. Then he taught him how to put it on a person in such a way that he could never get out of it.

Late that night, Judy got a call from Dorothy Turner. "There's another one," Turner said.

"Another what?"

"Another personality we didn't know about. A nineteen-year-old girl named Adalana."

"Oh my God!" Judy whispered. "That makes ten."

Dorothy described her late-night visit to the jail, how she had seen him sitting on the floor and heard him talking in a soft voice about needing love and affection. Dorothy had sat beside him, comforting him, wiping away his tears. Then "Adalana" talked of writing poetry in secret. She explained, tearfully, that only she had the ability to *wish* any of the others off the spot. Only Arthur and Christene, up to now, had known of her existence.

Judy tried to imagine the scene: Dorothy sitting on the floor, hugging Milligan.

"Why did she choose to reveal herself now?" Judy asked.

"Adalana blames herself for what happened to the boys," Dorothy said. "She's the one who stole the time from Ragen at the time of the rapes."

"What are you saying?"

"Adalana said she did it because she was desperate to be held and caressed and loved."

"Adalana did the—"

"Adalana's a lesbian."

When Judy hung up, she stared at the telephone for a long time. Her husband asked her what the call was about. She opened her mouth to tell him, but then she shook her head and instead turned out the light.

CHAPTER THREE

(1)

Billy Milligan was transferred from the Franklin County Jail to Harding Hospital two days ahead of schedule, on the morning of March 16. Dr. George Harding had assembled and briefed a therapy team for Milligan, but when he arrived unexpectedly, Dr. Harding was away at a psychiatric meeting in Chicago.

Judy Stevenson and Dorothy Turner, who had followed the police car to Harding Hospital, knew what a terrible blow it would be to Danny to be taken back to jail. Dr. Shoemaker, a staff physician, agreed to take personal charge of the patient until Dr. Harding returned, and the sheriff's deputy signed his prisoner over.

Judy and Dorothy walked with Danny to Wakefield Cottage, a locked psychiatric unit with facilities for fourteen difficult patients requiring constant observation and personal attention. A bed was found and prepared, and Danny was assigned to one of two "special care" rooms whose heavy oak doors had peepholes for around-the-clock observation. A psychiatric aide (called "psych-tech" at Harding Hospital) brought him a lunch tray, and both women stayed with him while he ate.

After lunch, Dr. Shoemaker and three nurses joined them. Turner—feeling it was important for the staff to see the multiple personality syndrome for themselves—suggested to Danny that Arthur come out and meet some of the people who would be working with him.

Nurse Adrienne McCann, the unit coordinator, had been briefed as part of the therapy team, but the other two nurses were taken completely by surprise.

Donna Egar, mother of five daughters, found it difficult to sort out her emotions at meeting the Campus Rapist. The

61

nurse watched closely as first the little boy talked and then his eyes became fixed in a trance, lips moving silently, conducting an inner conversation. When he looked up, his expression was austere and haughty, and he spoke in a British accent.

She had to keep from laughing, not convinced by Danny or Arthur of either's existence—it could be an act by a brilliant actor to avoid prison, she thought. But she was curious about what Billy Milligan was like; she wanted to know what kind of person would do the things he had done.

Dorothy and Judy spoke to Arthur, reassuring him that he was in a safe place. Dorothy told him she would be coming by in a few days to do some psychological testing. Judy said she and Gary would visit from time to time to work with him on the case.

Psych-tech Tim Sheppard observed the new patient every fifteen minutes through the peephole and made entries on the special-procedures record for that first day:

5:00   sitting cross-legged on bed, quiet
5:15   sitting cross-legged on bed, staring
5:32   standing, looking out window
5:45   dinner served
6:02   sitting on edge of bed, staring
6:07   tray removed, ate well.

At seven-fifteen, Milligan began pacing.

At eight o'clock, Nurse Helen Yaeger went into his room and stayed with him for forty minutes. Her first entry in the nurses' notes was brief:

3/16/78 Mr. Milligan remains in special care—observed closely for special precautions. Spoke of his multiple personalities. "Arthur" did most of the talking—he has an English accent. Stated that one of the persons—namely Billy—is suicidal and he has been asleep since 16 years of age in order to protect the others from harm. Eating well. Voiding well. Taking foods well. Pleasant and cooperative.

After Nurse Yaeger left, Arthur silently informed the others that Harding Hospital was a safe and supportive environment. Since it would take insight and logic to assist the physicians in therapy, he, Arthur, would henceforth assume complete domination of the spot.

At two twenty-five that morning, Psych-tech Chris Cann heard a loud noise from the room. When he went to check, he saw the patient sitting on the floor.

Tommy was upset at having fallen out of bed. Seconds later, he heard the footsteps and saw the eye at the peephole. As soon as the footsteps faded away, Tommy pulled the taped razor blade from the sole of his foot and carefully hid it, retaping it to the underside of one of the bed slats. He would know where to find it when the time came.

(2)

On his return from Chicago on March 19, Dr. George Harding, Jr., was annoyed that his careful arrangements had been upset by the early transfer. He had planned to greet Milligan in person. He had gone to a great deal of trouble to assemble a therapy team: psychologist, art therapist, adjunctive therapist, psychiatric social worker, doctors, nurses, psych-techs and the Wakefield unit coordinator. He had discussed with them the complexities of multiple personality. When some of the staff admitted openly that they didn't believe in the diagnosis, he listened to them patiently, spoke of his own skepticism and asked them to assist him in fulfilling the charge of the court. They would all have to keep open minds and work together to get an insight into William Stanley Milligan.

Dr. Perry Ayres gave Milligan a physical examination the day after Dr. Harding returned. Ayres wrote in the medical history that frequently Milligan's lips moved and his eyes were diverted to the right, usually before responding to a question. Ayres noted that when he asked the patient why he did that, he responded that he was talking to some of the others, especially Arthur, to get the answers to the questions.

"But you're supposed to call us Billy," Milligan said, "so no one will think we're crazy. I'm Danny. It was Allen that filled out that form. But I'm not supposed to talk about the others." Dr. Ayres quoted this in his report and added:

We agreed early that we would try to talk only about Billy, with the understanding that Danny would give us the health information related to all of them. It was his inability to stick to this agreement that led to the disclosure of the other names. The only ailment he recalls is the hernia repair when Billy was 9—

"David's always been 9," and it was David who had the hernia repair. Allen has tunnel vision, but everyone else has normal vision . . .

Note: Before going into the examining room, I discussed with him the nature of the examination contemplated, describing it in detail. I emphasized that it would be important to check his hernia repair and his prostate by rectal examination, the latter because of the urinary abnormality [pyuria]. He became very anxious and his lips and eyes moved rapidly as he apparently held a conversation with the others. He nervously but politely told me "that might mess up Billy and David because that's where Chalmers raped each of them 4 times when we lived on the farm. Chalmers was our stepfather." He also added at about this point that the mother described in the family history is Billy's mother, "but she's not my mother—I don't know my mother."

Rosalie Drake and Nick Cicco, co-therapists in Wakefield Cottage's "mini-group" program, became most closely involved with Milligan on a day-to-day basis. At ten each morning and three each afternoon, seven or eight of the Wakefield patients would be brought together to work on projects and activities as a group.

On March 21, Nick brought Milligan from the special-care room, now locked only at night, to the activities room. The slender twenty-seven-year-old psych-tech, who sported a full beard and wore two earrings—a delicate gold loop and a jade stone—in his left ear lobe, had heard of Milligan's hostility toward males because of the sexual abuse he had suffered as a child. He was curious about multiple personality, though he was skeptical about the whole idea.

Rosalie, a blond, blue-eyed occupational therapist in her late twenties, had never dealt with a multiple personality before. But after the briefing by Dr. Harding, she became aware that the staff had quickly divided into two camps: those who believed Milligan was a multiple and those who believed he was a con man—faking this exotic illness to gain attention and to avoid going to prison for rape. Rosalie was struggling hard to keep an open mind.

When Milligan seated himself at the end of the table, apart from the others, Rosalie Drake told him that the mini-group patients had decided the day before to make collages that would say something about themselves to someone they loved.

"I don't have anyone I love to make one for," he said.

"Then do it for us," Rosalie said. "Everyone is doing it." She held up a sheet of construction paper she was working on. "Nick and I are doing them too."

Rosalie watched from a distance as Milligan took a sheet of eight-by-eleven construction paper and started cutting photographs from magazines. She had heard of Milligan's artistic ability, and now, looking at the shy, quiet patient, she was curious to see what he would do. He worked silently, calmly. When he was done, she walked over and looked at it.

His collage startled her. It showed a frightened, tearful child looking out of the center of the page, and beneath him the name MORRISON. Looming over him was an angry man and, in red, the word DANGER. In the lower right corner was a skull.

She was touched by its simplicity of statement, the depth of emotion. She hadn't asked for anything like this, and it wasn't what she'd expected. It revealed, she felt, a painful history. She shivered when she looked at it, and right then and there she knew she was hooked. No matter what doubts the others in the hospital might have about him, this, she knew, was not the product of an unfeeling sociopath. Nick Cicco agreed.

Dr. George (so called by staff and patients to distinguish him from his father, Dr. George Harding, Sr.) began to read the relevant psychiatric journals and discovered that the disease known as multiple personality seemed to be on the increase. The doctor made calls to various psychiatrists, and all of them said much the same thing: "We'll share with you the little we know, but this is an area we don't understand. You'll have to blaze your own trail."

It was going to take much more time and effort than Dr. George had first imagined, and he wondered if he had done the right thing accepting this patient in the middle of a fund-raising campaign and expansion program for the hospital. He reassured himself that it was important to Billy Milligan, and important to the profession, to help psychiatry probe the limits of knowledge about the human mind.

Before he could provide the court with an evaluation, he would have to learn Billy Milligan's history. Considering the massive amnesia, that posed a serious problem.

On Thursday, March 23, Gary Schweickart and Judy Stevenson visited their client for an hour, going over his vague memory of events, comparing his story with those of the three victims, planning alternative legal strategies, depending on Dr. Harding's report to the court.

Both attorneys found Milligan more at ease, though he complained about being locked up in special care and having to wear "special precaution" clothes. "Dr. George says I can be treated just like the other patients here, but nobody here trusts me. The other patients are allowed to go off the grounds in the van on excursions, but not me. I have to stay here. And I just get furious when they insist on calling me Billy."

They tried to calm him, to explain that Dr. George had gone out on a limb for him, and that he had to be careful not to try the doctor's patience. Judy sensed he was Allen, but she didn't ask, always afraid he might be insulted that she didn't know him.

Gary said, "I think you should try to cooperate with the staff here. It's your only chance to stay out of jail."

As they left, both agreed that they were relieved he was safe and that the day-to-day responsibility and worry were off their backs for a while.

Later that day the first therapy session was a strained fifty-minute hour for Dr. Harding. Milligan sat on the chair facing the window in the interview room at Wakefield, but he would not, at first, make eye contact. He seemed to remember very little of his past, although he talked freely of the abuse by his adoptive father.

Dr. Harding knew he was being overcautious in his approach. Dr. Wilbur had told him to find out as soon as possible how many personalities there were, to establish their identities. The alternates needed to be encouraged to tell why they existed and to be permitted to relive the specific situations that had caused their creation.

Then all of the alternates had to be encouraged to know one another, to communicate and to help one another with their different problems, sharing things instead of being separated. The strategy, Wilbur had said, was to bring the others together and eventually introduce Billy—the core personality—to the memories of those incidents. Then, finally, fusion might be attempted. Though the temptation was great to try her approach, the way she had skillfully brought the personalities out in the jail, George Harding had long ago learned his lesson. What worked for someone else didn't always work for him. He considered himself a very conservative man, and he would have to learn in his own way, and in his own good time, who and what he had here.

As the days went by, Nurse Donna Egar discovered that she was pretty much on a one-to-one basis with Milligan. He slept very little, far less than most of the other patients, and waked early, so she got to talk to him a great deal. He spoke about the other people who lived with him inside his body.

One day he handed her a sheet of paper with writing all over it and signed "Arthur." He seemed quite frightened, saying, "I don't know anybody named Arthur, and I don't understand what's written on the paper."

Soon the staff was complaining to Dr. George that they found it increasingly difficult to deal with someone who constantly said, "I didn't do that, someone else did," when they had seen it happen with their own eyes. Milligan, they said, was undermining the treatment of other patients, manipulating the staff by going from one to the other to get what he wanted. He constantly hinted that Ragen might come out and handle matters, and the staff saw this as a veiled threat.

Dr. George suggested that he be the one to deal with Milligan's alter personalities, and then only in therapy sessions. The staff should not mention or discuss the other names on the unit, especially not in front of the other patients.

Helen Yaeger, the nurse who had spoken to Arthur on the first day, now entered this treatment plan on the nursing-goal sheet dated March 28:

Within one month Mr. Milligan will accept responsibility for acts which he denies as evidenced by no statements of denial of these behaviors.
Plan: (1) When denies ability to play piano—staff replies they saw or heard him play—maintain a matter of fact attitude.
    (2) When observed writing notes that he denies knowledge of—staff should tell him he was seen writing notes.

(3) When patient refers to himself as another personality—staff should remind him his name is Billy.

Dr. George explained his approach to Allen during the therapy session by pointing out that the other patients on the unit became confused when they heard the various names of the personalities.

"Some people call themselves Napoleon or Jesus Christ," Allen said.

"But it's different if I and the staff do it—call you Danny one day and Arthur or Ragen or Tommy or Allen another time. I suggest that to the staff and to the patients, all your personalities answer to the name of Billy, while in—"

"They're not 'personalities,' Dr. George. They're people."

"Why do you make the distinction?"

"When you call them personalities, it's as if you don't think they're real."

(3)

On April 8, several days after Dorothy Turner had begun a program of psychological testing, Donna Egar saw Milligan walking back and forth in his room angrily. When she asked him what was wrong, he answered in his British accent, "No one understands."

Then she saw his face change again and then his whole posture, walk and speech, and she knew it was Danny. At that point, seeing how consistent he was, how real these different personalities were, she no longer assumed he was faking. She had to admit that she, alone of the nursing staff, had come around to being a believer.

A few days later, he came to her, very upset. She could tell quickly that it was Danny. He stared at her and said pathetically, "Why am I here?"

"Where do you mean?" she asked. "Here in this room, or in this building?"

He shook his head. "Some of the other patients asked me why I'm in this hospital."

"Maybe Dorothy Turner can explain it to you when she comes to do your testing," she said.

That evening, after his testing session with Dorothy Turner was over, he wouldn't talk to anyone. He ran into his room and went to the bathroom to wash his face. A few seconds later,

Danny heard his front door open and close. He looked out and saw a young woman patient named Dorine. Though he often listened to her problems sympathetically and talked about his own, he had no other interest in her.

"Why are you here?" he asked.

"I wanted to talk to you. Why did you get so upset tonight?"

"You know you can't come in here. It's against the rules."

"But you look so depressed."

"I found out what someone did. It's terrible. I'm not fit to live."

Just then footsteps approached, followed by a knock on the door. Dorine jumped into the bathroom with him and closed the door behind her.

"What'd you do that for?" he whispered harshly. "I'll get into worse trouble. Now it'll be a mess."

She giggled.

"All right, Billy and Dorine!" Nurse Yaeger called. "You two can come out whenever you're ready."

In the nurses' notes for April 9, 1979, Nurse Yaeger wrote:

Mr. Milligan—found in his bathroom with female peer—light off—When questioned about this stated he needed to be alone to talk to her about something he found out he did—Related with questioning that during his psychological testing this evening with Mrs. Turner, he learned he had raped three women. Became very tearful, saying he wanted "Ragen and Adalana to die." Dr. George called—incident explained. Placed in special care room and on special precautions. Few minutes later patient observed sitting on bed with bathrobe tie in hand. Still tearful, saying he wanted to kill *them*. After speaking to him for a while he gave up bathrobe tie. Prior to doing this placed around neck.

In her testing, Dorothy Turner discovered significant IQ variation among the different personalities:

	VERBAL IQ	PERFORMANCE	FULL SCALE
Allen	105	130	120
Ragen	114	120	119
David	68	72	69
Danny	69	75	71
Tommy	81	96	87
Christopher	98	108	102

Christene was too young to be tested, Adalana would not come out and Arthur declined to take the IQ portion of the tests, saying it was beneath his dignity.

Turner discovered that Danny's Rorschach responses revealed poorly concealed hostility and a need for external support to offset the feelings of inferiority and inadequacy. Tommy showed more maturity than Danny and more potential for acting out. He had the most schizoid characteristics and the least concern for others. Ragen showed the most potential for violent acting out.

Arthur she found strongly intellectual, and she felt he relied on this to maintain his position of direction over the others. He also appeared to her to maintain a compensatory feeling of superiority to the world at large, but had feelings of uneasiness and was threatened by emotionally stimulating situations. Emotionally, Allen appeared to be an almost detached personality.

She found some things in common: evidence of a feminine identity and of a strong superego, which anger threatened to override. She did *not* find evidence of psychotic process, nor of schizophrenic thought disorder.

When Rosalie Drake and Nick Cicco announced that the mini-group would be doing trust exercises on April 19, Arthur allowed Danny to take the spot. The staff had prepared the rec room with tables, chairs, couches and boards, turning it into an obstacle course.

Knowing Milligan's fear of men, Nick had suggested that Rosalie blindfold and lead him through. "You've got to work with me, Billy," she said. "It's the only way to build enough confidence in other people so you can live in the real world."

He finally allowed her to blindfold him.

"Now hold my hand," she said, leading him into the room. "I'm going to take you over and around the obstacle course, and I'll keep you from being hurt."

As she led him, she could see and feel his uncontrolled terror at not knowing where he was moving or what he might crash into. They moved slowly at first and then faster, around chairs, under tables, up and down ladders. Seeing his panic, both she and Nick admired him for going through with it.

"I didn't let you get hurt, did I, Billy?"

Danny shook his head.

"You've got to learn that there are some people you can trust. Not everyone, of course, but some."

Rosalie noticed that more and more in her presence, he assumed the little-boy role she had come to know as Danny. It upset her that so many of his drawings contained death images.

The following Tuesday, Allen was permitted to go for the first time to the adjunctive therapy building to attend expressive-art class, where he would be able to sketch and paint.

Don Jones, the mild-mannered art therapist, was impressed by Milligan's natural talent, but Jones could see he was anxious and restive about being in the new group. The bizarre drawings, he realized, were Billy's way of attracting attention and seeking approval.

Jones pointed to a sketch of a tombstone engraved with the words "DO NOT R.I.P."

"Could you tell us something about that, Billy? What were your feelings when you drew that?"

"It's *Billy's* real father," Allen said. "He was a comedian and a master of ceremonies in Miami, Florida, before he killed himself."

"Why don't you tell us what you felt? We want to get in touch with feelings rather than details at this point, Billy."

Allen threw down his pencil in disgust at still having Billy get credit for his artwork, and looked up at the clock. "I've got to get back to the unit to make my bed."

The next day he talked to Nurse Yaeger about the treatment, complaining that it was all wrong. When she told him he was interfering with the staff and the patients, he became upset. "I'm not responsible for things that are done by my other people," he said.

"We can't relate to your other people," Yaeger said, "only to Billy."

He shouted, "Dr. Harding isn't treating me the way Dr. Wilbur told him to. This treatment is no good."

He demanded to read his chart, and when Yaeger refused, he said he knew he could make the hospital allow him access to his records. He was certain, he said, that the staff was not recording his changes of behavior and that he wouldn't be able to account for his lost time.

That evening, after a visit by Dr. George, Tommy announced to the staff that he was firing his doctor. Later Allen came out of his room and said he was reinstating him.

* * *

After she was given permission to visit, Milligan's mother, Dorothy Moore, came almost every week, often with her daughter, Kathy. Her son's reactions were unpredictable. Sometimes after her visit he would be happy and outgoing. Other times he would be depressed.

Joan Winslow, the psychiatric social worker, reported in the team meeting that she had interviewed Dorothy after each of her visits. Winslow found her a warm and giving person, but speculated that her shy and dependent nature had prevented her from interfering with the reported abuses. Dorothy had told her she always felt there were two Billys—one a kind and loving boy, the other someone who didn't care if he hurt people's feelings.

It was Nick Cicco who noted on the chart that after a visit from Mrs. Moore on April 18, Milligan seemed very upset and isolated himself in his room with a pillow over his head.

By the end of April, with six of the twelve weeks gone, Dr. George felt things were going too slowly. He needed some way to establish lines of communication between the personalities and the original personality, the core Billy. But first he had to break through and reach Billy, whom he had not seen since that Sunday when Dr. Wilbur had convinced Ragen to let him come out.

It occurred to Dr. George that it might be effective to confront the core personality and the alter egos with videotaped records of their speech and behavior. Dr. George told Allen about his idea and how important it was for the personalities to communicate with one another and with Billy. Allen agreed to it.

Later, Allen told Rosalie he was very pleased about the videotape they were going to make of him. He was nervous about it, but Dr. George had convinced him that he would learn a lot about himself.

Dr. George held the first videotaped session on May 1. Dorothy Turner was present because he knew Billy felt at ease with her and because he intended to try to bring out Adalana. Though he had at first resisted bringing out new people, he realized it was necessary to understand the significance of this female aspect of Milligan's personality.

He repeated several times how helpful it would be if Adalana would come out and talk to them. Finally, after several switches to the others, Milligan's face changed to a soft, tearful expression. The voice was choked and nasal. The face became almost feminine. The eyes drifted.

"It hurts to talk," Adalana said.

Dr. George tried to hide his excitement at the switch. He had wanted her to come out; he had expected it. But when it happened, it came as a surprise. "Why does it hurt?" he asked.

"Because of the boys. I got them into trouble."

"What did you do?" he asked.

Dorothy Turner, who had met Adalana in the jail the night before the transfer, sat by silently and watched.

"They don't understand what love is," Adalana said, "what it means to be held and cared for. I stole that time. I felt Ragen's alcohol and pills. Oh, it hurts to talk about it . . ."

"Yes, but we need to talk about it," Dr. George said, "to help us understand."

"I did it. It's a little too late to say I'm sorry now, isn't it? I ruined the boys' lives . . . But they just didn't understand . . ."

"Understand what?" Turner asked.

"What love is. What the need for love is. To be held by someone. Just to feel warm and cared for. I don't know what made me do it."

"During that time," Turner asked, "did you feel warm and cared for?"

Adalana paused and whispered, "Just for a few moments . . . I stole that time. Arthur didn't put me on the spot. I wished Ragen off the spot . . ."

She glanced around tearfully. "I don't like to go through this. I can't go into the courtroom. I don't want to say anything to Ragen . . . I want out of the boys' lives. I don't want to mess them up anymore . . . I feel so damned guilty . . . Just why did I do it?"

"When did you first begin to be on the spot?" Dr. George asked.

"Last summer I started stealing time. And when the boys were in solitary confinement in Lebanon, I stole some time to write poems. I love to write poems . . ." She wept. "What are they going to do to the boys?"

"We don't know," Dr. George said softly. "We're trying to understand as much as we can."

"Just don't hurt them too bad," Adalana said.

"When these incidents occurred last October, were you aware of what was being planned?" he asked.

"Yes. I know everything. I know things Arthur doesn't even know . . . But I couldn't stop it. I was feeling the pills and the alcohol. I don't know why I did it. I was so lonely."

She sniffled and asked for a Kleenex.

Dr. George watched Adalana's face closely as he questioned her very cautiously, afraid of frightening her away. "Were there friends you found . . . some pleasure in? To deal with some of your loneliness?"

"I never talk to anybody. Not even to the boys . . . I talk to Christene."

"You said it was during the summer that you were on the spot some of the time, and in Lebanon. Were you on the spot before that time?"

"Not on the spot. But I was there. I've been there for a long time."

"When Chalmer—"

"Yes!" she snapped. "Don't talk about him!"

"Can you relate with Billy's mother?"

"No! She couldn't even relate with the boys."

"Billy's sister, Kathy?"

"Yes, I talked to Kathy. But she didn't know it, I think. We went shopping together."

"Billy's brother, James?"

"No . . . I don't even like him."

Adalana wiped her eyes and then sat back, looking at the videotape machine, startled, sniffling. Then she was silent for a long time and Dr. George knew she was gone. He watched the glazed expression and waited to see who would come on the spot.

"It would be very helpful," he said, gently, persuasively, "if we could talk to Billy."

The face changed to a startled, frightened look as Billy glanced around quickly to take in his surroundings. Dr. George recognized the expression he had seen in the Franklin County Jail that day Dr. Wilbur had brought out Billy, the core personality.

Dr. George spoke to him gently, afraid he would disappear before he could make contact. Billy's knees jiggled nervously, eyes glanced around fearfully.

"Do you know where you are?" Dr. George asked.

"No?" He shrugged and said it as if answering a yes-or-no question on a school test and uncertain whether he had the right answer.

"This is a hospital and I'm your doctor."

"Jesus, he'll kill me if I talk to a doctor."

"Who will?"

Billy glanced around and saw the videotape camera pointed at him.

"What's that?"

"That's for recording this session. It's a videotape machine, and we thought it would be helpful to have a record of this session so that you could see what was happening."

But then he was gone.

"That thing frightened him," Tommy said in disgust.

"I explained it was a videotape recorder and—"

Tommy snickered. "He probably didn't know what you were talking about."

When the session was over and Tommy had gone back to Wakefield Cottage, Dr. George sat alone in his office and thought about it for a long time. He knew he would have to tell the court that although William S. Milligan was not insane in the usual sense of being psychotic (since dissociation was considered a neurosis), it was his best medical judgment that because Milligan was so far removed from reality that he couldn't conform his conduct to the requirements of the law, he was not responsible for those crimes.

What remained to be done was to continue treating this patient and in some way make him competent to stand trial.

But with less than six weeks left of the three months provided by the court, how did you cure an illness that had taken psychoanalysts like Cornelia Wilbur in her work with Sybil more than ten years to accomplish?

The next morning, Arthur decided it was important to share with Ragen what he had learned about Adalana during Dr. George's videotaping session. He paced back and forth in the special-care room and spoke aloud to Ragen: "The mystery of the rapes has been solved. I know now who did it."

His voice changed quickly to Ragen's: "How you know?"

"I have learned some new facts and put the information together."

"Who it vas?"

"I guess, since you have been blamed for those crimes you didn't commit, you have a right to know."

The conversation went on with rapid-fire switching, sometimes aloud, sometimes in the mind as speech without sound.

"Ragen, do you recall at times in the past hearing female voices?"

"Yes, I have heard Christene. And—yes, other voices of vomans."

"Well, when you went out stealing, three times last October, one of our females got involved."

"Vat you mean?"

"There is a young woman you have never met, called Adalana."

"I never hear of her."

"She's a very sweet and gentle person. She's the one who has always done the cooking and cleaning up for us. She did the flower arrangements when Allen got the job at the florist's shop. It just never occurred to me that—"

"Vat she have to do about it? Did she take money?"

"No, Ragen. She's the one who raped your victims."

"*She* raped girls? Arthur, how does a *she* rape a girl?"

"Ragen, have you ever heard of a lesbian?"

"All right," Ragen said, "how does a lesbian rape another girl?"

"Well, that's why they accused you. When one of the males is on the spot, some of them have the physical ability to perform sex, even though we both know I have laid down the rule that we are to be celibate. She used your body."

"You mean I am blamed all this time for a rape this bitch committed?"

"Yes, but I want you to talk to her and let her explain."

"So that is vat all this rape talk is about? I kill her."

"Ragen, be reasonable."

"Reasonable?"

"Adalana, I want you to meet Ragen. Since Ragen is our protector, he has a right to know what happened. You will have to explain yourself and justify your actions to him."

A soft, delicate voice echoed in his mind, as if from the darkness beyond. It was like a hallucination or a dream voice. "Ragen, I'm sorry for the trouble—"

"Sorry!" Ragen snarled, pacing. "You filty slut. Vy for you go around raping vomans? Do you realize vat you put us all through?"

He turned sharply, stepping off the spot, and suddenly the room was filled with a sound of a woman crying.

Nurse Helen Yaeger's face appeared at the peephole. "Can I help you, Billy?"

"Blast you, madam!" Arthur said. "Leave us alone!"

Yaeger left, upset that Arthur had snapped at her. When she was gone, Adalana tried to explain herself: "You have to understand, Ragen, my needs are different from the rest of you."

"Vy in hell you have sex vit vomans anyvay? You are voman yourself."

"You men don't understand. At least the children know what love is, what compassion is, what it means to put your arms around somebody and say, 'I love you, care about you, have feelings for you.'"

"I must interrupt," said Arthur, "but I have always felt that physical love is illogical and anachronistic, considering the most recent advancements in scientific—"

"You're crazy!" Adalana screamed. "Both of you!" Then her voice softened again. "If you could just experience what it's like to be held and cared for, you'd understand."

"Look, bitch!" Ragen snapped. "I do not care who or vat you are. If you so much as speak to another person on this unit—or to any other person again—I vill make sure you die."

"One moment," Arthur said. "*You* do not make those decisions at Harding. Here I am dominant. You listen to me."

"You are going to allow her to get avay vit this shit?"

"By no means. I will handle it. But you are not the one to tell her she can no longer take the spot. You have nothing to say about it. You were idiotic enough to allow her to steal that time from you. You had not enough control. Your stupid vodka and marijuana and amphetamines made you so vulnerable that you put Billy's and everyone else's life in danger. Yes, Adalana did it. But the responsibility was yours, because you are the protector. And when you became vulnerable, you put not only yourself but everyone else in danger."

Ragen started to speak, but backed away. Seeing the plant on the windowsill, he swung his arm and swept it to the floor.

"Having said that," Arthur continued, "I agree that Adalana will henceforth be classified as 'undesirable.' Adalana, you will never again take the spot. You will no longer take time."

She moved to the corner, facing the wall, and wailed until she left the spot.

There was a long silence, and David came and wiped the tears from his eyes. Seeing the plant in the broken pot on the floor, he watched it, knowing it was dying. It hurt to see it lying there with its roots exposed. He could feel it withering away.

Nurse Yaeger came back to the door with a tray of food. "Are you sure I can't help you?"

David cringed. "Are you going to put me in jail for murdering the plant?"

She set the tray down and put her hand reassuringly on his shoulder. "No, Billy. No one is going to put you in jail. We're going to take care of you and make you better."

Dr. George took time from his busy schedule to attend the American Psychiatric Association meeting in Atlanta on Monday, May 8. He'd seen Milligan the previous Friday and arranged for him to begin intensive therapy, while he was gone, with the Director of Psychology, Dr. Marlene Kocan.

Marlene Kocan, a New Yorker, was among those at Harding Hospital who had from the beginning doubted the diagnosis of multiple personality, although she never expressed this openly. Then one afternoon as she was talking to Allen in her office, Nurse Donna Egar greeted her: "Hi, Marlene. How've you been?"

Allen turned instantly and blurted out, "Marlene is the name of Tommy's girl friend."

That moment, seeing how spontaneous his remark was, spoken with no time for reflection, Dr. Kocan decided he was not faking.

"That's my first name too," Kocan said. "You say she's Tommy's girl friend?"

"Well, she doesn't know it's Tommy. She calls all of us Billy. But Tommy's the one who gave her an engagement ring. She never knew the secret."

Dr. Kocan said pensively, "It's going to be quite a shock when she finds out."

* * *

At the APA meeting, Dr. Harding brought Dr. Cornelia Wilbur up to date on Milligan's progress. He told her he now believed fully that Milligan was a multiple personality. He described Milligan's refusal to recognize the other names in public and the problems it was causing.

"He's used it in Dr. Pugliese's group therapy and caused problems with the other patients. When he's asked to share *his* problems, he just says, 'My doctor told me not to talk about it.' You can imagine the effect of that and of his tendency to play junior therapist. He's been dropped from group."

"You've got to understand," Wilbur said, "what it does to the alter personalities not to be recognized. Sure, they're used to responding to the original name, but once the secret is out, it makes them feel not wanted."

Dr. George considered that and asked Wilbur what she thought about his attempting to treat Milligan in the brief time left.

"I think you should ask the court for at least another ninety days," she said. "And then I think you should try to fuse him so that he can help his attorneys and stand trial."

"The state of Ohio is sending a forensic psychiatrist down to look him over about two weeks from now, on May 26. I was wondering if you'd consider coming to the hospital for a consultation. I could use your support."

Wilbur agreed to come.

Although the APA meeting was scheduled to run until Friday, Dr. George left Atlanta on Wednesday. He called a team meeting at Wakefield the following day and told the staff that after discussing the case with Dr. Wilbur, he had decided that not recognizing the alternate personalities was countertherapeutic.

"We thought if we ignored the multiple personalities, perhaps that would integrate them, but actually it's just caused them to go underground. We've got to continue to stress the need for responsibility and accountability, but we've got to avoid repressing the various personalities."

He pointed out that if there was to be any hope of achieving fusion so that Milligan could go to trial, all the personalities would have to be recognized and dealt with as individuals.

Rosalie Drake felt relieved. Secretly, she had always responded to them anyway, especially Danny. It would be easier now for everyone, having it all out in the open instead of pretending it didn't exist just because of the few who still didn't believe.

Donna Egar smiled when she entered the new plan on the nursing-goal sheet of May 12, 1978:

> Mr. Milligan will feel free to refer to other personalities in order to allow him to discuss feelings which he otherwise finds hard to express. Evidence will be his frank discussion with staff.
> Plan: (A) Do not deny that he experiences these dissociations.
> (B) When he believes he is another personality, elicit his feelings in that situation.

(4)

When the mini-group began working in the garden in mid-May, Rosalie Drake and Nick Cicco discovered that Danny was terrified of the hand-run Rototiller. They began a deconditioning program, telling Danny to come closer and closer to the machine. When Nick said that one of these days he'd lose his fear of it and even be able to run it, Danny nearly fainted.

Several days later, one of Rosalie's other male patients refused to cooperate in the gardening project. Allen had noticed that from time to time the man seemed to enjoy picking on her.

"This is stupid," the patient shouted. "It's obvious you don't know a goddamned thing about gardening."

"Well, all we can do is try," Rosalie said.

"You're just a fucking stupid broad," the patient said. "You don't know a goddamned thing more about gardening than you do about group therapy."

Allen saw her near tears, but he said nothing. He let Danny out for a while to work with Nick. Back in his room later, Allen started to come on the spot but felt himself jerked back and slammed into a wall. That was something only Ragen could do, and only close to the moment of switching.

"Jesus, what's that for?" Allen whispered.

"In garden this morning you permit that big mouth to offend a lady."

"Well, it's none of my doing."

"You know rules. You do not stand by and see voman or child hurt or offended vithout taking action."

"Well, why didn't *you* do something?"

"I vas not on spot. It vas your responsibility. Remember that, or next time ven you are coming on spot, I break your head."

The next day, when the aggressive patient insulted Rosalie again, Allen grabbed him by the collar and glared ferociously. "Watch your goddamned mouth!"

He hoped the man wouldn't start anything. If he did, Allen decided, he was going to leave and let Ragen do the fighting. That was for sure.

Rosalie Drake found that she constantly had to defend Milligan against those in the hospital who said he was nothing more than a con man faking to get out of a prison sentence and against those who were offended by Allen's demands for special privileges, pitting one staff member against another, by Arthur's arrogance and by Tommy's antisocial attitude. She was furious when she heard some of the nurses complain that Dr. George's pet patient was taking up too much of the hospital's time and facilities. And she cringed when she heard the sneering remark again and again: "They worry more about that rapist than they do about his victims." When you were trying to help the mentally disordered, she insisted, you had to put aside feelings of vengeance and deal with the individual.

One morning, Rosalie watched as Billy Milligan sat on the steps outside Wakefield Cottage, moving his lips, talking to himself. A change came over him. He looked up, startled, shook his head, touched his cheek.

Then he noticed a butterfly, reached out and caught it. When he peeked between his cupped palms, he jumped to his feet with a cry. He moved his open hands, sweeping them upward as if to help the butterfly take flight again. It fell to the ground and lay there. He looked at it in anguish.

As Rosalie approached him, he turned, obviously frightened, tears in his eyes. She had the feeling, without knowing why, that this was someone different from the others she had met.

He picked up the butterfly. "It don't fly anymore."

She smiled at him warmly, wondering if she should risk calling him by his right name. Finally she whispered, "Hello, Billy. I've been waiting for a long time to meet you."

She sat beside him on the steps as he hugged his knees and looked in awe at the grass and the trees and the sky.

A few days later, in mini-group, Arthur allowed Billy to take the spot again and work with clay. Nick encouraged him to model a head, and Billy worked at it for nearly an hour, rolling the clay into a ball, adding pieces for eyes and a nose, and pushing in two pellets for the irises.

"I made a head," he said proudly.

"That's very good," said Nick. "Who is it supposed to be?"

"Does it have to be someone?"

"No, I just thought it might be."

As Billy glanced away, Allen took the spot and looked at the clay head in disgust—it was just a gray blob with pellets of clay stuck on it. He picked up the modeling tool to reshape it. He'd turn it into a bust of Abraham Lincoln or maybe Dr. George, and show Nick what real sculpture was.

As he moved toward the face, the tool slipped, digging into his arm and drawing blood.

Allen's mouth fell open. He knew he hadn't been that clumsy. Suddenly, he felt himself thrown against the wall. Damnit. Ragen again.

"What'd I do now?" he whispered.

The answer echoed in his head. "You do not *ever* touch Billy's vork."

"Hell, I was only going to—"

"You ver going to show off. To show you are talented artist. But now is more important for Billy to have therapy."

That evening, alone in his room, Allen complained to Arthur that he was sick and tired of being pushed around by Ragen. "If he's so finicky about everything, let him or one of the others handle it."

"You've been quite argumentative," Arthur said. "Creating dissension. Because of you, Dr. Pugliese dropped us from group therapy. Your constant manipulation has created hostility in many of the Wakefield staff."

"Well, then, let someone else handle things. Put on someone who doesn't talk much. Billy and the children need the treatment. Let them deal with these people."

"I've been planning to let Billy take the spot more frequently," Arthur said. "After he meets Dr. George, it will be time for Billy to meet the rest of us."

(5)

As Milligan entered the interview room on Wednesday, May 24, Dr. George noticed the frightened, almost desperate look in his eyes, as if he would flee or collapse at any moment. He stared at the floor, and Dr. George felt there was a tenuous thread holding him in the here and now. They sat silently for a while, Billy's knees jiggling nervously, and then Dr. George said softly, "Maybe you can tell me just a little bit how you feel about coming up and talking with me here this morning."

"I don't know anything about it," Billy said, his voice nasal and whining.

"You didn't know you were going to come up and meet with me here? When did you come on the spot?"

Billy looked confused. "The spot?"

"When did you become aware that you and I were going to be talking?"

"When that guy came and told me to come with him."

"What did you think was going to happen?"

"He told me I was gonna go see a doctor. I didn't know why." His knees were jiggling up and down uncontrollably.

The conversation moved slowly, with agonizing silences, as Dr. George worked to establish a rapport with what he felt certain was the core Billy. Like a fisherman handling his pole with delicacy to work the line but keep it from breaking, he whispered, "How are you feeling?"

"Fine, I guess."

"What kinds of problems have you been having?"

"Well . . . I do things and I don't remember 'em . . . I go to sleep . . . and people tell me I do things."

"What kind of things do they say you do?"

"Bad things . . . criminal stuff."

"Things that you thought of doing? Most of us think of doing a whole lot of different things at different times."

"Just every time I wake up, somebody says I did something bad."

"What do you think of it when they tell you you've done something bad?"

"I just wanna die . . . 'cause I don't wanna hurt nobody."

He was trembling so badly that Dr. George quickly changed the subject. "You were telling me about sleeping. Just how much do you sleep?"

"Oh, it don't seem like a long time, but it is. I keep hearing things, too . . . somebody trying to talk to me."

"What are they trying to say?"

"I can't really understand 'em."

"Because it's in whispers? Or garbled? Or indistinct, so you can't make out the words?"

"It's real quiet . . . and it sounds like it's from somewhere else."

"Like from another room or another country?"

"Yeah," Billy said. "Like from another country."

"Any particular country?"

After a long pause as he searched his memory, he said, "It sounds like people on James Bond. And the other sounds like Russian. Is that the people the lady told me was inside me?"

"Could be," Dr. George whispered, almost inaudibly, worried as he saw the look of alarm cross Billy's face.

Billy's voice rose to a cry: *"What are they doin' in there?"*

"What are they saying to you? That might help us to understand. Are they giving you directions or guidance or counsel?"

"Sounds like they keep saying, 'Listen to what he says. Listen to what he says.'"

"Referring to whom? To me?"

"I guess so."

"When I'm not with you, when you're alone, do you hear them talking to you too?"

Billy sighed. "Kinda like they're talking *about* me. With other people."

"Do they act as if they need to protect you? Talk about you to other people, but as if they need to shield you?"

"I think they make me go to sleep."

"When do they make you go to sleep?"

"When I get too upset."

"Do you feel it's when you can't handle the upset? Because that's one of the reasons people go to sleep, to get away from whatever's upsetting them. Do you feel as if you're getting strong enough now so that they wouldn't have to be so protective of you?"

"Who's *they*?" he cried out, his voice rising in alarm again. "Who *are* these people? Why don't they let me stay awake?"

Dr. George realized he had to take another direction. "What are the things that are hardest for you to deal with?"

"Somebody going to hurt me."

"Does that frighten you?"

"It would make me go to sleep."

"But you still could get hurt," Dr. George insisted. "Even though you didn't know it."

Billy put his hands on his jiggling knees. "But if I go to sleep, I don't get hurt."

"What happens then?"

"I dunno . . . Every time I wake up, I'm not hurt." After a long silence, he looked up again. "Nobody said why these people are here."

"The ones who have been talking to you?"

"Yeah."

"Maybe it's because of what you've just been saying, that somehow when you didn't know how to protect yourself from some danger, another side of you has been able to figure out a way to protect yourself from being hurt."

"Another side of me?"

Dr. George smiled and nodded, waiting for a response. Billy's voice quivered, "How come I don't know the other side?"

"Because there must be some great fear inside of you," Dr. George said, "that prevents you from taking the actions that are necessary to protect you. Somehow it's too frightening for you to do this. And so you have to go to sleep in order for that side of you to take those corrective actions."

Billy seemed to be considering it, and then he looked up, as if struggling to understand. "Why am I that way?"

"There must have been things that frightened you terribly when you were very small."

After a long silence, Billy sobbed, "I don't want to think about those things. They hurt."

"But you were asking me why you had to go to sleep when there were situations you were afraid of being hurt in."

Billy looked around and in a choked voice said, "How'd I get here in this hospital?"

"Mrs. Turner, Dr. Karolin and Dr. Wilbur felt that perhaps if you came to the hospital, you wouldn't have to go to sleep. That you'd be able to learn how to deal with problems and frightening experiences, and that you'd be able to deal with them."

"You mean you guys c'n do that?" sobbed Billy.

"We certainly would like to try to help you do that. Would you like us to try?"

Billy's voice rose to a cry again: *You mean, you'll get these people outta me?*

Dr. George settled back. He had to be careful not to promise too much. "We'd like to help you so that you don't have to go to sleep. So that these sides of you can help make you a strong and healthy person."

"I won't hear 'em anymore? And they won't be able to put me to sleep?"

Dr. George chose his words carefully: "If you become strong enough, there won't be any need to put you to sleep."

"I didn't think nobody'd ever be able to help. I—I didn't know . . . Anytime I turned around, I'd wake up . . . I was locked in a room—back in the box . . ." He choked up, eyes flicking back and forth in terror.

"That would be very frightening," Dr. George said, trying to reassure him. "Terribly frightening."

"*I always got put in a box,*" Billy said, his voice rising. "Does he know I'm here?"

"Who?"

"My dad."

"I've had no contact with him. I don't know if he knows you're here."

"I—I'm not supposed to tell things. If he knew you was talking to me, he'd . . . oh! . . . he'd kill me . . . and bury me in the barn . . ."

The painful expression on Billy's face was terrible to see as he cringed and then looked down. The line had snapped. Dr. George knew he'd lost him.

Allen's voice came out softly. "Billy's asleep. Arthur didn't even put him to sleep. He just went to sleep because he started remembering again."

"Talking about those things was just too difficult, is that right?"

"What was you talking about?"

"About Chalmer."

"Oh, well, that would—" He glanced up at the video recorder. "What's this film machine on for?"

"I told Billy that I would like to video-record. I explained to him about it. He said it was okay. What made you come here now?"

"Arthur told me to get on the spot. I guess you were scaring Billy with that remembering. He kinda felt trapped in here."

Dr. George started to explain what he and Billy had talked about, and then he got an idea. "Tell me, would it be possible for me to talk with you and Arthur both here? All three of us talking together about what just happened?"

"Well, I can ask Arthur."

"I want to ask you and also get Arthur's opinion about whether perhaps Billy is stronger now, not suicidal, and could maybe deal with more things—"

"He's not suicidal."

The voice came out in a soft, clear, upper-class British accent, and Dr. George knew Arthur had decided to come out and speak for himself. He had not seen Arthur since the examination with Dr. Wilbur and others that Sunday morning at the jail. Trying to remain composed and show no surprise, he continued the conversation: "But does he still have to be handled with kid gloves? Is he still vulnerable?"

"Yes," Arthur said, placing the tips of his fingers together. "Easily frightened. Very paranoid."

Dr. George pointed out that he hadn't really meant to talk about Chalmer at that point, but that Billy had seemed to need to talk about it.

"You touched a memory of the past," Arthur said, choosing his words carefully, "and that's the first thing that popped into his mind. Common fear triumphed as well, and that was more than enough to put him to sleep. There was nothing I could do to control it. I let him wake up before he came—"

"Are you aware of all that he says when he's awake?"

"Partially and not always. I can't always tell exactly what he's thinking. But when he is thinking, I can sense fear. For some reason, he can't actually hear what I'm saying to him all very clearly. But it sounds as if he knows that there are times when we put him to sleep, and that he *can* go to sleep on his own."

Dr. George and Arthur reviewed the backgrounds of some of the alter personalities, but just as Arthur began to recall memories, he suddenly stopped, cocked his head and ended the discussion.

"Someone is at the door," he said, and then he was gone.

It was Psych-tech Jeff Janata, who had said he'd be back at a quarter to twelve.

Arthur let Tommy go back with Jeff to Wakefield Cottage.

The following day, two days before Dr. Wilbur's visit, Dr. George knew, by the jiggling knees, that it was the core Billy who had come to therapy again. Billy had heard the names Arthur and Ragen, and now he wanted to know who they were.

How could he tell him? Harding wondered. He had a horrible vision of Billy killing himself when he learned the truth. The patient of a colleague in Baltimore had hung himself in prison after he learned he was a multiple personality. Dr. George took a deep breath and then said it: "That voice that sounds like a James Bond movie is Arthur. Arthur is one of your names."

The knees stopped moving. Billy's eyes widened.

"A part of you is Arthur. Would you like to meet him?"

Billy began to tremble, knees moving so violently that he noticed it and put his hands out to still them. "No. It makes me want to sleep."

"Billy, I think if you tried real hard, you could stay awake when Arthur comes out and talks. You could hear what he says, and then you'd understand what your problem is."

"That's scary."

"Will you trust me?"

Billy nodded.

"All right then. While you're sitting there, Arthur is going to come on the spot and talk to me. You won't go to sleep. You'll hear everything he says, and you'll remember. Just the way some of the others do. You'll be off the spot, but you'll remain conscious."

"What's 'the spot'? You said that last time, but you didn't tell me what it is."

"That's Arthur's explanation of what happens when one of your inner people comes out into the reality and takes over. It's like a big spotlight, and whoever steps on it holds the consciousness. Just close your eyes and you'll see it."

Harding held his breath as Billy closed his eyes.

"I can see it! It's like I'm on a dark stage and the spotlight's shining on me."

"All right now, Billy. If you'll just step to one side, out of the light, I'm sure Arthur will come on and talk to us."

"I'm out of the light," Billy said, and his knees stopped jiggling.

"Arthur, Billy needs to talk to you," Harding said. "I'm sorry to disturb you and call you out, but it's essential to Billy's therapy that he know about you and the others."

Harding felt his palms moisten. As his patient's eyes opened, the expression changed from Billy's frown to Arthur's heavy-lidded haughty gaze. And out came the voice he had heard the day before: clipped upper-class British speech out of a tightly clenched jaw, lips barely moving.

"William, this is Arthur. I want you to know that this is a safe place, and that the people here are trying to help you."

Instantly Billy's facial expression changed, eyes opened wide. He looked around, startled, and asked, "Why didn't I know about you before?"

He switched again to Arthur. "It was my judgment that it would do you no good to know until you were ready. You were very suicidal. We had to wait until the right time before you were told the secret."

Dr. George watched and listened, awed but pleased as Arthur spoke to Billy for nearly ten minutes, telling him about Ragen and the other eight people and explaining how Dr. George's job was to bring all the minds together into one to make him whole again.

"Can you do that?" Billy asked, turning to Dr. George.

"We call it fusion, Billy. We'll do it slowly. First Allen and Tommy because they've got a great deal in common. Then Danny and David, both of whom need a great deal of therapy. Then we'll merge the others, one by one, until you're whole again."

"Why do you have to fuse 'em with me? Why can't you get rid of 'em?"

Dr. George put his fingertips together. "Because other therapists have tried that in conditions like yours, Billy. And it doesn't seem to work. The best hope you have of improving is to bring all these aspects of yourself together, first by communicating with each other, then by remembering everything each of them is doing, getting rid of the amnesia. We call that co-consciousness. Finally, you work at bringing the different people together. That's fusion."

"When you gonna do this?"

"Dr. Wilbur is coming to see you the day after tomorrow, and we're going to have a presentation and a discussion with most of the hospital staff who work with you. We'll show the videotapes to help some of our staff—who have never experienced this mental condition—to help them understand you better so that they can help you."

Billy nodded. And then his eyes went wide as his attention turned inward. He nodded several times, and then he looked up at Dr. George in astonishment.

"What is it, Billy?"

"Arthur says to tell you he wants to approve who can come to see me at the meeting."

(6)

Harding Hospital was abuzz with excitement. Dr. Cornelia Wilbur had lectured there in the summer of 1955, but this was different. Now they had a notorious patient, the first multiple personality to be observed around the clock in a mental hospital. The staff was still divided in their belief about the diagnosis, but everyone wanted to be in that room to hear Dr. Wilbur talk about Billy Milligan.

Though the Wakefield staff had been led to believe that ten or fifteen people would be present, the room in the basement of the administration building was packed with nearly a hundred. Doctors and administrators brought their wives; staff members from other branches of the hospital—who had nothing to do with Milligan's treatment—crowded into the back of the room, sitting on the floor, lining the walls and standing out in the nearby lounge.

Dr. George showed the audience the recent videotapes of himself and Dorothy Turner working with different personalities. Arthur and Ragen stirred interest, since no one on the staff outside of Wakefield had ever seen them. Adalana, whom no one but Dorothy Turner had ever met before, caused some awe, some scoffing. But when the core Billy came on the video monitor, there was rapt silence. And when he cried out, "Who are these people? Why don't they let me stay awake?," Rosalie Drake, among others, had to fight back tears.

When the viewing was finished, Dr. Wilbur brought Billy into the room and interviewed him briefly. She spoke with Arthur, Ragen, Danny and David. They answered questions, but Rosalie could see how upset they were. When the session was over, Rosalie realized from the buzz of conversation that everyone on the Wakefield staff was annoyed. Nurse Adrienne McCann and Nurse Laura Fisher complained that once again Milligan was being made to feel special and had another chance to be in the spotlight. Rosalie, Nick Cicco and Donna Egar were angry that Billy had been put on display.

After Dr. Wilbur's visit, the therapy strategy changed again, and Dr. George concentrated on fusing the personalities.

Dr. Marlene Kocan set up regular sessions, and the personalities began to recall their memories of abuse and torture, working them through and reliving the anguish that led to the major dissociation at the age of eight.

Dr. Kocan disagreed with the plan of fusion. She said she knew it had been Dr. Wilbur's method with Sybil, and in other circumstances it might be the right thing. But they had to consider what would happen if Ragen was fused with the others and Milligan was then sent to prison. In a hostile environment, he'd have no way of defending himself, and with his only defense removed, he might be killed.

"He survived in prison before," someone said.

"Yes, but Ragen was around to protect him. If he's once again raped by a hostile male—you know that often happens in prison—he'd probably commit suicide."

"It's our job to fuse him," Harding said. "That's our charge from the court."

The core Billy was encouraged to listen to and answer his other people, acknowledge their existence, and get to know them. Through constant suggestion, Billy was able to remain on the spot longer and longer. The fusing was to be done in stages. Those people who were similar or who had compatible qualities would be fused first, in pairs, and then the results of those pairings would be fused, by intensive suggestion, until all would be merged into the core Billy.

Because Allen and Tommy were most alike, they were to be fused first. Hours of argument and analysis with Dr. George were followed, Allen reported, by even more hours of internal discussion with Arthur and Ragen. Allen and Tommy worked hard with Dr. George on fusing, but it was difficult because Tommy had fears that Allen didn't have. Allen loved baseball, for example, but Tommy was afraid to play it because once when he was younger and played second base, he had made mistakes and was beaten for them. Dr. George suggested that Nick Cicco, Allen and the other people should help Tommy by talking to him about his fear and by encouraging him to play baseball. Art therapy would continue, including oil painting.

The younger ones, Allen said, were unable to understand the concept of fusion until Arthur explained it to them through an analogy. Arthur compared it to Kool-Aid, something the children knew about, and explained that Kool-Aid powder is made up of individual crystals, each grain separate. When you added water, they dissolved. But if the mixture was allowed to stand, the water would evaporate, leaving a solid mass. Nothing had been added or lost. It was just changed.

"Everyone understands it now," Allen said. "Fusion is just mixing the Kool-Aid."

Nurse Nan Graves recorded on June 5: "Mr. Milligan has stated he has fused for an hour as 'Tommy' and 'Allen' and it felt 'weird.'"

Donna Egar reported that Milligan told her he was worried about the fusion because he didn't want to let any of the others die or any of their talents or strengths be weakened. "But we're working on it," Allen assured her.

The next day, Gary Schweickart and Judy Stevenson visited and passed along good news. The court had approved an extension of Billy's observation and treatment at Harding Hospital, giving him at least another three months to complete the fusion.

On Wednesday evening, June 14, in the music building, Rosalie Drake watched and listened as Tommy played the drums. She knew that only Allen had played them before. In this fused state he was obviously not as good as Allen had been on his own.

"I feel I'm stealing Allen's talent," he told her.

"Are you still Tommy?"

"I'm a combination and I don't really have a name now. That bothers me."

"Yet you respond when people call you Billy."

"I've always done that," he said, tapping out a slow riff on the drum.

"Any reason why you can't go on doing that?"

He shrugged. "I guess it would be less complicated for everyone. Okay." He tapped it out. "You can just keep calling me Billy."

The fusion did not come all at once. At different times, for varying lengths of time, seven of the alternate personalities— all except Arthur, Ragen and Billy—fused into one. To avoid confusion, Arthur gave the fusion a new name—"Kenny." But the name didn't take and everyone went back to calling him Billy.

In the evening, another patient brought Nurse Yaeger a note she had found in Milligan's wastebasket. It looked very much like a suicide note. He was immediately placed on special precautions. The rest of the week, Nurse Yaeger reported that though he was fusing and unfusing, he seemed to be fused for longer and longer periods of time. By July 14, he was fused most of the day and seemed peaceful.

As the days passed, the partial fusions continued to hold most of the time, but there were brief periods when he blanked out, unable to control the spot at all.

Judy and Gary visited their client again at the hospital on August 28 and pointed out that Dr. George's report to the judge was due in about three weeks. If Dr. George decided he was fused and competent, it would be up to Judge Flowers to set a date for his trial.

"I think we should discuss trial strategy," Arthur said. "We want to change our plea. Ragen is willing to plead guilty and to accept punishment for the three robberies, but he has no intention of pleading guilty to rape."

"But four of the charges in the ten-count indictment include rape."

"According to Adalana's story, each of the three women cooperated," Arthur said. "Not one of them was injured. Each one had a chance to run away. And Adalana says she gave each of them part of the money back so that they'd come out ahead when the insurance companies paid off."

"That's not what the women say," Judy said.

"Who are you going to believe?" Arthur snorted. "Them or me?"

"We might question it if only one of them had contradicted Adalana's story. But all three do, and you realize these women didn't know or have any contact with each other."

"They could still each be unwilling to admit the truth."

"How do you know what really happened?" Judy asked. "You weren't there yourself."

"But Adalana was," Arthur said.

Neither Judy nor Gary accepted the idea that the victims had cooperated, but they realized Arthur was talking about Adalana's perceptions of what had happened.

"Can we talk to her?" Gary asked.

Arthur shook his head. "She's been banished from the spot forever for what she did. There can be no further exceptions."

"Then I'm afraid we stay with the plea we've entered," Gary said. "Not guilty, and not guilty by reason of insanity."

Arthur looked at him coldly and his lips barely moved. "You will never plead insanity on my behalf."

"It's our only hope," Judy said.

"I am not insane," Arthur insisted, "and that ends the discussion."

The following day, Judy and Gary received another note on lined yellow legal paper saying that William S. Milligan no longer wished to be represented by them, that he intended to handle his own defense.

"He's fired us again," Gary said. "What do you think?"

"I think I never saw this one, either," Judy said, putting it into a folder. "Papers get lost and mislaid. I mean, with our great filing system, it might take six or seven months to find it."

In the says that followed, four other dismissal letters to his attorneys were misfiled, and when they refused to answer his letters, Arthur finally gave up trying to fire them.

"Can we win with an insanity plea?" Judy asked.

Gary lit his pipe and puffed away at it. "If Karolin, Turner, Kocan, Harding and Wilbur will testify that Billy was legally insane at the time of the crimes, under the Ohio definition, I think we've got a pretty good shot at it."

"But you're the one who told me no multiple personality has ever been found not guilty by reason of insanity for a major crime."

"Well, then," Gary said, grinning through his beard, "William Stanley Milligan will be the first."

(7)

Dr. George Harding, Jr., now found himself struggling with his conscience. There was no doubt in his mind that Billy was fused or close to fusion now and probably could be fused enough to stand trial. That wasn't the problem. As Dr. George lay awake nights in late August, going over the material for the report to Judge Flowers, he wondered if it was morally right to use the diagnosis of multiple personality as a defense against these major crimes.

He was deeply concerned with the issue of criminal responsibility. It troubled him that his words might be misused, bringing discredit to the multiple personality diagnosis, to other patients who had this syndrome, to the profession and to psychiatric testimony. If Judge Flowers accepted his judgment that this dissociative disorder, classified thus far as a neurosis, was reason to find a patient not guilty by reason of insanity, he knew it would set legal precedent in Ohio, and perhaps in the country.

Dr. George believed Billy Milligan had not had control over his actions on those three fateful days last October. It was his job to learn more and to push into new areas. It was his responsibility to understand this case, to understand Billy in a way that would be useful to society in dealing with similar problems. He again phoned other professionals for advice and guidance, conferred with his staff, and then on September 12, 1978, he sat down and wrote his nine-page report to Judge Flowers, in which he described Billy Milligan's medical, social and psychiatric history.

"The patient reports," he wrote, "that the mother and children were subject to physical abuse and that he suffered sadistic and sexual abuse including anal intercourse from Mr. Milligan. According to the patient this occurred when he was eight or nine over the course of a year, generally on a farm where he would be alone with the stepfather. He indicates that he was afraid that the stepfather would kill him insomuch as he threatened to 'bury him in the barn and tell the mother that he had run away.'"

In analyzing the psychodynamics of the case, Harding pointed out that Milligan's natural father's suicide had deprived him of a father's involvement and attention, and left him with "a feeling of irrational power and overwhelming guilt leading to anxiety, conflict and increased fantasy formulation." He was thus "vulnerable to exploitation by the stepfather Chalmer Milligan, who preyed upon his needs for closeness and caring to satisfy his own frustrations through sexual and sadistic exploitation . . ."

Since young Milligan identified with his mother, when she was beaten by her husband, it caused young Milligan to "experience her terror and pain . . ." It also led to a "kind of separation anxiety which left him in an unstable fantasy world with all the unpredictable and unintelligible characteristics of a dream. This along with the stepfather's put-downs, sadistic abuses and sexual exploitation led to recurrent dissociations . . ."

Dr. George Harding concluded: "It is now my opinion that the patient is competent to stand trial having accomplished a fusion of his multiple personalities . . . it is also my opinion that the patient is mentally ill and that as a result of his mental illness he was not responsible for his criminal conduct at the time the criminal conduct did occur in the last half of October 1977."

On September 19, Judy Stevenson filed a motion to amend the defendant's plea to "not guilty, and not guilty by reason of insanity."

(8)

Up to this point in Milligan's case, the multiple personality diagnosis had not been made public. It was known only to those treating him, the prosecutors and the judge. The public defenders continued to insist that the diagnosis be kept secret, since it would be difficult to treat him and then try his case if it exploded into a media event.

Bernie Yavitch agreed, feeling it was well within his ethics as prosecutor not to reveal what was going on with the suspect, since there had been no testimony in court about it.

But on the morning of September 27, the *Columbus Citizen-Journal* broke the story with banner headlines:

PERSONALITIES "FUSED" FOR COURT TRIAL
10 PEOPLE "EXIST" IN RAPE SUSPECT

When the word got out at Harding Hospital about the morning paper, the staff encouraged Billy to tell the other patients about it before they learned of it from outside sources. He told the mini-group that he had been charged with these crimes but he wasn't sure he had done them, since he was defused at the time.

The evening news on television carried the story, and Billy went to his room in tears.

A few days later, Billy did a painting of a beautiful young woman with a tortured gaze, and Nurse Nan Graves reported his statement that it was Adalana.

Gary Schweickart visited Milligan on October 3, driving in his station wagon so that he could take some of Billy's paintings back with him. Judy Stevenson was on vacation with her husband in Italy, he explained, and wouldn't be at the competency hearing, but she'd be back in time for the trial. They walked and talked together as Gary tried to prepare Billy for the transfer to the Franklin County Jail to await his competency hearing, and for the possibility that they might lose the case.

Dr. George felt certain Billy was fused. He could tell by the lack of observable dissociation episodes, and also by the way Billy seemed to have taken on the characteristics of the separate personalities. At first he'd see part of one and part of another, but by degrees there had been a blending, a homogenization. The staff had seen it too. All the aspects of the different personalities were now seen in one—Billy Milligan. Dr. George said his patient was ready.

On October 4, two days before Billy was to return to the Franklin County Jail, Harry Franken of the *Citizen-Journal* broke a second major story about Milligan. He had gotten a copy of the Harding report from an unnamed source, and he came to Gary and Judy for comment, telling them he was going to run the story. Gary and Judy informed Judge Flowers, who decided the story should be released to the *Columbus Dispatch* as well. The public defenders agreed to comment on the report, since it had been leaked already. They allowed photographers to take pictures of the paintings Gary had brought back from the hospital—Moses about to break the tablet containing the Ten Commandments, a Jewish musician playing a horn, a landscape and the portrait of Adalana.

The newspaper stories upset Billy, and he was depressed during his final session with Dr. Kocan. He was afraid of what other prisoners might do to him now that the word was out that he had a lesbian personality.

He told her, "If they find me guilty and send me back to Lebanon, I know I'll have to die."

"Then Chalmer will have won."

"Well, what do I do? I have all this hate bottled up inside me. I can't handle it."

Although she rarely gave advice or instructions, preferring the nondirective method of allowing the patient to lead the way, she knew there was no time for such therapy.

"You could put hate to positive use," she suggested. "You suffered from child abuse. You could defeat those horrible memories, and the man you say inflicted them, by dedicating your life to the fight against child abuse. Alive, you can work for a cause and win. If you die, then the man who abused you wins, and you lose."

Later that day, talking to Donna Egar in his room, Billy reached under his bed and pulled out the razor blade Tommy had taped to the slat nearly seven months earlier.

"Here," he said, handing it to her. "I don't need this anymore. I want to live."

There were tears in her eyes as she hugged him.

He told Rosalie, "I don't want to go to mini-group. I've got to prepare myself to be alone. I've got to harden myself. No good-bys."

But the mini-group made farewell cards for him, and when Rosalie brought them to him, he let himself cry.

"For the first time in my life," he said, "I think I'm having a normal human reaction. I've got what I used to hear referred to as 'mixed emotions.' I've never been able to have them before."

Friday, October 6, the day he was to be taken away, was Rosalie's day off, but she came down to the hospital to be with him. She knew she would face raised eyebrows and sarcastic comments from some of the Wakefield staff, but she didn't care. She walked into the rec room and saw him, dressed in his blue three-piece suit, pacing, waiting, apparently calm and in control.

She and Donna Egar walked with him to the administration building, where a sheriff's deputy, in dark glasses, waited at the front desk.

When the deputy whipped out the handcuffs, Rosalie stepped in front of Billy and demanded to know if it was really necessary to handcuff him like an animal.

"Yes, ma'am," the deputy said. "It's the law."

"Well, for God's sake," Donna shouted. "When he was brought over here, he was escorted by two females, and now you're going to be a big bad cop and handcuff him?"

"That's the way it has to be, ma'am. I'm sorry."

Billy held out his wrists, and when the cuffs snapped into place, Rosalie saw him wince. He climbed into the paddy wagon, and they walked beside it as it slowly moved along the curving road toward the stone bridge. They waved good-by, went back to the unit and a had a long, hard cry.

CHAPTER
FOUR

(1)

When Bernie Yavitch and Terry Sherman read Dr. George Harding's report, they agreed it was one of the most thorough mental examinations they had ever seen. All the things they as prosecutors had been trained to attack in the testimony of psychiatrists, all the positions they might normally object to, were unassailable in Harding's report. It hadn't been a three- or four-hour checkup. It had been a hospital study of more than seven months. And it was not just Harding's opinion alone, but included consultation with a great many other psychologists and psychiatrists.

On October 6, 1978, Judge Flowers, after holding a brief competency hearing, ruled on the basis of the Harding report that Milligan was now capable of standing trial. He set the date for December 4.

Schweickart said that was satisfactory, with one proviso: that the trial be conducted under the law that existed at the time of the crimes. (The Ohio law would change on November 1, placing the burden of proof of insanity on the defendant rather than placing the burden of proof of sanity on the prosecution.)

Yavitch disagreed.

"I will take that motion under advisement," Judge Flowers said. "I know similar motions where amendments have been made—specifically, the new criminal code, for example. I know in most instances they have held, almost without exception, that the defendant is entitled to the better of the acts as to one way or the other. But I know of no decision or court cases in that regard."

On the way out of the courtroom, Schweickart told Yavitch and Sherman that he intended to waive jury trial on behalf of his client and was asking Judge Flowers to hear the case.

As Schweickart walked off, Yavitch said, "There goes our case."

"Not as locked up as it looked at the beginning," Sherman said.

Judge Flowers later said he felt that the prosecutors, in agreeing to accept Dr. Harding's report but not agreeing that Milligan was insane, had "put the monkey on my back."

Back at the Franklin County Jail, Gary and Judy noticed that once again Billy had become depressed and was spending most of his time drawing and brooding. The increasing publicity was bothering him. As the days went by, he spent more and more time sleeping, withdrawing from the cold, bare surroundings.

"Why can't I stay at Harding until the trial?" he asked Judy.

"It's not possible," she told him. "We were lucky the court gave you the seven months there. Just hold on. The trial's less than two months away."

"Now, you've got to keep yourself together," Gary said. "I have a strong feeling that if you stand trial, you'll be found not guilty. If you break down and can't stand trial, they'll send you to Lima."

But one afternoon, one of the guards watched Milligan lying on his bunk, drawing with a pencil. He looked down through the bars and saw the sketch—a Raggedy Ann doll with a noose around its neck, hanging in front of a shattered mirror.

"Hey, why're you drawing that, Milligan?"

"Because I am angry," came the deep Slavic accent. "Is time for someone to die."

The guard, hearing the accent, quickly hit the alarm button. Ragen just studied him in mild amusement.

"Now, just back up slow there, whoever you are," the guard said. "Leave the drawing on the bunk and back up against the wall."

Ragen obeyed him. He saw the other guards now crowding around the bars of the cell. They unlocked the door, quickly came in, grabbed the drawing and slammed the door shut again.

"Jesus," said one of the guards, "that's a sick picture."

"Call his attorney," someone said. "He's cracked up again."

When Gary and Judy arrived, they were met by Arthur, who explained to them that Billy had never been totally fused.

"He is sufficiently fused, however, to go to trial," Arthur assured them. "Billy now understands the nature of the charges against him, and he can cooperate in his own defense. But Ragen and I have stood apart. As you can see, this is a hostile place and Ragen is dominant. But if Billy isn't moved from here to a hospital, I can't guarantee that he'll stay even partially fused."

Franklin County Sheriff Harry Berkemer told a reporter from the *Columbus Dispatch* that his deputies witnessed an extraordinary feat of strength and endurance when Milligan was in the personality of Ragen. Ragen had been taken to the prisoner recreation area, and he chose to punch a large body bag. "He hit it hard for nineteen and a half minutes straight," Berkemer said. "An average man can't hit it for more than three minutes straight without becoming exhausted. He hit it so hard we thought he had perhaps broken an arm, and took him to a doctor to have him checked out." But Ragen had not hurt himself.

On October 24, Judge Flowers again ordered Southwest Community Mental Health Center to examine Milligan and submit a report on his competency to stand trial. Dr. George Harding, Jr., could, at his discretion, attend the defendant. The judge also ordered Milligan immediately transferred from prison to the Central Ohio Psychiatric Hospital.

On November 15, Marion J. Koloski, director of the Court Assistance Program of Southwest's Forensic Psychiatric Center, reported that when Dr. Stella Karolin and Dorothy Turner last saw him, they had found Milligan competent to stand trial and capable of assisting his attorney in his defense, but added: "His mental condition is viewed as being very fragile, however, and it is possible that at any given time there could be a disintegration of the present fused personality into the dissociated personalities which have been evidenced previously."

On November 29, the *Dayton Daily News* and the *Columbus Dispatch* published Chalmer Milligan's denials of the widely circulated report that he had sexually abused his stepson. The following Associated Press story appeared in the *Columbus Dispatch:*

STEPFATHER SAYS HE DIDN'T ABUSE YOUNG MILLIGAN
Chalmers [*sic*] Milligan says he has become "very upset" by published reports that he physically and sexually abused his

stepson William S. Milligan, whom doctors say has 10 personalities.

"Nobody has talked to me," complains Milligan, who asserts the abuse claims by his stepson are "completely false. . . ."

According to a report signed by Dr. George T. Harding, the psychiatrists also concluded that Milligan exhibited multiple personality behavior and that he had personalities unaware of the actions of others. They blamed his condition partly on abuse he suffered as a child. . . .

Chalmer Milligan said he has suffered considerable hardship as a result of the published reports.

"You always have the misunderstanding bunch. It's very upsetting," he said.

He said he particularly was upset by published accounts that failed to attribute the abuse claim to William or the psychiatrists.

"It all goes back to the boy," Milligan said. "All they're (the publications) doing is repeating what they (the psychiatrists and young Milligan) said," he added.

He would not say whether he planned any legal action regarding the abuse claims.

Feeling increasingly confident that Billy would be found not guilty by reason of insanity, Judy and Gary realized there was still another hurdle. Up to this time, all such verdicts resulted in the defendant being sent to Lima. But within three days, on December 1, a new Ohio law dealing with mentally ill patients would go into effect, requiring that someone found not guilty by reason of insanity be treated as a mentally ill patient and not as a criminal. The new law would require that he be sent to the least restrictive environment consistent with safety to himself and others, and his commitment to a state mental institution would come under the jurisdiction of the probate court.

Since the trial date was set for December 4 and Billy would be the first to come under the new Ohio law, there was a good chance that after the trial, the probate court would agree to send him to a place other than Lima if the defense could demonstrate an alternative where he would receive proper treatment.

Harding Hospital was out of the question because of the expense. It would have to be a state hospital where someone could be found who knew about and could treat a multiple personality.

Dr. Cornelia Wilbur mentioned that at a state mental hospital less than seventy-five miles from Columbus, there was a physician who had treated several multiple personalities and who was recognized as being skilled in the field. She recommended Dr. David Caul, medical director of the Athens Mental Health Center in Athens, Ohio.

The prosecutor's office requested a pretrial meeting with Probate Judge Richard B. Metcalf to clarify procedures under the new Ohio law. Judge Jay Flowers agreed and arranged the meeting. But Judy and Gary knew that the meeting would range far beyond that. Judge Flowers would join the meeting, and it would be decided which evidence was to be admitted on Monday by stipulation and where Billy Milligan would be sent for treatment in the event he was declared not guilty by reason of insanity.

Gary and Judy decided it was important to know if Dr. Caul would accept Billy as a patient at the Athens Mental Health Center. Though Judy had heard Caul's name before and had written him in July for information about multiple personality, she had not mentioned Billy's name. Now she phoned to ask if he would accept Billy Milligan as a patient and if he could come to Columbus on Friday to attend the meeting.

Caul said he would have to check with the hospital superintendent, Sue Foster, who would discuss it with her superiors in the state Department of Mental Health. Caul said he would consider accepting Milligan as a patient, and he agreed to drive to Columbus on Friday to attend the meeting.

On December 1, Judy waited impatiently for Dr. Caul. The lobby outside Judge Metcalf's chambers was filling up with the others who had become involved in the case, including Dr. George Harding, Dr. Stella Karolin, Dorothy Turner and Bernie Yavitch. Shortly after ten o'clock, she saw the receptionist point her out to a middle-aged, fat little man. His olive-skinned, fleshy face was fringed with gray hair. His fierce, penetrating eyes were the eyes of an eagle.

She introduced him to Gary and the others, and led him into Judge Metcalf's chambers.

Dr. David Caul settled back in the second row and listened as the attorneys discussed how the new law applied to the

Milligan case. A short while later, Judge Flowers entered the chambers and, together with Judge Metcalf, summarized the case and the procedures up to this point. Bernie Yavitch spoke of the professional information that had been assembled and agreed that it would be difficult to refute the evidence regarding Milligan's condition at the time of the offenses. He would not challenge the reports by Southwest and Harding. Gary pointed out that the defense had no intention of challenging the prosecution's evidence that Milligan had actually committed the crimes.

It dawned on David Caul that they were all talking about what was going to be happening at that trial on Monday. It was his impression that here was a meeting of the minds about the scenario of that trial. Gary and Judy agreed that the victims' names be deleted from the record. What remained was to determine what would happen to Billy if Judge Flowers found him not guilty by reason of insanity.

Gary rose and said, "We have Dr. Caul here from Athens. He has had experience in treating patients with multiple personalities at the Athens Mental Health Center, a state facility, and he was highly recommended by both Dr. Ralph Allison in California and Dr. Cornelia Wilbur in Kentucky, who themselves are recognized experts in this area of psychiatry."

Caul found all eyes suddenly focused on him. Judge Flowers asked, "Dr. Caul, would you accept him for treatment?"

Something suddenly triggered his alarm instinct. He decided that all these people were passing along a hot potato and he had better clarify his position.

"Yes, I'll take him," Caul said. "But if he comes to Athens, I want to be able to treat him in the same manner that I've treated other multiples, in an open—and the most therapeutic—setting we have." He looked around at the others who were watching him, then back at Flowers and Metcalf, and said emphatically, "And if I can't do that, don't send him."

When he looked around, he saw all heads nodding.

As he drove back to Athens, Dr. Caul mulled over what he had seen and heard at the meeting, and it occurred to him that almost everyone there, even the prosecutor Yavitch, accepted the fact that Milligan was a multiple personality. He knew that if it went at the trial as it seemed to be going at that meeting, Milligan was about to become the first multiple personality charged with major crimes ever to be declared not guilty by reason of insanity. He realized the meeting he had just attended foreshadowed the making of legal and psychiatric history on Monday in that courtroom.

(2)

When Billy Milligan awoke on December 4, the morning they were to take him from the Columbus Ohio Psychiatric Hospital back to the Franklin County Courthouse, and looked into the mirror, he was startled to see that his mustache was gone. *But he didn't remember shaving it*, and he wondered who had done it. The mustache had been shaved off between the first and second rapes, and he had grown it back. Now he had lost time again. He had the same odd sensation he had known in those last days at Harding and in the Franklin County Jail—that somehow Ragen and Arthur had stood apart, and they couldn't or wouldn't fuse until they were sure he wouldn't be sent to prison. Well, he was partially fused, enough to stand trial.

He would continue to answer to the name Billy, though he knew he was neither the core Billy nor a completely fused Billy. He was somewhere in between. He wondered, as they walked to the police van, what it would feel like if he was ever completely fused.

When he got into the police van at the entrance to the hospital, he saw the deputies looking at him strangely. On the way to the courthouse, the paddy wagon made a five-mile detour to throw off any news reporters or TV news people who might be following. But as it swung around Front Street into the cruiser entrance of the Franklin County Jail, a young woman and a man with a TV camera stepped inside just before the sally-port door closed behind them.

"All right, Milligan," said the driver, opening the door.

"I'm not getting out," Billy said. "Not with that TV camera and that reporter there. If you don't protect me here in jail, I'm gonna tell my lawyers as soon as I get in."

The driver turned and saw them. "Who are you?"

"Channel Four News. We've got permission to be here."

The driver looked at Billy, who shook his head defiantly. "My lawyers told me not to get near any reporters. I'm not getting out."

"Well, he won't come out while you're here," the officer told the reporter.

"We have a right—" the woman began.

"It's a violation of my rights," Billy called from the van.

"What's going on here?" another officer shouted from inside the security gate.

The driver said, "Milligan refuses to get out while these people are here."

"Look, folks," Sergeant Willis said, "I'm afraid you'll have to leave so we can get him inside."

When the TV cameraman and the reporter stepped outside the sally port and the steel door clanged down, Billy let Willis lead him out through the doors. Inside, black-shirted sheriff's deputies gathered to watch Milligan being brought in, and Willis made a path for Billy to go through.

Sergeant Willis took him up to the third floor. "You remember me, son?"

Billy nodded as they stepped out of the elevator. "You were pretty decent to me."

"Well, you never caused me no trouble. Except them toilets." Willis handed him a cigarette. "You're a pretty famous man."

"I don't feel famous," said Billy. "I feel hated."

"Well, I seen Channel Four out front and Channel Ten and ABC and NBC and CBS. There's more TV cameras and reporters out there than I've seen in a lot of big murder trials."

They stopped at the barred exit to a small anteroom, beyond which the court passage gate would lead him to the Franklin County Hall of Justice.

The guard at the desk nodded to him. "Almost didn't recognize you without your mustache." Then he pressed the buzzer to call the central control room and tell them to stand by and unlock the court gate for Milligan.

The court passage door opened. The court escort braced him against the wall and frisked him carefully.

"All right," the man said, "walk on ahead of me down that passageway to the courthouse."

When they reached the seventh floor of the Hall of Justice, Judy and Gary joined them. They noticed that Billy's mustache was gone.

"You look better without it," Judy said. "More clean-cut."

Billy put his finger to his lip, and Gary had the fleeting impression that something was wrong. He was about to say something when an officer with a walkie-talkie and an earphone came up, took Billy's arm and said the sheriff wanted Milligan brought down to the second floor.

"Wait a minute," Gary said. "The trial's on this floor."

"I don't know what's going on, sir," the deputy said, "but the sheriff wants him brought down immediately."

"Wait here," Gary told Judy. "I'll go down with him and see what's going on."

He got into the elevator with Billy and the deputy, but when the doors opened at the second floor and he stepped out, Gary saw what it was. A flashbulb went off. It was a photographer and a reporter from the *Columbus Dispatch*.

"What the hell is this?" Gary shouted. "Do I look dumb to you? I won't stand for this."

The reporter explained that they wanted to take some photographs and hoped to get pictures not showing the manacles. The sheriff, he said, had okayed it.

"The hell with that," Gary snapped. "You have no right to do this to my client." He turned Billy around and led him back to the elevator.

The deputy took them up and directed them to the holding room outside the court of common pleas.

Dorothy Turner and Stella Karolin came into the holding room, hugged Billy and calmed him. But when they left to go into the courtroom and Billy was alone with the officer, he began to tremble and gripped the sides of the chair.

"All right, Milligan," the officer said. "You can go into the courtroom now."

Gary noticed that when Billy was led in, the sketch artists all stared at him. Then, one by one, they picked up their erasers and started rubbing. He smiled. They were erasing the mustache.

"Your Honor," said Gary Schweickart as he approached the bench, "both the prosecution and the defense are now agreed that there is no need to call witnesses nor to put Mr. Milligan on the stand. The facts of the case will be read into the record as stipulations, agreed upon by both sides."

Judge Flowers consulted his notes. "You are not contesting the charges nor denying that your client committed the crimes he is charged with, except for the first count of sexual assault."

"That's right, Your Honor, but we plead not guilty by reason of insanity."

"Mr. Yavitch, do you plan to contest the findings of the psychiatrists from Southwest Community Mental Health Center and Harding Hospital?"

Yavitch rose. "No, Your Honor. The prosecution agrees to the evidence presented by Dr. Harding, Dr. Turner, Dr. Karolin and Dr. Wilbur, supporting the defendant's mental condition at the time the crimes were committed."

Judy Stevenson read the defense testimony, taken by deposition, into the court record. As she read to the hushed courtroom, she glanced at Billy from time to time and saw how pale his face was. She hoped the pain of hearing all this wouldn't make him unfuse.

Mrs. Margaret Changett can testify that she saw Billy's mother on several occasions after being beaten by Mr. Milligan. She will testify that on one occasion Bill called her and said his mother was beaten rather badly. Mrs. Changett went to the Milligan house and found Mrs. Moore in bed. Mrs. Moore, according to Mrs. Changett, was in bed, shaking and battered. Mrs. Changett said she called a doctor and priest; she stayed with Mrs. Moore all day.

Dorothy Moore, the defendant's mother, will, if called, testify that her ex-husband, Chalmer Milligan, was very abusive to her and would often beat her when he was drinking. He would generally lock the children in their bedroom while he beat her. She will testify that "Chalmer often became sexually aroused" after the beatings. Mrs. Moore said that Mr. Milligan was jealous of Bill and beat him quite often "for punishment." He once tied Bill to a plow and later tied him to a barn door in order to "keep him in line." Mrs. Moore will testify that she was not aware of the severity of the beatings, and sodomy, administered to Bill until the present offense came to light . . .

Gary saw Billy put his hands over his eyes when he heard the testimony. "Got a tissue?" Billy asked.

Gary turned and saw a dozen people around him pulling tissues out and handing them over.

And Mrs. Moore will testify that on one occasion Bill's effeminate side was displayed when he prepared breakfast for her. She said that Bill was walking like a girl and even talking effeminately. Mrs. Moore will testify that she found Bill on the fire escape of a building in the downtown area of Lancaster, in a "trance like" state. He had left school without permission and the principal called her to inform her that Bill had left school. Mrs. Moore said that she has found Bill in a "trance" on numerous occasions. She will testify that when Bill came out of the "trance" he could not remember anything about what transpired during his "trance."

Mrs. Moore will also testify that she did nothing about her marital situation with Mr. Milligan because she wanted to keep the family together. It was only after her children gave her an ultimatum that she divorced Mr. Milligan.

The report from Southwest by Karolin and Turner was read into the record.

Then came the deposition of Billy's brother, Jim:

If James Milligan was called to testify, he would state that on many occasions Chalmers [*sic*] Milligan would take James and Bill to family property on which there was a barn. That he, James, would be sent out to the field to hunt rabbits and Bill would always be told to remain with his step-father Chalmers. On all these occasions, when he, James, would return to the barn area, Bill would be crying. On many occasions, Bill told James that his step-father hurt him. Whenever Chalmers saw Bill relating these incidents to James, he, Chalmers Milligan would say to Bill—now nothing happened in the barn did it. Bill who was very afraid of his step-father would say No. Chalmers would further state we don't want to upset your mother do we. He would then take James and Bill to the ice cream store prior to going home.

He would also verify all of the home life trauma directed at Billy.

At twelve-thirty Judge Flowers asked if either side wished to make closing arguments. Both sides waived the right.

The judge dismissed the first count of rape, pointing out the lack of corroborating evidence and the lack of a similar *modus operandi*.

"Now, proceeding as to the defense of insanity," Judge Flowers said, "all of the evidence is stipulated medical evidence, and from that, without question, the doctors all testify that at the time of the acts in question, that the defendant was mentally ill at the time of the offense with which he was charged. That by virtue of his mental illness he was unable to distinguish between right and wrong, and further that he did not have the ability to refrain from doing these acts."

Gary held his breath.

"Lacking any evidence to the contrary," Flowers continued, "this court has no alternative other than to determine from the evidence before me that as to counts two to ten, inclusive, that the defendant is not guilty by reason of insanity."

Judge Flowers placed Billy Milligan under the authority of the probate court of Franklin County, struck his gravel three times and adjourned.

Judy felt like crying, but held it back. She squeezed Billy and pulled him toward the holding cell to avoid the crowd. Dorothy Turner came in to congratulate him, as did Stella Karolin and the others, who Judy could see were crying.

Only Gary stood apart, leaning against the wall thoughtfully, arms folded. It had been a long battle, with sleepless nights and a marriage ready to break up, but now it was almost over.

"All right, Billy," he said. "We've got to go down to probate court before Judge Metcalf. But we're going to have to go out in the lobby and run the gauntlet of those reporters and TV cameras."

"Can't we go the back way?"

Gary shook his head. "We've won. I don't want you to have bad relations with the press. They've been waiting there for hours. You'll have to face the cameras and answer a few questions. We don't want them to say we sneaked out the back way."

When Gary led Billy out into the lobby, reporters and cameramen gathered around, filming as they followed him.

"How do you feel, Mr. Milligan?"

"Okay."

"Are you very optimistic now that the trial is over?"

"Nope."

"What do you mean by that?"

"Well," Billy said, "there's a lot to come."

"What are your goals now?"

"I want to be a citizen again. I'd like to learn life all over."

Gary pushed him with gentle pressure in the center of his back, and Billy moved on. They went up to the eighth-floor probate court and Judge Metcalf's chambers, but he'd gone to lunch. They would have to come back to the court at one o'clock.

Bernie Yavitch called each of the victims, as he had promised he would, and told them what had happened in court. "Based on the evidence and the law," he said, "there's no doubt in my mind that Judge Flowers made the right decision." Terry Sherman agreed with him.

After lunch, Judge Metcalf reviewed the recommendations of the psychiatrists and committed Milligan to the Athens Mental Health Center in custody of Dr. David Caul.

Billy was taken down to the conference room again, where Jan Ryan of Channel 6, who had been working on a documentary about Billy's life for the Child Abuse Foundation, asked him a few questions and shot some more footage for the TV special. Judy and Gary were called away, and before they got back, the officer knocked and said that Billy had to leave for Athens.

He felt bad, leaving without being able to say good-by to Judy and Gary, but the officer slapped the handcuffs on him, needlessly tight, and hustled him downstairs into the police van. A second officer shoved a container of hot coffee into his hand and slammed the door.

As the van turned the corner, some of the hot coffee spilled onto his new suit, and he threw the cup down behind the seat. He felt lousy, and the feeling was getting worse and worse.

He had no idea what the Athens Mental Health Center would be like. It might be a prison for all he knew. He had to remember that the torment was far from over, that a lot of people still wanted to put him behind bars. He knew the Adult Parole Authority had notified Gary that because of the guns, he was in violation of his parole and probation, and as soon as he was cured they would send him back to prison. Not Lebanon, he imagined. Because of his violent behavior, probably a hell called Lucasville. Where was Arthur? And Ragen? Would they ever join the fusion?

They drove along snow-covered Route 33, passing through Lancaster, where he's been raised, gone to school and tried to kill himself. It was too much to bear. He was very tired and he had to let go. He closed his eyes and let it all slip away . . .

Seconds later, Danny looked around and wondered where he was being taken. He was cold and lonely, and afraid.

CHAPTER FIVE

(1)

It was nearly dark when they reached Athens and turned off the highway. The mental hospital was a complex of Victorian buildings on a snowy hill overlooking the campus of Ohio University. When they crossed the wide avenue and turned up the narrow, curving road, Danny began to tremble. The two officers led him out of the van and up the steps to the ancient red brick building with its thin white pillars.

They ushered him directly through the old entrance corridor into the elevator and up to the third floor. As the elevator door opened, the policeman said, "You got pretty damned lucky, mister."

Danny started to hang back, but the officer pushed him through a heavy metal door marked ADMISSIONS AND INTENSIVE TREATMENT.

Instead of a prison or hospital, the ward resembled a long lobby of a small residential hotel, with carpeting, chandeliers, drapes and leather chairs. Both walls were lined with doors. The nurses' station looked like a reception desk.

"Jesus Christ," said the officer. "A regular resort."

A large elderly lady stood at the entrance of an office on the right. Her broad, friendly face was framed in black ringlets, as if she'd just had a hair dye and permanent. She smiled when they stepped into the small admissions office and said softly to the policeman, "Can I have your name?"

"I ain't the one being admitted, lady."

"Well," she said, "I am receiving the patient from you, and I need your name to document who brought the patient in."

The officer grudgingly gave her his name. Danny stood aside awkwardly, stretching his fingers, numb from the tight handcuffs.

Dr. David Caul, who had seen the policeman push Milligan into the office, glared and snapped, "Take those goddamned handcuffs off him!"

The officer fumbled with his key and removed the cuffs. Danny rubbed his wrists and looked at the deep marks on his skin. "What's gonna happen to me?" he whined.

"What's your name, young man?" Dr. Caul asked.

"Danny."

The officer who had removed the handcuffs laughed and said, "Jesus Christ!"

Dr. Caul jumped up and slammed the door in his face. He was not surprised that dissociation had taken place. Dr. Harding had told him the fusion seemed fragile at best. His own experience with multiples had taught him that a stressful situation, such as a trial, could cause unfusion. Right now he had to gain Danny's confidence.

"I'm glad to meet you, Danny," he said. "How old are you?"

"Fourteen."

"Where were you born?"

He shrugged. "I don't remember. Lancaster, I think."

Caul thought about it a few minutes and, seeing how exhausted Milligan was, put his pen down. "I think we can let these questions go for another time. Just take it easy tonight. This is Mrs. Katherine Gillott, one of our mental health technicians. She'll show you your room, and you can put your suitcase away and hang up your jacket."

When Dr. Caul had left, Mrs. Gillott took him across the lobby to the first room on the left. The door was open.

"My room? That can't be for me."

"C'mon, young'un," Mrs. Gillott said, walking in and opening the window. "You've got a nice view of Athens and Ohio University. It's dark now, but you'll see it in the morning. Make yourself t'home."

But when she left him alone, he stayed in the chair outside his room and sat, afraid to move, until one of the other mental health technicians started turning out the lights in the corridor.

He went into his room and sat on the bed, his body trembling, tears in his eyes. He knew that whenever people were nice to you, you had to pay in the long run. There was always a catch.

He lay on the bed, wondering what was going to happen to him. He tried to stay awake, but it had been a long day, and finally he fell asleep.

(2)

In the morning of December 5, 1978, Danny opened his eyes and saw the light streaming through the window. He looked out and saw the river and the university buildings on the other side. While he was standing there, someone knocked at the door. It was a rather handsome, mature woman with short hair and wide-set eyes.

"I'm Nórma Dishong, your morning case manager. If you'll come along, I'll take you around and show you where you get breakfast."

He followed her as she showed him the TV room, the billiard room, the snack area. Through one set of double doors was a small cafeteria with one long table in the center and four square tables the size of card tables along the walls. At the far end was the serving counter.

"Get yourself a tray and some tableware, and you can help yourself."

He took a tray and then reached for a fork, but when it came out of the canister and he saw it was a knife, he flung it away. It hit the wall and clattered to the floor. Everyone looked up.

"What's the matter?" Dishong asked.

"I—I'm afraid of knives. I don't like 'em."

She retrieved the knife, then pulled a fork for him and put it on his tray. "Go ahead," she said, "get something to eat."

After breakfast she greeted him as he walked by the nurses' station. "By the way, if you want to go for a walk through the building, just sign that piece of paper up on the wall there so that we'll know you're off the ward."

He stared at her, dumfounded. "You mean I can go out of here?"

"This is an open ward. As long as you stay in the hospital, you're free to come and go as you please. Eventually, when Dr. Caul feels you're ready, you'll be able to sign yourself out of the building to walk on the grounds."

He looked at her in astonishment. "The grounds? But there are no walls or fences?"

She smiled. "That's right. This is a hospital, not a prison."

* * *

That afternoon Dr. Caul dropped in to visit Billy in his room. "How are you feeling?"

"Fine, but I didn't think you let people like me come and go without being watched the way they watched me at Harding Hospital."

"That was before your trial," Caul said. "There's one thing I want you to remember. You've had your day in court, and you were found *not guilty*. To us you're not a criminal. No matter what you did in the past, or whatever *anyone else inside you* did, that's over with. This is a new life. What you do here, how you progress, how you accept things—how you work with Billy, and bring yourself together in terms of yourself—that's what's going to make you get well. You've got to *want* to get well. Nobody here is going to look down on you."

Later that day the *Columbus Dispatch*, carrying the story of Milligan's transfer to Athens, summarized the case, including the evidence presented in court of Chalmer Milligan's alleged abuses of his wife and children. It also published a sworn statement submitted to the *Dispatch* by Chalmer Milligan and his attorney:

I, Chalmer J. Milligan, married the mother of William Stanley Milligan in October of 1963. I adopted William, along with his brother and sister shortly thereafter.

William has accused me of threatening, abusing and sodomizing him, particularly over the period of the year when he was 8 or 9 years old. This accusation is completely false. Furthermore, none of the psychiatrists or psychologists, who examined William for the report prepared for Judge Flowers, interviewed me prior to that document's preparation and release.

There is no doubt in my mind that William has lied repeatedly and extensively to those who have been examining him. During my 10 years of marriage to his mother, William was a habitual liar. I feel that William is continuing a pattern of lying which he established many years ago.

The accusations by William and their subsequent publication by numerous newspapers and magazines have caused me extreme embarrassment, mental anguish and suffering. I make this statement in order to set the record straight and clear my good name.

One morning a week after Milligan's arrival, Dr. Caul stopped by again. "I thought you and I ought to begin your therapy today. Let's go to my office."

Danny followed him, frightened. Caul pointed to a comfortable chair and sat across from him, clasping his hands across his potbelly.

"I want you to understand that I know a great deal about you from your case files. It's pretty damned thick. Now we're going to do something like Dr. Wilbur did. I've talked to her, and I know she made you relax and she was able to talk to Arthur and Ragen and the others. That's what we're going to do."

"How? I can't make 'em come."

"You just settle back comfortably and listen to my voice. I'm sure Arthur will understand that Dr. Wilbur and I are friends. She suggested that you be sent here for treatment because she has confidence in me, and I hope you'll have confidence in me too."

Danny squirmed in his seat, then sat back and relaxed, eyes drifting from side to side. Seconds later he looked up, suddenly alert.

"Yes, Dr. Caul," he said, placing his fingertips together, "I appreciate the fact that Dr. Wilbur recommended you. You will have my full cooperation."

Caul had expected the Englishman, so he wasn't startled by the change. He'd seen too many multiples to be taken by surprise at the emergence of an alter ego.

"Ahem . . . ah . . . yes. And would you please tell me your name? For the record."

"I'm Arthur. You wanted to speak with me."

"Yes, Arthur. Of course I knew who it was, by your distinctive British accent, but I'm sure you realize it's necessary for me not to make assumptions about—"

"I don't have the accent, Dr. Caul. You do."

Caul stared at him blankly for a moment. "Ah, yes," he said. "I'm sorry. I hope you won't mind answering a few questions."

"Not at all. That's why I'm here, to help in any way I can."

"I would like to review with you the vital facts about the various personalities—"

"*People*, Dr. Caul. Not 'personalities.' As Allen explained to Dr. Harding, when you call us 'personalities,' it gives us the impression that you don't accept the fact that we are real. That would make therapy difficult."

Caul studied Arthur carefully and decided he didn't care much for the arrogant snob. "I stand corrected," he said. "I'd like to know about the *people*."

"I will give you as much information as I can."

Caul questioned and Arthur reviewed the ages, appearances, traits, abilities and reasons for the emergence of the nine people recorded by Dr. Harding.

"Why did the baby come into existence? Christene. What was her role?"

"Companionship for a lonely child."

"And her temperament?"

"Shy, but she can be set off by fear that Ragen will do something mean or violent. He adores her, and she can usually distract him from some intended violence by going into a tantrum and banging her feet."

"Why did she remain three?"

Arthur smiled knowingly. "It became important to have someone who knew little or nothing about what was happening. Her not knowing was an important protective device. If William had to hide something, she would come on the spot and draw or play hopscotch or cuddle the little Raggedy Ann doll Adalana made for her. She's a delightful child. I have a particular fondness for her. She's British, you know."

"I didn't know that."

"Oh, yes. She's Christopher's sister."

Caul regarded him a moment. "Arthur, do you know all the others?"

"Yes."

"Have you always known all the others?"

"No."

"How did you learn of their existence?"

"By deduction. When I realized I was losing time, I began watching other people closely. I discovered that it was different with them, and I began to brood about it. Then, by asking some questions—both in and outside my head—I discovered the truth. Slowly, over many years, I've established contact with all the others."

"Well, then, I'm glad we've met. If I'm to be of any help to Billy—to all of you—I'll need your assistance."

"You may call upon me anytime."

"There is one important question I'd like to ask before you go."

"Yes?"

"Gary Schweickart mentioned something that has since appeared in the press. He said that from the facts of the case, discrepancies among statements made by all of you and the comments of the victims—things like foul language, statements about criminal activities, and the name 'Phil'—he believed there might be more personalities than the ten already revealed. Would you know anything about that?"

Instead of answering him, Arthur's eyes glazed and his lips began to move. Slowly, imperceptibly, he withdrew. After a few seconds the young man blinked and looked around him. "Oh my God! Not again!"

"Hello," Caul said. "I'm Dr. Caul. Would you mind giving me your name—for the record?"

"Billy."

"I see. Well, hello, Billy. I'm your doctor. You were sent here and placed under my care."

Billy put his hand to his head, still slightly dazed. "I was coming out of the courtroom. I went into the van . . ." He looked quickly at his wrists and then at his clothes.

"What are you remembering, Billy?"

"The cop put the handcuffs on very tight. And then he shoved a hot container of coffee into my hands and slammed the van door. When he started up, I spilled hot coffee all over my new suit. That's the last thing I—Where's my suit?"

"It's in your closet, Billy. We can send it out for dry cleaning. The spots should come out."

"I feel very strange," he said.

"Would you try to describe it for me?"

"Like something is missing in my head."

"A memory?"

"No. It's like before the trial I was more together with all the others, you know? But now it's like there's more pieces missing up here." He tapped his head.

"Well, Billy, maybe in the next few days and weeks we can try to find those pieces and put them back together."

"Where am I?"

"This is the Athens Mental Health Center in Athens, Ohio."

He settled back. "That's what Judge Metcalf said. I remember he said I had to be sent here."

Sensing that he was dealing now with a partially fused core Billy, the host personality, Caul spoke to him softly, careful to ask neutral questions. It struck him how the change of personality caused a definite facial alteration. Arthur's tight-jawed, pressed-lipped, heavy-lidded gaze that made him appear arrogant had given way to Billy's wide-eyed, hesitant expression. He seemed weak and vulnerable. In place of Danny's fear and apprehension, Billy showed bewilderment. Although he answered the questions eagerly, trying to please his doctor, it was clear he didn't know, or didn't remember, much of the asked-for information.

"I'm sorry, Dr. Caul. Sometimes when you ask me a question I think I'm going to know the answer, but when I reach for it, it's not there. My Arthur or my Ragen would know. They're smarter than I am, and they've got good memories. But I don't know where they've gone."

"That's all right, Billy. Your memory will get better, and you'll discover you know much more than you expect."

"Dr. Harding said that. He said it would happen when I fused, and it did. But then, after the trial, I came apart. Why?"

"I don't have the answer, Billy. Why do you think it happened?"

Billy shook his head. "All I know is Arthur and Ragen aren't with me right now, and when they're not with me, I don't remember things too good. I missed out a lot on my life because they kept me asleep for a long time. Arthur told me."

"Does Arthur talk to you a lot?"

Billy nodded. "Ever since Dr. George introduced me to him at Harding Hospital. Now Arthur tells me what to do."

"I think you should listen to Arthur. People with multiple personalities usually have someone inside them who knows all the others and tries to be helpful. We call that an 'inner self helper'—or ISH for short."

"Arthur? He's an ISH?"

"I think so, Billy. He fits the role: intelligent, aware of the others, highly moral—"

"Arthur's very moral. He's the one who made up the rules."

"What rules?"

"How to act, what to do, what not to do."

"Well, I think Arthur will be very helpful in curing you, if he will cooperate with us."

"I'm sure he will," Billy said, "because Arthur's always saying how it's important for us to get all together and get well so I can become a useful citizen and a contributing member of society. But I don't know where he's gone now."

As they spoke, Caul had the feeling Billy was gaining confidence in him. Caul brought him back to the ward, showed him his room and introduced him once again to his case manager and some of the other people on the ward.

"Norma, this is Billy," Caul said. "He's new here. We ought to get someone to show him around AIT."

"Of course, Dr. Caul."

But when she walked him back to his room, she looked at him steadily. "You know your way around here by now, Billy, so we won't have to go through that again."

"What's AIT?" he asked.

She led him to the main entrance to the ward and opened the heavy door, pointing to the sign: "Admissions and Intensive Treatment. We call it AIT for short." Then she turned and left.

Billy wondered what he had done to make her so curt with him, but try as he might, he couldn't figure it out.

When he learned that his sister and mother were coming to visit that evening, he became tense. He had seen Kathy, his sister, at the trial, and as soon as he had gotten over the shock of seeing his fourteen-year-old sister transformed into an attractive twenty-one-year-old woman, he felt comfortable with her. But his mother hadn't been at the trial, at his own insistence. Though Kathy had assured him that his mother had visited him often at Harding Hospital, and before that at Lebanon prison, he had no recollection of any of it.

The last time he'd seen Mom was when he was sixteen, before they'd put him to sleep. But the image in his mind was from an earlier time: her beautiful face covered with blood, and a big chunk of hair ripped out of her scalp . . . That was the face he remembered, from when he was fourteen.

When they came to AIT, he was shocked to see how his mother had aged. Her face was lined. Her hair, curled into tight dark ringlets, looked like a wig. But the blue eyes and the pouting lips were still beautiful.

She and Kathy reminisced about the past, each trying to outdo the other in recalling moments which had been confusing in his childhood but which they could now explain as having been caused by one of the other personalities.

"I always knew there were two," his mother said. "I always said there was *my* Billy and that *other* one. I tried to tell them you needed help, but no one would listen to me. I told the doctors and I told that lawyer who plea-bargained you into Lebanon. But no one would listen to me."

Kathy sat back and glared at her mother. "But someone would have listened if you told them about Chalmer."

"I didn't know," Dorothy Moore said. "Kathy, as God is my witness, if I'd known what he did to Billy, I'd have cut his heart out. I'd never have taken that knife away from you, Billy."

Billy frowned. "What knife?"

"I remember it like it was yesterday," his mother said, smoothing her skirt over her long tanned legs. "You was about fourteen. I found the kitchen knife under your pillow and I asked you about it. You know what you said to me? I think it was the *other* one who said it. 'Madam, I thought your husband would be dead by this morning.' Those was your exact words, as God is my witness."

"How's Challa?" Billy asked, changing the subject.

His mother looked down at the floor.

"Something's wrong," Billy said.

"She's all right," his mother said.

"I feel something's wrong."

"She's pregnant," said Kathy. "She's left her husband and she's coming back to Ohio to live with Mom until she has the baby."

Billy passed his hands over his eyes as if to clear away smoke or fog. "I knew something was wrong. I felt it."

His mother nodded. "You always did have a way of telling things. What do they call that?"

"ESP," said Kathy.

"And you too," said his mother. "Between the two of you, you always knew things. And you two could always know what was going on in each other's minds without talking. That always gave me the creeps, I can tell you that."

They stayed for over an hour, and when they left, Billy lay on his bed and stared out the window at the lights from the city of Athens.

(3)

In the days that followed, Billy jogged around the hospital grounds, read, watched TV and had therapy sessions. The Columbus newspapers ran stories about him regularly. *People* magazine published a long article on his life, and his picture appeared on the cover of *Columbus Monthly*. Calls began to flood the hospital switchboard from people who had read about or seen pictures of his artwork and wanted to buy his paintings. With Dr. Caul's permission, he sent for art supplies, set an easel up in his room and painted dozens of portraits, still lifes and landscapes.

Billy told Dr. Caul that a lot of people had contacted Judy and Gary about the rights to his life story, and others wanted him to appear on *The Phil Donahue Show, Dinah!* and *60 Minutes*.

"Do you want someone to write about you, Billy?" Caul asked.

"I guess I could use the money. When I get better and go out into society, I'll need something to support me. Who would give me a job?"

"Aside from the money, how do you think you'd feel about the whole world reading about your life?"

Billy frowned. "I think people should know. It could help them understand what child abuse can lead to."

"Well, if you really decide you want someone to write your story, you might want to meet a writer I know and trust. He teaches here in Athens, at Ohio University. One of his books was made into a movie. I mention this only so that you can examine all the possibilities."

"You think a real writer would want to write a book about me?"

"It wouldn't hurt to meet him and see what he thinks."

"Okay, that's a good idea. I'd like that."

That night Billy tried to imagine what it would be like to talk to an author. He tried to visualize the man. Probably be wearing a tweed jacket and smoking a pipe, like Arthur. How good could he be if he had to teach at a university? An author should be someone who lived in New York or Beverly Hills. And why was Dr. Caul recommending him? He had to be careful. Gary had said there could be a lot of money in a book. And a movie. He wondered who would play his part.

He tossed and turned through the night, excited and frightened at the prospect of talking to a real author whose own book had been made into a movie. When he finally fell asleep at dawn, Arthur decided that Billy was incapable of handling the interview with the writer. Allen would have to take the spot.

"Why me?" Allen asked.

"You're the manipulator. Who is better qualified to be on the alert and make sure Billy's not being conned?"

"Always the front man," grumbled Allen.

"That's what you're best at," Arthur said.

The next day, when Allen met the writer, he was shocked and disappointed. Instead of a tall, glamorous author, he saw a short, thin man with a beard and glasses, wearing a tan corduroy sports coat.

Dr. Caul introduced them, and they went into his office to talk. Allen settled back on the leather settee and lit a cigarette. The writer sat across from him and lit his pipe. Just like Arthur. They chatted for a while and then Allen brought up the subject.

"Dr. Caul said you might be interested in the rights to my story," Allen said. "What do you think it's worth?"

The writer smiled and puffed away. "That depends. I'd have to know more about you to be sure there's a story a publisher might be interested in. Something that goes beyond what's already been published in the newspapers and *Time* and *Newsweek*."

Caul smiled and laced his fingers across his stomach. "You can be sure of that."

Allen hunched forward, elbows on his knees. "There is. A lot more. But I'm not giving it away for nothing. My lawyers in Columbus told me that a lot of people are after the rights. A guy came out from Hollywood to make an offer for TV and movie rights, and there's a writer flying in this week with an offer and a contract."

"That sounds promising," the writer said. "With all the publicity you've had, I'm sure a lot of people would like to read the story of your life."

Allen nodded and smiled. He decided to check the man out a little further.

"I'd like to read something you've written to get an idea of your work. Dr. Caul says one of your books was made into a movie."

"I'll send you a copy of the novel," the writer said. "After you've read it, if you're interested, we can talk about it again."

When the writer left, Dr. Caul suggested that before things went any further, Billy should get a local attorney to look after his interests. Columbus public defenders would no longer be able to represent him.

That week Allen, Arthur and Billy took turns reading the novel the author had sent. When they were finished, Billy said to Arthur, "I think he's the one who should do the book."

"I agree," Arthur said. "The way he gets into the mind of his character is the same way I would like him to tell our story. If anyone is to understand Billy's problem, it must be told from the inside. The writer will have to stand in Billy's shoes."

Ragen spoke out: "I disagree. I do not think book should be written."

"Why not?" Allen asked.

"Let me put it this vay. Billy vill talk to this man and so vill you and the others. You might tell him things for vich I could still be charged—other crimes."

Arthur thought about it. "We don't have to tell him those things."

"Besides," Allen said, "we have an out anytime we want to use it. If things come out in the conversations that could be used against us, Billy can always destroy the book."

"How is possible?"

"Just deny the whole thing," Allen said. "I can say I just pretended to have a multiple personality. If I say it's a fake, no one will buy the book."

"Who vould believe that?" Ragen said.

Allen shrugged. "It doesn't matter. What publisher would take a chance on publishing a book if the man it's about says the whole thing is a lie?"

"Allen has a point," Arthur said.

"The same holds true for any contracts Billy might sign," Allen added.

"You mean, pretend he is incompetent to sign it?" Ragen asked.

Allen smiled. " 'Not guilty by reason of insanity,' right? I talked to Gary Schweickart on the phone about it. He said I can always say I was too crazy to sign a contract, that I was pressured by Dr. Caul. That'll make it null and void."

Arthur nodded. "Then I think we can safely go ahead and tell the writer to seek a publisher for the book."

"I still do not think it is vise," Ragen said.

"I believe it is very important," Arthur said, "that this story be told to the world. Other books have been written about multiple personalities, but never a story like Billy's. If people can be made to see how these things come about, then we might make a contribution to mental health."

"And besides," Allen said, "we'll make a lot of money."

"That," said Ragen, "is best and most intelligent argument I have heard today."

"I thought money would appeal to your nature," Allen said.

"It is one of Ragen's more interesting contradictions," said Arthur. "He's a dedicated communist who loves money so much he steals it."

"But you vill agree," said Ragen, "that I always give vatever is not needed to pay our own bills to the poor and needy."

"So?" laughed Allen. "Maybe we can take a charitable tax deduction."

(4)

On December 19, the city editor of the *Athens Messenger* telephoned the hospital for an interview with Billy Milligan. Billy and Dr. Caul agreed.

Caul led Billy into the conference room, where he introduced him to city editor Herb Amey, reporter Bob Ekey and photographer Gail Fisher. Caul showed them Billy's paintings, and Billy answered their questions about his past, the abuse, his attempted suicide, his domination by the other personalities.

"What about the stories of violence?" Amey asked. "How could the community of Athens be assured—if you were allowed to leave the grounds, as so many patients in this open ward do—that you wouldn't be a threat to them or their children?"

"I think," said Caul, "the question of violence should be answered not by Billy, but by one of his other personalities."

He took Billy out of the conference room into his office across the hall and sat him down. "Now, Billy, I think it's important for you to establish good relations with the media in Athens. The people have to be shown you're not a danger to them. One of these days you're going to want to be allowed to go downtown without a supervisor, to buy art supplies or go to a movie or buy a hamburger. These newspapermen are obviously sympathetic. I think we should let them talk to Ragen."

Billy sat silently, his lips moving. After a few moments he leaned forward and glared. "Are you crazy, Doc-tor Caul?"

Caul caught his breath at the harshness of the voice. "Why do you say that, Ragen?"

"Is wrong to do this. Ve haf struggled to keep Billy awake."

"I wouldn't have called you out if I hadn't thought it was important."

"Is not important. Is exploitation for newspapers. I am against. I am angry."

"You're right," Caul said, eyeing him warily, "but the public has to be reassured that you're what the court has said you are."

"I do not care vat public thinks. I do not vant to be exploited and embarrassed by headlines."

"But it's necessary to have good relations with the press in Athens. What the people in this town think is going to have an effect on your therapy and your privileges."

Ragen thought about it. He sensed that Caul was using him to give weight to his statements to the press, but Caul's arguments were logical. "You think is right thing?" he asked.

"I wouldn't have suggested it if I didn't."

"All right," Ragen said. "I vill talk to reporters."

Caul led him back to the conference room, and the reporters looked up apprehensively.

"I vill answer questions," Ragen said.

Startled by the accent, Ekey hesitated. "I—I mean we—were asking . . . We wanted to assure the community that you—that Billy isn't violent."

"I vould be violent only if someone vould try to hurt Billy or to harm a female or a child in his presence," Ragen said. "Only in such case I vould intervene. Let me put it this vay. Vould you allow person to hurt your child? No. You vould protect vife, child or any voman. If someone try hurt Billy, I vould protect. But to attack without provocation is barbaric. I am not barbarian."

After a few more questions, the reporters asked to speak to Arthur. Caul relayed their request, and they saw Ragen's hostile expression change as if melting. An instant later it hardened into a haughty, thin-lipped frown. Arthur looked around, preoccupied, took a pipe from his pocket, lit it and blew a long stream of smoke. "This is quite mad," he said.

"What is?" Dr. Caul asked.

"Putting William asleep to bring us out on display. I have been trying my hardest to keep him awake. It's important for him to stay in control. However"—he turned his attention to the reporters—"to answer your question about violence, I can assure the mothers of this community that they do not have to bolt their doors. William is improving. He is gaining logic from me and the ability to express anger from Ragen. We are teaching him and he is consuming us. When William has learned everything we have to teach him, we shall disappear."

The reporters wrote quickly in their note pads.

Caul brought Billy back, and as he came out, he began to choke on the pipe. "God! That junk's terrible!" he said, and threw it on the table. "I don't smoke."

Answering more questions, Billy said he did not remember anything that had happened from the time Dr. Caul had taken him into the other room. He spoke hesitantly about his aspirations. He hoped to sell some of his paintings and put part of his money into a child-abuse-prevention center.

As the *Messenger* staff left the room, Caul noticed all three looked quite dazed. "I think," he said, walking with Billy back to AIT, "we've got some more believers."

Judy Stevenson was busy on a case, so Gary Schweickart brought the head of the public defender's office with him to Athens to visit Billy. Gary wanted to know more about the writer who was going to do the book, and about L. Alan Goldsberry, the Athens attorney Billy had hired to handle his civil affairs. They met at eleven o'clock in the conference room, along with Dr. Caul, Billy's sister and her fiancé, Rob. Billy insisted he had come to his own decision, and that he wanted this writer to do the book. Schweickart turned over to Goldsberry a list of publishers, potential writers and a producer who had shown interest in the rights to the story.

After the meeting, Gary went off alone with Billy to chat briefly. "I've got another case that's in the headlines now," he said. "The twenty-two-caliber killer."

Billy looked at him very seriously and said, "You've got to promise me one thing."

"What's that?"

"If he did it," Billy said, "don't defend him."

Gary smiled. "Coming from you, Billy, that's really something."

When Gary left the Athens Mental Health Center, he had mixed feelings, knowing that Billy was in other hands now. It had been an incredible fourteen months, all-demanding, all-consuming.

It had contributed to breaking up his marriage with Jo Anne. The time the case had taken away from his family, and the notoriety it was still causing—the late-night phone calls from people who were blaming him for having successfully defended a rapist—had become an intolerable burden. One of his children had been jumped in school because his dad had defended Milligan.

All during the case he had wondered how many of his other clients were being cheated out of the time and effort that he and Judy couldn't give them because Billy Milligan had been so complicated and had taken priority. As Judy had put it, "The fear that you might be slighting someone else makes you work ten times as hard so you won't short-change the others. Our homes and families paid the price."

Gary looked up at the huge, ugly Victorian building as he got into the car, and he nodded. Now Billy Milligan was someone else's care and responsibility.

(5)

Billy awoke on December 23, nervous at the thought of talking to the writer. There was so little he could actually remember of his early years, just bits and pieces, the things he had picked up from others. How could he tell the writer the story of his life?

After breakfast, he walked to the end of the lobby, filled a second cup of coffee from the urn and sat in an armchair to wait for him. Last week his new lawyer, Alan Goldsberry, represented him on the book, and they had signed contracts with the writer and the publisher. That had been hard enough. But now panic was setting in.

"Billy, you have a visitor." Norma Dishong's voice startled him, and he jumped up, splashing coffee on his jeans. He saw the writer coming through the door of the ward, down the steps into the corridor. God, what had he gotten himself into?

"Hi," the writer said, smiling. "Ready to start?"

Billy led the way to his room, then watched as the slight, bearded writer unpacked his tape recorder, notebook, pencils, pipe and tobacco, and settled back in a chair. "Let's make it a practice to start each session with your name. For the record, who am I talking to?"

"Billy."

"Okay. Now, when you first met me in Dr. Caul's office, he mentioned something about 'the spot,' and you said you didn't know me well enough to tell me about it. How about now?"

Billy looked down, embarrassed. "That wasn't me you met that first day. I'd have been too shy to talk to you."

"Oh? Who was it?"

"Allen."

The writer frowned and puffed at his pipe thoughtfully. "Okay," he said, making a note in his memo book. "Can you tell me about the spot?"

"I learned about it, as I learned about most other things in my life, at Harding Hospital when I was partially fused. That was Arthur's explanation to the younger ones about being in the real world."

"What does the spot look like? What do you actually see?"

"It's a big white spot shining on the floor. Everybody is standing around it or lying on their beds near it in the dark, some watching, others sleeping or busy with their own interests. But whoever steps on the spot holds the consciousness."

"Do all your personalities respond to the name 'Billy' when spoken to?"

"When I was asleep and outsiders were calling for Billy, my *people* started answering to the name. As Dr. Wilbur explained to me once, the others do everything they can to conceal the fact that they're a multiple. The truth about me came out only by mistake when David got scared and told Dorothy Turner."

"Do you know when your people first came into existence?"

He nodded and leaned back to think. "Christene came when I was very little. I don't remember when. Most of the others came when I was about eight, going on nine. When Chalmer . . . when Daddy Chal . . ."

His speech grew halting.

"If it bothers you to talk about it, don't."

"That's all right," he said. "The doctors say it's important for me to get it out of my system."

He closed his eyes. "I remember it was the week after April Fool's Day. I was in fourth grade. He took me down to the farm to help him get the garden ready for planting. He took me into the barn and tied me to the Rototiller. Then . . . then . . ." Tears came into his eyes, his voice thickened, became hesitant, boyish.

"Maybe you shouldn't—"

"He beat me," he said, rubbing his wrists. "He started the motor, and I thought it was going to pull me in and rip me apart with the blades. He said if I told my mother, he'd bury me in the barn, and then he'd tell my mother I ran away because I hated her."

Tears ran down Billy's cheeks as he spoke. "The next time it happened, I just closed my eyes and went away. I know now, from the things Dr. George helped me remember at Harding Hospital, that it was Danny who was tied to the motor, and then David came at that time to accept the pain."

The writer found himself trembling with anger. "God, it's amazing you survived at all."

"I realize now," Billy whispered, "that when the police came to get me in Channingway, I wasn't really *arrested*. I was *rescued*. I'm sorry people had to be hurt before it happened, but I feel God finally smiled down at me after twenty-two years."

CHAPTER SIX

(1)

The day after Christmas, the writer drove up the long, curving road to the Athens Mental Health Center for his second interview with Billy Milligan. He had the feeling Billy would be depressed after having spent the holiday in the hospital.

The writer had learned that the week before Christmas, Billy had pressured Dr. Caul to be allowed to spend the holiday with his family at his sister's house in Logan, Ohio. Caul told him it was too soon—just over two weeks since he'd arrived. But Billy insisted. Other patients at AIT were allowed to go home on brief furloughs. If what his doctor said about treating him like the other patients was true, then he should try to get permission for him to do the same.

Knowing his patient was testing him, and realizing how important it was to gain Billy's trust and confidence, Caul agreed to make the request. He was certain it would be turned down.

It created a furor at the Adult Parole Authority, at the state Department of Mental Health, and at the prosecutor's office in Columbus. When Yavitch phoned Gary Schweickart and asked what the hell was going on out there in Athens, Gary said he would try to find out. "But I'm not his attorney anymore," he added.

"Well, I'd call his doctor in Athens if I were you," Yavitch said, "and tell them to cool it. If anything in the state of Ohio is going to stir up an outcry for new legislation on the controls over the criminally insane, Milligan going out on furlough two weeks after commitment will sure as hell do it."

As Caul had expected, the request was denied.

As he pushed open the heavy metal door and walked to Billy's room, the writer noticed that AIT was nearly deserted. He knocked on Billy's door.

"Just a second," came a sleepy voice.

When the door opened, the writer saw that Billy looked as if he'd just gotten out of bed. He seemed confused as he looked at a digital watch on his wrist. "I don't remember this," he said.

He went to his desk and glanced at a paper. Then he showed it to the writer. It was a hospital commissary receipt for twenty-six dollars.

"I don't remember buying it," he said. "Somebody is spending my money—money I've been making from selling my paintings. I don't think that's right."

"Maybe the commissary will take it back," the writer suggested.

Billy examined it. "I guess I'll keep it. I need a watch now. It's not a very good one, but—I'll see."

"If you didn't buy it, who do you think did?"

He glanced around, bluish-gray eyes scanning the room as if to see whether anyone else was there. "I've been hearing strange names."

"Like what?"

" 'Kevin.' And 'Philip.' "

The writer tried not to show his surprise. He had read about the ten personalities, but no one had ever mentioned the names Billy had just given him. The writer checked to make sure the tape recorder was running. "Have you told Dr. Caul about this?"

"Not yet," he said. "I guess I will. But I don't understand what it means. Who are they? Why am I thinking about them?"

As Billy spoke, the writer recalled the last passage of the December 18 *Newsweek* article: "There remain, however, unanswered questions . . . what about his conversations with his rape victims in which he claimed to be a 'guerrilla' and a 'hit man'? Doctors think that Milligan may have personalities yet unfathomed—and that some of them may have committed undiscovered crimes."

"Before you say anything more, Billy, I think we ought to set some ground rules. I want to be sure that nothing you tell me can ever be used to hurt you. If you're ever about to tell me something that you think might be used against you, just say, 'This is off the record,' and I'll stop the tape recorder. There'll be nothing in my files to implicate you. If you forget, I'll stop you and turn off the recorder. Is that clear?"

Billy nodded.

"Another thing. If you ever plan to break the law in any way, don't tell me. If you do, I'll have to go directly to the police. Otherwise I'd be guilty of complicity."

He looked shocked. "I don't plan to commit any more crimes."

"I'm glad to hear that. Now, about those two names."

"Kevin and Philip."

"What do those names mean to you?"

Billy looked into the mirror over his desk. "Nothing. I can't remember. But one thing keeps popping to my mind—the 'undesirables.' It has something to do with Arthur, but I don't know what."

The writer hunched forward. "Tell me about Arthur. What kind of person is he?"

"No emotions. He reminds me of Mr. Spock in *Star Trek*. He's the kind of person who doesn't hesitate to complain in a restaurant. He doesn't bother to explain himself to people, but he gets annoyed when someone doesn't understand what he's saying. He just doesn't have time to be tolerant. Says he has a busy schedule—things to arrange, to plan, to organize."

"Doesn't he ever relax?"

"Sometimes he'll play chess—usually with Ragen, with Allen moving the pieces—but he doesn't believe in wasting time."

"You sound as if you don't like him."

Billy shrugged. "Arthur isn't someone you like or dislike. He's someone you respect."

"Does Arthur look different from you?"

"He's about my height and weight—six foot, a hundred and ninety pounds. But he wears wire-rimmed glasses."

This second interview lasted three hours, touching on some of the personalities that had been mentioned in the newspapers, facts about Billy's real family, memories of his childhood. The writer found himself groping for a method of handling the material coming his way. His major problem would be the amnesia. With so many gaps in Billy's memory, it would be impossible to learn much about his childhood or the crucial

seven years when Billy had been asleep and the other personalities were living his life. The writer was determined that
although he might dramatize some of the experiences, he
would always stick to Billy's own facts. Except for the unsolved
crimes, it would all be as Billy reported it. The problem was,
he was afraid it would be a story filled with unacceptable holes.
And in that case, there could be no book.

(2)

Dr. Caul looked up; loud voices outside his office were dis-
tracting him. His secretary was talking to a man with a strong
Brooklyn accent.

"Dr. Caul is busy. He can't see you right now."

"Cheez, lady, I don't give a fuck how busy he is. I gotta see
him. I got sumpin' t'give him."

Caul started out of his chair, but then the door to his office
opened and Billy Milligan was standing there.

"You Billy's shrink?"

"I'm Dr. Caul."

"Yeah, well, I'm Philip. Some of us tink you should oughta
have dis." He slapped a sheet of yellow legal paper on the
desk, then turned and walked out. Caul glanced at it and saw
immediately that it was a long list of names: Billy's ten personalities and others as well. The last one wasn't really a name,
just "The Teacher."

He started to follow his patient, but then thought better of
it. He picked up the phone and asked to speak to the technician at medical microwave.

"George," he said. "I've got a session planned for today with
Billy Milligan and Dave Malawista. I'd like you to videotape
it."

Then he hung up and studied the list. So many unfamiliar
names—twenty-four in all. Caul didn't dare allow himself to
think what was starting to dawn on him. How did one handle
something like this? And who in God's name was "The
Teacher"?

After lunch Caul went up to AIT and knocked on the door of
Milligan's room. Seconds later Billy opened it, sleepy-eyed
and tousled. "Yeah?"

"We've got a session this afternoon, Billy. C'mon, shake it."

"Yeah, sure. Okay, Dr. Caul."

Billy followed the energetic little man up the steps and through the door out of AIT.

They walked down the corridor to the modern geriatrics building, past the soft-drink and candy machines, through doors leading to the medical microwave room.

George was inside the conference room, setting up the television camera, and he nodded as Billy and Dr. Caul walked in. On the right, chairs were grouped as if for a nonexistent audience. On the left, just beyond the open accordion doors, stood the television camera and a bank of monitoring equipment. Billy took the chair Caul motioned to, and George helped Billy fasten the cord of the microphone around his neck. At that moment a young dark-haired man entered the room, and Caul turned to greet Dave Malawista, a senior staff psychologist.

George signaled that the TV camera was ready and Caul began the session. "Would you tell us for the record who you are?"

"Billy."

"All right, Billy, I need your help to get some information. We know there are some new names of what you've called 'your people' that keep coming up. Are there, to your knowledge, any others?"

Billy looked surprised and glanced from Caul to Malawista and back. "Well, there was a psychologist in Columbus who asked me about someone named 'Philip.'"

Caul noted that Billy's knees were moving up and down in a nervous jiggling motion.

"Do the names 'Shawn' or 'Mark' or 'Robert' mean anything to you?"

Billy thought for a moment, looked distant, his lips moving in inner conversation. Then he mumbled, "I just heard talking in my head. Arthur and somebody were arguing. The names ring out. I don't know what they mean." He hesitated. "Arthur said 'Shawn' wasn't retarded. Not mentally. He was born deaf, and he slowed down. He's not normal for his age . . . There's been a war going on in me ever since Dr. Wilbur woke me up and before I went to sleep."

His lips moved again, and Caul signaled with his eyes for George to pan the camera in closer to get Billy's facial expression.

"Do you want someone to explain?" Billy asked nervously.

"Who do you think I should talk to?"

"I'm not sure. There's been a lot of mix-up time the last few days. I'm not sure who you could get information out of."

"Can you get off the spot yourself, Billy?"

Billy looked surprised and a little hurt, as if he felt Dr. Caul was sending him away.

"Now, Billy, I didn't mean—"

Billy's eyes glazed. He sat rigid for a few seconds. Then he looked around, as if suddenly wakened and suspiciously alert. He cracked his knuckles and glared.

"You have made quite a few enemies, Dr. Caul."

"Could you explain that?"

"Vell, I am not one at the moment. It is Arthur."

"Why?"

"There vas penetration by the undesirables."

"Who are 'the undesirables'?"

"Those who vas silenced by Arthur because their functions ver no longer necessary."

"If they were no longer necessary, why are they still around?"

Ragen glared at him. "Vat do you vant us to do—murder them?"

"I see," Caul said. "Go on."

"I am not satisfied vit Arthur's decisions. He should be protector, too, as vell as me. I cannot do everything."

"Could you tell me more about these undesirables? Are they violent? Criminals?"

"I am only violent one. And then only for reason." Suddenly he noticed the watch on his wrist and looked surprised.

"Is that your watch?" Caul asked.

"I have no idea vere it come from. Billy must have bought it ven I vas not looking. As I say, the others are not thieves." He smiled. "Arthur is stuck-up type person about the undesirables, and the other people ver told never to mention them. They ver to be kept secret."

"Why wasn't it revealed before that there are others?"

"No one ever asked."

"Never?"

He shrugged. "Maybe they ask Billy or David, who did not know they existed. The undesirables ver not to be revealed until total trust was available."

"Then why were they revealed to me?"

"Arthur is losing domination. Undesirables are now in rebellion and decided to reveal themselves to you. Kevin wrote list. Is very necessary step. But is bad to reveal too much ven there is still lack of trust. Ve lost defense mechanism. I vas sworn to secrecy not to tell, but I vould not lie."

"What's going to happen, Ragen?"

"Ve vill be solidified. All together. In complete control. There vill be no more amnesia. Only one vill be dominant."

"Who will that be?"

"The Teacher."

"Who is the Teacher?"

"He is very likable person. He has good and bad, as most humans. You know Billy as he is now. His emotions change by circumstances. The Teacher keeps his own name silent, but I know who Teacher is. If you know who Teacher is, you vould definitely classify us all as insane."

"What is that?"

"You have met parts of the Teacher, Dr. Caul. Let me put it this vay. The main question is, How did all of us learn the things ve know? From the Teacher. He taught Tommy electronics and escape. He taught Arthur biology and physics and chemistry. He taught me about veapons and how to control adrenaline for maximum power. He taught us all to draw and paint. The Teacher knows all."

"Ragen, who is the Teacher?"

"The Teacher is Billy all in one piece. But Billy does not know."

"Why are you on the spot now telling me this, Ragen?"

"Because Arthur is angry. He made mistake of relaxing control, letting Kevin and Philip reveal undesirables. Arthur is intelligent, but he is only human. Now is rebellion inside."

Caul motioned to Malawista to pull his chair closer. "Do you mind if Dave Malawista joins us?"

"Billy vas nervous in front of both of you, but I have no fear." Ragen glanced around at the coiled wires and the electronic equipment and shook his head. "This looks like Tommy's playroom."

"Could you tell me more about the Teacher?" Malawista asked.

"Let me put it this vay. Billy was child prodigy ven he vas little. He vas all of us in one. He does not know that now."

"Then why did he need you?" Malawista asked.

"I vas created for physical protection."

"But you know, don't you, that you are really just a figment of Billy's imagination."

Ragen leaned back and smiled. "I have been told. I have accepted that I am figment of Billy's imagination, but Billy has not accepted that. Billy has failed at many things. That is vy there are undesirables."

"Do you think Billy should know he's the Teacher?" Malawista asked.

"It vould upset him to know. But ven you talk to Teacher, you vill be talking to Billy all in one person." Ragen examined the watch again. "Is not fair to spend Billy's money vithout him knowing it. But this vill let him know how much time he loses."

Caul said, "Ragen, don't you think it's time all of you faced reality and worked on your problems?"

"I don't *have* problem, I am *part* of problem."

"How do you think Billy would react if he learned he was the Teacher?"

"It vould destroy him if he finds out."

At the next therapy session, Ragen told Dr. Caul that he and Arthur, after a long and heated discussion, had agreed that Billy should be told he was the Teacher. Arthur had felt, at first, that the shock would be too much for Billy to bear and that it would drive him insane if he found out. Now both of them agreed that if Billy was to get well, it was necessary for him to know the truth.

Caul was pleased with the decision. Ragen's report of the conflict between himself and Arthur and of the rebellion of the undesirables suggested that things were reaching a crisis point. The time had come, he felt, for Billy to see the others and to learn that *he* was the one who had amassed all the knowledge, learned all the skills and passed them on. It would strengthen him to learn that he was the Teacher.

Caul asked to speak to Billy, and when he saw the knees jiggling and knew who he was speaking to, he told him of the decision made by Arthur and Ragen. Caul saw the combination of excitement and fear as Billy nodded and said he was ready. The doctor put the tape cartridge into the recorder, adjusted the sound and then settled back to watch his patient's reactions.

Billy, smiling self-consciously, watched himself on the monitor. When he saw the image of his jiggling legs and noticed he was still doing it, he put his hands on both knees to stop them. And when the monitor showed his lips moving silently, he put his hand to his mouth, eyes wide, not really comprehending. Then came Ragen's face, looking exactly like his own, and Ragen's voice, for the first time not in his own head but out there on the screen. And the words: "You have made quite a few enemies, Dr. Caul."

To this moment Billy had accepted on faith what others had told him—that he was a multiple personality—even though nothing inside him made him feel that was true. All he had known until now was that occasionally he heard voices and he lost time. He had believed what the doctors told him, but he never felt it. Now for the first time he saw it with his own eyes, and for the first time he understood.

He watched in fearful fascination as Ragen spoke of the twenty-four names on the paper and of the undesirables. His mouth stayed open as Ragen spoke of the Teacher, who had taught everyone all they knew. But who was the Teacher?

"The Teacher is Billy all in one piece. Billy does not know he is Teacher," Ragen said from the screen.

Caul watched as Billy went limp. He looked weak. He was sweating.

Billy walked out of the medical microwave room and took the stairs up to the third floor. People passed and greeted him, but he didn't respond. He walked through the nearly empty lobby of AIT. Suddenly weak and trembling, he dropped into an easy chair.

He was the Teacher.

He was the one with the intelligence, the artistic talent, the strength, the escape-artist abilities.

He tried to understand it. At first, there had been only the core Billy, the one who was born and who had the birth certificate. Then he had broken into many parts, but all the while behind these many parts there was a presence without a name—someone that Ragen had said was the Teacher. In a sense, the unseen, fragmented, spiritlike thing called the Teacher had created all the others, children as well as monsters—and therefore he alone bore the responsibility for their crimes.

If the twenty-four people fused into one, that would be the Teacher. That would be the whole Billy. What would it feel like? Would he know it? Dr. Caul had to meet the Teacher. It was important for the therapy. And the writer needed the Teacher, too, to learn everything that had happened . . .

He closed his eyes and felt a strange warmth flow up from his legs to his trunk and out to his arms, up to his shoulders and his head. He felt himself vibrating and pulsing. He looked down and saw the spot, the bright white light that hurt his eyes. And looking down, he knew they had to take the spot, all of them, all together at once, and then they were on the spot and he was on the spot and in the spot . . . and through the spot . . . falling . . . hurtling through inner space . . . all the people flowing together . . . sliding together . . . interlocking . . .

And then he was out the other side.

He clasped his hands and held them in front to look at them. Now he knew why he hadn't been completely fused before. The others hadn't been revealed. All the others he had created, all their actions, thoughts, memories, from Billy's early childhood to this moment, now came back to him. He knew the successful ones as well as the failures—the undesirables Arthur had tried to control and then vainly to hide. He now knew his history: their absurdities, their tragedies, their undisclosed crimes. And he also knew that as he thought of something or remembered it and spoke of it to the writer, the twenty-three others would come to know it, too, and would learn the story of their own lives. Once knowing, amnesia erased, they could never be the same again. That made him sad, as if he had lost something. But for how long?

He sensed someone walking down the lobby, and turned to see who was coming toward him. Parts of himself, he knew, had met the little doctor.

Dr. Caul walked through the AIT lobby toward the nurses' station and saw what he thought at first was Billy, sitting in the chair outside the TV room. But the moment his patient stood and turned, Caul knew it wasn't Billy or any of the personalities he had seen before. There was an easiness to the stance, a disarmingly open gaze. Caul guessed something had happened, and he felt it was important to show the patient his doctor was sensitive enough to know without asking or being told. He had to risk it. Caul folded his arms across his chest and looked directly into the penetrating eyes.

"You're the Teacher, aren't you? I've been expecting you."

The Teacher looked down at him and nodded, a quiet strength in his half smile. "You've stripped away all my defenses, Dr. Caul."

"I didn't do it. You know that. It was time."

"Things can't ever be the same again."

"Do you want them to?"

"I guess not."

"So now you'll be able to tell the writer the whole story. How far back can you recall?"

The Teacher looked at him steadily. "Total recall. I remember Billy being brought back to the hospital in Florida when he was a month old and nearly died because there was an obstruction in his throat. I remember his real father, Johnny Morrison, the Jewish comedian and master of ceremonies, who committed suicide. I remember Billy's first imaginary playmate."

Caul nodded, smiling, and patted his arm. "It's good to have you with us, Teacher. We've all got a lot to learn."

BOOK TWO
BECOMING THE TEACHER

CHAPTER
SEVEN

(1)

Dorothy Sands recalled March of 1955, holding her one-month-old baby in her arms after giving him his medicine, suddenly seeing the infant's bright-red face and the ring of white around his mouth.

"Johnny!" she screamed. "We got to get Billy to the hospital!"

Johnny Morrison rushed into the kitchen.

"Can't get nothing down," Dorothy said. "Keeps throwing up. And now look what this medicine is doing to him."

Johnny shouted for Mimi, the housekeeper, to keep an eye on baby Jim, and he ran out to start the car. Dorothy met him with baby Billy, and they drove to the Mount Sinai Hospital in Miami Beach.

In the emergency room, a young intern glanced at the baby and said, "Lady, you're too late."

"He's alive!" she shouted. "You son of a bitch, you do something for my baby!"

Jolted by the mother's words, the intern took the baby and stammered, "We—we'll do what we can."

The nurse at the reception desk filled out the admissions form.

"Child's name and address?"

"William Stanley Morrison," Johnny said. "1311 North East 154th Street. North Miami Beach."

"Religion?"

He paused and looked at Dorothy. She knew he was about to say "Jewish," but seeing the look on her face, he hesitated.

"Catholic," she said.

Johnny Morrison turned away and walked to the waiting room. Dorothy followed, slumped into the plastic couch and watched him chain-smoke. She guessed he was still wondering if Billy was really his. Billy looked different from dark-haired, dark-complexioned Jim, who'd been born almost a year and a half earlier. Johnny had been so happy about Jimbo he'd talked of finding his wife and getting a divorce. But he never did. Still, he'd bought the pink stucco house with the palm tree in the backyard because, he said, it was important for people in show business to have a home life. It was a better home life than she'd had with her ex-husband, Dick Jonas, in Circleville, Ohio.

But Johnny was going through a bad time now, she realized. His jokes weren't getting across. The younger comedians were getting the bookings, and Johnny was getting the dregs. He used to be a top-notch M.C. and musician, but now instead of working on his act he was gambling and drinking. It had reached the point where he would take one belt before the first nightclub performance, "for starters," and then be unable to go on for the last show. Though he still publicized himself as "half music and half wit," now he could add "and a fifth of bourbon."

He was not the same Johnny Morrison who used to fix up her singing arrangements and saw her home safely, "to protect my twenty-year-old, rosy-cheeked Ohio farm girl." Not the same Johnny Morrison she felt so secure about that she'd warn would-be mashers, "Hey, look out, I'm Johnny Morrison's girl."

At thirty-six, blind in his left eye, stocky and built like a fighter, Johnny was more like a father to her, she thought.

"You shouldn't smoke so much," she said.

He stubbed a cigarette out in the ashtray and jammed his hands into his pockets. "I don't feel like doing the show tonight."

"You've missed too many this month, Johnny."

His sharp glance cut her words. He opened his mouth to say something, and she braced herself for a wisecrack just as the doctor came into the reception room. "Mr. and Mrs. Morrison, I think your baby's going to be all right. He has a growth blocking his esophagus. We can get it under control. His condition is stable. You two can go home now, and we'll call you if there's any change."

* * *

Billy survived. For the first year, he was in and out of hospitals in Miami. When Dorothy and Johnny had out-of-town bookings together, Billy and Jimbo were left with Mimi or in a children's care center.

Dorothy became pregnant, for the third time, a year after Billy was born. Johnny suggested an abortion in Cuba. She refused, she told her children years later, because it was a mortal sin. Kathy Jo was born on New Year's Eve, December 31, 1956. Meeting the medical expenses overwhelmed Johnny. He borrowed more, gambled more, drank more, and Dorothy learned he was into the loan sharks for six thousand dollars. She argued with him. He beat her.

Johnny was hospitalized for acute alcoholism and depression in the fall of 1956, but was allowed home from the hospital on October 19 for Jimbo's fifth birthday party, which was to be the next day. When Dorothy returned late that night from work, she found him slumped over the table, half a bottle of Scotch and an empty bottle of sleeping pills on the floor.

(2)

The Teacher remembered that Billy's first inner friend had no name. One day four months before his fourth birthday when Jimbo wouldn't play with him, Kathy was still too little and Daddy was too busy reading a book, Billy sat alone in his room with his toys, feeling lonely and bored. Then he saw a little boy with black hair and dark eyes who sat across from him and just stared. Billy pushed a toy soldier toward him. The boy picked it up, put it into the truck and moved it back and forth, back and forth. They didn't speak, but even without talking, it was better than being all alone.

That night Billy and the little boy with no name saw his father go to the medicine cabinet and take out a bottle of pills. The mirror reflected Daddy's face as he emptied the bottle of yellow capsules into his hand and swallowed them. Then Daddy sat down at the table, Billy lay down in his crib and the little boy with no name disappeared. In the middle of the night his mother's scream woke Billy. He watched her rush to the telephone to call the police. With Jimbo standing beside him at the window, Billy looked on while they wheeled the stretcher and the cars with the flashing lights took Daddy away.

In the days that followed, Daddy didn't come back to play with him, and Mommy was too upset and busy, and Jimbo wasn't around and Kathy was too little. Billy wanted to play with Kathy, talk to her, but Mommy said she was a little girl and he had to be very, very careful. So when he got lonely and bored again, he closed his eyes and went to sleep.

"Christene" opened her eyes and went to Kathy's crib. When Kathy cried, Christene knew by the expression on her face exactly what she wanted, and she went to tell the beautiful lady that Kathy was hungry.

"Thank you, Billy," Dorothy said. "You're a good boy. You watch your little sister and I'll get dinner ready. Then I'll come and read you a bedtime story before I go to work."

Christene didn't know who Billy was or why she was being called that, but she was happy she could play with Kathy. She took a red crayon and went to the wall beside the crib to draw Kathy a picture of a doll.

Christene heard someone coming; she looked up to see the beautiful lady glaring at the drawing on the wall and the red crayon in her hand.

"That's bad! Bad! Bad!" Dorothy shouted.

Christene closed her eyes and went away.

Billy opened his eyes and saw the anger in his mother's face. When she grabbed and shook him, he got scared and cried. He didn't know why he was being punished. Then he saw the drawing on the wall and wondered who had done that naughty thing.

"Me not bad!" he cried.

"You drew that on the wall!" she shouted.

He shook his head. "Not Billy. Kathy did it," he said, pointing to the crib.

"You mustn't lie," Dorothy said, jabbing her forefinger hard against his little chest. "Lying . . . is . . . bad. You'll go to hell if you're a liar. Now get to your room."

Jimbo wouldn't talk to him. Billy wondered if Jimbo had drawn the picture on the wall. He cried for a while and then he closed his eyes and went to sleep . . .

When Christene opened her eyes, she saw a bigger boy asleep on the other side of the room. She looked around for a doll to play with, but all she saw were toy soldiers and trucks.

She didn't want those toys. She wanted dolls and bottles with nipples and Kathy's cuddly Raggedy Ann.

She slipped out of the room to look for Kathy's crib, peeking into three rooms before she found it. Kathy was asleep, so Christene took the Raggedy Ann doll and went back to bed.

In the morning, Billy was punished for taking Kathy's doll. Dorothy found it in his bed and shook him and shook him until he felt his head was going to fall off.

"Don't you ever do that again," she said. "That's Kathy's doll."

Christene learned that she had to be careful how she played with Kathy when Billy's mother was around. At first she thought the boy in the other bed might be Billy, but everyone called him Jimbo, so she knew he was the older brother. Her own name was Christene, but since everyone called her Billy, she learned to answer to it. She loved Kathy very much, and as the months went by, she played with her, taught her words, watched as she learned to walk. She knew when Kathy was hungry and what foods Kathy liked. She knew when something was hurting Kathy and she told Dorothy if anything was wrong.

They played house together, and she enjoyed playing dress-up with Kathy when her mommy wasn't there. They'd put on Dorothy's clothes and shoes and hats and pretend they were singing in the nightclub. Most of all, Christene liked to draw pictures for Kathy, but she didn't do it on the walls anymore. Dorothy got her lots of paper and crayons, and everyone said how good Billy was at making pictures.

Dorothy was worried when Johnny came home from the hospital. He seemed fine when he played with the children or tried to work up new songs and routines for the show, but when her back was turned, he'd be on the phone with the bookies. She tried to stop him, but he turned on her, cursed her and hit her. He moved out to the Midget Mansions Motel, missing Christmas with the children and Kathy's third birthday on New Year's Eve.

On January 18, Dorothy was awakened by a call from the police department. Johnny's body had been found in his station wagon, parked outside the motel, with a hose leading from the tailpipe into the back window. He'd left an eight-page suicide note attacking Dorothy and giving instructions to pay a few personal debts from the insurance money.

When Dorothy told the children that Johnny had gone to heaven, Jimbo and Billy went to the window and looked up at the sky.

The following week the loan sharks said she'd better pay up Johnny's six-thousand-dollar debt or something would happen to her and the kids. She fled with the children, first to the home of her sister Jo Ann Bussy in Key Largo and then back to Circleville, Ohio. There she met her ex-husband, Dick Jonas, again. After a few dates and promises that he would change, she remarried him.

(3)

Billy was almost five when he went into the kitchen one morning and reached on tiptoe to get the dishtowel from the counter. Suddenly the cookie jar standing on it came crashing to the floor. He tried to put the pieces together, but they wouldn't stick. Hearing someone coming, he began trembling. He didn't want to be punished. He didn't want to be hurt.

He knew he had done something bad, but he didn't want to know what was going to happen, didn't want to hear Mommy screaming at him. He closed his eyes and went to sleep . . .

"Shawn" opened his eyes and looked around. He saw the broken jar on the floor and stared at it. What was it? Why was it broken? Why was he here?

A pretty lady came in, glared at him and moved her mouth, but he heard no sounds. She shook him hard, again and again, and jabbed her forefinger into his chest, her face red, her mouth still moving. He had no idea why she was angry with him. She dragged him to a room, pushed him in and closed the door. He sat there in the dead silence, wondering what was going to happen next. Then he went to sleep.

When Billy opened his eyes, he cringed, expecting to be hit for breaking the cookie jar, but the blows didn't come. How had he gotten back into his room? Well, he was getting used to being somewhere, then closing his eyes and opening them to find himself somewhere else at a different time. He supposed it was that way with everyone. Up to now, he would find himself in a situation where he would be called a liar and punished for something he hadn't done. This was the first time he had done something and waked to find nothing had happened to him. He wondered when his mom was going to punish him for the broken cookie jar. It made him nervous, and he spent the rest of the day alone in his room. He wished Jimbo would come home from school, or that he could see the little dark-haired boy who used to play with his soldiers and trucks. Billy squeezed his eyes closed, hoping the little boy would be there. But nothing.

The strange thing was, he never felt lonely anymore. Whenever he would start to feel lonely or bored or sad, he would just close his eyes. When he opened them, he would be in a different place and everything would be changed. Sometimes he would close his eyes when the sun was shining brightly outside, and when he opened them again, it would be nighttime. Sometimes it would be the opposite. Other times he would be playing with Kathy or Jimbo, and when he blinked he would be sitting on the floor alone. Sometimes when this happened he would have red marks on his arms or an ache in his behind, as if he had been spanked. But he never got spanked or shaken again.

He was glad no one punished him anymore.

(4)

Dorothy stayed with Dick Jonas for a year. Then the situation became too much for her, and she left him for the second time. She supported herself and her children as a waitress at the Lancaster Country Club and by singing in cocktail lounges like the Continental and the Top Hat. She placed the children in St. Joseph's School in Circleville, Ohio.

Billy got along well in first grade. The nuns praised him for his drawing ability. He could sketch quickly, and his use of light and shadow was uncanny for a six-year-old. But in second grade, Sister Jane Stephens was determined he would use only his right hand for writing and drawing. "The devil is in your left hand, William. We have to force him out." He saw her pick up her ruler, and he closed his eyes . . .

Shawn looked around and saw the lady with the black dress and the starched white bib coming toward him with the ruler. He knew he was here to be punished for something. But what? She moved her mouth, but he couldn't hear what she was saying. He just cringed and stared at her red, angry face. She grabbed his left hand, lifted her ruler and brought it down on his palm silently over and over again.

Tears rolled down his cheeks, and again he wondered why he was here to be punished for something he hadn't done. It wasn't fair.

When Shawn left, Billy opened his eyes and saw Sister Stephens walking away. He looked at his left hand and saw the red welts, felt the burning. He felt something on his face, too, and touched his cheek with his right hand. Tears?

Jimbo never forgot that although he was a year and four months older than his brother, it was Billy who, at the age of seven, instigated running away from home that summer. They would pack some food, Billy told him, and take a knife and some clothes, and they would go off and have adventures. They would come back rich and famous. Impressed with his younger brother's planning and determination, Jimbo agreed to go along.

They slipped out of the house with their packs and hiked from Circleville through the outskirts of town, past the built-up area, to the big field overgrown with clover. Billy pointed to a stand of five or six apple trees in the center of the field and said that was where they'd stop for a lunch break. Jimbo followed.

As they sat there leaning against the trees, eating apples and talking about the adventures they would have, Jimbo felt a strong wind coming up. Apples started falling all around them.

"Hey," Jimbo said. "Gonna be a storm."

Billy glanced around. "And look at the bees!"

Jimbo saw that the whole field seemed to be filled with swarming, buzzing bees. "They're all over the place. We'll get stung to death. We're trapped. Help! Help!" he screamed. "Somebody help us!"

Billy packed quickly. "Okay, we didn't get stung on the way into the field. So the best thing is to go out the way we come in—but we go out running. Let's go now!"

Jimbo stopped screaming and followed him.

They took off, racing across the field, and made it back to the road without getting stung.

"That was quick thinking," Jimbo said.

Billy looked at the darkening sky. "It's getting mean-looking. We got stopped, so let's call it off for today. We'll go back, but we won't say anything. Then we can do it another time."

All the way home, Jimbo kept wondering why he was letting himself be led by his younger brother.

Later that summer they went exploring in the woods around Circleville. When they got to Hargis Creek, they saw a rope hanging from a branch over the water.

"We can swing across," Billy said.

"I'll check it out," Jimbo said. "I'm the oldest. I'll go first. Then, if it's safe, you can swing across after me."

Jimbo pulled the rope, backed up to get a running start and swung out. Three quarters of the way across, he fell and dropped into mud, which started sucking him down.

"Quicksand!" Jimbo shouted.

Billy moved fast. He found a large stick and threw it across to him. Shimmying up the tree, Billy climbed out on a branch, down the rope, and pulled his brother to safety. When they were on the bank, Jimbo lay back and looked at him.

Billy said nothing, but Jimbo put his arm around his kid brother's shoulder. "You saved my life, Bill. I owe you."

Unlike Billy and Jimbo, Kathy loved Catholic shool and admired the sisters. She was, she decided, definitely going to be a nun when she grew up. She adored the memory of her father and tried to find out all she could about Johnny Morrison. Her mother had told the children that their father had been ill, was taken to the hospital, and had died. Now that she was five and in school, whatever she did, Kathy asked herself first, "Is that what Daddy Johnny would want me to do?" It was something she would continue into adulthood.

Dorothy saved some money from her singing engagements and bought part interest in the Top Hat Bar. She met a handsome, fast-talking young man who had a wonderful idea about the two of them opening a supper club in Florida. They had to move fast, he explained. She should take the children to Florida to look over a couple of places. He would stay here in Circleville, sell her interest in the bar and then join her. All she had to do was sign her share over to him.

She did what he suggested, took the children to her sister's place in Florida, checked out some clubs for sale and waited a month. He never showed up. Realizing she had been taken by a con man, she came back to Circleville again—broke.

In 1962, while she was singing at a lounge of a bowling alley, Dorothy met Chalmer Milligan, a widower. He now lived with his daughter, Challa, who was the same age as Billy, and he had a grown daughter who was a nurse. He began to date Dorothy and got her a job at the company where he was a job steward on press machines, molding parts for telephones.

From the beginning, Billy didn't like him. He told Jimbo, "I don't trust him."

The Pumpkin Festival in Circleville, famous throughout the Midwest, was the annual highlight of the town. In addition to parades and floats, the streets were turned into a pumpkin fair, vendors in their booths selling pumpkin donuts, pumpkin candies and even pumpkin hamburgers. The city was transformed into a pumpkin fairyland of lights and streamers and carnival rides. The Pumpkin Festival of October 1963 was a happy time.

Dorothy felt her life had taken a good turn. She had met a man with a steady job who would be able to take care of her and who said he would adopt her three children. He would, she felt, be a good father, and she would be a good mother to Challa. On October 27, 1963, Dorothy married Chalmer Milligan.

Three weeks after their marriage, on a Sunday in mid-November, he took them out to visit his father's small farm in Bremen, Ohio, just fifteen minutes away. It was exciting to the children to go through the white farmhouse, swing on the porch swing, poke around the springhouse out back and the old red barn a little ways down the hill. The boys would have to come out weekends, Chalmer said, to work on the place. There was a lot to do to get the soil ready for planting vegetables.

Billy looked at the rotting pumpkins in the fields and fixed the barn and the landscape in his mind. He decided that when he got home, he would draw a picture of it as a present for his new Daddy Chal.

* * *

The following Friday, Mother Superior and Father Mason came into the third-grade room and whispered quietly to Sister Jane Stephens.

"Will all you children please stand and bow your heads?" Sister Stephens said, tears running down her face.

The children, puzzled at the solemnity in Father Mason's voice, listened as he spoke, his voice trembling: "Children, you may not understand the way the world situation is going. I don't expect you to. But I must tell you that our President, John F. Kennedy, was assassinated this morning. We will now say a prayer."

After he said the Lord's Prayer, the children were sent outside to wait for the buses to take them home. Sensing the awesome sadness of the adults, the children stood and waited silently.

That weekend, as the family watched the news and the funeral procession on TV, Billy saw that his mother was crying. It pained him. He couldn't stand to see her that way or hear her sobbing, so he closed his eyes . . .

Shawn came and stared at the silent pictures on the TV screen and at everybody watching it. He went up to the set and put his face close to it, feeling the vibrations. Challa pushed him out of the way. Shawn went to his room and sat on the bed. He discovered that if he let air out of his mouth slowly, with his feet clenched, it would make the same funny vibrations in his head—something like zzzzzzzz . . . He sat and did it alone in his room for a long time. Zzzzzzzz . . .

Chalmer took the three children out of St. Joseph's and enrolled them in the Circleville city school system. As an Irish Protestant, he wasn't having anyone in his family going to Catholic school; they would all have to go to the Methodist Church.

The children resented having to change their prayers from the Ave Maria and the Lord's Prayer—grown-up prayers they all were used to by now—to the children's prayers Challa had to say, especially "Now I lay me down to sleep."

Billy decided if he was going to change his religion he was going to be what his father, Johnny Morrison, had been— Jewish.

CHAPTER EIGHT

(1)

Soon after her marriage, when they all moved to the nearby city of Lancaster, Dorothy discovered that Chalmer was unusually strict with the four children. No talking at the dinner table. No laughing. The salt had to be passed clockwise. When company came, the children had to sit up straight, feet flat on the floor, hands on their knees.

Kathy was not allowed to sit on her mother's lap. "You're too old for that," Chalmer said to the seven-year-old.

Once when Jimbo asked Billy to pass the salt, and Billy, unable to reach that far, slid it over partway, Chalmer shouted at him, "Can't you do anything right? Nine years old, acting like a baby."

They became afraid of Daddy Chal. It was even worse when he was drinking beer.

Afraid to show his anger, Billy withdrew into himself. He didn't understand the strictness, the hostility, the punishment. Once when Chalmer shouted at him and Billy looked directly into his face, Chalmer's tone changed to an icy hiss: "Bend them eyes while I'm talkin' to you."

The voice made Billy cringe and look down . . .

Often when Shawn opened his eyes and looked around, someone was watching him with lips moving, face angry. Sometimes it was the pretty lady. Sometimes it was one of the girls or the boy, who was a little bigger than he was, who would push him or take his toy away. When they moved their lips, he moved his, too, and made the buzzing through his teeth. Then they would laugh when he did that. But not the big angry man. The man would glare at him. Then Shawn would cry, and that would make a funny feeling in his head, too, and Shawn would close his eyes and go away.

Kathy later remembered Billy's favorite childhood game.

"Do the bee, Billy," Kathy said. "Show Challa."

Billy looked at them, puzzled. "What bee?"

"The bee thingie you do. You know. *Zzzzzzzz!*"

Puzzled, Billy imitated the buzzing of a bee.

"You're funny," Kathy said.

"Why do you make that buzzing sound at night?" Jimbo asked later in their room. They slept in the antique wooden double bed together, and Jimbo had been awakened several times by his brother making the vibrating buzzing sound.

Embarrassed that Jimbo should mention the buzzing, just as the girls had, which Billy knew nothing about, he thought quickly. "It's a game I invented."

"What kind of game?"

"It's called 'Little Bee.' I'll show you." He put both hands under the covers and moved them in circles. "*Zzzzzzzz* . . . You see, that's a family of bees under there."

To Jimbo, it was almost as if the buzzing sound *was* coming from under the covers. Billy brought one hand out, cupped, and it seemed the buzzing was coming from inside his hand. Then with his fingers he walked the bee up and down the pillow and the covers. He did this several times with different bees until suddenly Jimbo felt a sharp pinch on his arm.

"Ow! What'd you do that for?"

"That was one of the bees stung you. Now you gotta catch it. Smack that bee or hold it down with your hand."

Several times Jimbo slapped or trapped a bee that stung him. Then once, as he trapped one, the buzzing filled the darkened room, became louder and angrier, and the other hand came out and pinched him harder and harder.

"*Ow! Ow!* Hey, you're hurting me."

"It's not me," Billy said. "You trapped Little Bee. His daddy and his big brother came buzzing around to punish you."

Jimbo let go of Little Bee, and Billy had the whole family of bees circling around Little Bee on the pillow.

"That's a good game," Jimbo said. "Let's play it again tomorrow night."

Billy lay there in the dark before falling asleep, thinking that was probably the real explanation for the buzzing. He had probably been inventing the game in his head—making the buzzing sounds without realizing the others in the house could hear him. That probably happened to a lot of people. Just like losing time. He figured everybody lost time. He'd often heard his mother or one of the neighbors say, "God, I don't know where the time went" or "Is it that late?" or "Where on earth did the day go?"

(2)

The Teacher remembered one Sunday vividly. It was a week after April Fool's Day. Billy, who had turned nine seven weeks earlier, had noticed Daddy Chal watching him constantly. Billy picked up a magazine and glanced through it, but when he looked up he saw Chalmer staring, sitting stone-faced with his hand to his chin, his empty blue-green eyes watching everything he did. Billy got up, put the magazine neatly back on the coffee table and sat on the couch the way he'd been told to, feet flat on the floor, hands on his knees. But Chalmer kept looking at him, so he got up and went out on the back porch. Restless, not knowing what to do, he thought of playing with Blackjack. Everyone said Blackjack was a vicious dog, but Billy got along with him. When he looked up, he saw Chalmer staring at him through the bathroom window.

Frightened now, wanting to get away from Chalmer's gaze, he went around the house to the front yard and sat there shivering although it was a warm evening. The paper boy tossed the *Gazette* to him, and he got up and turned to bring it into the house, but there was Chalmer watching him through the front window.

All the rest of that Sunday and that evening, Billy felt Chalmer's eyes boring into him. He began to tremble, not knowing what Chalmer was going to do. Chalmer didn't say anything, didn't speak, but the eyes were there, following every move.

The family watched *Walt Disney's Wonderful World of Color,* and Billy stretched out on the floor. From time to time, he would look back and see Chalmer's cold, empty stare. When he moved to sit close to his mother on the couch, Chalmer got up and stomped out of the room.

Billy couldn't sleep much that night.

Next morning, before breakfast, Chalmer came into the kitchen, looking as if he hadn't slept much either, and announced that he and Billy were going to the farm. There was a lot to be done.

Chalmer drove the back way, the long way, to the farm, never speaking a word the whole trip. He opened the garage and drove the tractor into the barn. Then Billy closed his eyes. He felt pain . . .

Dr. George Harding's statement to the court recounts the event: "The patient reports . . . that he suffered sadistic and sexual abuse including anal intercourse from Mr. Milligan. According to the patient this occurred when he was eight or nine over the course of a year, generally on a farm when he would be alone with his stepfather. He indicates that he was afraid that the stepfather would kill him insomuch as he threatened to 'bury him in the barn and tell the mother that he had run away.'"

. . . at that moment his mind, his emotions and his soul shattered into twenty-four parts.

(3)

Kathy, Jimbo and Challa later confirmed the Teacher's memory of their mother's first beating. According to Dorothy, Chalmer had become enraged after he saw her talking to a black co-worker on the job at a nearby bench. She had been operating a tape-controlled punch drill, and when she noticed the man was starting to doze on the assembly line, she went over, shook him and told him it was dangerous. He smiled and thanked her.

As she went back to her work table, she saw Chalmer glaring at her. All the way home he was silent, sulking.

In the house she finally said to him, "What's the matter? You want to talk about it?"

"You and that nigger," Chalmer said. "What's going on?"

"Going on? What in God's name are you talking about?"

He hit her. The children watched from the living room as he beat her. Billy stood there, terrified, wanting to help her, wanting to stop Chalmer from hurting his mother. But he smelled the liquor and he was afraid Chalmer would kill him and bury him and tell her he ran away.

Billy ran to his room, slammed the door shut with his back against it and covered his ears with his hands. But he couldn't shut out his mother's screaming. Crying, he slowly slid down the door until he was sitting on the floor. He closed his eyes tight, and in Shawn's deafness everything went silent . . .

That was the first of the bad mix-up times, the Teacher recalled. Life became tangled as Billy wandered about, losing time, not knowing the day or week or month. His fourth-grade teachers noticed his odd behavior, and when one of the personalities, not knowing what was going on, would say something strange or get up and wander around the room, Billy would be sent to stand in the corner. Three-year-old Christene was the one who kept her face to the wall.

She could stay there for a long time and not say anything, keeping Billy out of trouble. Mark, who had a short attention span for anything but manual labor, would have wandered away. Tommy would have rebelled. David would have suffered. "Jason," the pressure valve, would have screamed. "Bobby" would have gotten lost in a fantasy. "Samuel," who was Jewish, like Johnny Morrison, would have prayed. Any one of them or the others might have done something wrong and gotten Billy into a worse mess. Only Christene, who never got older than three, could stand there patiently and say nothing.

Christene was the corner child.

She was also the first to hear one of the others. She was on the way to school one morning and stopped to pick a bunch of wildflowers in the field. She found sumac and mulberries and tried to put them into a bunch. If she brought them to her fourth-grade teacher, Mrs. Roth, maybe she wouldn't be put in the corner so much. When she passed the apple tree, she decided to bring a fruit instead. She threw away the wildflowers and tried to reach the apples. She felt sad they were too high, and tears came to her eyes.

"Vat is wrong, little girl? Vat for you are crying?"

She looked around but didn't see anyone. "The tree won't let me have the apples," she said.

"Don't cry. Ragen gets apples."

He shimmied up the tree, and summoning all his strength, "Ragen" broke a thick branch and brought it down. "Here," he said. "I have for you many apples." He loaded his arms with apples and led Christene toward the school.

When Ragen left, Christene dropped them in the middle of the street. A car was speeding toward the biggest, shiniest apple, the one she wanted to give Mrs. Roth, and when she tried to reach it, Ragen bumped her out of the way to save her from being hit. She saw the car had squashed the pretty apple, and she cried, but Ragen picked up another one, not nearly as nice, wiped it off and gave it to her to take to school.

When she put the apple on the desk, Mrs. Roth said, "Why, thank you, Billy."

That upset Christene, because *she* had brought the apple. She went to the back of the room, wondering where to sit. She sat down on the left side of the room, but a few minutes later a big boy said, "Get outta my seat."

She felt bad, but when she sensed Ragen coming to hit the boy, she got up quickly and walked to another chair.

"Hey, that's my seat," a girl called from the blackboard. "Billy's sitting in my seat."

"Don't you know where you sit?" Mrs. Roth asked.

Christene shook her head.

Mrs. Roth pointed to an empty seat on the right side of the room. "You sit in that chair right there, Billy. Now go to it."

Christene didn't know why Mrs. Roth was angry. She had tried so hard to make the teacher like her. Through her tears she felt Ragen coming out to do something bad to the teacher. So she squeezed her eyes shut, stamped her feet and made Ragen stop. Then she left too.

Billy opened his eyes, looked around, dazed, to find himself in class. God, how had he gotten here? Why were they staring at him? Why were they giggling?

On the way out of class, he heard Mrs. Roth call to him, "Thank you for the apple, Billy. It was very nice of you. I'm really sorry I had to scold you."

He watched as she went down the corridor, and wondered what in the world she was talking about.

(4)

The first time Kathy and Jimbo heard the British accent, they thought Billy was clowning. Jimbo was in the room with him while they were sorting their laundry. Kathy came to the door to see if Billy was ready to walk with her and Challa to school.

"What's the matter, Billy?" she asked, seeing the dazed look on his face.

He looked at her, around the room and at the other boy, who was staring at him too. He had no idea who these two were or how or why he was here. He didn't know anyone named Billy.

All he knew was that his name was Arthur and he was from London.

He looked down and saw the socks he was wearing, one black and the other purple. "Oh, I say, these are most certainly not mates."

The girl giggled and so did the boy. "Oh, you're silly, Billy. That's good. You sound just like Dr. Watson on those Sherlock Holmes movies you're always watching, doesn't he, Jimbo?"

Then she skipped off, and the boy called Jimbo ran out, shouting, "Better hurry up or you'll be late."

Why, he wondered, were they calling him Billy when his name was Arthur?

Was he an impostor? Had he come into this house among these people as a spy? A detective? It would take some logical thinking to put the pieces of the puzzle together. Why was he wearing two different-color socks? Who had put them on? What was going on here?

"You coming, Billy? You know what Daddy Chal will do if you're late again."

Arthur decided that if he was going to be an impostor, he might as well go all the way. He joined Challa and Kathy on their walk to the Nicholas Drive school, but he said nothing all the way there. When they passed a room, Kathy said, "Where you going, Billy? You'd better get in there."

He hung back until he could figure out—by the last empty seat—where it would be safe to sit. He walked to it without looking right or left, holding his head high, not daring to speak; he had figured out that the others had laughed because he spoke differently.

The teacher handed out the mimeographed arithmetic test. "When you're done," she said, "you may leave your papers in your books and go out to recess. After you come back, check your answers. Then I'll collect the papers and grade them."

Arthur looked at the test and sneered at the multiplication and long-division problems. He picked up a pencil and quickly went down the paper, doing the problems in his head and writing in the answers. When he was done, he put the paper into the book, crossed his arms and stared into space.

This was all so very elementary.

Out in the schoolyard the rowdy children annoyed him, and he closed his eyes . . .

After recess the teacher said, "Take your papers out of your books now."

Billy looked up, startled.

What was he doing in class? How had he gotten here? He remembered getting up in the morning, but not getting dressed or coming to school. He had no idea what had happened between waking up at home and now.

"You may check your answers before turning in the math papers."

What math papers?

He had no idea what was going on, but he decided if she asked him why he didn't have his math, he'd tell her he forgot it or lost it outside. He'd have to tell her something. He opened his book and stared in disbelief. There was the test paper with all the answers written in—to all fifty problems. He noticed that it wasn't his handwriting—similar, but as if it had been written very quickly. He'd often found papers in his possession and just assumed they were his. But he knew there was no way in the world someone as bad as he was in math could have done those problems. He peeked over at the desk next to his and saw a girl working on the same test. He shrugged, picked up a pencil and wrote "Bill Milligan" at the top. He had no intention of checking it. How could he double-check the answers if he didn't know how to work the problems?

"Are you finished already?"

He looked up and saw the teacher standing over him.

"Yeah."

"You mean you didn't check your answers?"

"Nope."

"Do you have *that* much confidence you're going to pass this test?"

"I dunno," Billy said. "Only way to find out is to grade it."

She took the test paper up to her desk, and a few seconds later he saw the frown on her face. She walked back to his seat. "Let me see your book, Billy."

He handed it to her and she leafed through it.

"Let me see your hands."

He showed her his hands. Then she asked to see his shirt cuffs and the contents of his pockets and the inside of his desk.

"Well," she said finally, "I don't understand. There's no way you could have the answers, because I just ran the test off on the mimeograph this morning and the only answers are in my purse."

"Did I pass?" Billy asked.

She gave him back his paper reluctantly. "You got a perfect score."

Billy's teachers called him truant, troublemaker, liar. From fourth to eighth grade, he was in and out of offices of advisers, the principal, the school psychologist. Growing up was a constant battle of making up stories, bending the truth, manipulating explanations to avoid admitting that most of the time he didn't know what had happened to him days, hours, even just minutes ago. Everyone noticed his trances. Everyone said he was strange.

When he came to understand that he was different from other people, that not everyone lost time, that everyone around him agreed he had done and said things he, and he alone, couldn't recall, he assumed he was insane. He hid it.

Somehow he kept the secret.

It was in the spring of 1969, the Teacher recalled, when Billy was fourteen and in eighth grade, that Chalmer took him to the farm, out beyond the cornfield, handed him a shovel and told him to start digging . . .

Dr. Stella Karolin was later to describe this alleged event in her statement read into the court record: "[His stepfather] abused Billy sexually and threatened to bury him alive if he told his mother. He even buried the child, leaving a pipe over his face for air . . . Before he shoveled the dirt off the child, he urinated through the pipe onto the child's face" (Newsweek, December 18, 1978).

. . . from that day, Danny feared the earth. He would never again lie in the grass, touch the ground or paint a landscape.

(5)

Several days later Billy went into his room and reached over to switch on his bedside lamp. Nothing happened. He clicked it again and again. Still nothing. He shuffled out to the kitchen, got a new bulb and came back to change it as he had seen his mother do. He got a shock that sent him back against the wall . . .

"Tommy" opened his eyes and looked around, not knowing what to expect. He saw the light bulb on the bed, picked it up, peered under the lampshade and started to screw it in. As he touched the metal collar he got a shock. Son of a bitch! What the hell was that? He pulled off the lampshade and looked into the hole. He touched it and felt the shock again. He sat there trying to puzzle it out. Where was this shit coming from? He followed the electric cord to where it plugged into the wall. He pulled out the plug and touched the collar again. Nothing. So the goddamned shock was coming from the wall. He stared into the two little holes, then jumped up and ran downstairs. He followed the wires from the ceiling to the fuse box, followed the cable from the fuse box outside the house, and stopped in amazement as he saw the lines leading to the telephone poles along the streets. So that's what those goddamned things were for!

Tommy followed the poles to see where they led to. It was nearly dark when he found himself outside the building with the wire fence around it and the sign OHIO POWER. Okay, he thought, so where do *they* get the stuff that lights the lights and shocks the shit out of you?

Back home he got out the phone book, looked up Ohio Power and wrote down the address. It was too dark now, but tomorrow morning he would go there and see where the power came from.

The next day Tommy went downtown to Ohio Power. He walked inside and stared, dumfounded. Just a lot of people sitting at desks, answering telephones and typing. A business office! Jesus Christ, struck out again! As he wandered along Main Street trying to figure out how he was going to find out where this junk came from, he passed the library sign in front of the Municipal Building.

Okay, he'd go look it up in the books. He went up to the second floor, searched the card catalog under "power," found the books and began to read. It astonished him to learn about dams, hydroelectric power and the burning of coal and other combustible fuels to create energy to work machinery and light the lights.

He read until dark. Then he wandered the streets of Lancaster, looking at all the lights that had been turned on, excited that now he knew where the power was coming from. He was going to learn all about those machines and everything that had to do with electricity. He stopped in front of a store window and looked at the display of electronic equipment. A crowd had gathered around the TV sets in the window, and they were watching the man in a spacesuit climb down a ladder.

"Can you believe it?" someone said. "Seeing this all the way from the moon?"

". . . *one giant step for mankind*," the voice from the TV was saying.

Tommy looked up at the moon and then back at the TV screen. That was something else he had to learn about.

Then he saw a woman's reflection in the window.

Dorothy said, "Billy, you'd better come on home now."

He looked up at Billy's pretty mother and started to tell her that his name was Tommy, but she put her hand on his shoulder and led him to the car.

"You got to stop this wandering around downtown, Billy. You got to be home before Chal gets back from work or you know what'll happen."

All the way back in the car Dorothy kept looking at him sideways, as if trying to size him up, but he kept quiet.

She gave Tommy something to eat, and then she said, "Why don't you just go in and do some painting, Billy? You know that always settles you down. You look so edgy."

He shrugged and went into the room where the art supplies were. With quick strokes, he painted a night scene of a road with telephone poles. When he was done, he stood back and looked at it. Pretty damned good for a beginner. The next morning he got up early and painted a landscape with the moon showing, even though it was a day scene.

(6)

Billy loved flowers and poetry and helping his mother around the house, but he knew that Chalmer called him "a sissy" and "a little queer." So he stopped helping his mother and writing poetry. "Adalana" came to do them for him in secret.

One evening Chalmer settled down to watch a World War II movie in which a Gestapo interrogator beat his victim with a hose. When the movie was over, Chalmer went out into the yard and cut a four-foot length of garden hose, doubled it and wrapped the cut ends together with black tape for a handle.

When he came inside he saw Billy washing the dishes.

Before she knew what was happening, Adalana felt a blow in the small of her back that knocked her to the floor.

Chalmer hung the hose by the looped end on his bedroom door and went to bed.

Adalana learned that men were violent and hateful and never to be trusted. She wished Dorothy or one of the girls—Kathy or Challa—would hug her and kiss her and make the fear and the bad feelings go away. But she knew that would cause trouble, so she went to bed and cried herself to sleep.

Chalmer used that hose often, mostly on Billy. Dorothy recalled hanging her robe or nightgown over it on the back of the bedroom door, hoping that if Chalmer didn't see it, he wouldn't use it. Then one day, after he hadn't used it for a long time, she threw it away. He never did know what had happened to it.

In addition to secretly playing with motors and electrical equipment, Tommy began to study methods of escape. He read about the great escape artists Houdini and Sylvester, and was disappointed to discover that some of their great escapes were tricks.

In later years Jimbo remembered his brother telling him to tie his hands tightly with a rope and then to leave. When Tommy was alone he would study the knots and figure out the easiest way to turn his wrists to make them mobile so that the ropes would slide. He practiced tying one wrist with a rope and then untying it with his hand behind his back.

After reading of African monkey traps—used to capture the animals when they reached through narrow slots for food and were then unable to pull their fists free because they wouldn't let go—Tommy began to think about the structure of the human hand. He studied the encyclopedia pictures of bone structure, and it occurred to him that if the hand could be compressed smaller than the wrist, it could always get free. He measured his own hands and wrists and began a series of exercises, squeezing and conditioning his bones and joints. When he finally reached the point of being able to compress his hands smaller than his wrists, he knew that nothing could ever again keep him in harness or chains.

Tommy decided he also needed to know how to get out of locked rooms. When Billy's mother was out and he was alone in the house, he got a screwdriver and unscrewed the lock plate of the door, studying the mechanism to see how it worked. He drew a picture of the inside of the lock and memorized the shapes. Whenever he saw a different lock, he would take it apart, study it and put it back together.

One day he wandered downtown into the shop of a locksmith. The old man let him look at the different kinds of locks to memorize how they worked. He even lent Tommy a book about magnetic-invoked tumblers, spinner-type tumblers and different kinds of vaults. Tommy studied hard, testing himself constantly. At the sporting goods store he saw handcuffs and decided that as soon as he had the money he would get a pair to learn how to unlock those as well.

One evening when Chalmer was particularly nasty at dinner, Tommy searched for a way he could hurt him without getting caught. He had an idea.

He got a file from the toolbox, took the cover off Chalmer's electric rotary razor and carefully filed all three rotary blades dull. Then he put the cover back on and went out.

Next morning he stood outside the bathroom while Chalmer was shaving. He heard the click of the razor and then the shouts of pain as the dull blades yanked at the hairs instead of cutting them.

Chalmer raced out of the bathroom. "What're you looking at, you stupid bastard? Don't stand there like a goddamned moron!"

Tommy shoved his hands into his pockets and walked off, turning his head away so Chalmer wouldn't see him smiling.

"Allen's" first time out on the spot was when he tried to talk some neighborhood tough guys out of throwing him down into a construction-site hole dug for the foundation of a building. He argued with them, using all of his con-man abilities, but it didn't work. They tossed him down into the pit anyway and threw rocks at him. Well, he figured, no use in sticking around . . .

Danny heard the clunk of the rock hitting the ground in front of him. Then another one and another. He looked up to see the gang of boys at the top of the excavation tossing rocks at him. One hit him in the leg and another hit his side. Danny ran to the far end, going in circles, trying to find a way out. Finally, realizing the sides were too steep for him to climb, he sat down in the dirt and crossed his legs . . .

Tommy looked up when a rock hit him in the back. Quickly sizing up the situation, he realized an escape was called for. He had been practicing picking locks and untying ropes, but this was a different kind of escape. This needed strength . . .

Ragen got to his feet, pulled out his pocket knife and stormed up the incline toward the boys, flicking open the knife, looking from one of the bullies to the other, holding his anger in control, waiting to see which one would jump him. He had no hesitation about stabbing any of them. They had picked on someone a foot shorter than they were, but they had not expected him to confront them. The boys scattered and Ragen walked home.

Jimbo later recalled that when the parents of the boys complained that Billy had threatened their sons with a knife, Chalmer listened to their side of it, took Billy out back and beat him.

(7)

Dorothy knew that her younger son had changed and was acting strangely.

"Billy wasn't Billy at times," she recalled later. "He was moody, he was off to himself. I would say something to him and he wouldn't answer me, like he was far off and thinking about it, staring into space. He would go wandering downtown like he used to when he would sleepwalk. He'd do it from school. Sometimes if they caught him in school before he had a chance to wander off, they would keep him and call for me to come and get him. Sometimes he'd just leave and they'd call me. I'd go looking for him everywhere, find him wandering downtown and bring him home, and I'd say to him, 'Okay, Billy, you go lay down.' But that child didn't even know which direction his bedroom was. I'd go in there and I'd think, 'My God!' 'Well, how do you feel?' I'd ask him when he'd wake up. He'd look real bewildered and say, 'Did I stay home today?'

"And I'd say, 'No, Billy, you did not stay home today. Don't you remember me coming after you? You were at school and Mr. Young called me and I come up to the school after you. Don't remember coming home with me?'

"He'd look dazed and nod and say, 'Oh.'

" 'Don't you remember?'

" 'I guess I just wasn't feeling well today.'

"They tried to tell me it was drug-related," Dorothy said, "but I knew it wasn't. That boy never took drugs. He wouldn't even take an aspirin. I'd have to fight him to take medicine. Sometimes he'd come home on his own, confused and in a trace. He wouldn't talk to me until he had a nap. Then he'd come out and it would be *my* Billy again. I told them. I told everyone, '*That boy needs help*.'"

(8)

Arthur appeared in school occasionally to correct a teacher when they were studying world history, especially when the subject was England and the Colonies. He spent most of his time in the Lancaster Public Library, reading. There was more to be gained from books and firsthand experience than from these narrow-minded, provincial teachers.

The schoolteacher's explanation of the Boston Tea Party made Arthur angry. He had read the truth in a Canadian book called *The Raw Facts*, which debunked the phony patriotic explanation for what had really been a group of drunken sailors. But when Arthur spoke, everyone laughed, and he walked out of the class, leaving the sound of giggling behind him. He went back to the library, where he knew the pretty librarian wouldn't laugh at his accent.

Arthur knew very well there were others around, because as he checked the dates on the calendar, he knew something was wrong. According to everything he read and observed, other people didn't sleep as long as he seemed to be sleeping.

He began to question people. "What did I do yesterday?" he would ask Kathy or Jim or Challa or Dorothy. Their descriptions of his behavior would be completely strange to him. He would have to check it out by logical deduction.

One day as he was about to sleep, he felt someone else's presence in his mind and he forced himself to stay awake.

"Who are you?" he asked. "I demand to know who you are."

He heard the voice answer, "Well, who in the hell are you?"

"My name's Arthur. Who are you?"

"Tommy."

"What are you doing here, Tommy?"

"What are *you* doin' here?"

The questiining went back and forth in his mind.

"How did you get here?" Arthur asked.

"I dunno, d'you?"

"No, but I've bloody well got to find out."

"How?"

"We must be logical about it. I have an idea. Let's you and I keep track of the time we're awake, to see if that accounts for all the hours of the day."

"Hey, that's a good idea."

Arthur said, "Make a mark inside the closet door for every hour you can account for. I'll do the same thing. We'll tally it up and check it with the calendar to see if all the time is accounted for."

It wasn't.

There had to be others.

Arthur spent every conscious moment working out the puzzle of the missing time and searching for other people who seemed too be sharing his mind and body. After meeting Tommy, one by one he discovered all the others, a total of twenty-three, including himself and the one the outside people referred to as Billy or Bill. He had learned through logical deduction who they were, how they behaved and the things they did.

Only the child called Christene seemed to have been aware, before Arthur, of the existence of the others. She could, he learned, experience what went on in their minds when they were conscious. Arthur wondered if that was a skill that could be developed.

He brought up the subject to the one called Allen, the manipulator who was always there to fast-talk himself out of a tight situation.

"Allen, next time you are holding the consciousness, I want you to think real hard and tell me everything that's going on around you."

Allen agreed to try it, and the next time he found he was out, he told Arthur everything he saw. Arthur visualized it until it came into focus, and then, with a tremendous effort, he was able to see it through Allen's eyes. He discovered, however, that it worked only when he paid attention and when he was awake, even though not out in the consciousness. He had achieved his first intellectual triumph of mind over matter.

Arthur realized that because of his knowledge, he had become responsible for a large, diverse family. They were all involved with the same body, and something had to be done to create order out of what was proving to be a chaotic situation.

Since he was the only one capable of handling the task unemotionally, he would put his mind to it and come up with something that would be fair, workable and—above all—logical.

(9)

The kids at school teased Billy when he wandered around the halls in a daze. They saw him talking to himself, behaving at times like a little girl, and they picked on him. One cold afternoon during recess, some of the boys started taunting him in the schoolyard.

Someone threw a rock at him, hitting him in the side. At first he didn't know what had happened, but he knew he wasn't permitted to show anger or Chalmer would punish him.

Ragen turned and glared at the laughing boys. Another boy picked up a rock and threw it, but Ragen caught it and whipped it back swiftly hitting the boy in the head.

Astonished, the boys backed off as Ragen pulled a switchblade out of his pocket and approached them. They fled. Ragen stood looking around, trying to understand where he was and how he had come to be there. He closed the knife, put it into his pocket and walked off. He had no idea what was going on.

But Arthur observed him, his swiftness, his anger, and he deduced why Ragen was there. He realized that Ragen's sudden emotional outbursts would have to be dealt with. But it would be necessary to study and understand him before he introduced himself. What surprised him most of all was that Ragen was thinking in a Slavic accent. Arthur felt the Slavs had been the first barbarians. In dealing with Ragen, he was dealing with a barbarian. Dangerous, but the kind of person who might prove necessary in times of danger, a power to be harnessed. Arthur would bide his time and approach him when he felt it was right.

Several weeks later "Kevin" joined some tough boys in a dirt-clod fight against kids from another neighborhood. The battleground was a mound of dirt behind a big pit where a housing development was under construction. Kevin was feeling rough and tough, tossing the clods, laughing as he missed, watching them explode like dirt bombs.

Then he heard a strange voice from somewhere beside him say, "Lowah. Trow dem lowah!"

He stopped and looked around, but no one was close by. Then he heard it again: "Lowah . . . lowah . . . trow dem tings lowah." It was a voice like the Brooklyn soldier's in the war movie he had seen on TV. "Y' should trow dem damned doit clods lowah!"

Kevin was baffled. He stopped throwing and sat down on the dirt pile, to figure out who was talking to him.

"Where are you?" Kevin asked.

"Where are *you*?" echoed the voice.

"I'm standing on the dirt behind the pit."

"Yeah? Me too."

"What's your name?" Kevin asked.

"Philip. What's yours?"

"Kevin."

"Dat's a funny name."

"Yeah? I'd bust you if I could see you."

"Where ya live?" Philip asked.

"On Spring Street. Where you from?"

"I'm from Brooklyn, Noo Yawk, but now I live on Spring Street too."

"It's 933 Spring. A white house. Owned by some guy named Chalmer Milligan," Kevin said. "He calls me Billy."

"Cheeze, dat's where I live. I know da same guy. He calls me Billy too. I ain't never seen you dere."

"I ain't never seen you there, either," said Kevin.

"Well, shit, pal!" Philip said. "Let's go bust out some windows at the school."

"That's cool," Kevin said, and they ran down to the school and broke a dozen windows.

Arthur listened and watched and decided that those two were definitely criminal types who could prove to be a very serious problem indeed.

Ragen knew some of the other people who shared his body. He knew Billy, whom he had known from the beginning of his own consciousness; David, who accepted the pain; Danny, who lived in constant fear; and three-year-old Christene, whom he adored. But he knew there were others as well—many others he hadn't met. The voices and the things that happened couldn't be explained by just the five of them.

Ragen knew his last name was Vadascovinich, that his homeland was Yugoslavia and that his reason for existence was to survive and to use any means to protect the others—especially the children. He was aware of his great strength and his ability to sense danger as a spider feels the tingling presence of an intruder on his web. He was able to absorb all the others' fear and transform it into action. He vowed to train himself, perfect his body, study the martial arts. But that was not enough in this hostile world.

He went downtown to the local sporting-goods store and bought a throwing knife. Then he went out to the woods and practiced pulling it quickly from his boot and tossing it into a tree. When it got too dark to see, he headed for home. Never again, he decided, as he slipped the knife back into his boot, would he be without a weapon.

On the way home, he heard a strange voice with a British accent. He turned quickly, bending down and whipping out the knife, but there was no one there.

"I'm in your head, Ragen Vadascovinich. We are sharing the same body."

Arthur talked to him as they walked, explaining what he had discovered about the other people inside.

"You are really in my head?" Ragen asked.

"That's right."

"And you know vat I am doing?"

"I've been observing you lately. I think you're very good with a knife, but you should not limit yourself to one weapon. In addition to the skills of the martial arts, you should learn about guns and bombs as well."

"I am no good vit explosives. I don't understand about all those vires and connections."

"Tommy could specialize in that. The lad is good with electronics and mechanical things."

"Who is Tommy?"

"One of these days I'll introduce you. If we are to survive in this world, we'll have to bring some order out of this chaos."

"Vat you mean 'chaos'?"

"When Billy wanders around, and one person after another switches in front of people, starting things and not finishing them, getting into scrapes that the others have to do mental handsprings to get out of, I call that chaos. There's got to be a way to control things."

"I don't like too much control," Ragen said.

"The important thing," said Arthur, "is to learn to control events and people so that we can survive. That I place as the highest priority."

"And next to highest?"

"Self-improvement."

"I agree," Ragen said.

"Let me tell you about a book I read that explains how it's possible to control one's adrenaline, to channel it for maximum power."

Ragen listened as Arthur described his readings in biology, especially his interest in the idea of harnessing fear and transforming it into energy by adrenaline and thyroid secretion. Ragen found himself annoyed at Arthur's assumption of superiority, but he could not deny that the Englishman knew a great deal he himself had never heard of.

"You play chess?" Arthur asked.

"Of course," said Ragen.

"All right then, pawn to king four."

Ragen thought a moment and answered: "Knight to queen's bishop three."

Arthur visualized the board and said, "Ah, an Indian defense. Very good."

Arthur won the game, and every chess game they played after that. Ragen had to admit that when it came to mental concentration, Arthur was his superior. He consoled himself with the knowledge that Arthur couldn't fight if his life depended on it.

"We will need you to protect us," Arthur said.

"How you can read my mind?"

"A simple technique. You should be able to pick it up someday yourself."

"Does Billy know about us?"

"No. He hears voices from time to time and he sees visions, but he has no notion we exist."

"Should he not be told?"

"I don't think so. I believe it would drive him insane."

CHAPTER
NINE

(1)

In March 1970, Robert Martin, school psychologist at Stanbery Junior High, reported:

> On several occasions Bill couldn't remember where he was, couldn't recall where his belongings were, and could not walk without assistance. The pupils of his eyes were pinpoint in size at these times. Recently Bill has had frequent altercations with teachers and peers which result in his leaving class. During these episodes he is depressed, cries and becomes incommunicative. During one of these recent episodes Bill was observed attempting to step in front of a moving car. Bill was taken to a physician for this behavior. It was reported that the diagnosis was "psychic trances."
>
> During my evaluation Bill appeared depressed, but well in control of his behavior. The evaluation revealed a strong dislike for his stepfather and strong aversion to his home because of this. Bill sees his stepfather as an extremely rigid, tyrannical individual with little feeling for others. This impression was verified by Bill's mother in a parent conference. She reported that Bill's natural father committed suicide and that Bill's stepfather often compared Bill to his natural father. He frequently states that Bill and his mother were responsible for the natural father's suicide (mother's statement).

(2)

John W. Young, principal of Stanbery Junior High, discovered that Billy Milligan frequently cut class and sat on the steps outside his office or at the rear of the auditorium. Young would always sit beside the boy and talk with him.

Sometimes Billy spoke of his dead father and said he would like to be an entertainer when he grew up. He spoke of how bad things were at home. But often, Principal Young realized, the boy was in a trance. He would lead Billy to his car and take him home. After a great many of these episodes, Principal Young referred him to the Fairfield County Clinic for Guidance and Mental Health.

Dr. Harold T. Brown, psychiatrist and director, first saw Billy Milligan on March 6, 1970. Brown, a slight man with gray muttonchops and a receding chin, gazed at the boy through black-rimmed glasses. He saw a neat-looking, slender fifteen-year-old in apparent good health, sitting passively, neither tense nor anxious, but avoiding looking him in the eyes.

"His voice is soft," Dr. Brown wrote in his notes, "with little modulation, almost trancelike."

Billy stared at him.

"What are your feelings?" Brown asked him.

"Like a dream that comes and goes. My dad hates me. I hear him screaming. I have a red light in my room. I see a garden and a road—flowers, water, trees and nobody there to yell at me. I see lots of things that aren't real. There's a door with all the locks on it, and someone is pounding to get out. I see a woman falling down, and suddenly she's turning into a pile of metal and I can't reach her. Hey, I'm the only kid who can take a trip without LSD."

"How do you feel about your parents?" asked Brown.

"I'm afraid he's going to kill her. It's because of me. They fight over me because he hates me so much. I get these nightmares that I can't describe. Sometimes my body feels funny, like I'm real light and airy. There are times I think I can fly."

Brown's first report noted: "Despite the reported experiences, he seems to know reality, and no clearly psychotic ideation elicited. He is reasonably able to focus and sustain attention. He is oriented. Memory is good. Judgment is severely impaired by the above ideation and his seeming need to be dramatic. Insight is insufficient to modify behavior. *Diagnostic Impression:* Severe hysterical neurosis with conversion reactions—APA Code 300.18."

According to the Teacher, who later recalled the session, Dr. Brown had not been interviewing Billy. It was Allen describing David's thoughts and visions.

* * *

Five days later Milligan came to the clinic without an appointment, but Dr. Brown, noticing that he was in a trance, agreed to see him. He observed that the boy seemed to know where he was and that he responded to directions.

"We'll have to call your mother," Brown said, "and tell her you're at the clinic."

"Okay," David said, and got up and walked out.

It was Allen who came back a few minutes later and waited to be called in for an interview. Brown watched as he sat quietly and stared across the room.

"What happened today?" Brown asked.

"I was in school," Allen said. "It was about eleven-thirty, and I started dreaming. When I woke up, I was on top of the Hickle Building looking down, like I was getting ready to jump. I went down and went to the police station and told them to call the school so they wouldn't worry about me. Then I came here."

Brown studied him for a long time, stroking his gray muttonchops. "Billy, do you take any drugs?"

Allen shook his head.

"Right now, you're staring. What do you see?"

"I see people's faces, but only the eyes and noses and weird colors. I see bad things happening to people. They fall in front of cars, they fall down cliffs, they're drowning."

Dr. Brown observed Milligan sitting silently, as if watching an inner screen. "Tell me about things at home, Billy. The family."

"Chalmer likes Jim. He hates me. He's yelling at me all the time. He's driving two people into hell. I lost my job at the grocery. I wanted to lose it so I could stay home with Mom, so I pretended to steal a bottle of wine, and they fired me."

On March 19, Brown noticed that his patient was wearing a turtleneck shirt and blue jacket that gave him an almost effeminate look. "It is my opinion," he wrote after the session, "that this patient should no longer be managed on an outpatient basis and could well benefit from residential therapy in the Columbus State Hospital Children's Adolescent Unit. Arrangements were made with Dr. Raulj for his admission. Final diagnosis is hysterical neurosis with many passive-aggressive features."

Five weeks after his fifteenth birthday, Billy Milligan was committed by Dorothy and Chalmer to the children's unit of the Columbus State Hospital as a "voluntary" patient. Billy believed that because of all his complaining and his bad behavior, his mother had decided to keep Chalmer and give him away.

(3)

COLUMBUS STATE HOSPITAL RECORD—CONFIDENTIAL

March 24—4:00 P.M. Injury occurred during a fight between this patient and another patient, Daniel M—Injury involved a cut below the right eye. Injury occurred while fighting in the hall outside sleeping rooms on RV3 about 4.00 PM. Apparently William and Daniel were playing. William became angry and struck Daniel and then Daniel struck William. Patients separated.

March 25—Patient was found with a case knife on his person also found a small file on the ward which he had taken out of the wood shop. Dr. Raulj talked with the patient and he stated he wanted to kill himself. Placed in seclusion and suicidal precautions.

March 26—Patient has been fairly cooperative. Complains periodically of seeing weird things. Patient did not participate at recreation. Just sat alone most of the time.

April 1—Patient was screaming that the walls were closing in on him and he didn't want to die. Dr. Raulj took him in seclusion and warned him about having cigarettes and matches.

April 12—Patient starts acting out about bedtime the last few nights. He asks us if he is in a trance. Patient wanted extra medication tonight. I explained to patient he should try to get to bed. Patient became hostile and belligerent.

(4)

"Jason" threw the temper tantrums. He was the safety valve who could siphon off excess pressure by screaming and shouting. He was introverted until it came time to release tension. Jason was the one put into seclusion in the "quiet room" at Columbus State Hospital.

Jason had been created, at the age of eight, ready to explode with emotion, but he was never allowed to come out—if he did, Billy would be punished. Here in the Columbus State Hospital, when the fear and pressure became too strong, Jason cried and screamed and vented his emotions.

He did it when he heard on TV about the killing of the four students at Kent State. The attendants locked him up.

When Arthur discovered that Jason was locked away whenever he exploded, he decided to take action. It was no different here from home. Showing anger was not permitted; if one did, all of them got punished. So Arthur forced Jason from consciousness, designated him "an undesirable" and informed him that he was never again to hold the consciousness. He would stay in the shadows beyond the spot.

The others kept themselves busy with art therapy. When Tommy wasn't unlocking doors, he painted landscapes. Danny painted still lifes. Allen painted portraits. Even Ragen tried his hand at artwork but limited himself to sketching in black and white. That was when Arthur discovered that Ragen was colorblind, and recalling the unmatched socks, deduced that it had been Ragen who put them on. Christene drew pictures of flowers and butterflies for her brother, Christopher.

The attendants reported that Billy Milligan seemed calmer and more cooperative. He was given privileges, and when the weather turned warm, he was allowed to go outside to walk and sketch.

Some of the others came out, looked around, didn't like what they saw and left. Only Ragen, impressed with Dr. Raulj's Slavic name and accent, took the Thorazine and obeyed his instructions. Danny and David, being obedient children, took the antipsychotic medication as well. But Tommy would keep it in his mouth and spit it out. So would Arthur and the others.

Danny made friends with a little black boy, and the two of them talked and played together. They would sit up late describing for hours the things they'd like to do when they grew up. It was the first time Danny ever laughed.

One day Dr. Raulj moved Danny from RB-3 to RB-4, where all the boys were bigger. Danny didn't know anyone or have anyone to talk to, so he went into his room, crying because he was lonely.

Then Danny heard a voice say, "Why're you crying?"

"Go away and don't bother me," Danny said.

"Where can I go?"

Danny looked around quickly and saw that there was no one else in the room. "Who said that?"

"I said that. My name's David."

"Where are you?"

"I don't know. I think I'm right where you are."

Danny looked under the bed, in the closet, but the speaker was nowhere to be found. "I can hear your voice," he said, "but where are you?"

"I'm right here."

"Well, I can't see you. Where are you?"

"Close your eyes," David said. "I can see you now."

They spent long hours talking privately about things that had happened in the past, getting acquainted with each other, never realizing that Arthur was listening all the while.

(5)

Philip met a fourteen-year-old blond-haired patient so lovely that everyone admired her beauty. She would walk and talk with him, trying to arouse him sexually, though he never made a pass at her. She watched him sitting with a sketch pad at a picnic table near the pond. Usually there would be no one else around.

One warm day early in June she sat beside him and looked at his drawing of a flower. "Hey, that's good, Billy."

"Ain't nothin'."

"You're a real artist."

"Aw. C'mon."

"No, I mean it. You're different from the other kids here. I like boys that don't just have their minds on one thing."

She put her hand on his leg.

Philip jumped back. "Hey, whatcha doin' that for?"

"Don't you like girls, Billy?"

"Sure I do. I ain't no queer. It's just I—I don't—I—"

"You look real upset, Billy. What's wrong?"

He sat down next to her again. "I don't go in much fuh dat sex stuff."

"How come?"

"Well," he said. "We—I mean, when I was little, I got raped by a man."

She looked at him, shocked. "I thought only girls could be raped."

Philip shook his head. "Well, you got another think comin'. I was beat and raped. And it did somethin' to my head, I can tell ya. I dream about it a lot. A part of me does. All my life I always thought sex was somethin' painful and dirty."

"You mean you never had regular sex with a girl?"

"I ain't never had regular sex with no one."

"It doesn't hurt, Billy."

He blushed as he pulled away.

"Let's go swimming," she said.

"Yeah, great idea," he said, jumping up and taking a running dive into the pond.

When he came up sputtering, he saw that she had dropped her dress on the bank of the pond and was coming in naked.

"Holy shit!" he said, and dived for the bottom.

When he came up, she reached him and put her arms around him. He felt her legs around him in the water, felt her rubbing her breasts into his chest, reaching down to touch him.

"It won't hurt, Billy," she said. "I promise."

Swimming with one hand, she led him toward the cove to a big flat rock angled into the water. He climbed up after her and she pulled his shorts down. He knew he was being awkward as he touched her, and he was afraid if he closed his eyes it would all disappear. She was so beautiful. He didn't want to find himself someplace else and not remember what was happening. He wanted to remember this time. He felt good. She hugged him and squeezed him as he did it, and when it was over he felt like jumping up and shouting with joy. As he rolled off her, he lost his balance and went sliding down the wet, slippery rock, splashing back into the water.

She laughed. He felt like a fool. But he felt happy. He wasn't a virgin anymore, and he wasn't a queer. He was a man.

(6)

On June 19, at the request of his mother, Billy Milligan was discharged from the hospital by Dr. Raulj. The social worker's summary for discharge read:

Prior to discharge, Bill was manipulative with staff members and patients. He would maliciously lie his way out of trouble, harming anyone's reputation and feeling no remorse. His peer group relations were superficial on his part and his peers were mistrusting of him due to his constant lies.

Staff Recommendations: The patient's behavior became increasingly disruptive to the ward program, therefore the patient is being discharged with the recommendation to seek outpatient treatment for the patient and counseling for the parents.

Medication at Time of Release: Thorazine 25 mg t.i.d.

Back home, in a deep depression, Danny painted a nine-by-twelve still life—a withering yellow flower in a cracked drinking glass against a black and dark-blue background. He brought it upstairs to show Billy's mother what he had done, but then he froze. Chalmer was there. Chalmer took it from him, looked at it and threw it on the floor.

"You're a liar," he said. "You didn't do that."

Danny picked it up and fought back the tears as he took it down to the painting room. Then, for the first time, he signed it: "Danny '70." On the back of the canvas board, he filled in the information it called for:

ARTIST	Danny
SUBJECT	Dyeing Alone
DATE	1970

From that time, unlike Tommy and Allen, who continued to seek approval for their painting, Danny never volunteered to show his still lifes to anyone again.

In the fall of 1970, Billy entered Lancaster High School, the rambling glass-and-concrete complex of modern buildings on the north side of Lancaster. Billy did not do well in his classes. He hated his teachers and he hated school.

Arthur cut many of his high school classes to study medical books at the library and became especially fascinated by the study of hematology.

Tommy spent his spare time fixing appliances and practicing his escape procedures. By this time, no ropes could hold him. He could work his hands to undo any knot or slide out through any ropes that tied him. He bought himself a pair of handcuffs and practiced getting out of them using a split ball-point pen plastic cap as a key. He made a mental note that it would always be best to have two handcuff keys on you at all times—one in a front pocket and one in back—so you could get to one no matter which way they handcuffed you.

In January 1971, Billy got a job as a part-time delivery boy at an IGA grocery store. He decided to use part of the money from his first paycheck to buy a steak for Chalmer. Things had gone pretty well over the Christmas holidays. He thought if he showed his stepfather now that he cared for him, maybe Chalmer would stop picking on him.

He came up the back steps and saw that the door to the kitchen had been knocked off its hinges. Grandma and Grandpa Milligan were there, and so were Kathy and Challa and Jim. Mom was holding a bloody towel to her head. Her face was black-and-blue.

"Chalmer knocked her through the door," Jim said.

"Ripped her hair right out of her head," said Kathy.

Billy said nothing. He just looked at his mother, threw the steak on the table, walked into his room and closed the door. He sat in the dark for a long time with his eyes closed, trying to understand why there was so much pain and hurting in this family. If only Chalmer was dead, it would solve all their problems.

The feeling of hollowness came over him . . .

Ragen opened his eyes, feeling the rage that could no longer be bottled up. For what Chalmer had done to Danny and to Billy and now to Billy's mother, the man had to die.

He rose slowly and went to the kitchen, hearing the lowered voices from the living room. He opened the drawer where the cutlery was kept, took a six-inch steak knife, slipped it into his shirt and went back to his room. He put the knife under the pillow and lay down to wait. After they all went to sleep, he would come out and stab Chalmer in the heart. Or perhaps he would cut his throat. He lay there rehearsing it in his mind, waiting for the house to grow quiet. At twelve o'clock they were still awake, talking. He fell asleep.

The morning light woke Allen and he jumped out of bed, unsure of where he was or what had happened. He went quickly to the bathroom, and Ragen told him what he had planned. When he came out, Dorothy was in his room. She had started to make up his bed, but she was holding the knife.

"Billy, what's this?"

He looked at it calmly and said in a monotone, "I was going to kill him."

She looked up quickly, surprised at the low, emotionless tone of voice. "What do you mean?"

Allen stared at her. "Your husband was supposed to be dead this morning."

She went pale and clutched her throat. "Oh my God, Billy, what are you saying?" She grabbed his arms and shook him, hissing the words softly so that no one else would hear. "You mustn't say that. You mustn't think it. Look what it would do to you. What would happen to you?"

Allen gazed at her and said calmly, "Look at what's happened to you." Then he turned and walked out.

Sitting in class, Billy tried to ignore the snickering and teasing of the other kids. The word had gotten around that he was an outpatient at the mental health clinic. There were giggles and circling of index fingers at temples. Girls stuck out their tongues at him.

Between classes, several of the girls crowded around him in the corridor near the girls' lavatory.

"C'mere, Billy. We wanna show you something."

He knew they were teasing him, but he was too shy to resist girls. They pushed him into the lavatory, forming a barrier, knowing he wouldn't dare touch them.

"Is it true you're a virgin, Billy?"

He blushed.

"You ain't never made it with a girl?"

Not knowing about Philip's experience with the girl at the hospital, he shook his head.

"He probably made it with animals up on the farm."

"Do you play with animals on the farm in Bremen, Billy?"

Before he knew what they were doing, they had him against the wall and they were pulling his trousers down. He slipped and fell to the floor, trying to hang on to his pants, but they got them off and ran away, leaving him lying in the girls' lavatory in his shorts. He started to cry.

One of the women teachers came in. When she saw him, she left, returning in a little while with his trousers.

"Those girls should be whipped, Billy," she said.

"I guess it was the guys that put 'em up to it," Billy said.

"You're such a big, strong boy," she said. "How could you let them do that to you?"

He shrugged. "I couldn't hit a girl."

Then he shuffled off, knowing he would never again dare face the girls in his classroom. He wandered the halls. There was no sense in going on living. He looked up, noticing the workmen had left open the door to the passageway that led to the roof. Then he knew. Slowly he walked through the empty halls, up the staircase, out the door onto the roof. It was cold. He sat down and wrote a note inside the cover of his book: "Good-by, sorry, but I can't take it anymore."

He put the book on the ledge, then backed up to get a running start. He got ready, took a deep breath and ran . . .

Before he reached the edge of the building, Ragen slammed him to the ground.

"I say, that was close," Arthur whispered.

"Vat ve do vit him?" Ragen asked. "Is dangerous to let him valking around like this."

"He is a danger to all of us. In his depressed state, he might succeed in killing himself."

"Vat is solution?"

"Keep him asleep."

"How?"

"From this moment forward, Billy is not to hold the consciousness again."

"Who can control it?"

"You or I. We'll share the responsibility. I'll spread the word to the others that no one is to allow him to take the consciousness under any circumstances. When things are going along their fairly normal course, in relative safety, I'll control things. If we find ourselves in a dangerous environment, you take over. Between us we will determine who may or may not hold the consciousness."

"I agree," said Ragen. He looked down at the page in the book on which Billy had written his suicide note. He tore out the page, ripped it into pieces and threw it into the wind. "I vill be protector," he said. "It vas not right for Billy to endanger lives of children."

Then Ragen thought of something. "Who vill speak? Other people laugh ven they hear my accent. And yours too."

Arthur nodded. "I've thought of that. Allen has, as the Irish say, 'kissed the Blarney stone.' He can do the talking for us. I think as long as we control things and keep the secret from the rest of the world, we should be able to survive."

Arthur explained matters to Allen. Then he spoke to the children and tried to help them understand what was going on.

"Think of it," he said, "as if all of us—a lot of people, including many you have never met—are in a dark room. In the center of this room is a bright spot of light on the floor. Whoever steps into this light, onto the spot, is out in the real world and holds the consciousness. That's the person other people see and hear and react to. The rest of us can go about our regular interests, study or sleep or talk or play. But whoever is out must be very careful he or she doesn't reveal the existence of the others. It is a family secret."

The children understood.

"All right," said Arthur. "Allen, go back to class."

Allen took the spot, picked up his books and went down.

"But where's Billy?" asked Christene.

The others listened to hear Arthur's answer.

Arthur shook his head gravely, put his finger to his lips and whispered, "We mustn't wake him. Billy is sleeping."

CHAPTER
TEN

(1)

Allen got a job at a flower shop in Lancaster, and things started out fine. "Timothy," who loved flowers, did most of the work, though Adalana came out from time to time to do the flower arranging. Allen convinced the owner it would be a good idea to hang some of his paintings in the window, and if one sold, he could take a commission. The idea of making money from his artwork appealed to Tommy, and after the first few paintings sold, Tommy worked harder than ever, investing some of the income to buy more paints and brushes, He turned out dozens of landscapes, which sold more quickly than Allen's portraits or Danny's still lifes.

One Friday evening in June, after closing, the owner, a middle-aged man, called Timothy into the back office and made a pass at him. Frightened, Timothy left the spot and withdrew into his own world. Danny looked up and saw what the man was trying to do. Remembering what had happened to him on the farm, Danny screamed and fled.

When Tommy came to work the following Monday, eager to see if any of his paintings would be sold that day, he discovered the store was empty. The owner had moved out, leaving no forwarding address, and taken all the paintings with him.

"Goddamned son of a bitch," shouted Tommy at the empty store window. "I'll get you, you bastard!" He picked up a rock, threw it through the window and felt better.

"Rotten capitalist system is to blame," Ragen said.

"I don't see the logic in that," Arthur said. "The man was obviously afraid of being exposed as a homosexual. What does one frightened man's dishonesty have to do with the economic /system?"

188

"Is result of profit motive. Is contaminate the minds of young people like Tommy."

"I say, I didn't know you were a bloody communist."

"Someday," said Ragen, "all capitalist societies vill be destroyed. I know you are capitalist, Arthur, but I varn you. All power belongs to the people."

"Be that as it may," Arthur said in a bored voice, "the florist's shop is gone, and somebody's going to have to find another bloody job."

Allen got a job as an orderly on the night shift at the Homestead Nursing Home on the east end of Lancaster. It was a modern low brick building with a wide glass-fronted lobby always filled with elderly residents wearing their bibs, parked in their wheelchairs. Most of the work was menial, and "Mark" handled it without complaint, sweeping and mopping the floors, changing the linens and the bedpans.

Arthur was most interested in the medical aspects of the position. When he found that some of the nurses or attendants were loafing on the job, playing cards, reading or dozing, Arthur would make the rounds himself, attending to the sick and dying. He listened to their complaints, cleaned infected bedsores and generally devoted himself to what he felt was his destined profession.

One night as he watched Mark on his knees, scrubbing the floors in a room from which someone had been taken away, Arthur shook his head. "That's all you'll spend your life doing—manual labor. Bloody slave work that could be done by a zombie."

Mark looked at his rag, then at Arthur, and shrugged. "To control one's own destiny takes a mastermind. To execute the plans takes a fool."

Arthur raised his eyebrows. He had not given Mark credit for such insight. But it made it all the worse, to see a mind with a spark of intelligence wasted on mindless work.

Arthur shook his head and strolled off to see his patients. He knew Mr. Torvald was dying. He went into the old man's room and sat beside his bed, as he had done every night for the past week. Mr. Torvald talked of his youth in the old country, of coming to America and settling on the land in Ohio. Blinking his rheumy, heavy-lidded eyes, he said wearily, "I am an old man. I talk too much."

"Not at all, sir," Arthur said. "I have always believed that older people, who are wiser and have had much experience, should be listened to. Your knowledge, which cannot be written down in books, should be passed on to the young."

Mr. Torvald smiled. "You're a good boy."

"Are you in much pain?"

"I don't believe in complaining. I've lived a good life. I'm ready to die now."

Arthur put his hand on the withered arm. "You are dying very gracefully," he said, "with great dignity. I would have been proud to have you for a father."

Mr. Torvald coughed and pointed to his empty water pitcher.

Arthur went out to fill it, and when he came back, he saw Mr. Torvald staring upward blankly. Arthur stood there silently for a moment, gazing at the serene old face. Then he brushed the hair out of the eyes and closed them.

"Allen," he whispered, "call the nurses. Tell them Mr. Torvald is deceased."

Allen took the spot and pressed the button over the bed.

"That," whispered Arthur, stepping back, "is proper procedure."

Allen thought for a moment that Arthur's voice was husky with emotion. But he knew that couldn't be. Before Allen could question him, Arthur was gone.

The job at Homestead lasted three weeks. When the administration office discovered Milligan was only sixteen, they informed him he was too young to work the night shift, and he was discharged.

A few weeks after the fall term began, Chalmer said Billy had to go down to the farm that Saturday to help cut the grass. Tommy watched as Chalmer backed his new yellow tractor-mower up two boards onto the back of the truck.

"What do you need me for?" Tommy asked.

"Don't ask dumb questions. You're coming. You wanna eat, you're gonna work. I need someone to rake up the leaves before I mow. That's about all you're good for, anyway."

Tommy watched as Chalmer secured the tractor in the truck by setting it in reverse gear and slipping the U-pin into place to keep the lever from popping out.

"Now pick up them goddamn boards and get them into the truck."

Shit, Tommy thought, pick 'em up yourself. And he left the spot.

Danny stood there, wondering why Chalmer was glaring at him.

"Well, get them boards in, stupid."

Danny wrestled with the two huge boards, even though they were too big and heavy for a fourteen-year-old.

"Goddamn clumsy bastard," Chalmer said. Knocking him to the side, he pushed the boards in himself. "Get in before I beat your ass."

Danny scrambled into the seat and looked straight ahead. But he could haear Chalmer popping the top of a can of beer, and as he smelled it, a cold fear went through him. When they got to the farm, Danny was relieved that he was put right to work raking leaves.

Chalmer mowed and Danny was afraid when the tractor came too close to him. He'd been terrorized by tractors before. Chalmer's new yellow one frightened him. He switched to David and then to Shawn, switching back and forth until the work was done and Chalmer finally shouted, "Get them boards outta the truck. Let's go!"

Danny stumbled forward, still terrified of the tractor, and used all his strength to pull the heavy planks out of the truck. With the planks in place, Chalmer backed the tractor up onto the truck bed. After he hauled the planks back in, Danny waited while Chalmer popped another can of beer, finishing it before he was ready to take off.

Tommy, who had seen what happened, took the spot. That sonofabitchin' tractor frightened Danny. That tractor had to go. Quickly, while Chalmer's head was turned, Tommy climbed up into the truck bed, pulled the U-pin out and popped the clutch into neutral. As Chalmer went around to the driver's seat, Tommy jumped down and flipped the U-pin into the bushes. Then he got in the front, stared straight ahead and waited. He knew the minute Chalmer made one of his jack-rabbit starts, that new yellow tractor of his would be gone.

Chalmer started out slowly and drove without a stop into Bremen. Nothing happened. Tommy thought it would go after they stopped in front of the General Mills plant. But Chalmer pulled away real easy and drove all the way into Lancaster. All right, thought Tommy, it'll happen the first time he stops for a red light.

It happened in Lancaster. When the light turned green, Chalmer took off, squealing his tires, and Tommy knew the tractor was gone. He tried to keep his face straight, but he couldn't. He looked away, toward the window, so the old fart wouldn't see his grin. When he glanced back, he saw the little yellow tractor tumbling back down the street, end over end. Then he saw Chalmer looking in his rear-view mirror, his mouth wide open. He jammed the brakes, stopped the truck, jumped out and started running back, picking up pieces of metal scattered on the street.

Tommy broke up with laughter. "Goddamn you," he said. "That tractor'll never hurt Danny or David again." Double revenge with one blow. He had gotten the machine, and at the same time he got Chalmer.

Most of the grades sent home on Billy's report cards were C's, D's and F's. In all his school years he got an A only once: the third quarter in tenth-grade biology. Arthur, who had developed an interest in the subject, started paying attention in class and doing the homework.

Knowing people would laugh if he spoke, he had Allen answer for him. He amazed the teacher by his sudden change, his brilliance. Though Arthur never lost his interest in biology, things at home got so bad that the spot kept changing. Much to the regret of the biology teacher, the flame died out and the last two quarters were failures. Arthur drifted off to study on his own, and the final report card registered a D.

Arthur was having his hands full with the others coming and going on and off the spot more and more frequently. He diagnosed this period of mental instability as "a mix-up time."

When the school had to be evacuated because of a bomb scare, everyone suspected it was Billy Milligan, though no one could prove it. Tommy denied making the bomb. It wasn't a real one anyway, though it might have been if the liquid in the flask had been nitro instead of water. Tommy hadn't lied about not making it. He would never have lied. Though he had taught one of the other boys how to do it, even drew the diagram, he had never touched it himself. He wasn't that stupid.

Tommy enjoyed the excitement and the chagrin on the principal's face. Principal Moore looked like a man with a lot of problems, like someone who couldn't solve all the things that were bothering him.

He solved one of them by expelling Milligan, the trouble-maker.

So, five weeks after Billy Milligan turned seventeen—a week before Jim was to leave for the Air Force—Tommy and Allen joined the Navy.

CHAPTER
ELEVEN

(1)

On March 23, 1972, Allen went with Dorothy to the recruiting office, and he and Tommy signed the enlistment papers. Dorothy had mixed feelings about letting her younger son join the Navy, but she knew it was important to get him out of the house, away from Chalmer. The expulsion from school had made things worse.

The recruiting officer moved quickly through the paperwork and the questions. Dorothy did most of the answering.

"Have you ever been in a mental institution or been diagnosed as mentally ill?"

"No," Tommy said. "Not me."

"Wait just a minute," Dorothy said. "You did spend three months in Columbus State Hospital. Dr. Brown said it was hysterical neurosis."

The recruiter looked up, pen poised. "Ah, we don't have to put that down," he said. "Everybody's a little neurotic."

Tommy gave Dorothy a triumphant look.

When the time came to take the General Education and Development Test, Tommy and Allen both looked it over. Seeing that it had nothing to do with any of Tommy's abilities or knowledge, Allen decided to take the test himself. But then Danny came and looked at the paper, not knowing what to do.

The proctor, seeing his confused look, whispered, "Go ahead, you just black in your answers between the little lines."

Danny shrugged and, without reading any of the questions, went down the columns and blacked in between the lines.

He passed.

Within a week Allen was on his way to the Naval Training Center at Great Lakes, Illinois, and was assigned to Company 109, Battalion 21, to begin his basic training.

Because Milligan had been in the Civil Air Patrol when he was in high school, he was appointed RPOC (Recruit Petty Officer in Charge) of 160 young recruits. He was a strict disciplinarian.

When Allen learned that the company most proficient in the sixteen-count manual would be made the honor company, he and Tommy set to work to find where they could whittle minutes off the morning schedule.

"Cut out showers," Tommy suggested.

"Regulations," Allen said. "They've got to go into the showers even if they don't use soap."

Tommy sat down and figured out an assembly-line method of showering.

The next evening Allen instructed the men: "You roll up your towel and put it into your left hand. You put your bar of soap into your right. There's sixteen showers this way, twelve across and sixteen this way. Now, they're all even water temperature, so you won't get scalded or froze out. What you do is walk through and keep walking as you wash the left side of your body. When you get to the corner, flip the soap over to your other hand and keep moving, going backwards as you wash the other side of your body and your hair. By the time you get to the end shower you've rinsed off, ready to dry."

The recruits watched in astonishment as he demonstrated by walking through the showers with his uniform on, checking his watch. "This way it takes only forty-five seconds for each one to shower. All hundred and sixty of you should be able to get through, out of the shower and dressed in less than ten minutes. I want us to be the first company out on the grinder in the morning. We're gonna be the honor company."

Next morning, Milligan's company was the first out on the parade grounds. Allen was pleased, and Tommy told him he was working on a few more time-saving methods. He was awarded the Service Medal for good conduct.

Two weeks later things started to go bad. Allen called home and found out that Chalmer was beating Dorothy again. Ragen became angry. Arthur, of course, didn't really care. But it bothered Tommy and Danny and Allen a great deal. They became depressed and it caused another mix-up time.

Shawn started wearing his shoes on the wrong feet and leaving them untied. David became slovenly. Philip found out where he was and didn't give a damn. The men of Company

109 soon realized there was something wrong with their RPOC. One day he would be a crack leader and the next day he would sit around talking and letting the paperwork pile up.

They observed that he began walking in his sleep. Someone told him about it, and Tommy started tying himself to the bed at night. When he was relieved of the RPOC job, Tommy became depressed and Danny went to sick bay whenever he could.

Arthur became interested in the hematology lab.

The Navy sent an investigator to observe him one day, and he found Philip stretched out on his bunk in uniform, his white hat on his feet, flipping cards off the top of a deck.

"What's going on here?" Captain Simons demanded.

"Get on your feet, mister," said his aide.

"Fuck off!" Philip said.

"I'm a captain. How dare you—"

"I don't give a damn if you're Jesus Christ! Get outta here. You're making me miss."

When Chief Petty Officer Rankin came in, Philip told him the same thing.

On April 12, 1972, two weeks and four days after Tommy joined the Navy, Philip was assigned to the Recruit Evaluation Unit.

The report from his company commander stated: "This man was my RPOC at first, but then he didn't do anything except try to boss everyone all the time. Then he started going to sick call after I relieved him of his RPOC job. Each day it got worse, and every class he found a reason to get out of it. This man is way behind the rest of the company and is going downhill all the time. This man will require watching."

A psychiatrist interviewed David, who didn't understand what was going on. After a check of the records from Ohio, the Navy discovered that he had been in a mental hospital and had lied on recruitment papers. The psychiatric report stated, "He lacks the necessary maturity and stability to function effectively in the Navy. It is recommended that he be discharged as temperamentally unsuitable for further training."

On May 1, a month and a day after his enlistment, William Stanley Milligan was discharged from the U.S. Navy "under honorable conditions."

He was given his pay and an airline ticket to Columbus. But on the way from Great Lakes to O'Hare Airport in Chicago, Philip learned that two other recruits on leave to go home were heading for New York City. Instead of using his United Airlines ticket, Philip joined them on the bus. He was going to see New York, the place he knew he was from but had never seen.

(2)

At the New York bus terminal Philip said good-by to his traveling companions, slung his duffle bag over his shoulder and started walking. He picked up maps and brochures at the information desk and headed for Times Square. He felt at home. The streets, the voices that sounded natural to his ear, assured him that this was where he belonged.

Philip spent two days exploring the city. He took a trip on the Staten Island Ferry and one to the Statue of Liberty. Then, starting at the Battery, he wandered the narrow streets around Wall Street and walked up to Greenwich Village. He ate in a Greek restaurant and slept at a cheap hotel. The next day he went to Fifth Avenue and Thirty-fourth Street and stared up at the Empire State Building. He took the tour to the top and studied the city.

"Which way is Brooklyn?" he asked the tour guide.

She pointed. "Over there. You can see the three bridges— the Williamsburg, the Manhattan and the Brooklyn Bridge."

"That's where I'm going next," he said.

He took the elevator down, hailed a cab and said, "Take me to the Brooklyn Bridge."

"The Brooklyn Bridge?"

Philip flung his duffel bag inside. "That's what I said."

"You gonna jump off it or buy it?" the driver asked.

"Fuck you, doc. Just drive and save the smart-ass jokes for the out-of-towners."

The driver let him out at the bridge and Philip started walking across it. There was a cool breeze and he felt good, but when he reached the halfway point, he stopped and looked down. All that water. God, it was beautiful. Suddenly he felt very depressed. He didn't know why, but in the middle of this beautiful bridge he felt so down he couldn't go on. He slung his duffel bag over his shoulder and turned back toward Manhattan.

His depression grew deeper. Here he was in New York and not having a good time. There was something he had to see, someplace he had to find, but he didn't know what or where it was. He got on a bus, took it as far as it went, then transferred to another bus and another, looking at the houses and the people but not knowing where he was going or what he was searching for.

He got off at a shopping mall and wandered. In to middle of the mall he saw a wishing fountain. He flipped a couple of coins. As he started to toss a third quarter in, he felt a tugging at his sleeve. A little black boy was looking up at him with big pleading eyes.

"Oh shit," Philip said, flipping him the coin. The boy grinned and ran.

Philip picked up the duffel bag. The depression began to eat at his gut with such a feeling of pain that he stood there for a few moments, shuddered and left the spot . . .

David staggered under the weight of the duffel bag and dropped it. That was too heavy for an eight-year-old—almost nine—to carry. He dragged it along behind him, looking at the store windows, wondering where he was and how he had gotten here. He sat down on a bench, looked around and watched children playing. He wished he could play with them. Then he got up and started pulling the duffel bag again, but it was too heavy, so he just left it and wandered off.

He went into an Army and Navy store and looked at the surplus CB's and sirens. He picked up a big plastic bubble and pressed a switch. A siren went off and the red light inside started flashing. Terrified, he dropped the bubble and ran, knocking over an ice cream vendor's bicycle parked outside and scraping his elbow. He kept running.

When he saw no one coming after him, David stopped running and walked the streets, wondering how he was going to get back to the house. Dorothy was probably worried about him. And he was getting hungry. He wished he had an ice cream. If he could find a policeman, he would ask him how to get home. Arthur always said if he was lost, he should ask the bobbies to help him . . .

Allen blinked his eyes.

He bought an ice cream on a stick from a vendor and started off, unwrapping it, but then he saw a little dirty-faced girl watching him.

"Jesus Christ," he said, handing it to her. He was a sucker for kids, especially those with big hungry eyes.

He went back to the vendor. "Gimme another one."

"Boy, you must be humgry."

"Shut up and gimme the ice cream."

As he walked, eating his ice cream, he decided he had to do something about letting kids get to him. What kind of con artist lets kids make a sucker of him?

He wandered around, looking at the big buildings of what he thought was Chicago, and then took a bus downtown. He knew it was too late to get down to O'Hare Airport tonight. He'd have to spend the night here in Chicago and take the plane to Columbus in the morning.

Suddenly he saw an electronic sign on a building that flashed: MAY 5, TEMPERATURE 68°. *May 5?* He pulled out his wallet and looked through it. About five hundred dollars' separation pay. His discharge was dated May 1. His plane ticket from Chicago to Columbus was dated May 1. What the hell? Here he'd been wandering around in Chicago for four days since his discharge without knowing it. Where was his duffel bag? He had an empty feeling in his stomach. He looked down at his dress blue uniform. It was filty. The elbows were ripped and his left arm was scraped.

All right. He'd get something to eat, get a night's sleep and take the flight back to Columbus in the morning. He grabbed a couple of hamburgers, found a flophouse and spent nine dollars for a room.

The next morning he hailed a cab and told the driver to take him to the airport.

"La Guardia?"

He shook his head. He didn't know there was a La Guardia in Chicago.

"Nah, the other one, the big one."

All during the trip to the airport he tried to understand what had happened. He closed his eyes and tried to reach Arthur. Nothing. Ragen? Nowhere around. So it was another mix-up time.

At the airport, he went up to the United Airlines counter and handed the clerk his ticket.

"When can I get outta here?" he asked.

She looked at the ticket and then at him. "This is for a flight from Chicago to Columbus. You can't go from here to Ohio on this."

"What are you talking about?"

"Chicago," she said.

"Yeah? So?"

A supervisor came over and examined the ticket. Allen didn't understand what the problem was.

"You all right, sailor?" the man said. "You can't fly from New York to Columbus on this."

Allen rubbed his unshaven face. "New York?"

"That's right, Kennedy Airport."

"Oh God!"

Allen took a deep breath and started talking fast. "Well, look, what happened is somebody made a mistake. You see, I've been discharged." He pulled out his papers. "I got on the wrong plane, you see. And it was supposed to take me to Columbus. Somebody must've slipped something in my coffee, because I was unconscious, and when I came to, I was here in New York. Left my bags on the plane and everything. You'll have to do something about it. It's the airline's fault."

"It's going to cost you a surcharge to change this ticket," the woman said.

"Well, you just call the Navy in Great Lakes. They're the ones who have got to get me back to Columbus. You just bill them for it. I mean, a serviceman on his way home has a right to be given proper transportation without going through a hassle. You just pick up that phone and call the Navy."

The man looked at him and then said, "Okay, why don't you just wait here and I'll see what we can do for a serviceman?"

"Where's the men's room?" Allen asked.

She pointed and Allen walked to it quickly.

Once inside, seeing there was no one else there, he grabbed a loose roll of toilet paper off the ledge and flung it across the room. "Shit! Shit! Shit!" he shouted. "Goddamn it, I can't take any more of this shit!"

When he settled down, he washed his face, brushed his hair back and put his white cap on at a jaunty angle to face the people at the ticket coounter

"All right," the woman said. "It's been worked out. I'll write you up a new ticket. You've got a seat on the next flight out. It leaves in two hours."

During the flight back to Columbus, Allen mulled over his annoyance at having been in New York for five days without seeing any of it except the inside of a taxi and Kennedy International Airport. He had no idea how he had gotten there, who had stolen the time or what had happened. He wondered if he would ever find out. On the bus to Lancaster, he settled back for a nap and mumbled—hoping Arthur or Ragen would hear it—"Somebody sure screwed up."

(3)

Allen got a job selling vacuum cleaners and trash compactors door-to-door for Interstate Engineering. Fast-talking Allen did well for about a month. He observed his co-worker Sam Garrison making dates with waitresses and secretaries as well as customers. Allen admired his hustle.

On the Fourth of July, 1972, Garrison asked, as they sat talking, "How come you don't date some of these chicks?"

"I don't have time," Allen said. He squirmed, always uncomfortable when the conversation turned to sex. "I'm not really that interested."

"You're not queer, are you?"

"Hell no."

"Seventeen, and you're not interested in girls?"

"Look," Allen said, "I've got other things on my mind."

"For God's sake," Garrison said, "haven't you ever been laid?"

"I don't wanna talk about it." Unaware of Philip's experience with the girl in the psychiatric hospital, Allen felt his face go red and he turned away.

"You don't mean to tell me you're a virgin."

Allen said nothing.

"Well, my boy," Garrison said. "We'll have to do something about that. Leave it to Sam. I'll pick you up at your house tonight at seven o'clock."

That evening, Allen showered, dressed up and used some of Billy's brother's cologne. Jim was in the Air Force now and wouldn't miss it.

Garrison arrived on time and drove him up town. They pulled up in front of the Hot Spot on Broad Street and Garrison said, "Wait in the car. I'll be right out with something."

Allen was startled when Garrison returned a few minutes later with two bored-looking young women.

"Hi, honey," the blonde said, leaning into the car window. "I'm Trina and this is Dolly. You're a good-looking guy." Dolly flipped her long black hair back and got into the front of the car with Garrison. Trina got in the back with Allen.

They drove out into the country, talking and giggling all the way. Trina kept putting her hand on Allen's leg and playing with his fly zipper. When they got to a deserted spot, Garrison pulled off the road. "C'mon, Billy," he said. "I got blankets in the trunk. Help me get them out."

As Allen walked to the trunk with him, Garrison handed him two thin tinfoil-wrapped packages. "You know what to do with these, don't ya?"

"Yeah," Allen said. "But I don't need to put two on, do I?"

Garrison punched his arm gently. "Always the comedian. One's for Trina, and the other one's for Dolly. I told them we'd switch. We'll each fuck 'em both."

Allen looked down into the trunk and saw a hunting rifle. He looked up quickly, but Sam handed him a blanket, took one for himself and shut the trunk. Then he and Dolly walked off behind a tree.

"C'mon, we'd better get started," Trina said, unbuckling Allen's belt.

"Hey, you don't have to do that," Allen said.

"Well, if you're not interested, honey—"

A short time later, Sam called for Trina, and Dolly came over to Allen. "Well?" asked Dolly.

"'Well' what?"

"Can you make it again?"

"Look," Allen said, "like I told your friend over there, you don't have to do anything and we can still be friends."

"Well, honey, you can do anything you want, but I don't want Sam to get mad. You're a pretty nice guy. He's kind of busy with Trina, so I guess he won't notice."

When Sam was done, he went to the trunk, pulled a couple of beers out of the cooler and handed one to Allen.

"Well," he said, "how'd you like the girls?"

"I didn't do anything, Sam."

"You mean *you* didn't do anything? Or *they* didn't do anything?"

"I told them they didn't have to. When I'm ready, I'll get married."

"Shit."

"Now, that's okay, take it easy," Allen said. "Everything's cool."

"Cool, crap!" He stormed over to the girls. "I told you this guy was a virgin. It was up to you two to turn him on."

Dolly walked to the back of the car where Garrison was standing and saw the rifle in the trunk. "You're in trouble, buddy."

"Shit. Get in the car," Garrison said. "We'll take you back."

"I'm not getting in the car."

"Well, then, fuck you!"

Garrison slammed the trunk shut and jumped behind the wheel. "C'mon, Billy. Let the goddamn bitches walk."

"Why don't you get in?" Allen asked them. "You don't want to stay out here alone."

"We'll get back okay," Trina said. "But you guys are gonna pay for this."

Garrison gunned the motor and Allen got into the car.

"We shouldn't leave them here alone."

"Shit. Just a couple of crummy broads."

"It wasnt their fault. I didn't want it."

"Well, at least it didn't cost us nothing."

Four days later, on July 8, 1972, Sam Garrison and Allen went to the sheriff's office in Circleville to answer some questions. Both were immediately arrested for kidnapping, rape and assault with a deadly weapon.

When the judge in Pickaway County heard the facts at pretrial, he dismissed the charge of kidnapping and set a bond of two thousand dollars. Dorothy raised two hundred dollars for the bondsman's fee, and took her son back home.

Chalmer argued to have him sent back to jail but Dorothy arranged with her sister to take Billy into her home in Miami, Florida, until his October hearing before the Pickaway County Juvenile Court.

With Billy and Jim away, the girls began to work on Dorothy. Kathy and Challa gave her an ultimatum: If she didn't start divorce proceedings against Chalmer, they were both going to leave home. Dorothy finally agreed that Chalmer had to go.

In Florida, Allen went to school and did well. He got a job at a paint supply store and impressed the owner with his organizational ability. "Samuel," the religious Jew, learned Billy's father had been Jewish. Along with many of the other Jewish residents in Miami, he was outraged at the killing of the eleven Israeli athletes at the Munich Olympic Village. Samuel went to Friday night services to pray for their souls and the soul of Billy's father. He also asked God to have the court find Allen innocent.

When he came back to Pickaway County on October 20, Milligan was turned over to the Ohio Youth Commission for evaluation. He was held in the Pickaway County Jail from November 1972 to February 16, 1973—two days after his eighteenth birthday. Though he had turned eighteen while in custody, the judge agreed that he should be tried as a juvenile. His mother's attorney, George Kellner, told the judge that in his view, whatever the decision of the court, it was imperative that his young man not be sent back to his destructive home environment.

The judge handed down a verdict of guilty and ordered William S. Milligan sent to an Ohio Youth Commission facility for an indefinite period. On March 12, the same day Allen was transported to the youth camp in Zanesville, Ohio, Dorothy's divorce decree from Chalmer Milligan became final. Ragen mocked Samuel and told him there was no God.

CHAPTER TWELVE

(1)

Arthur decided that the younger ones should be on the spot at the Zanesville Youth Camp. After all, it would give them experiences every child should have: hiking, swimming, horseback riding, camping, sports.

He approved of Dean Hughes, the tall black recreation director with the flattop haircup and the Vandyke beard. He seemed like a sympathetic and trustworthy young man. All in all, there seemed to be no danger here.

Ragen agreed.

But Tommy bitched about the rules. He didn't like having his hair cut, having to wear state-issue clothing. He didn't like being here with thirty juvenile delinquents.

Charlie Jones, the social worker, explained the setup to the new boys. The camp was divided into four progress zones, and they were expected to move through a zone each month. Zones 1 and 2 were the dormitories in the left wing of the T-shaped building. Zones 3 and 4 were in the right wing.

Zone 1, he admitted, was "the pits." Everyone dumped on you, and you had to wear your hair cropped close. In zone 2, the boys could wear their hair longer. In zone 3, they could wear their own clothes instead of state-issue clothes after their daily work assignments. In zone 4, instead of living in a dorm, they could have their own private cubicles. Zone 4 boys didn't have to do regularly scheduled events. Most of them were trusties, and they didn't even have to go to the Scioto Village Girls Camp for the dances.

The boys laughed at that.

They would move through zones 1 to 4, Mr. Jones explained, by the merit system. Each of them started out the month with

120 merits to his credit, but he had to have 130 to move on to the next zone. A boy could earn credits by special work and good behavior, or he could lose them by disobedience or antisocial behavior. Merits could be removed by the staff or by one of the trusties from zone 4.

If any of those people said the word "Hey," that cost a merit. If someone said, "Hey, cool it," two merits were lost. "Hey, cool it, bed," meant that in addition to losing two merits, the offender had to stay in bed for two hours. If he left his bed and someone said, "Hey, cool it, bed! Hey, cool it," that was a loss of three merits. But if someone said, "Hey, cool it, bed! Hey, cool it, county," that cost four. And "county" meant the boy would cool off in the county jail.

Tommy felt like throwing up.

There were lots of things to do around there, Charlie Jones said. He expected the boys to put in their time and behave themselves. "Any of you boys think you're too good or too smart for this place or try to run off, the state of Ohio has another place for you. The Training Institution of Central Ohio is called TICO for short. And if you get sent to TICO, you'll sure as hell wish you were right back here. All right, now get your bedding in the storeroom and then go to the mess hall for chow."

That evening Tommy was sitting on his bunk wondering who had gotten him into this and why he was here. He didn't give a shit about merits and rules and zones. As soon as he got the chance, he was busting out. He hadn't been on the spot coming in, so he didn't know the way out, but he noticed there was no barbed wire or walls around the camp, just woods. It shouldn't be hard to get away.

As he passed the mess hall, he smelled good cooking. Hell, no sense jumping into the fire until he knew what was in the frying pan.

One of the other new boys in zone 1 was a little kid with glasses who couldn't have been more than fourteen or fifteen. Tommy had noticed him in the line-up, wondering if he'd blow over in a breeze. He was struggling under the weight of his mattress and bedding when a tall guy with long hair and weight lifter's muscles tripped him. The kid bounced back up from the ground and butted the big guy right in the stomach, knocking him over.

Musclebound looked up surprised at the kid standing over him with his tiny fists clenched. "Okay, you little prick," Musclebound said. "Hey!"

"Stuff it up your ass!" the boy said.

"Hey, cool it!" the big guy snapped, getting up and brushing himself off.

The little kid had tears in his eyes. "C'mon and fight, you big bastard."

"Hey, cool it, bed!"

Another boy, scrawny but taller and two or three years older, pulled the little kid away.

"Back off, Tony," he said. "You've lost two merits already, and now you gotta stay in your bed for two hours."

Tony calmed down and picked up his mattress. "Hell, Gordy, I wasn't hungry anyway."

In the mess hall, Tommy ate in silence. The food wasn't half bad. But he was starting to worry about the place. If they let the big boys rag you and take your merits away, he knew he would have to be very careful of his temper.

Back in the dorm, he noticed that the scrawny boy called Gordy had the bunk next to his and had brought part of his dinner to the little one. They were sitting and talking.

Tommy sat on his bunk and watched. He knew one of the rules was no eating in the dorm. Out of the corner of his eye, he saw Musclebound coming in the door.

"Look out!" he whispered. "That big bastard is coming."

The kid called Tony slid his plate under the bed and leaned back. When Musclebound checked things out and was satisfied that the kid was in his bed, he left.

"Thanks," the kid said. "I'm Tony Vito. What's your name?"

Tommy looked him in the eye. "They call me Billy Milligan."

"This here is Gordy Kane," he said, pointing to the scrawny boy. "He's in for selling pot. What did they get you for?"

"Rape," Tommy said, "but I didn't do it."

Tommy could tell by their smiles that they didn't believe him. Well, he didn't really give a damn. "Who's the bully?" he asked.

"Jordan. From zone four."

"We'll get even with the bastard," Tommy said.

* * *

Tommy was on the spot most of the time, and he talked to Billy's mother when she visited. Tommy liked and felt sorry for her. So when she told him that she'd divorced Chalmer, he was glad.

"He hurt me, too," Tommy said.

"I know. He always had it in for you, Billy. But what could I do? I needed a roof over our heads. Three children of my own, and Challa just like my own daughter too. But now Chalmer's gone. You be a good boy and do what they tell you, and you'll be able to come home soon."

Tommy watched her leave and decided she was the most beautiful mother he'd ever seen. He wished she was his. He wondered who his own mother was and what she looked like.

(2)

Dean Hughes, the young recreation director, noticed that Milligan lay around most of the time, reading or staring in a trance. One afternoon he approached the boy directly.

"You're here," Hughes told him. "You're going to have to do the best you can. Be happy. Get involved in something. What do you like to do?"

"I like to paint," Allen said.

The following week, at his own expense, Dean Hughes bought Milligan paints, brushes and canvases.

"Want me to paint you a picture?" Allen asked, setting the canvas up on a table. "What would you like me to paint you?"

"Make it a old barn," Hughes said. "Windows broken. Tire hanging down off an old tree. Old country road. Make it look like it just got done rainin'."

Allen worked all day and all night and finished the painting. The next morning he gave it to Dean Hughes.

"Man, that's good," Hughes said. "You could make a lot of money with your artwork."

"Sure would like that," Allen said. "I just love to paint."

Hughes realized he was going to have to work at getting Milligan out of his trancelike behavior. One Saturday morning, he took the boy out to Blue Rock State Park. Hughes supervised as Milligan painted. People came by and watched, and Hughes sold them some of the artwork. Hughes took Milligan out again the next day, and by Sunday night they had sold four hundred dollars' worth of paintings.

"Arthur." Pencil sketch by Allen

"Ragen Holding Christine." Pencil sketch by Allen
(Christine spells her own name with an "e"—Christene—
whereas the other personalities spell it as usual,
with an "i.")

"Shawn." Oil painting by Allen

"David." Oil painting by Allen

"Adalana." Oil painting by Allen

"The Bitch: Portrait of April." Oil painting by Allen

"Christine." Pencil sketch by Allen

"Christine's Rag Doll." Drawn by Ragen in the Franklin County Jail (Christine is holding this rag doll in the above sketch.)

Why do I gots to say in A cage And cant
got out AN play
Do you Like Icrgam
I Love you
Mp AntFen say you going to help us

A giant big hug AN A Kiss For Miss Judey

From
CHristong

Christine's note to Attorney Judy Stevenson

"Dr. David Caul." Oil painting by Allen

"Landscape." Oil painting by Tommy

"The Grace of Cathleen." Oil, painted in Billy's cell at
Lebanon prison by Allen and Danny. (Originally signed by
Billy, but note the lower right-hand corner where Allen and
Danny later signed their names.)

Left to right: **Jim, Kathy, Billy.** *Center bottom:* **Dorothy**

Billy in 1965 at age ten

Billy at the Dayton Forensic Center, February 20, 1981

On Monday morning the director called Hughes into the office and informed him that since Milligan was a ward of the state, it was against policy for him to be selling artwork. He had to contact the people, return their money and get the paintings back.

Hughes hadn't known of the policy, and he agreed to refund the money. On the way out, he asked, "How'd you find out about the sales?"

"People have been calling here," the director said. "They want more of Milligan's paintings."

April passed quickly. As the weather warmed, Christene played in the garden. David chased butterflies. Ragen worked out in the gym. Danny, who was still afraid of the outdoors from having been buried alive, stayed indoors and painted still lifes. Christopher, who was thirteen, rode horseback. Arthur spent most of his time in the library reading law statutes in the Ohio Revised Code, saying he would get on a horse only if he were playing polo. They were all happy to move to zone 2.

Milligan and Gordy Kane were assigned to work in the laundry, where Tommy enjoyed tinkering with the old washer and the gas-fired dryer. He was looking forward to moving to zone 3, where he would be allowed to wear his own clothes in the evenings.

One afternoon Frank Jordan, the musclebound bully, walked in with a load of laundry. "I want these washed right away. I'm expecting company tomorrow."

"That's nice," Tommy said, going on about his business.

"I mean wash them now," Jordan said.

Tommy ignored him.

"I'm a zone-four trusty, you prick. I can take your merits away. You'll get bumped out of going to zone three."

"Look," said Tommy, "I don't give a damn if you're in the twilight zone. I don't have to wash your goddamn personal clothes."

"Hey!"

Tommy looked up at him furiously. What right had this common thief to remove one of his merits? "Stuff it," Tommy said.

"Hey, cool it!"

Tommy clenched his fists, but Jordan walked off to report to the man in charge that he had given Milligan a hey-cool-it.

When Tommy got back to the dorm, he learned that Jordan had given Kane and Vito each a hey-cool-it as well. All because he knew the three of them were friends.

"We gotta do something about this," Kane said.

"I'll do something," Tommy said.

"What?" Vito asked.

"Never mind," Tommy said. "I'll come up with something."

Tommy lay back in his bed thinking about it, and the more he thought, the angrier he got. Finally he got up, went around back, found a section of a two-by-four and started toward zone 4.

Arthur explained the situation to Allen and told him he'd better get over there before Tommy got into trouble.

"Don't do it, Tommy," Allen said.

"Shit, I'm not letting that big bastard get away with taking my merits, bumping me outta going to zone three."

"You're going off half-cocked."

"I'll half-cock that son of a bitch with a busted head."

"Hey, Tommy, cool it."

"Don't say those words to me!" Tommy shouted.

"Sorry. But you're going about this all the wrong way. Let me handle it."

"Shit," said Tommy, throwing the two-by-four down. "You can't handle your own ass."

"You always did have a fresh mouth," Allen said. "Beat it."

Tommy left the spot. Allen walked back to the zone-2 barracks and sat down with Kane and Vito.

"Now, this is how we're going to do it," Allen said.

"I know how we'll do it," Kane said. "We'll blow the damned office up."

"No," Allen said. "We assemble the facts and figures, and tomorrow we march into Mr. Jones' office and tell him how unfair it is to have our own peers—kids who are common criminals, no better than we are—stand in judgment on us."

Both Kane and Vito stared, open-mouthed, at Allen. They'd never heard him talk this smooth, slick way before.

"Get me a paper and pencil," Allen said, "and let's get this worked out properly."

Next morning the three of them, with Allen as spokesman, went to see Charlie Jones, the social worker.

"Mr. Jones," said Allen, "you've told us that when we come in here, we can air our feelings without getting into trouble."

"That's right."

"Well, we've got a complaint about this system of having our peers punish us by removing our merits. If you'll just look at this chart I've drawn up, you'll see how unfair it is."

Allen reviewed the tally of hey-cool-its Frank Jordan had issued against them, describing in each case how it had come about as a result of a personal grudge or refusal to do his chores or run his errands.

"We've used this system for a long time, Bill," Jones said.

"That doesn't mean it's right. A place like this is meant to prepare us to fit into society. How's it going to do that if it shows us society is unfair? How's it right to place kids like Vito here at the mercy of a bully like Frank Jordan?"

Jones pulled at his ear as he thought about it. Allen kept hammering away at the unfairness of the system, while Kane and Vito kept silent, impressed by the fast-talking of their spokesman.

"I'll tell you what," Jones said. "Let me think about this. Come back and see me on Monday, and I'll let you know my decision."

Sunday evening Kane and Vito were playing cards on Kane's bunk. Tommy was lying around, trying to piece together what had happened in Mr. Jones' office from what Kane and Vito were saying.

Kane glanced up and said, "Look what the cat drug in."

Frank Jordan walked up to Vito and dropped a pair of muddy shoes on top of the cards. "I need these polished for tonight."

"Well, then, you can do them yourself," Vito said. "I ain't polishing your damned shoes."

Frank punched him in the side of the head, knocking him off the bunk. Vito began to cry. When Frank walked off, Tommy moved quickly. Halfway down the aisle, he tapped Frank on the shoulder. As Frank turned, Tommy swung a roundhouse punch, catching him on the nose and slamming him against the wall.

"I'm gonna have you in the county, you bastard!" Frank shouted.

Kane, who had come up alongside, lashed out with his foot, knocking Frank's legs out from under him and dropping him between two bunks. Tommy and Kane piled on, punching away.

Ragen watched as Tommy fought to be sure he was in no danger. Had there been a real threat, he would have intervened. He would not have swung wildly and in anger, as Tommy did. He would have moved in, planning where to hit and what bones to break. This was none of his affair and he wasn't needed.

The next morning Allen decided they'd better tell Mr. Jones what had happened before Frank Jordan gave a damaging version of the incident.

"You can see Vito's head, swelled up where Frank hit him without provocation," Allen said to the social worker. "He's been taking advantage of a system that gives him authority over kids like Vito. Like we said the other day, it's wrong and potentially dangerous to put that kind of power into the hands of criminals."

On Wednesday, Mr. Jones announced that henceforth the reduction of merits would be done only by the professional staff. The merits that Frank Jordan had unjustly removed from others were to be paid back out of his own account. Jordan was bumped all the way back to zone 1. Vito, Kane and Milligan now had enough merits to move on to zone 3.

(3)

One of the privileges of zone 4 was being allowed to go home on trial visit. Tommy looked forward to his furlough. When the time came, he packed his bag and waited for Dorothy to pick him up. But the more he thought about leaving, the more confused he felt. He liked the place, but he still wanted to be back at Spring Street, knowing that Chalmer would never be there again. Just him and Challa and Kathy. There would be good times at home for a change.

Dorothy picked him up and they drove back to Lancaster without talking very much. He was surprised when, a few minutes after he got home, a man he had never seen before dropped in for a visit. He was a big, beefy-faced man with a barrel chest. And he chain-smoked.

Dorothy said, "Billy, this is Del Moore. He owns the bowling alley and lounge where I used to sing in Circleville. He's staying for dinner."

Tommy could tell by the way they were looking at each other that there was something between them. Shit! Chalmer out of the house not more than two months, and now there was another guy hanging around.

That evening at dinner Tommy announced, "I'm not going back to Zanesville."

"What are you talking about?" Dorothy asked.

"I can't take that place no more."

"Now, that ain't right, Billy," Del Moore said. "Your ma tells me you only got about a month to go."

"That's my business."

"Billy!" Dorothy said.

"Well, I'm a friend of the family now," Del said. "It's not right to be causing your ma so much worry. You got just a little time to serve. You stick it out or you'll have to go over me."

Tommy looked down at his plate and ate his dinner in silence.

Later he asked Kathy, "What's with this guy?"

"Mom's new boyfriend."

"Well, Jesus, he's acting like he thinks he can tell me what to do. He been coming around here a lot?"

"He's got a room in town," Kathy said, "so I guess no one can really say they're living together. But I've got eyes."

During the next weekend furlough, Tommy met Del Moore's son, Stuart, and liked him right away. About Billy's age, Stuart was a football player and an all-around athlete. But what Tommy liked most about Stuart was the way he handled his motorcycle. He could make that bike do things Tommy had never seen before.

Allen liked Stuart too, and Ragen respected him for his athletic ability and his skill and daring. It was an exciting weekend, and they all found themselves looking forward to spending more time with this new friend, who accepted them without questioning their strange behavior. Stuart never called any of them absent-minded or a liar. Tommy thought he would like to be like Stuart someday.

Tommy told Stuart that after he got out of the youth camp, he didn't feel he could live at home anymore. He didn't think it was right, with Del spending so much time there. Stuart told him that when the time came, they'd share an apartment together.

"You really mean it?" Tommy asked.

"I mentioned it to Del," Stuart said, "and he thinks it's a great idea. He figures we'll sort of keep an eye on each other."

But a few weeks before he was due to be released from Zanesville, Tommy learned that Dorothy wouldn't be coming up for her regular visit.

On August 5, 1973, Stuart Moore had been riding his motorcycle in Circleville. Turning a fast corner, he crashed into the back of a boat on a trailer; both cycle and boat burst into flames on collision. Stuart was killed instantly.

Hearing about it, Tommy went into shock. Stuart—his brave, smiling friend who was going to conquer the world—engulfed in flames. Tommy couldn't stand it any longer. He didn't want to be here anymore. Then David came to feel Stuart's agony and to cry Tommy's tears . . .

CHAPTER THIRTEEN

(1)

A month after Stuart's death, Billy Milligan was released from Zanesville. A few days after his return, Allen was reading in his room when Del Moore came in and asked if he'd like to go fishing. He knew Del was trying to score points with Dorothy—Kathy said they'd probably get married. "Sure," Allen said. "Love fishing."

Del made all the arrangements, took the next day off from work and came by to pick Billy up.

Tommy looked at him in disgust. "Fishing? Shit, I don't want to go fishing."

When Tommy came out of his room and Dorothy confronted him with his inconsiderate behavior—first promising to go fishing with Del and then changing his mind—Tommy looked at them both in astonishment. "Christ! He never even *asked* me to go fishing."

Del stormed out of the house swearing that Bill was the damnedest bald-faced liar he had ever met.

"I can't take it anymore," Allen said to Arthur when he was alone in his room. "We've got to get out of here. I feel like an intruder with Del hovering around all the time."

"Same here," said Tommy. "Dorothy's been like a mother to me, but if she's going to marry Del, I want out."

"All right," Arhtur said. "Let's find a job, put a few quid aside and get an apartment of our own."

The others applauded the idea.

Allen got a job at Lancaster Electro-Plating on September 11, 1973. It didn't pay much and it was dirty work, not the kind of employment Arthur had in mind.

It was Tommy who did the boring work as a zinc-tank operator, pulling the cage that hung from the overhead moving chain and lowering it into the acid for the plating. He moved from one square tank to the next; they were lined up the length of a bowling alley. Lower it, wait, raise it, move it, lower it, wait.

Sneering at such menial labor, Arthur turned his attention to other matters. He had to prepare his people to move out on their own.

All during Zanesville, he had been studying the behavior of those he allowed to come on the spot, and he was beginning to understand that the key to survival in society was self-control. Without rules there would be chaos, endangering them all. It occurred to him that the rules at the youth camp had a salutary effect. The constant threat of being bumped back to zone 1 or 2 had kept all those unruly lads in check. That is what would be needed when they were on their own.

He explained his code of behavior to Ragen. "Because someone became involved with women of ill repute," Arthur said, "we were accused of rape by those two women in Pickaway County—a crime we did not commit—and they sent us to prison. It must never happen again."

"How you vill prevent it?"

Arthur paced. "I can usually prevent someone from taking the spot. And I have observed your ability to bump someone off immediately after the vulnerable moment of switching. Between us, we ought to control the consciousness. I have decided that certain undesirable individuals should be permanently banished from the spot. The rest of us will be required to live by a code of conduct. We are like a family. We must be strict. A single infraction will result in someone being classified as undesirable."

With Ragen's agreement, Arthur communicated the rules to all the others:

FIRST: *Never lie*. All their lives they had been accused unjustly of being pathological liars for denying knowledge of things one of the others had done.

SECOND: *Behave properly to ladies and children*. This included avoiding foul language and adhering to proper etiquette, such as opening doors. The children were to sit straight at table, with napkins across laps. Women and children must be protected at all times, and everyone should come to their defense. If any one saw a woman or a child being hurt by a man, he or she must step off the spot immediately and let Ragen deal with the situation. (If one of their own were in personal physical danger, that would not be necessary, since Ragen would take the spot automatically.)

THIRD: *Be celibate*. Never again should the males be placed in a position where they could be accused of rape.

FOURTH: *Spend all your time on self-improvement*. No one was to waste time with comic books or television, but each should study in his or her own specialty.

FIFTH: *Respect the private property of each member of the family*. This was to be most strictly enforced with regard to the selling of paintings. Anyone was permitted to sell an unsigned painting or one signed "Billy" or "Milligan." But the private paintings done and signed by Tommy, Danny or Allen were personal, and no one was ever to sell something that did not belong to him or her.

Anyone violating these rules would be banished forever from taking the spot and would be relegated to the shadows with the other undesirables.

Ragen thought about it and asked, "Who are these—vat you call—undesirables?"

"Philip and Kevin—both unmistakably antisocial, criminal types—are banished from the spot."

"Vat about Tommy? He is antisocial sometimes."

"Yes," Arthur agreed, "but Tommy's belligerency is needed. Some of the younger ones are so obedient that they would harm themselves if a stranger told them to. As long as he does not violate other rules or use his escape talents and lock-picking abilities for criminal purposes, Tommy may take the spot. But I will rattle his cage from time to time to let him know we're watching him."

"Vat about me?" Ragen asked. "I am criminal. I am violent and antisocial."

"There must be no breaking of the law, no crimes." Arthur said, "even so-called victimless crimes, for any reason."

"You must realize," Ragen said, "is always possible for me to be in situation vere crime could be necessary for defense, for survival. Necessity knows no laws."

Arthur placed the tips of his fingers together for a few moments and considered Ragen's argument. Then he nodded. "You will be the exception to the rule. Because of your great strength and power, you alone may have the right to hurt others, but only in self-defense or in defense of women and children. As the protector of the family, you alone may commit victimless crimes or crimes necessary for survival."

"Then I accept idea of rules," Ragen said softly. "But system vill not always vork. During mix-up periods, people steal time. Then ve do not even know—not you, not me, not Allen—vat is happening."

"True," Arthur said, "but we have to do the best we can with what we have. Part of the challenge will be to keep the family stable and prevent those mix-up times."

"Is difficult. You vill have to communicate this to the others. I do not yet know all of the—how you say?—the family. They come, they go. I am not sure sometimes if one is outside people or one of ours."

"That's natural. It is as it was in the hospital or even in the youth camp. One learns the names of some of the people who live around you and becomes aware of the existence of others. But quite often even outside people don't communicate with each other although they're living in close proximity. I will communicate with each of our people and tell them what they need to know."

Ragen mused. "I am strong, but vit all the things you have learned, you have gained much power."

Arthur nodded. "And that is why I can still beat you at chess."

Arthur reached the others one by one and told each one what was expected of him or her. In addition to the code of behavior, there were other responsibilities for those who were on the spot.

Christene had stayed three years old and constantly embarrassed them. Yet Ragen insisted, and it was agreed that since she had been the first and was still "the baby" of the family, she would never be removed or classified as undesirable. She might even prove useful at times when it was necessary to have someone on the spot who couldn't communicate and wouldn't know what was going on. But she, too, was expected to work at her own goals. With Arthur's help, she was to learn to read and write and struggle to overcome her dyslexia.

Tommy was to pursue his interest in electronics and strengthen his mechanical abilities. Though he could pick locks and crack vaults, the techniques he had learned were to be used for only one purpose—not to penetrate, but to escape. He was never to aid anyone in stealing. He was not to be a thief. He was to practice the tenor saxophone in his spare time and to perfect his talent in painting landscapes. He was to control his belligerent attitude, but use it to deal with other people when necessary.

Ragen was to take karate and judo lessons, to jog and to keep the body in perfect physical condition. With Arthur's help and direction, Ragen would learn to control his adrenaline flow so as to fucus all his energies in times of stress or danger. He was to continue to study munitions and demolition. Part of the next paycheck would go toward buying him a gun for target practice.

Allen was to practice his verbal skills, to concentrate on painting portraits. He would play the drums to help release excess tension. He would generally be the front man to help manipulate others when it was necessary. As the most sociable one, it was important for him to get out and meet people.

Adalana was to continue writing her poetry and perfecting her cooking skills for the time when they would be leaving home and getting their own apartment.

Danny would concentrate on still lifes and learn to master the airbrush. Since he was a teen-ager, he would baby-sit and help care for the younger children.

Arthur would concentrate on his scientific studies, especially those in the medical arts. He had already sent for a mail-order study course in the fundamentals of clinical hematology. He would also use his logic and clear reasoning to study law.

All the others were made aware of the need to use every moment of their time to improve themselves and expand their knowledge. They must never be still, Arthur warned, never waste time, never allow their minds to stagnate. Each member of the family must strive to achieve his or her own goals, and at the same time be educated and cultured. They should think of these things even while off the spot and practice them intensively when they were holding the consciousness.

The young ones were never to drive a car. If any of them found himself on the spot behind the steering wheel, he was to slide over to the passenger's side and wait for someone older to come and do the driving.

Everyone agreed that Arthur had been very thorough and had thought things out logically.

"Samuel" read the Old Testament, ate only kosher food and loved to sculpt sandstone and carve wood. He took the spot on September 27, Rosh Hashanah, the Jewish New Year, and said a prayer in memory of Billy's Jewish father.

Samuel knew of Arthur's strict rule concerning the selling of paintings, but one day when he needed money and no one from the family was around to give him advice or to tell him what was going on, he sold a nude signed by Allen. Nudes offended his religious sensibilities, and he did not want it where he could see it. He told the purchaser, "I am not the artist, but I know the artist."

Then he sold Tommy's painting of a barn, a painting that clearly had fear surrounding it.

When Arthur learned what Samuel had done, he was outraged. Samuel should have realized he was selling paintings the others held dear to themselves, paintings so personal they were never meant for the eyes of strangers. He ordered Tommy to find Samuel's favorite creation—a draped Venus surrounded by cupids, done in plaster.

"Destroy it," Arthur said.

Tommy took it out back and smashed it with a hammer.

"For this terrible crime of selling other people's art, Samuel is henceforth an undesirable. He is hereby banished from the spot."

Samuel argued his fate. He pointed out to Arthur that he should not be banished, since he was the only one among all of them who believed in God.

"God was invented by those who are afraid of the unknown," Arthur said. "People worship figures like Jesus Christ only because they fear what might happen to them after they die."

"Exactly," Samuel said. "But look, it wouldn't be such a terrible idea to have a little insurance. If after we die we find out there *is* a God, what should be so bad that there should be at least one of us who did believe in Him? That way one of us has a shot at getting the soul into heaven."

"If there is a soul," Arthur said.

"So what's the rush to take the gamble? What would it cost to give me another chance?"

"I've made the rule," Arthur said, "and my decision stands. October sixth is your holiest day, Yom Kippur. You may take the spot to fast on your Day of Atonement, but then you are banished."

Later, he admitted to Tommy that in making his judgment in anger, he had made a mistake. Since he couldn't know for sure that there was no God, he should not have acted so hastily in banishing from the spot the only one of them who believed.

"You could change it," Tommy said, "and let Samuel take the spot sometimes."

"Not while I dominate the consciousness," Arthur said. "I admit I made an error in allowing my emotions to affect my decisions. But having decided, I will not change it."

Thinking about heaven and hell bothered Tommy. He found himself going over and over the thought in his mind, and he wondered, if they did get sent to hell, whether there would possibly be a way to escape.

(2)

A few days later, Allen ran into a school acquaintance downtown. He vaguely remembered that Barry Hart was a friend of someone he used to know. Now, with his long hair, he looked like a hippie. Barry Hart invited him up to his place to have a beer and talk.

It was a big rundown apartment. While Allen sat in the kitchen talking with Hart, people came and went, and Allen got the impression there was a lot of drug dealing going on. When Allen got up to leave, Hart said he was going to have a lot of friends over Saturday night for a party and Allen was invited.

He accepted. What better way to follow Arthur's instructions to get out and socialize?

But when Allen got there on Saturday night, he didn't like what he saw. It was a heavy drug scene, with people drinking booze, smoking pot and popping pills. Most of them, he thought, were making fools of themselves. He'd stay for just a little while and have a beer. But after a few minutes, he got so uncomfortable he left the spot.

Arthur looked around, disgusted at the goings on, but he decided to sit back and observe this species of lowlife. It was interesting to see how different people made fools of themselves under different drugs: belligerent on alcohol, giggling on marijuana, trancelike on amphetamines, tripping on LSD. It was, he decided, a laboratory of drug abuse.

Arthur noticed one couple sitting apart, as he was. The girl, tall and slender, with long dark hair, full lips and smoky eyes, kept looking his way. He had the impression she would talk to him soon. The very idea annoyed him.

The fellow she was with made the first move. "Come to Hart's parties often?" the young man asked.

Arthur let Allen take back the spot. He looked around, dazed. "What did you say?"

"My friend says she thinks she's seen you here at a party before," the young man said. "I have the feeling I've seen you before too. What's your name?"

"They call me Billy Milligan."

"Challa's brother? Hey, I'm Walt Stanley. I've met your sister."

The young woman came over and Stanley said, "Marlene, this is Billy Milligan."

Stanley wandered off, and Marlene talked with Allen for nearly an hour, trading observations about the other people in the room. Allen found her amusing and warm. He could tell she was attracted to him. Her dark catlike eyes gave him an odd feeling and he was drawn to her. But he knew that because of Arthur's rules, nothing would come of it.

"Hey, Marlene!" Stanley called from across the room. "You wanna split?"

She ignored him.

"Your boyfriend is calling you," Allen said.

"Oh," she said smiling, "he's not my boyfriend."

She was getting him nervous. Here he had just gotten out of Zanesville after serving time on a phony rape charge, and this girl was making moves on him.

"Excuse me, Marlene," he said. "I've gotta leave."

She seemed surprised. "Maybe we'll run into each other again sometime."

Allen took off fast.

The following Sunday, Allen decided, was a perfect fall day for a round of golf. He tossed his clubs into the car, drove to the

Lancaster Country Club and rented an electric cart. He played several holes but did poorly; when he put his third shot into a sand bunker, he got so disgusted with himself that he left the spot.

"Martin" opened his eyes, surprised to find himself with a sand wedge in his hand, addressing the ball from a bunker. He hit it out and finished the hole. Not knowing how many strokes it had taken him to do the par four hole, he scored it as a birdie three.

Martin was annoyed when he saw how crowded the next tee was, and he complained loudly that slow play was ruining the game for better players like himself. "I'm from New York," he said to a middle-aged man with a group of four ahead of him, "and I'm used to private clubs that are much more exclusive than this and particular about the class of people they allow to play."

When the man looked flustered, Martin stepped forward. "You don't mind if I play through, do you?" And without waiting for an answer, he stepped up, teed off, put his ball in the right rough and zoomed ahead in his golf cart.

He played through the next threesome as well, but then hit his ball into a water hazard. He parked the golf cart near the pond to see if he could retrieve it. Unable to find it, he hit a second ball across the pond and returned to the cart, but he cracked his knee against the side as he jumped in.

David came to take the pain, wondering where he was and why he was in this little car. When the pain subsided, David sat there playing with the steering wheel, making engine noises with his mouth and kicking the foot pedals. The brake released and the cart rolled down, sinking the front wheels into the pond. Frightened, David left and Martin returned, wondering what had happened. It took him nearly half an hour, rocking the cart back and forth, to free the front wheels from the mud, and he was furious as group after group played through.

When the cart was back on dry land, Arthur took the spot and told Ragen he was banishing Martin as undesirable.

"Is severe punishment for mistake of golf cart in pond."

"That is not the reason," Arthur said. "Martin is a worthless braggart. Ever since Zanesville, all he has thought about is wearing flashy clothes and driving big cars. He puts on airs.

He thinks nothing of improving himself or being creative. He's a fraud and a phony, and worst of all, he is a snob."

Ragen smiled. "I did not know being snob is reason for being undesirable."

"My dear chap," Arthur said coolly, knowing what Ragen was alluding to, "no one has the right to be a snob unless he is very intelligent. I have that right; Martin doesn't."

Arthur finished the last four holes in par.

On October 27, 1973, almost ten years from the day she had married Chalmer Milligan, Dorothy married her fourth husband—Delmos A. Moore.

He tried to be like a father to Billy and the girls, but they resented him. When he started to lay down rules, Arthur scorned him.

One of the things Dorothy forbade her younger son was to ride a motorcycle. Tommy knew it was because of Stuart, but he didn't think it was right to deprive him because of what had happened to someone else.

One day he borrowed a friend's Yamaha 350 and drove it right past the house. As he headed back along Spring Street, Tommy looked down and saw the tailpipe was coming loose. If it hit the ground . . .

Ragen threw himself off the cycle.

He picked himself up, brushed off his jeans and wheeled the cycle back to the yard. Then he went into the house to wash the blood off his forehead.

When he came out of the bathroom, Dorothy began screaming at him. "I told you I didn't want you on a motorcycle! You're doing this to torment me!"

Del came in from the yard and shouted, "You did that on purpose! You know how I've felt about cycles, ever since . . ."

Ragen shook his head and left the spot. He'd let Tommy explain about the tailpipe.

Tommy looked up to see Dorothy and Del glaring at him.

"It *was* on purpose," Del said, "wasn't it?"

"That's crazy," Tommy said, checking his bruises. "The tailpipe came down and—"

"That's another lie," Del said. "I went out and looked at that cycle. Ain't no way that tailpipe could have come down and flipped that cycle without bending in two. That tailpipe ain't bent."

"Don't you ever call me a liar!" Tommy shouted.

"You're a goddamned liar!" Del shouted back.

Tommy stormed out of the room. What good would it do to tell them the reason it wasn't bent was that Ragen had seen the thing coming down and had thrown the bike just in time to prevent a worse crack-up? No matter how he explained it, they were going to call it a lie.

Feeling the anger building up, too strong for him to handle, Tommy gave up the spot . . .

Dorothy, sensing the fury in her son, followed him as he went into the garage. She stood outside and watched him, unseen, through the window. She saw the look of murderous rage as he went to the lumber pile, picked up a two-by-four and snapped it in half. Again and again he broke the boards, venting a deep and violent anger.

Arthur made a decision. They had to move out.

A few days later, Allen found a cheap two and a half room apartment in a white frame house at 808 Broad Street, just a short drive east of where Dorothy lived. It was a rundown place, but it had a refrigerator and a stove. He added a mattress, a couple of chairs and a table. Dorothy let him buy a Pontiac Grand Prix in her name with the understanding that he would make the payments on it.

Ragen bought a .30-caliber carbine with a nine-shot clip and a .25-caliber semiautomatic.

At first, the freedom of having his own apartment was exhilarating. He could paint when he wanted, with no one hassling him.

Arthur made sure aspirin and other medication were purchased in bottles with child-proof caps so that the little ones wouldn't get into them. He even insisted that Ragen find a child-proof cap that could be adapted to fit his vodka bottle, and he reminded him to make sure his guns were always under lock and key.

A rivalry developed between Adalana and "April" in the kitchem, and though Arthur sensed there was going to be trouble, he decided not to take sides. He had little enough time for his own study, research and planning for the future, so he tried not to pay attention to the women constantly haranguing and arguing in the back of his mind. When the nagging got too bad, he suggested that Adalana do the cooking and April do the sewing and washing, and let it go at that.

Arthur had been quite taken by the thin, black-haired, brown-eyed April when he first descovered her along with the others. She was more attractive than the plain, almost homely Adalana, and certainly more intelligent. Almost as bright as Tommy or Allen, or even Arthur himself. And he was intrigued, at first, by her Boston accent. But he had lost interest in her when he became aware of her thoughts. April was obsessed with ideas of torturing and killing Chalmer.

She worked things out in her mind. If she could lure Chalmer to the apartment, she would tie him in the chair and burn his body, bit by bit, with a blowtorch. She would keep him awake with amphetamines, and the heat of the blowtorch would amputate each toe and each finger, cauterizing as it did, so there would be no blood. She wanted him to suffer here, before he went to hell.

April began to work on Ragen.

She whispered into his ear, "You have to kill Chalmer. You have to take one of your guns and shoot him."

"I am not murderer."

"It wouldn't be murder. It would be justice for what he did."

"I am not law. Justice is for courts. I use my strength only to defend the children and vomans."

"I'm a woman."

"You are crazy voman."

"All you would have to do is take your rifle and hide on the hill across from where he lives now with his new wife. You could take him. No one would ever know who did it."

"Is no scope for carbine. Vould be too far. Ve do not have money to buy scope."

"You're ingenious, Ragen," she whispered. "We have a telescope. You could adapt it and make cross hairs to do the job."

Ragen shook her off.

But April kept at it, reminding Ragen of the things Chalmer had done—especially to the children. Knowing how much he cared for Christene, she made it a point to remind him of the abuse Christene had taken.

"I do it," he said.

He took two hairs from his head and carefully wet them to the inside of the eyepiece. Then he went up to the roof and, sighting through the homemade scope, dropped BB's, to a small black spot on the ground below. Once he felt it was accurate enough to do the job, he glued the cross hairs in place, mounted the eyepiece on the carbine and took it out in the woods to test it. He would be able to hit Chalmer from the rise across from his new house.

The next morning, an hour before the time Chalmer usually went to work at his foreman job in Columbus, Ragen drove to his neighborhood, parked the car and slipped into the wooded area across from the house. He positioned himself behind the tree, waiting for Chalmer to come out. He trained his scope on the door he knew Chalmer would have to walk through to get to his car.

"Don't do it," Arthur said aloud.

"He must die," Ragen said.

"This does not come under the heading of being necessary for survival."

"It comes under protect vomans and children. He has hurt children. He must die to pay for it."

Arthur, knowing that argument was useless, brought Christene to the edge of the spot and showed her what Ragen was doing. She cried and stamped her feet and pleaded with Ragen not to do bad things.

Ragen clenched his teeth. Chalmer was coming through the door. Ragen reached over and removed the nine-shot clip. With the rifle chamber empty, he sighted through the eyepiece, centered Chalmer in the cross hairs and gently pulled the trigger. Then he put the rifle over his shoulder, went back to the car and drove home to the new apartment.

That day Arthur said, "April is insane, a menace to all of us." And he banished her from the spot.

(3)

"Kevin" was alone in the apartment when the doorbell rang. He opened the door and saw a beautiful young woman smiling at him.

"I called Barry Hart," Marlene said, "and he told me you had this place of your own. I enjoyed our talk at his party that time, and I thought I'd see how you were."

Kevin had no idea what she was talking about, but he motioned for her to come in. "I was feeling pretty low," he said, "until I opened this door."

Marlene spent the evening with him, looking at his paintings and talking about people they knew. She was glad she'd made the first move and come to see him. It made her feel very close to him.

When she got up to leave, he asked if she would come to see him again. She said she would if he wanted her to.

On November 16, 1973, the day he was officially discharged from the custody of the Ohio Youth Commission, Kevin sat in a neighborhood bar and recalled Gordy Kane's words the day he left the Zanesville Youth Camp. "If you ever need a dope connection," Kane had said, "look me up."

Well, that's just what he intended to do.

Late in the afternoon he drove out to the Reynoldsburg area on the east side of Columbus. The address he had for Kane was an expensive-looking ranch house on a corner lot.

Gordy Kane and his mother were glad to see him. Julia Kane said, in her sexy, throaty voice, that he was a welcome visitor in their home at any time.

While Julia was busy making herself a cup of tea, Kevin asked Gordy if he could lend him enough money to make a buy and start dealing. He was broke now, but he'd pay him back.

Kane took him to a house in the neighborhood where an acquaintance sold him three hundred and fifty dollars' worth of pot.

"You should be able to deal that for over a thousand," Kane said. "You can pay me back after you sell it."

Kane's hands were shaking and he looked spaced out.

"What drugs do you do?" Kevin asked.

"Morphine, when I can get it."

Later that week, Kevin sold the pot to some of Hart's friends in Lancaster and cleared seven hundred dollars' profit. Kevin went back to the apartment, smoked a joint and phoned Marlene.

She came over and told him she was worried about what she'd learned from Barry—that he'd been dealing pot.

"I know what I'm doing," he said. He kissed her, turned out the lights and pulled her down on the mattress. But as soon as their bodies touched, Adalana wished Kevin off the spot. This was what she needed. Holding and tenderness.

Adalana understood Arthur's rule of celibacy. She had heard him tell the males that a single violation would make them undesirable. But, proper British gentleman that Arthur was, it had never occurred to him to talk to *her* about sex. *She* had never agreed to his puritanical rules, and he would probably never even suspect.

When Allen woke up next morning, he had no idea what had happened. He saw the money in the drawer and it worried him, but he couldn't reach Tommy or Ragen or Arthur or anyone else for an explanation.

Several of Barry Hart's friends dropped by that afternoon for dope, but Allen didn't know what they were talking about. Some of them were belligerent, shoving money into his face, and Allen began to suspect someone in the family was dealing.

The next time he was at Hart's place, one of the men showed him a .38 Smith and Wesson. He wasn't sure why he wanted it, but he offered the man fifty bucks, and he accepted, even throwing in some bullets.

Allen took the gun out to the car and put it under the seat . . .

Ragen reached down and took the .38 into his hand. He'd wanted Allen to buy it. Not his favorite weapon. He would have preferred a 9-millimeter. But it would be a good one to add to his weapons collection.

Allen decided to move out of the crummy apartment. Looking through the apartment ads in the *Lancaster Eagle-Gazette*, he saw a familiar phone number.

He searched through his address book until he found it and the name that went with it: George Kellner, the lawyer who had plea-bargained him into Zanesville. Allen had Dorothy call him about renting the apartment to her son. Kellner agreed to let him have it for eighty dollars a month.

The apartment at 803 1/2 Roosevelt Avenue was a clean one-bedroom second-floor apartment in a white house set back from the street behind another building. Allen moved in a week later and fixed up the place comfortably. No more messing around with drugs, he decided. We've got to keep away from those people.

He was astonished when Marlene, whom he had not seen since the night of Barry Hart's party, came in one day and made herself at home. He had no idea which of the others was dating her, but he decided she was not his type and he wanted nothing to do with her.

She would come in after work, make his dinner, spend part of the evening, then go home to her parents' house. She was practically living there, and it made everything a lot more complicated than Allen liked.

Whenever she started to get affectionate, he'd leave the spot. He didn't know who came on and he didn't really give a damn.

Marlene thought the apartment was great. Billy's periodic shifts into foul language and his explosions of rage shocked her at first, but she got used to his changing moods—one minute tender and affectionate, the next minute angry and storming all over the place, then funny, clever and articulate. Without warning sometimes, he'd become clumsy and pathetic, like a little boy who didn't know which foot to put his shoe on. She knew he surely needed someone to look after him. It was all the drugs he was doing and the crowd he was hanging out with. If she could convince him that Barry Hart's friends were just using him, maybe he would see that he didn't need them at all.

At times the things he did frightened her. He talked about being worried that some other people would show up and cause trouble if they found her there. He hinted it was "the family," and she assumed he was being a big shot and boasting that he was working with the Mafia. But when he went to all the trouble to devise a signal, she found herself believing it *was* the Mafia. Whenever she was in the apartment, he would put a painting in the window. That, he said, would be a message to the "others" that she was there and that they should stay away.

When he made love to her, what often started with foul language and rough talk would always turn into tender caresses and softness. But something bothered her about his love-making. Though he was strong and manly, she had the feeling he was only pretending his passion, that he never really climaxed. She wasn't sure, but she knew she loved him and decided all it would take was time and understanding.

One evening Adalana slipped away and David found himself on the spot, frightened and sobbing.

"I've never seen a man cry," Marlene whispered. "What's wrong?"

David curled up like a baby, tears rolling down his cheeks. She felt touched and close to him when he was so vulnerable like this. She cuddled him in her arms.

"You have to tell me, Billy. I can't help you if you don't let me know what's the matter."

Not knowing what to tell her, David left the spot. Tommy found himself in the arms of a beautiful woman. He pulled away.

"If you're going to act that way, I might as well go home," she said, angry that he was trying to make a fool of her.

Tommy watched her as she walked to the bathroom.

"Holy shit!" he whispered, looking around in a panic. "Arthur'll kill me!"

He jumped out of bed and pulled his jeans on, walking back and forth, trying to figure this out. "Who the hell is she?"

He saw her purse on the chair in the living room and went through it quickly. He read the name *Marlene* on her driver's license, then shoved it back into her purse.

"Arthur?" he whispered. "If you can hear me, I didn't have nothing to do with that. I didn't touch her. Believe me. I'm not the one who's breaking the rules."

He went over to the easel and picked up a brush to work on a landscape he had started. Arthur would know he was doing what he was supposed to, perfecting his talents.

"I think you care more about your painting than you do about me."

Tommy turned and saw that Marlene was dressed, brushing her hair. He said nothing but went on painting.

"Painting, painting, that's all you think about is your damned painting. Talk to me, Billy."

Remembering Arthur's rule about being polite to women, Tommy put the brush down and sat in the chair across from her. She was beautiful. Though she was fully dressed now, he visualized her slender body, every curve, every hollow. He had never painted a nude before, but he would love to paint her. He knew he wouldn't, though. Allen was the one who painted people.

He spoke to her for a while, fascinated by her dark eyes, her full, pouting lips, her long throat. He knew that whoever she was, whatever had brought her here, he was crazy about her.

* * *

(4)

No one could understand why Billy Milligan started missing days at work or why he became so clumsy and stupid. Once he climbed up to fix the chain over the tanks and fell into the acid bath. They had to send him home. He walked off the job one day, and on December 21, 1973, he was fired from Lancaster Electro-Plating. He stayed home alone painting for a few days. Then one day Ragen took his guns and drove out into the woods for target practice.

By this time Ragen had bought himself quite a few guns. In addition to the .30-caliber carbine, the .25-caliber semiautomatic and the .38 Smith and Wesson, he had a .375 magnum, an M-14, a .44 magnum and an M-16. He liked his Israeli grease gun because of its compactness and quietness. He'd also bought a .45 Thompson barrel clip, which he thought of as a collector's item.

When the mix-up time reached its peak, Kevin asked Gordy Kane for an introduction to his connection. Kevin was ready to deal drugs full-time. Kane called an hour later and gave him directions to Blacklick Woods, near Reynoldsburg, east of Columbus.

"I told him about you. He wants to see you alone so he can size you up. If he likes you, you've got it made. He goes under the name of Brian Foley."

Kevin drove out, following instructions carefully. He had never been in this area, but he reached the appointed location near a culvert ten minutes early. He parked and waited in the car. Nearly a half-hour later, a Mercedes drove up and two men got out. One was tall, with a pitted face and a brown leather jacket. The other was of medium height, with a beard and a pinstriped suit. Someone was watching from the back of the car. Kevin didn't like it—not at all. He sat behind the wheel, sweating, wondering what he had gotten himself into and whether or not he should drive off.

The tall guy with the pitted face leaned over and looked at him. The man's tight jacket showed a bulge under his left armpit. "You Milligan?"

Kevin nodded.

"Mr. Foley wants to talk to you."

Kevin slid out from behind the wheel. When he turned, he saw that Foley had gotten out of the back seat of the Mercedes and was leaning against the door. He looked no older than himself, eighteen or so. His blond hair came down to his shoulders and blended into a camel's-hair coat and a matching muffler, knotted at the throat.

Kevin started toward him but suddenly found himself spun around and braced against his own car. The tall man held an automatic at his head, while the bearded one reached to frisk him. Then Kevin was gone . . .

Ragen caught the bearded man's hand, spun him and flipped him at the tall one with the gun. He jumped the man, wrested the gun from his grip and held him as a shield as he pointed the gun at Foley, who had been watching from the Mercedes.

"It is not good to move," he said calmly. "I put three bullets betveen eyes before you take step."

Foley put his hands up.

"You," Ragen said to the bearded man. "Take gun from under jacket vit two fingers and put it on ground."

"Do what he says," Foley ordered.

When the man moved slowly, Ragen said, "Do it now or you vill be smiling out of your sleeve."

The man opened his jacket, removed his gun and placed it on the ground.

"Now, vit foot, kick it easy over here."

The man kicked the gun toward him. Ragen released his captive and picked up the second gun, covering all three of them. "Is not good manners to treat visitor this vay."

He emptied both clips, spun both guns, catching them by the barrels, and flipped them back to their owners. He turned his back on them and walked toward Foley.

"I vould say you need better bodyguard than these two."

"Put your guns away," Foley said. "And go stand over by his car. I'm going to have a talk with Mr. Milligan."

He nodded for Ragen to get into the back of the car and slipped in beside him. He pressed a button and a traveling bar opened.

"What do you drink?"

"Vodka."

"I expected that from your accent. So you're not Irish, as your name would suggest."

"I am Yugoslavian. Names mean nothing."

"Can you use a gun as well as your hands?"

"You have gun for demonstration?"

Foley reached under the seat and handed Ragen a .45.

"Is good veapon," Ragen said, testing its heft and balance. "I prefer nine-millimeter, but this vill do. Choose target."

Foley pressed the button, lowering the window. "That beer can on the other side of the road, the one near the—"

Before he finished, Ragen's hand moved out and fired. The can clattered. He hit it again twice as it bounced away.

Foley smiled. "I can use a man like you, Mr. Milligan or whatever your name is."

Ragen said, "I need money. You have job, I do it."

"Do you have any objections to breaking the law?"

Ragen shook his head. "Except one thing. I do not hurt people unless my life in danger, and I do not harm vomans."

"Fair enough. Now go back to your own car and follow us closely. We'll go to my place, where we can talk business."

Both bodyguards glared at him as he brushed by them to get into his car.

"You ever do that again," the tall one said, "and I'll kill you."

Ragen caught him and spun him quickly against the car, twisting his arm upward just a fraction short of breaking it. "For that you have to be more faster and smarter than you are. Be careful. I am very dangerous person."

Foley called from his car. "Murray, damn you, get the hell over here. Leave Milligan alone. He's working for me now."

When they got into the car, Ragen pulled out to follow them, wondering what this was all about and why he had come here in the first place.

He was surprised when the car pulled into a luxurious estate not far from Reynoldsburg. There was a storm fence around it, and behind the fence, three Doberman pinschers ran back and forth.

It was a large Victorian mansion, thickly carpeted and decorated in a simple modern style with paintings and *objects d'art*. Foley showed Ragen around the house, obviously proud of his possessions. Then he led him to the bar in the den and poured him a vodka.

"Now, Mr. Milligan—"

"People call me Billy," Ragen said. "I do not like name Milligan."

"I understand. I imagine it's not your real name. All right, Billy, I can use a man like you—fast, intelligent, strong and damned good with a gun. I need someone who can ride shotgun for me."

"Vat is 'ride shotgun'?"

"I'm in the shipping business, and my drivers need protection."

Ragen nodded, feeling the warming effect of the vodka in his chest. "I am protector," he said.

"Good. I'll need a number where I can reach you. A day or two before each delivery, you'll sleep here. We have lots of rooms. You won't know what's being shipped or where until you're on the road with the driver. That way there will be less chance of a leak."

"Is sound very good," Ragen said, yawning. On the way back to Lancaster, Ragen slept while Allen drove home, wondering where he had been and what he'd been doing.

In the weeks that followed, Ragen rode shotgun for deliveries of narcotics to various dealers and customers in and around Columbus. He was amused to find marijuana and cocaine being shipped to prominent people whose names he had seen constantly in the newspapers.

He rode shotgun on a shipment of M-1's to a group of black men in West Virginia, and wondered what they wanted them for.

Several times Ragen tried to reach Arthur, but either Arthur was being stubborn and wanted nothing to do with him or it was a very bad mix-up time. He knew that Philip and Kevin were stealing time because occasionally he found open containers of barbiturates and amphetamines in the apartment. And once he discovered that one of his guns had been left out on the dresser. He was furious, because someone's carelessness could harm the children.

He decided that the next time one of the undesirables came on the spot, he would try to be alert and bump them into the wall to teach them a lesson. Drugs were bad for the body; vodka and grass in moderation, having natural ingredients, were not. But he wanted nothing to do with hard drugs. He began to suspect that Philip or Kevin had experimented with LSD.

* * *

A week later, after returning from delivering a shipment of marijuana to a car dealer in Indiana, Ragen stopped in Columbus for dinner. As he was getting out of his car, he saw an elderly man and woman distributing Communist party leaflets. There were several hecklers standing around, and Ragen asked the couple if he could help them.

"Are you sympathetic to our cause?" the woman asked.

"Yes," Ragen said. "I am communist. I have seen slave labor in sweatshops and factories."

The man handed him a stack of leaflets describing the philosophy of the Communist party and attacking the United States for supporting dictatorships. Ragen walked up and down Broad Street, pushing them into the hands of passers-by.

When he was down to the last leaflet, he decided to keep it for himself. He looked around for the old couple, but they were gone. He wandered for several blocks looking for them. If only he could find out where the meetings were held, he would join the Communist party. He had watched Tommy and Allen at Lancaster Electro-Plating and knew that the only way to improve the lot of the down-trodden masses was through the people's revolution.

Then he saw the bumper sticker on his car: WORKERS OF THE WORLD UNITE! The old couple must have put it there. The words sent a thrill through him. He kneeled, and in the lower right-hand corner of the sticker, he saw the name of a Columbus silkscreen company. Someone there might be able to tell him where the local communist group was meeting.

He looked up the address in the telephone directory and discovered that the silkscreen company wasn't far. He drove there and watched the store from the car for a few minutes. Then he drove to the phone booth up the block and, using his cable cutters, snipped the wires. He did the same to the other phone booth two blocks away. Then he went back to the store.

The owner, about sixty, with thick glasses and white hair, denied silkscreening the bumper stickers for the Communist party. "It was ordered by a printer in north Columbus," he said.

Ragen slammed his fist on the counter. "Give address."

The man paused nervously. "Do you have some identification?"

"No!" Ragen said.

"How do I know you're not from the FBI?"

Ragen grabbed him by the shirt front and pulled him close. "Old man, I vant know vere you send these bumper stickers."

"Why?"

Ragen pulled out his gun. "I am looking for my people and I cannot find them. Give me information or look for the hole in your body."

The man peered nervously over his glassses. "All right." He picked up a pencil and wrote down an address.

"I vant to see record to be sure," Ragen said.

The man pointed to the order book on the desk. "The records are over there, but—but—"

"I know," Ragen said. "Address of communist customer is not in there." He pointed the gun at him again. "Open your safe."

"Are you holding me up?"

"I vant only correct information."

The man opened the safe, pulled out a sheet of paper and laid it on the counter. Ragen checked it. Satisfied that he had the right address, Ragen jerked the phone cord out of the wall.

"If you vant call them before I get there, use pay telephone two blocks away."

Ragen walked out to the car. He estimated the printing shop to be about four miles away. He would have enough time to get there before the man could find a pay phone that hadn't been cut.

The address was a residence with a small sign in the first-floor window: PRINTING. Inside, he noticed that the business was run from the front living room. There was a long desk, a small hand printing press and a mimeograph machine. Ragen was surprised there were no hammer-and-sickle posters around. It looked like a simple operation. But the vibration under his feet told him that printing presses were running in the basement.

The man who came through the door was about forty-five, heavy-set, with a neat Vandyke beard. "I am Karl Bottorf. What can I do for you?"

"I vant to vork for the revolution."

"Why?"

"Because I believe 'U.S. government' is another vord for 'Mafia.' They take labor of vorking people and use money to support dictators. I believe in equality."

"Come in, young man. Let's talk awhile."

Ragen followed him into the kitchen and sat down at the table.

"Where are you from?" Bottorf asked.

"Yugoslavia."

"I *thought* you were a Slav. Of course we will have to check you out, but I see no reason why you cannot join us to help our cause."

"I vould like to go to Cuba someday," Ragen said. "I have great admiration for Dr. Castro. He took band of rebel vorkers from sugar-cane fields into hills and created revolution. Now all people in Cuba are equal."

They spoke for a while and Bottorf invited him to attend the meeting of the local communist cell that afternoon.

"Is here?" Ragen asked.

"No. It's near Westerville. You can follow me in your car."

Ragen followed Karl Bottorf to a wealthy-looking neighborhood. Ragen was disappointed. He had expected it to be in the slums.

He was introduced as "the Yugoslavian" to several nondescript people, and sat in the back to observe the meeting. But as the speakers droned on in abstractions and slogans, his mind wandered. He struggled to stay awake for a while, but finally he gave in. Just a short cat nap, and he would be alert again. He had found his people. This was what he had always wanted to be part of, the people's struggle against the oppressive capitalist system. His head nodded . . .

Arthur sat up straight, alert, on edge. He had observed just the last part of Ragen's trip and had become fascinated watching Ragen follow the other car. But now he was amazed that such a bright fellow should be taken in by all this. Communism indeed! He had a good mind to get up and tell these mindless robots that the Soviet Union was nothing more than a monolithic dictatorship that had never turned power over to the people. Capitalism was the system that had brought freedom of conscience and opportunity to people all over the world in a way that communism could never hope to. So inconsistent was the Yugoslavian that he would rob banks, live off the fruits of narcotics traffic and yet convince himself that he was involved in the liberation of the people.

Arthur stood up, gave the entire assembly a withering glance and, in an even, unemotional tone, said, "Balderdash." The others turned and stared in astonishment as he left.

He found the car and sat there for a few moments. He hated to drive on the right-hand side of the road. But try as he might, he couldn't reach anyone to come and take the car. "Damn these damnable mix-up times!" he said. Slowly he eased himself behind the wheel, and craning his neck to see the center line, he pulled away from the curb. He drove tensely at twenty miles an hour.

Arthur checked the street signs, and it occurred to him that Sunbury Road might be in the neighborhood of the Hoover Reservoir. He pulled over to the curb, took out the highway map and plotted the coordinates. He was indeed near the dam he had been intending to visit for a long time.

He had heard that ever since the Army Corps of Engineers had built the dam, the sludge had accumulated against the structure. He had been wrestling with the question of whether this sludge area, with its varied forms of microscopic life, might turn out to be an ideal breeding ground for mosquitoes. If he discovered this was indeed an infested area, he would inform the authorities that action must be taken. The important thing was for him to take some scrapings of the sludge and examine them under the microscope at home. It was not a major project, he realized, but someone had to do it.

He was deep in thought, driving slowly and carefully, when a truck passing him swerved back into the lane, drove a car ahead of him off the road, and kept going. The car hit the guardrail and went into the ditch end over end. Arthur pulled quickly off onto the berm. He got out calmly and climbed down. A woman was moving, crawling out of the car.

"I say, don't move any more," he said. "Let me help you."

She was bleeding, and he used direct pressure to stop it. She began to gag—he could see her teeth had been knocked out and she was choking. Discarding the idea of performing a tracheotomy, he decided to create an airway instead. Searching through his pockets, he found a plastic ball-point pen. He pulled out the ink sheath and, using his pipe lighter, softened the plastic shell and bent it. Then he slipped it into her throat to help her breathe, turning her head to the side to allow the blood to run out of her mouth.

A brief examination told him that her jaw was broken, as was her wrist. Her side was lacerated and he suspected her ribs were crushed. She must have hit the steering wheel when she went forward.

When the ambulance arrived, he quickly told the driver what had happened and what he had done. Then he walked off into the gathering crowd.

He discarded the idea of going to the Hoover Dam. It was getting rather late, and he really should be getting home before dark. He did not like the idea of driving on the wrong side of the road at night.

CHAPTER FOURTEEN

(1)

Arthur found himself growing increasingly irritated with the way things were going. Allen had been fired from his latest job—filling invoices and loading trucks at the J. C. Penney distribution center—when David came on the spot unexpectedly and crashed a forklift into a steel pillar. Tommy wandered around Lancaster and Columbus looking, unsuccessfully, for a new job. Ragen was working for Foley on a regular basis—guarding shipments of guns and drugs—and was drinking too much vodka and smoking too much marijuana. After Ragen had spent four days in Indianapolis tracing a confiscated shipment of guns, he ended up in Dayton. Someone took too many downers and Tommy, finding himself on Interstate 70 feeling dizzy and sick to his stomach, gave up the spot to David, who was arrested on a complaint from a motel owner. At the hospital, they pumped David's stomach and treated him for an overdose, but the police let him go when the motel owner decided not to sign the complaint. When Allen got back to Lancaster, Marlene stayed with him. Then one of the undesirables—the Brooklyn accent revealed it to be Philip—took an overdose of red capsules. Marlene called the emergency squad and went along to the hospital. After they pumped his stomach again, she stayed and comforted him.

She told him she knew he was mixed up with some bad people and she was afraid he was going to get into deep trouble, but even if he did, she was going to stand by him. Arthur was annoyed at the thought and knew that finding one of them helpless and vulnerable like this aroused the maternal instinct in her. He couldn't tolerate it.

Marlene began spending more and more time at the apartment, making life very difficult. Arthur had to be constantly vigilant to make certain she did not discover the secret. Increasingly, there was lost time he couldn't account for. He was certain that someone was dealing drugs—he had discovered a bail receipt in a pocket—and he learned that one of them had been arrested for filling illegal drug prescriptions. He was also quite certain that someone was having sex with Marlene.

Arthur decided he needed to get away from Ohio, and this would be the right time to use a passport he had asked Ragen to purchase through one of his underworld connections.

He examined the two passports Ragen had bought through Foley, one in the name of Ragen Vadascovinich and the other in the name of Arthur Smith. They were either stolen and altered or superb forgeries. They would certainly stand up under close scrutiny.

He called Pan American Airlines, booked a one-way ticket to London, took what money he could find in closets, drawers and books, and packed his bags. He was going home.

The flight to Kennedy and then across the Atlantic was uneventful. When he placed his bag on the counter at Heathrow Airport, the customs official waved him through.

In London, Arthur checked into a small hotel above a pub in Hopewell Place, thinking that the name might well be prophetic. He lunched alone at a small but select restaurant, then took a taxi to Buckingham Palace. He had missed the changing of the guard, but he planned to see it another day. He felt comfortable wandering about the streets of the city and greeted passers-by with a "Top of the day" or "Smashing afternoon." He decided tomorrow he would buy a bowler and an umbrella.

For the first time in his memory, there were people around him who spoke as he did. The traffic moved on the correct side of the street, and the bobbies gave him a sense of security.

He visited the Tower of London and the British Museum, and dined on fish and chips and warm English beer. When he went to his room that night, remembering his favorite Sherlock Holmes movies, he made a mental note to visit 221b Baker Street the next day. He would inspect the place and make sure it was being kept up as a suitable memorial to the great detective. He felt he had come home at last.

The next morning, the loud ticking of the wall clock was the first thing Allen heard. He opened his eyes and stared around him. He jumped out of bed. It was an old-fashioned hotel, with an iron bedstead, curlicue-patterned wallpaper and a threadbare rug on the floor. It sure was no Holiday Inn. He looked for the bathroom, but there was none. Allen pulled on his trousers and peered out in the hallway.

Where the hell was he? He went back to the room, dressed and headed downstairs to see if he could identify his surroundings. On the stairs, he passed a man coming up with a tray.

"Bit o' breakfast, gov'nah?" the man asked. "Bloomin' lovely day."

Allen ran down the steps, out the front door, into the street, and looked around. He saw the black taxicabs with the big license plates, the pub sign, the traffic on the wrong side of the street.

"Holy shit! What the hell's going on? What the hell's the matter with me?" He ran up and back, shouting, terrified and angry at the same time. People turned to look at him, but he didn't care. He hated himself for waking up in different places all the time, for not being able to control himself. He just couldn't take this anymore. He wanted to die. He dropped to his knees and beat his fists into the curb, tears rolling down his cheeks.

Then, realizing that if a policeman came by, he'd be hauled off to the nut house, Allen jumped to his feet. He dashed back to his room, where he found in his suitcase a passport with the name "Arthur Smith." Inside it was the receipt of a one-way plane ticket to London. Allen slumped on the bed. What had Arthur had in mind? Crazy bastard!

Searching through his pockets, he found seventy-five dollars. Where was he going to get the money to get home? A return ticket would probably cost three or four hundred bucks. "Goddamn! Jesus Christ! Holy hell!"

He started to pack Arthur's clothes to check out, and then he stopped. "The hell with it. It'll serve him right." He left the luggage and clothes.

He took the passport, walked out of the hotel without paying and hailed a cab. "Take me to the international airport."

"Heathrow or Gatwick?"

He rummaged through the passport and looked at the one-way ticket. "Heathrow," he said.

All the way there, he worked out how he was going to handle it. Seventy-five dollars wouldn't get him very far, but if he used his wits and put up a good front, there had to be a way to get on a plane back home. At the airport he paid the driver and ran into the terminal.

"Jesus Christ!" he shouted. "I don't know what happened! I got off the plane at the wrong time! I was drugged. I left my ticket, my luggage, everything on the plane. Nobody told me I wasn't supposed to get off. There must've been something in my food or drink. I fell asleep, and when I woke up, I got out to stretch my legs. Nobody told me I wasn't supposed to get off the plane. My tickets, my traveler's checks, everything's gone."

A guard tried to calm him down and led him to the passport-control office.

"I got off the plane at the wrong time!" he shouted. "I was coming over. I was supposed to go to Paris. But I got off the plane at the wrong time. I've been wandering dazed. There was something in my drink. It's the airline's fault. Everything's on the plane. I've only got a few dollars in my pocket. How'm I gonna get back to the United States? Ohmigod, I'm stranded. I can't afford a ticket home! I'm no deadbeat. Look, I wouldn't pull something to come over here and spend one day in London. You gotta help me get home."

A sympathetic young woman listened to his pleas and told him she would do what she could for him. He waited in the lounge, pacing back and forth, chain-smoking as he watched her making several phone calls.

"There is one thing we can do," she said. "We can put you on stand-by for a return flight to the States. Once you get home, you'll have to pay for the return ticket."

"Of course!" he said. "I'm not trying to beat the ticket. I've got money at home. All I want to do is get back, and I'll pay it right away."

He kept babbling away at whoever would listen to him, and finally he could see that they were desperate to get him off their hands. It was what he counted on. They finally put him on a 747 back to the States.

"Thank God!" he whispered as he sank into the seat and fastened his safety belt. He didn't trust himself to go to sleep, so he kept awake reading every magazine on board. When he got back to Columbus, a security official drove him to Lancaster. Allen found money from paintings he'd sold just where he'd hidden it—behind a loose board in the broom closet—and paid for the return ticket.

"I want to thank you," he told his escort. "Pan Am has been very understanding. As soon as I get a chance, I'm going to write a letter to the president of your company and tell them what a wonderful job you're doing."

Alone in the apartment, Allen became very depressed. He tried to communicate with Arthur. It took a long time, but Arthur finally came out and looked around. When he saw he was no longer in London, he refused to have anything to do with anyone.

"You're all a bunch of worthless blighters," he grumbled.

And then he turned his back and sulked.

(2)

At the end of September, Allen was hired by the huge Anchor Hocking Glass Corporation, where Billy's sister Kathy had once worked. His job was to pack the glassware as the women took it off the moving belt. But sometimes he worked as a selector, examining the product just off the belt. It was a torturous job to stand there—ears deafened by the roar of the flame jets and air blowers—pick up the still-warm glasses, examine them for defects and stack them on open trays for the packers to remove. There was a great deal of switching between Tommy, Allen, Philip and Kevin.

With Arthur's approval, Allen had rented a three-bedroom duplex apartment in Somerford Square in the northeast section of Lancaster—1270K Sheridan Drive. Everyone liked the place. Allen liked the gray, weathered fence that hid the apartments from view of the parking area and the highway. Tommy had a room of his own for his electronic equipment, and there was a separate room for a studio. Ragen had a walk-in closet that he could lock in one of the bedrooms upstairs, where he kept all his guns except the 9-millimeter automatic. He kept that on top of the refrigerator, back where none of the children would see or reach it.

Marlene came to the apartment every evening after her job at Hecks department store. When he worked the second shift, she would wait for him to get home around midnight, and she would stay most of the night. Before morning, she would always go back to her parents' home.

Marlene was finding Billy moodier and more unpredictable than ever before. At times he would storm around the apartment, smashing things. He would stare at the walls in a trance, or he would go to the easel and paint in a fury. Always, he was a soft-spoken, considerate lover.

Tommy didn't tell her that he was getting shaky. He was missing work. And he was missing time. Things seemed to be happening closer and closer together; they were moving into another bad mix-up time. Arthur should have been in control, but for some reason he was losing domination. No one was minding the store.

Arthur blamed the confusion on Marlene and insisted that the relationship be broken off. Tommy felt his heart jump. He wanted to protest, but he was too afraid of Arthur to tell him that he had fallen in love with Marlene. He knew he had shaved the rules close enough several times to be in danger of being classified as undesirable. Then he heard Adalana's voice.

"That's not fair," she said.

"I am always fair," Arthur said.

"It's not right for you to make rules and break all bonds and ties of love and affection between us and the people outside."

She's right, Tommy thought, but he kept silent.

"Marlene is suppressing the talents and skills of all of us," Arthur said. "She makes accusations, takes up time with foolish quarrels and interferes with the expansion of our minds."

"I don't think it's right to send her away," she insisted. "She's a caring person."

"For God's sake!" Arthur said. "Tommy and Allen still work in a bloody *factory*. I had expected them to be there a few months at the most, using that as a base from which to find a decent strategic or technical job that would utilize and expand their skills. No one is expanding their minds anymore."

"What's more important—expanding your mind or showing your feelings? Maybe that's the wrong question, because you don't *have* feelings. Oh, maybe it's possible to become a very productive and outstanding person by suppressing your emotions and living only with logic, but you'll be so lonely you're not going to be worth anything to anybody."

"Marlene goes," Arthur said, deciding he had demeaned himself long enough in arguing with Adalana. "I don't care who handles it, but this relationship must be terminated."

Marlene later described the events of that evening before their first breakup. They'd been arguing. He was acting weird and she thought he was on drugs. He was lying on the floor, really mad at her about something—she had no idea what it was. He had his gun in his hand, turning it on his finger, pointing it at his head.

He never pointed the gun at her and she wasn't frightened for herself, only for him. She saw him staring at a fish-cord lamp he had brought home one evening; then he jumped up, fired at the lamp, and it exploded. There was a hole in the wall.

He put the gun down on the bar, and when he turned away, she grabbed it, running out of the apartment. She got down the stairs and into the car before he caught up to her. Just as she pulled away from the curb, he jumped on the hood and glared at her through the windshield with a look of rage in his face. He had what looked like a screwdriver in his hand, and he was banging it on the glass. She stopped the car, got out and gave him the gun back. He took it and went back inside without a word.

She drove home, assuming it was over between them.

Later that evening, Allen went to Grilli's and ordered a hot "Stromboli hero" sandwich—Italian sausage, provolone cheese and extra tomato sauce—to go. He watched the counter man wrap it, steaming hot, in aluminum foil and put it into a white paper bag.

Back at the apartment, he set the paper bag on the counter and went to the bedroom to change his clothes. He felt like painting tonight. He kicked his shoes off and walked into the closet, bending over to find his slippers. As he stood up, he banged his head on the shelf and slumped down, angry and dazed. The closet door had swung shut behind him. He tried to push the door open, but it was stuck. "Oh, Christ!" he muttered as he jumped up and hit his head again . . .

Ragen opened his eyes to find himself holding his head and sitting on the floor amid a pile of shoes. He rose, kicked the door open and looked around. He was annoyed. These mix-up times were becoming more upsetting and confusing every day. At least he had gotten rid of that woman.

He wandered through the apartment, trying to sort things out. If he could only reach Arthur, perhaps he could find out what was going on. Well, what he did need was a drink. He walked into the kitchen and noticed the white paper bag on the counter. He didn't remember seeing it there before. He glared at the bag suspiciously and pulled out a bottle of vodka from under the bar. While he was pouring it over ice, he heard an odd noise coming from the bag. He backed away and stared as it moved gently, leaning to one side.

When the bag moved again, he let out his breath slowly and backed up. He remembered a defanged cobra he had once left in a paper bag in front of a slumlord's door as a warning. Perhaps this one was not defanged. He put his hand up to the top of the refrigerator behind him and felt for his gun. He pulled it down quickly, took aim and fired.

The paper bag flew off the counter against the wall. He ducked behind the bar and peered over it cautiously, keeping the gun trained on the bag. It lay on the floor. Very carefully, he walked around the bar and used the barrel of the gun to rip open the top of the bag. There he saw the bloody mess, jumped back and fired a second time, yelling, "I shoot you again, you bastard!"

He kicked it a few times, but when it didn't move, he opened it and stared inside in disbelief at the tomato-sauce-and-cheese sandwich with a big hole in it.

Then he laughed. He realized that the heat of the Stromboli in the aluminum foil had made it move. Feeling silly at wasting two rounds of ammunition on a sandwich, he put the bag on the kitchen counter, returned the gun to the top of the refrigerator and drank his vodka. He poured another, took it with him into the living room and turned on the television set. It was news time, and he thought he might find out what day it was. Before the news was over, he fell asleep . . .

Allen woke up, wondering how he had gotten out of the closet. He felt his head. Just a slight bump. Well, what the hell, he might as well paint that portrait of Billy's sister, Kathy, that he'd been planning. He started into the studio, then realized he'd forgotten to eat.

Back at the bar, he poured himself a Coke and looked for his sandwich. He was sure he'd left it on the bar. Then he saw it on the counter. The damned bag looked crumpled. What the hell? The sandwich was all messy, with the aluminum foil shredded and torn and tomato sauce all over the place. What kind of Stromboli sandwich was that?

He picked up the phone, dialed Grilli's and, when he got the manager, blasted him. "I buy a sandwich and this thing is all mangled. Looks like it's been put through a blender."

"I'm sorry, sir. If you'll bring it back, we'll make you another one."

"No thanks. I just wanted you to know you've lost a customer."

He slammed down the phone and stomped into the kitchen to fry himself some eggs. He sure as hell wasn't going to give Grilli's any more of his business.

Two weeks later, Tommy took advantage of the mix-up time and called Marlene. There were some things of hers in the apartment, he told her. She ought to come over and get them. She came by after work and they sat and talked through the evening. She started dropping in regularly again.

Things were back to what they had been before, and Ragen blamed it all on Arthur's inability to control the family.

CHAPTER FIFTEEN

(1)

"Walter" woke up in the apartment late in the afternoon of December 8, restless to go hunting, longing for the thrill of the chase. He loved being out in the woods alone with a gun.

Walter didn't find himself out on the spot very often, and he knew he would be called upon only when his uncanny sense of direction—a special skill he'd acquired from hunting in the bush in his native Australia—was needed. The last time he'd been out was years ago when Billy and his brother, Jim, had been on a summer bivouac with the Civil Air Patrol. Because of Walter's tracking ability, he had been pressed into service as a spotter.

But he had not hunted for a very long time.

So this afternoon he took it upon himself to borrow Ragen's handgun from the top of the refrigerator. Though it was hardly a substitute for a rifle, it was better than nothing. He listened to the weather report; hearing that it was cold, he decided to bring a mackinaw and gloves. Unable to find his Aussie hat with the pinned-up brim, he settled for a ski mask. He packed a lunch and set off south on Route 664. He knew instinctively what direction to follow. South would lead him to wooded areas where he could hunt to his heart's content. He got off the highway and followed the signs to Hocking State Park, wondering what game he would find.

He drove into the forest, parked the car and began to walk. As he pressed deeper into the woods, the pine needles felt slippery beneath his feet. He breathed deeply. It was good to be out on the spot, moving through the silence of the wilderness.

He walked for nearly an hour. Besides an occasional scurry that told him squirrels were about, there was no sign of game. It was almost dusk. He was growing impatient when he saw a fat black crow on the branch of a spruce. He quickly aimed and fired. The bird fell. Suddenly he felt dizzy and left the spot . . .

"Barbarian," Arthur said coldly. "Killing animals is against the rules."

"Vy he take my gun?" Ragen demanded.

"You left it unsecured," Arthur said. "That was against the rules too."

"Not true. Ve have agreed one veapon should alvays be available, out of children's reach, in case of intruder. Valter did not have right to take it."

Arthur sighed. "I really liked the chap. Energetic, reliant young man. Good sense of direction. Always reading about Australia, and after all, it *is* part of the British Empire. He once suggested I investigate the evolution of the kangaroo. Now I'm afraid he's undesirable."

"Is severe penalty for one crow," Ragen said.

Arthur gave him a withering stare. "The time may come when you have to kill a human being in self-defense, but I will not tolerate taking the life of a poor dumb creature."

Arthur buried the crow and walked back to the car. Allen, who had heard the last part of the conversation, moved onto the spot behind the wheel and drove home.

"Killing a dumb crow and thinking he's a big-game hunter—what a stupid twerp!"

(2)

Driving back to Lancaster at night, Allen felt groggy. He put down the quart bottle of Pepsi he'd been sipping, and as his lights illuminated the roadside-rest sign, he decided he'd better pull off for a while. He parked near the men's room, shook his head and closed his eyes . . .

Danny looked up, wondering what he was doing behind the wheel. Remembering Arthur's instructions, he slid over to the passenger's side to wait for someone to come and drive. Then he realized he was at the bathroom stop he'd used lots of times. He noticed two other cars with people in them. One was a lady with a floppy hat. The other one had a man in it. They were just sitting there. Maybe they had changed their spots, too, and were waiting for someone to come to drive them home.

He really wished someone would come. He was tired and he had to go to the bathroom. When he got out of the car and walked to the men's room, he noticed the lady getting out of her car.

Danny stood at the low urinal for little boys, unzipped his fly and shivered in the cold December air. He heard the footsteps and the creak of the door hinge. The lady came in. That surprised him, and he blushed and turned away so she wouldn't see him peeing.

"Hey, sweetheart," the lady said, "are you gay?"

It wasn't a lady's voice. It was a man dressed like a lady, with a floppy hat and lipstick and a lot of make-up and a black dot on his chin. He looked like Mae West in the movies.

"Hey, big boy," the man-lady said, "let me suck your cock."

Danny shook his head and started to edge past, but another man came in too. "Hey," he said, "this one's good-looking. Let's have a party."

The man grabbed his collar and pulled him back against the wall. The one dressed like a woman held the front of his jacket and grabbed for his fly. Danny felt fear at the roughness and closed his eyes . . .

Ragen grabbed the hand, twisted it and slammed the man into the wall. As the man slumped, Ragen caught him in the chest with his knee and a karate chop to the side of the throat.

He turned, saw the woman and paused. He could never hit a woman. But when he heard her say, "Oh my God, you bastard," he knew it was a man in woman's clothing. He reached out, twisted him around and pressed him against the wall with his elbow, watching to see if the other one was going to get up.

"Down on floor with friend!" Ragen ordered, punching the tranvestite hard in the stomach. The man doubled over and dropped to the floor. Ragen took their wallets, but as he started to walk away with the identification cards, the transvestite jumped up and grabbed him by the belt. "Give that back, you bastard!"

Ragen spun around and caught him in the groin with his foot. When he went down, Ragen kicked him with his other foot, smashing his face. Blood burst from the man's nose and he gagged through broken teeth.

"You vill live," Ragen said calmly. "I am very careful vat bones I break."

He looked at the other man on the floor. Though he had not been hit in the face, blood was trickling from his mouth. As Ragen had calculated when he struck, the blow to the solar plexus had put pressure on the epiglottis and ruptured the blood vessels. He, too, would live. Ragen stripped the Seiko watch from the man's wrist.

Outside, Ragen noticed the two empty cars. He picked up a rock and smashed the headlights. They would not follow on the highway without lights.

Ragen drove home, let himself into the apartment, looked around to make sure it was safe and left the spot . . .

Allen opened his eyes, wondering if he should bother to use the john. He shook his head when he found himself home. He no longer had to piss. And his knuckles were bruised. And what was that stuff on his right shoe? He touched it and examined it.

"Jesus Christ!" he yelled. "Whose blood is it? Who the hell's been in a fight? I wanna know. I have the right to know what's going on."

"Ragen had to protect Danny," Arthur said.

"What happened?"

Arthur explained to all of them: "It's very important for the young ones to know that roadside-rest areas are dangerous places at night. It's a well-known fact that homosexuals frequent these places after dark. Ragen had to get Danny out of a dangerous situation that Allen let him get into."

"Well, Jesus, it wasn't my fault. I didn't *ask* to leave the spot, and I didn't make Danny come. Who the hell knows who's coming and who's going and what all they're doing during a mix-up time?"

"I should a been dere," Philip said. "I'd like to have taken on dem fags."

"You'd have gotten yourself killed," Allen said.

"Or else you'd have done something stupid," Arthur said, "like killing one of them. And then we'd face a bloody murder charge."

"Ahhh . . ."

"Besides, you are not allowed on the spot," Arthur said firmly.

"I know, but I'da still of liked tuh be dere."

"I am beginning to suspect you've been stealing time, taking advantage of mix-up periods to go about your antisocial business."

"Who, me? Nah."

"I know you've been out. You're a drug addict and you've been abusing your body and your mind."

"You callin' me a liar?"

"That is one of your attributes. You are a defective android, and I assure you that as far as it is in my power to prevent it, you will never hold the consciousness again."

Philip slipped back into the darkness, wondering what an android was. He wasn't going to ask Arthur to explain. He wasn't going to give that goddamned limey the satisfaction of getting on his case again. He'd get out whenever he had the chance. He knew that ever since Zanesville, Arthur's domination had weakened. As long as there was pot or speed or even LSD, he was going to sneak out and keep hard-ass Arthur off balance.

The following week, while Philip was on the spot, he told Wayne Luft, one of his dope customers, what had happened at the Lancaster roadside rest.

"Shit," Luft said. "Didn't you know them roadside rests is infested with queers?"

"Sure as hell surprised me," Philip said. "Fuckin' faggots trollin' their bait. I hate 'em."

"No worsen I do."

"Why don't we get us some?" Philip said.

"How's that?"

"We know they're always parkin' around duh roadside rests at night. We go in and let 'em have it. We could clean out dese infected areas."

"We could rob 'em, too," Luft said. "Get us some Christmas money for our time and get rid of all the homos. Make the place safe for decent people."

"Yeah," Philip laughed. "Like us."

Luft got out his highway map and made marks on the roadside-rest areas in Fairfield and Hocking counties.

"We'll use my car," Philip said. "It's fast."

Philip took along a decorative sword he found in the apartment.

At the roadside-rest area near Rockbridge in Hocking County, they noticed a single Volkswagen Beetle with two occupants, parked in front of the men's room. Philip pulled the Grand Prix around to the other side of the highway, facing in the opposite direction. He took two Preludins that Luft handed him. Then they sat for half an hour, watching the VW. No one came or went.

Luft said, "That must be a couple of 'em. Who else would just stay parked so long at two in the morning in front of the men's room?"

"I'll go in foist," Philip said. "Wit my sword. If they folla me inside, you come up behind 'em wit the piece."

Philip felt good as he walked across the highway, the sword under his coat, to the men's room. Just as he expected, the two men followed him.

As they approached, he felt his skin crawling. He wasn't sure if it was them or the speed that was doing it, but he whipped out his sword and grabbed the queen. The guy with him was a fat slob. When Luft came up and shoved the gun in the guy's back, the faggot stood there stunned and shaking like a mountain of jelly.

"All right, fuckin' faggots!" Luft shouted. "Lay down on the fuckin' floor."

Philip stripped the fat one of his wallet, a ring and a watch. Luft did the same to the other one.

Then Philip ordered them into the car.

"Where are you taking us?" the fat one asked, sobbing.

"Fer a little stroll in the woods."

They drove off the highway onto a deserted country road, where they dropped the two men.

"That was easy," Luft said.

"Nothin' to it," Philip said. "It's duh poifect crime."

"How much we got?"

"A lot. Dey was loaded. And credit cards, too."

"Shit, man," Luft said. "I'm gonna give up my job and do this for a living."

"Public soivice," Philip said, grinning.

Back at the apartment, Philip told Kevin about the perfect crime. He knew he was going to crash. He took a couple of downers to help him land softly . . .

(3)

Tommy put up a Christmas tree, strung the lights and put out the presents he'd made for Marlene and the family. He looked forward to going over to Spring Street later to see Mom, Del, Kathy and her boyfriend Rob.

The early evening at Spring Street went well until Rob and Kathy came into the living room and Kevin found himself on the spot.

"Hey, that's a good-looking leather jacket," Rob said. "And I noticed you're wearing a new Seiko."

Kevin held the watch up. "Best there is."

"I've been wondering about that, Billy," Kathy said. "You haven't been making that much at Anchor Hocking. Where are you getting the money?"

Kevin smiled. "I've discovered the perfect crime."

Kathy looked up at him quickly. She felt there was something different again, that sneering, cold-blooded attitude. "What are you talking about?"

"I ripped off some fags at a roadside rest. No way they could ever find out who did it. Didn't leave any fingerprints or anything. And those guys won't even dare complain to the cops. Got money and credit cards." He held up the watch.

She couldn't believe what she was hearing. It wasn't like Billy to talk that way. "You're joking, aren't you?"

He smiled and shrugged. "Maybe I am and maybe I'm not."

When Del and Dorothy came in, Kathy excused herself and went out to the hall closet. Finding nothing in his new leather jacket, she went out to the car. Sure enough, there was a wallet in the glove compartment. There were also credit cards, a driver's license and the identification of a male nurse. So he hadn't been joking after all. She sat in the car for a while, wondering what to do. She put the wallet into her purse and decided she had to talk to someone.

After Billy left, she showed her mother and Del what she had found.

"God Almighty," Dorothy said. "I can't believe it."

Del looked at the wallet. "Why not? I believe it. Now we know how he's been buying all this stuff."

"You've got to call Jim," Kathy said. "He's got to come home and see what he can do to straighten Billy out. I have some money in the bank. I'll pay his plane fare."

Dorothy made the long-distance call and begged Jim to take an emergency leave to come home. "Your brother's in trouble.

He's into something very bad, and if he can't get it straight, I think we'll have to go to the police."

Jim applied for emergency leave from the Air Force and came home two days before Christmas. Del and Dorothy showed him the wallet and the clippings from the *Lancaster Eagle-Gazette* about the roadside-rest robberies.

"You got to see what you can do with him," Del said to Jim. "God knows, I've tried to be like a father to him. I thought for a time after Zanesville that Billy could take the place of my own boy—rest his soul—but Billy won't let no one tell him nothing."

Jim looked through the wallet, went to the phone and dailed the number on the I.D. card. He had to check it out for himself.

"You don't know me," he said when a man answered, "but I've got something that may be of importance to you. Let me ask you a hypothetical question. If someone was to know you were a male nurse by way of your identification card, what would you say to that?"

After a moment, the voice answered, "I'd say the person who knows that has my wallet."

Okay," Jim said, "and can you tell me what your wallet looks like and what else is in it?"

The man described the wallet and its contents.

"How'd you come to lose it?"

"I was in a roadside-rest area between Athens and Lancaster with a friend of mine. Two guys came into the men's room. One of them had a pistol, the other one had a sword. They took our wallets, watches and rings, then they drove us out into the woods and left us."

"What kind of car was it?"

"The guy who had the sword was driving a blue Pontiac Grand Prix." He gave Jim the license-plate number.

"How are you so sure about the car and the number?"

"I saw that car again in a store downtown the other day. I stood not fifty feet away from the guy who carried the sword, and I followed him to the car. He was the same one."

"Why didn't you turn him in?"

"Because I'm in a position to get an important new job, and I'm a homosexual. If I report this incident, I expose not only myself but several of my friends."

"Okay," Jim said, "on the premise that you don't want to report this incident and expose yourself and your friends, I'll see that you get back your wallet and personal effects. Let's just keep it anonymous. You'll get it in the mail."

When he got off the phone, he leaned back and took a deep breath. He looked at his mother and Del and Dathy. "Billy's in trouble," he said, and picked up the phone again.

"Who are you calling now?" Kathy asked.

"I'm going to tell Billy I'd like to come over tomorrow and see his new place."

Kathy said, "I'm going with you."

The following evening, Christmas Eve, Tommy greeted Kathy and Jim at the door in his bare feet. Behind him, in the corner, stood the brightly lit Christmas tree surrounded by presents. On the wall hung a plaque with decorative crossed swords.

While Jim and Tommy talked, Kathy excused herself and went upstairs. She was going to see if she could find further evidence of what he'd been doing.

"Hey, just one question," Jim said when they were alone. "Where are you getting all the bread for this stuff—this duplex apartment, all those presents, clothes, that watch?"

"My girl's working," Tommy said.

"Marlene's paying for all this stuff?"

"Well, a lot of it's on credit, too."

"Those credit cards'll get you if you don't watch out. I hope you're not getting in too deep."

Jim, who had just completed an Air Force course in interrogation techniques, decided to put his skill to use now to help his brother. If he could get him to talk about it, admit he was wrong, maybe there would still be a way to keep him from going to prison.

"Carrying credit cards around is dangerous," Jim said. "People steal 'em and bust 'em, and you're stuck with paying—"

"Aw, there's a fifty-dollar liability. After that, it's the company gets stuck. They can afford it."

"Like I've been reading in the papers," Jim said, "about these people who got held up in the roadside-rest areas, had their credit cards stolen. I mean, you know, it could happen to you."

Jim saw the strange look in Billy's eyes, a clouding over, tracelike. It reminded him of the way Chalmer Milligan would look before he went into one of his violent fits of rage.

"Hey, you all right?"

Kevin looked up at him and wondered what Jim was doing here, how long he had been in the apartment. He glanced quickly at his new watch. Nine forty-five. "What?" asked Kevin.

"I said, 'Are you all right?'"

"Sure. Why shouldn't I be?"

"I was telling you to be careful with credit cards. You know, all these holdups at roadside-rest areas and stuff."

"Yeah, I read about it."

"I've heard that some of those guys who were robbed were homosexuals."

"Yeah. They deserved it."

"What do you mean?"

"Why should them faggots have all that money and stuff?"

"But whoever did it has got to be careful. There's a long prison sentence attached to that kind of thing."

Kevin shrugged. "They'd have to find the guys. They'd have to prove it."

"Well, for example, you've got a sword on your wall just like the one the guys described."

"They can't tie that sword in with the one that was there."

"Maybe so, but there was also a gun used in the robbery."

"Hey, I didn't hold no piece. They can't get me."

"Yeah, but they'll nail the other guy, and then whoever was in on it with him will take the fall just as well."

"They can't connect me with it," Kevin insisted. "It's not the kind of thing the fags are gonna press charges about. There aren't any fingerprints or anything like that."

Kathy came down and sat with them a few minutes. When Billy went upstairs to the bathroom, she handed Jim what she had found.

"Jesus Christ," Jim muttered. "All these credit cards with different names on them. How the hell are we going to get him out of this one?"

"We've got to help him, Jim. That isn't like Billy."

"I know. Maybe the only thing is to confront him directly."

When Kevin came back downstairs, Jim showed him the credit cards. "This is what I meant, Billy. You did those robberies, and you've got the evidence right here in your own apartment."

Kevin became furious and shouted, "You had no right to come into my house and go through my stuff!"

Kathy said, "Billy, we're trying to help you."

"This is my property, and you two came in here and searched it without a warant."

"I'm your brother. Kathy's your sister. We're just trying to—"

"Evidence obtained without a search warrant wouldn't be admitted in court."

Jim told Kathy to wait for him in the car in case it came to blows. When Jim confronted him again, Kevin began to walk into the kitchen. "Billy, you're buying all this stuff on the credit cards. They'd get you on that."

"They'll never know," Kevin insisted. "I go buy one or two things and then I throw the card away. I only hold up queers and people who hurt other people."

"It's a crime, Billy."

"That's my affair."

"But you're getting yourself into trouble."

"Look, you got no right coming out here from Spokane and getting on my case about what I'm doing. I'm my own person. I'm old enough. I'm outta the house. What I do is my own business. Besides, you left the family a long time ago."

"True, but we care about you."

"I didn't ask you to come over here. I want you to get the hell out of here right now."

"Billy, I'm not leaving until we've had this out."

Kevin grabbed his leather coat. "Well, fuck you. Then I'll leave."

Jim, who had always been stronger than his younger brother and had been trained in the martial arts in the Air Force, stepped between Kevin and the door. He grappled with him and threw him backward. Jim hadn't intended to be so hard or violent, but Kevin crashed into the Christmas tree, knocking it against the wall and onto the presents. Boxes were crushed. Bulbs shattered. The wire was yanked out of the outlet and the lights went out.

Kevin got up and started for the door again. He was no fighter, and he had no intention of battling Jim, but he had to get out of there. Jim grabbed him by the shirt, throwing him against the bar.

Kevin lost the spot . . .

As Ragen hit the bar, he saw very quickly sho was attacking him, though he had no idea why. He had never liked Jim. He had never forgiven him for leaving home, for leaving the women and Billy to face Chalmer alone. Seeing that Jim was blocking the doorway, Ragen reached back, picked up a knife from the top of the bar and threw it with such force that it stuck in the wall beside Jim's head.

Jim froze. He had never seen such cold hate in Billy's face or seen him respond with such swift violence. He looked at the knife, still quivering in the wall inches from his head, and realized that his brother hated him enough to kill him. He stepped aside as Ragen walked silently past him, barefoot, out into the snow . . .

Danny found himself outside, wondering what he was doing walking on the freezing street in a torn shirt and without his shoes or gloves. He turned around and went back into the house, shocked to see Jim in the doorway staring at him as if he were crazy.

Danny looked past him and saw the toppled Christmas tree and the broken presents. He felt a sudden fear.

"I didn't mean to knock your tree over," Jim said, startled by another incredible change in his brother's face. The cold rage had vanished, and now Billy was cowed, trembling.

"You broke my Christmas tree," Danny sobbed.

"I'm sorry."

"I hope you have a very merry Christmas," Danny whined, "'cause you spoiled mine."

Kathy, who had been waiting in the car, came rushing in, her face pale. "The police are coming."

Seconds later there was a knock at the door. Kathy looked at Jim and then at Billy, who was crying like a little boy.

"What are we gonna do?" she said. "What if they—"

"I'd better let them in," Jim said. He opened the door and admitted two officers.

"We got a report about a disturbance," one of them said, looking past him into the living room.

"Your neighbors called in a complaint." said the other.

"I'm sorry, Officer."

"It's Christmas Eve," the first one said. "People are with their kids. What's going on?"

"Just a family quarrel," Jim said. "It's over. We didn't know we were so loud."

The officer made a notation in his memo book. "Well, cool it, folks. Just keep it down."

After they were gone, Jim got his coat. "All right then, Billy. I guess I'll have to say good-by. I'm only in Lancaster for another couple of days, then I've got to go back to the base."

As Jim and Kathy left, their brother was still crying.

The door slammed shut and Tommy looked around, startled. His hand was bleeding. He picked the pieces of glass out of his palm and washed the cuts, wondering where Kathy and Jim had gone and why the place was such a mess. He had worked so hard on that Christmas tree, and look at it now. All the presents he and the others had made with their own hands—not a single one bought. He had a painting upstairs for Jim—a seascape he knew Jim would love—and he'd wanted to give it to him.

He picked up the fallen tree and tried to made it look decent again, but most of the ornaments were busted. It had been such a beautiful Christmas tree. He just had time to arrange Marlene's present before she arrived. He had taken it on his own to call her to come over for Christmas Eve.

Marlene was shocked at the mess in the apartment. "What happened?"

"I don't really know," Tommy said, "and to tell you the truth, I don't give a damn. I just know I love you."

She kissed him and led him to the bedroom. She knew that at times like this, when everything was confused in his mind, he was most vulnerable and he needed her.

Tommy blushed and closed his eyes. He did wonder, as he followed her, how come he never kept the spot long enough to make it through the bedroom door.

On Christmas Day, Allen, who had no idea what had happened the night before, gave up trying to make sense of the mess in the living room. He asked around inside his head, but no one answered. God, how he hated these mix-up times. He salvaged what presents he could, rewrapping the torn packages, and loaded them, along with the painting Tommy had done for Jim, into the car.

When he got to Spring Street, he began to piece together quickly what had happened the previous night. Jim was sore as hell about him throwing a knife, and Kathy, Del and Mom jumped on him about some robberies.

"You did those roadside-rest robberies," Del shouted, "and used a car registered in your mother's name."

"I don't know what you're talking about," Allen shouted back. Throwing up his hands in disgust, he stomped upstairs.

While he was gone, Del went through his jacket pockets and found the keys to the car. He, Kathy, Jim and Dorothy went outside to check through the trunk of the car. They found credit cards, driver's licenses and a highway map. The roadside-rest areas along Route 33 were marked with X's.

When they turned, they saw him at the door watching them.

"You did it," Del said, waving the evidence in his face.

"Nothing to worry about," Kevin said. "I won't get caught. It's the perfect crime. I didn't leave any fingerprints or anything, and the fags won't report it."

"You goddamned fool," Del screamed. "Jim called the guy whose wallet you stole. He saw you in town. You dragged this whole family into your goddamned 'perfect crime.'"

They saw his face change; panic replaced coolness.

They decided to help Billy by getting rid of the evidence. Jim would take the Grand Prix back with him to Spokane and keep up the payments on it. Billy was going to move out of Somerford Square to a smaller apartment on Maywood Avenue.

Through it all, Danny listened, wondering what in the world they were talking about and when everyone was going to open the presents.

CHAPTER SIXTEEN

(1)

On Wednesday, January 8, as Tommy was meeting Marlene for lunch at the Memorial Plaza Shopping Center, he saw a delivery van pull up to the Gray Drug Store. While they watched the delivery man walk into the store with a large box, Tommy muttered, "Narcotics delivery. The pharmacist'll be working late tonight."

Marlene looked at him curiously. He didn't know why he had said that.

Kevin had been planning to rob the store. He'd gotten together with Wayne Luft and another friend, Roy Bailey, and laid it out for them. They would execute the robbery and get the lion's share of the money and drugs. For the planning, he would get 20 percent.

That night, following Kevin's instructions, the two men waited until one-thirty in the morning, forced the pharmacist back into the store at gunpoint, then robbed the safe and the narcotics cabinet.

Still following the plan, they drove out into the woods, spray-painted the white Dodge station wagon black and drove out to pick Kevin up. Back at Bailey's place, Kevin checked out the drugs for them: Ritalin, Preludin, Demerol, Seconal, Quäälude, Delaudid and more.

He estimated the drugs would bring in thirty to thirty-five thousand on the street, and he saw their faces change from curiosity to greed. As the night wore on, they all got high, and each of the men secretly approached Kevin, suggesting the two of them team up to rip off the third partner. By morning, when both Bailey and Luft were out cold, Kevin stuffed the money and the drugs into two suitcases and took off for Columbus on his own. Neither one, he knew, would have the guts to stand up to him. They were afraid of him. Time and again they had talked about how crazy he was, how he had put his fist through a door and used a Thompson machine gun to shoot up a guy's car.

They'd tip off the police. He expected that. But once he got rid of the dope, there was nothing they could do. The pharmacist had seen their faces, not his. There was nothing to tie him in with the robbery.

When Marlene picked up the *Lancaster Eagle-Gazette* the next day and read of the Gray Drug Store robbery, she had a sinking feeling.

A few days later, Tommy came to meet her for lunch. She was surprised to see that he had painted the old Dodge black—and so sloppily.

"You did it, didn't you?" she whispered.

"What, painted the car?" Tommy asked innocently.

"You did the Gray Drug Store robbery."

"Oh, for crying out loud! Now you're calling me a criminal? Marlene, I don't know a thing about it. I swear!"

She was confused. Something told her he was guilty, but he seemed truly upset at being accused. Unless he was the world's greatest actor, his denial had to be real.

"I just hope to God you're not involved in it," she said.

After they parted, Allen grew nervous about Marlene's accusations. He had a feeling something was wrong. Driving back to work, he decided he needed help.

"Come on, guys," he said out loud. "We're in trouble."

"That's all right, Allen," said Arthur. "Keep driving."

"Don't you want to take over?"

"I'd rather not drive. I'm never steady on American roads. Just keep going."

"Do you have any idea what's going on?" Allen asked.

"I've been so preoccupied with my research during this mix-up time that I don't really know, but I suspect some of the undesirables have been stealing time and committing crimes."

"I tried to tell you."

"I really do feel we need Ragen," Arthur said. "Can you find him?"

"I've tried. Jesus, he's never around when you need him."

"Let me try. Just keep your attention focused on your driving."

Arthur searched his mind, peering inward into the darkness beyond the spot. He saw images of the others, some asleep in their beds, some sitting in the shadows. The undesirables refused to look at him—having banished them from the spot, he no longer had any hold over them. Finally he found Ragen—playing with Christene.

"You're needed, Ragen. I believe someone has committed a crime or crimes, and we may now be in danger."

"Is not my problem," Ragen said. "I did not commit these crimes."

"I'm sure that's true, but may I remind you that if one of our people is sent to prison, the children will go too. Imagine Christene in that environment, a pretty little girl locked up with all those sex maniacs and perverts."

"All right," Ragen said. "You know my veakness."

"We've got to figure out exactly what's going on."

Arthur began a general inquiry. One after the other, he questioned the various people inside, and—though he was sure some of the undesirables were lying—he began to piece together a picture. Tommy told him of Marlene's suspicions that he had been involved in the Gray Drug Store robbery, and also told of having observed a shipment of drugs earlier.

Walter denied having touched Ragen's guns since his own banishment from the spot for shooting a crow, but he recalled having heard a voice with a Brooklyn accent talking about a perfect crime at a roadside rest. Philip finally admitted the roadside-rest assaults, but denied any involvement with the Gray Drug Store robbery.

Kevin then told of having planned it.

"But I wasn't there. I just set it up and then ripped them two guys off. It was a sting, that's all. Maybe those guys tipped off the police, but I'm clean. There's no way the cops can tie me to that robbery."

Arthur reported back to Allen and Ragen: "Now, both of you, think: Is there anything to which they can connect us, anything they can arrest us for?"

As far as they all knew, there was nothing.

Several days later, Billy Milligan was fingered by a fence in Columbus who owed a detective on the narcotics squad a favor. The fence reported that a quantity of drugs matching the description of those stolen from the Gray Drug Store had been sold to him by Milligan. The word was passed on to the Lancaster police department. A warrant was issued for Billy's arrest.

(2)

When Marlene came to the apartment on Monday after work, Tommy gave her an engagement ring.

"I want you to have this, Marveen," Tommy said, calling her by his pet name for her. "And if anything happens to me, I want you to know I'll always love you."

She stared in disbelief as he put it on her finger. It was a moment she had dreamed of for a long time, but now it was painful. Had he gone out and bought it because he expected something to happen to him? She felt the tears in her eyes but tried not to show her feelings. No matter what he had done, no matter what they did to him, she would stand by him.

In her calendar for January 20, 1975, she wrote: "Got engaged. Really surprised me to death."

They arrested Danny the following day.

They pushed him into the cruiser and took him down to the Fairfield County Jail. They read him his rights and began questioning him. He had no idea what they were talking about.

The questioning went on for hours. From what the detectives said, Danny began to piece together a picture. Wayne Luft had been picked up for drunken driving, and while being questioned, he had said that Milligan and Roy Bailey had robbed the drugstore.

Danny looked up at them, dazed. They wanted him to give a voluntary statement. As they asked him questions, he heard Allen's voice in his head, telling him exactly what to answer. When the interrogation was over, Danny was asked to sign his statement. Laboriously, his tongue between his teeth, Danny pressed hard with the pencil as he signed the name "William Stanley Milligan."

"Now can I go home?" he asked.

"If you can post ten thousand dollars' bail."

Danny shook his head, still very confused about all this, and they led him back to his cell.

Later that day, Marlene got a bondsman to post bail. Tommy went back to stay with Dorothy and Del, who got in touch with

George Kellner, the lawyer who had represented him on the rape case in Pickaway County two years earlier.

While awaiting trial, Arthur learned of other charges being brought against Milligan. Two victims had identified him as one of the assailants who had robbed them at a roadside-rest area. On January 27, 1975, the state highway patrol filed additional charges of aggravated robbery of motorists in the roadside-rest areas of Fairfield and Hocking counties.

Milligan was taken back to the Fairfield County Jail, two years to the day since he'd been sent to the Zanesville Youth Camp.

(3)

Allen wanted to take the stand in his own defense. Arthur wanted to try the case himself and prove that he was nowhere near Gray Drug Store the night of the robbery.

"What about the roadside-rest assaults?" Allen asked.

"Ragen did it. But that was self-defense."

"They say there were others. Just out-and-out robberies."

"Not true," Ragen insisted. "I not rob other victims at roadside-rest areas."

"Well, someone did," Allen said.

"Can they prove it?" Ragen asked.

"How the hell do I know?" Allen said. "I didn't see it."

"Vat ve do?" Ragen asked.

"It's a bloody mess," Arthur said. "Can we trust this attorney? He didn't keep us from being sent to Zanesville by the Ohio Youth Commission two years ago."

"This time he says we can plea-bargain," Allen said. "The way I understand it, if I plead guilty to the Gray drug robbery, they'll give me shock probation and we probably won't have to do any time in the slammer."

"Vat is this 'shock' probation?"

"That's when they lock you up without letting you know how long you're gonna be there, and then they shock you by letting you out unexpectedly so you'll be grateful and stay out of trouble."

"Well, if that's the case," Arthur said, "let's follow the barrister's advice. That's what we're paying him for."

"All right," Allen said. "So that's it. We plead guilty in exchange for getting off on probation."

* * *

On March 27, 1975, William Stanley Milligan pleaded guilty to, and was convicted of, robbery and aggravated robbery. Two months later, Allen learned the court gave him shock probation only for the roadside-rest assaults, but not for the lesser charge. He would have to serve a two- to five-year sentence for the Gray Drug Store robbery. They were all stunned.

On June 9, after forty-five days in Mansfield Reformatory, Allen was put on a blue Ohio State Reformatory bus with fifty-nine other inmates handcuffed in pairs to be transported to the Lebanon Correctional Institution.

He tried to avoid the eyes of the armed guard sitting in the cage at the front of the bus. How would he survive for two years? The fear expanded inside him as the bus pulled up to the prison and he saw the barbed-wire fence and the watch-towers around the walls of Lebanon. The prisoners were taken off the bus and marched into the receiving entrance.

The first of the two remote-controlled doors hissed open, then closed behind him. It reminded Allen of Chalmer's hiss, and the fear in his stomach exploded. He never got to the second door . . .

Ragen heard a hiss as the second door opened. He nodded and shuffled along to the cell block in the line of handcuffed prisoners. Now Arthur no longer had dominance. Here, Ragen knew, he would finally rule. He and only he would decide who came on and off the spot for the next two to five years. Ragen Vadascovinich heard a loud clang as the iron door closed behind them.

CHAPTER
SEVENTEEN

(1)

Ragen found Lebanon an improvement over Mansfield Reformatory. It was newer, cleaner, brighter. At the first day's orientation session, he listened to the lectures on rules and regulations, the descriptions of the prison schools and jobs.

A big man with heavy jowls and a football player's neck got up and, arms crossed, rocked back and forth.

"All right," he said. "Ah'm Cap'n Leach. So you guys think you're hot shit? Well, now you're mine! You done fucked up on the street, but you mess up down here, Ah'm gonna bust your heads. The hell with civil rights, human rights, everything else rights. Down here you all nothing but a piece of meat. You get outta line, Ah'm gonna grind you . . ."

He hammered away at them for fifteen minutes. Ragen decided the man was trying to whip them into line with words, just blowing hot air.

Then Ragen noticed that the psychologist, a thin, sandy-haired man with glasses, took the same tack. "You men are nothing now. Just numbers. You have no identity. No one cares who you are or that you're here. You're nothing but criminals and convicts."

As the little man insulted them, several of the new prisoners became upset and started shouting back.

"Who the hell are you to tell us that?"

"What kind of shit is that, man?"

"I ain't no number!"

"You fucking crazy, man!"

"Blow it out your asshole, shrink!"

Ragen observed the inmates' reactions to the verbal assaults. He suspected the psychologist was intentionally provoking them.

"See?" the psychologist said, jabbing his forefinger at them. "Look what's happening. You can't fit into society because when you're put into a pressure situation, you don't know how to control it. You counteract a verbal statement with raw hostility and violence. Maybe you can see now why society wants to lock you away in a cage until you learn to adjust."

The men, realizing he'd been teaching them a lesson, sat back and grinned at each other sheepishly.

In the main corridor, some of the veteran inmates watched and jeered as the new men walked out of the orientation room.

"Hey, lookit. New meat!"

"Hey, bitches, see ya later."

"That one's a good-looker. She's mine."

"Hell, I saw her first, she's my punk."

Ragen knew they were pointing to him, and he stared back coldly.

In his cell that night, he discussed things with Arthur.

"You're in charge here," Arthur said, "but I'd like to point out that a great deal of that teasing and joking is merely prisoners' letting off steam in a pressure-cooker situation. Anything to get a bit of laughter. You would do well to discriminate between the prison comedians and those who might really be dangerous."

Ragen nodded. "Is exactly vat I am thinking."

"I have another suggestion."

Ragen listened with a half smile. It amused him to hear Arthur making suggestions instead of issuing orders.

"I noticed that those inmates wearing green hospital uniforms are the only ones—except for the guards—allowed to walk in the center of the corridors. When the time comes to apply for a work detail, it might be advisable to have Allen request assignment to the prison hospital."

"For vat reason?"

"Working as a medic could provide a margin of safety—especially for the children. You see, in a prison community a medical attendant is respected, since every inmate knows that someday he might need emergency treatment. I would do the work, using Allen to communicate."

Ragen agreed it was a good idea.

The next day, when the guards talked to the new prisoners about work experience and previous specialization, Allen said he thought he would like to work in the prison hospital.

"Y'all got training?" asked Captain Leach.

Allen answered as Arthur had coached him: "When I was in the Navy, there was a pharmacists' school at Great Lakes Naval Base. I worked in the hospital there."

It wasn't exactly a lie. Arthur had studied those things on his own. He hadn't exactly said he'd been trained as a medic.

The following week the call came down from the prison hospital that Dr. Harris Steinberg, the medical director, wanted to see Milligan. Walking the wide halls, Allen noticed that Lebanon was laid out in the form of a giant nine-legged crab. The central corridor was lined with offices, but at various intervals the cell-block corridor branched off in all directions. At the hospital Allen waited in the outer room separated by unbreakable glass partitions, watching Dr. Steinberg, an elderly white-haired man with a kind, ruddy face and a gentle smile. Allen noticed there were paintings on the walls.

Finally Dr. Steinberg waved him into his office. "I understand you have lab experience."

"All my life I've wanted to be a doctor," Allen said. "I thought with a big prison population like this, you might be able to use someone who could do blood counts and urine tests."

"Ever do that before?"

Allen nodded. "Of course, it was a long time ago and I probably forgot a great deal, but I can learn. I'm fast. And like I say, working in this field is my great ambition when I get out of here. I've got medical books at home I've studied on my own. I'm particularly interested in hematology, and if you'd just give me a chance, I'd appreciate it."

He could tell Steinberg wasn't really taken in by his fast-talking, so he searched for other ways to impress the doctor. "Those paintings are fascinating," Allen said, quickly glancing at the wall. "I prefer oils to acrylics, but whoever did those has a good eye for detail."

He saw Steinberg's expression change to one of interest. "You paint?"

"All my life. Medicine is the career I've chosen, but ever since I was a kid, people said I had a natural talent. Maybe someday you'll let me paint your portrait. You've got a strong face."

"I collect art," Steinberg said. "And I paint a little myself."

"I've always felt art and medicine complemented each other."

"Ever sell any of your paintings?"

"Oh, quite a few. Landscapes, still lifes, portraits. I hope I'll get a chance to paint while I'm here."

Steinberg toyed with his pen. "All right, Milligan. I'll give you a chance to work in the lab. You can start by mopping up the floor, and when you're done with that, you can straighten up the place. You'll work with Stormy, the duty nurse. He'll show you the ropes."

(2)

Arthur was delighted. He didn't at all mind getting up earlier than the other prisoners to do the blood tests. Dismayed at what he considered inadequate medical records, he began to keep his own charts on the fourteen diabetics he soon came to think of as his patients. He spent most of the day at the lab working with the microscope and preparing slides. When he went back to his cell at three-thirty, tired but happy, he paid little attention to his new cell mate, a slight and taciturn man.

Adalana decorated the bare cell by spreading patterned towels on the floor and hanging them on the walls. Allen soon began wheeling and dealing—trading a flowered towel for a carton of cigarettes, then lending cigarettes out at two-for-one interest and ending up with two cartons at the end of the week. He kept pyramiding his barter. Along with what his mother and Marlene sent or brought him, he was able to buy food form the commissary and thus avoid the dining room in the evenings. He would plug his sink with a rubber stopper borrowed from the lab, fill it with hot water and let a can of chicken and dumplings, soup or beef stew heat up until it was warm enough to be palatable.

He wore his green uniform proudly, delighted at the privilege of being allowed to walk and even run down the main corridor instead of moving like a cockroach against the walls. He enjoyed being called "Doc," and he sent Marlene the names of some medical books to buy for him. Arthur was serious about studying medicine.

When Tommy learned that many of the other prisoners had their girl friends on the visitors' list as common-law wives so they would be allowed to visit the prison, he told Ragen he wanted Marlene down as his wife. Arthur was opposed at first, but Ragen overruled him. As Milligan's wife, she could bring things to the prison.

"Write to her," Ragen said, "to bring oranges. But first to use hypodermic and inject vodka. Is very good."

"Lee" took the spot for the first time in Lebanon. Comedian, wit, practical joker, he exemplified Arthur's theory that laughter was a safety valve appreciated by most inmates. The teasing by other inmates that had a first frightened Danny and angered Ragen was now practiced by Lee. Ragen had heard of Billy's father, the stand-up comic and M.C. who had billed himself as "half music and half wit." Ragen had decided that Lee had a role to play in prison.

But Lee went beyond funny stories. He loaded Allen's cigarettes by scraping the sulfur off a couple of matches, soaking a matchstick in sugar water, rolling it in sulfur and burying it in the tobacco. He'd carry a couple of these in Allen's pack, and when an inmate would ask for a cigarette, Lee would hand over a loaded one. By the time he was down the corridor or leaving the cafeteria, he could hear the shout of rage from the victim as the cigarette flared. Several of them exploded in Allen's face.

One morning when the blood work was done, Arthur, thinking about the incidence of sickle-cell anemia among black inmates, left the spot. Lee, finding himself with nothing to do, decided on some mischief. He opened a jar of onion-oil extract, dipped a swab into it and lined the eyepiece rims of the microscope.

"Hey, Stormy," he said, handing the medic a slide, "Dr. Steinberg wants this white-blood-cell count quick. You'd better check this under the microscope."

Stormy placed the slide on the microscope stage and focused. Suddenly his head snapped up, eyes filling with tears.

"What's the matter?" Lee asked innocently. "Is it that sad?"

Unable to control himself, Stormy roared, laughing through his tears. "Goddamn sonofabitch. You're a real funny motherfucker, ain't you?" He went to the sink and washed his eyes.

A short while later, Lee watched a prisoner come in and give Stormy five bucks. Stormy took Flask 11-C off a crowded shelf, pulled the cork and handed it to the man, who took a deep swig.

"What's that?" Lee asked when the prisoner had left.

"White lightning. Make it myself. I get five bucks a hit. If I'm ever not around when a customer comes in, you can handle the business for me and I'll cut you in for a buck."

Lee said he'd be happy to oblige.

"Look," Stormy went on, "Dr. Steinberg wants that first-aid cabinet straightened out. Would you do it? I got some things to take care of."

While Lee rearranged the first-aid supplies, Stormy took Flask 11-C off the shelf, emptied the alcohol into a beaker and filled the flask with water. Then he lined the rim with bittersweet concentrate.

"I gotta see Dr. Steinberg about something," he said to Lee. "Mind the store, will ya?"

Ten minutes later, a huge black prisoner came into the lab and said, "Gimme 11-C, man. I paid Stormy ten bucks for two hits. He said you'd know where it is."

Lee handed the flask to the black man, who quickly put it to his mouth and tilted it upward. Suddenly his eyes opened wide and he spat and gagged.

"Goddamned honkie sonofabitch! What kind of shit you pullin' on me?" He kept puckering his mouth, making odd movements with his lips, trying to wipe the taste off with his sleeve.

He grabbed the flask by the neck, brought it down sharply against the desk, shattering the bottom of it, splattering the liquid all over Lee's hospital greens. Then he brandished the jagged edge. "I gonna cut you up, honkie!"

Lee backed toward the door. "Ragen," he whispered. "Hey, Ragen."

Lee, feeling terror build, expected Ragen to come to his defense. But no one came. He dashed out the door and down the hall, with the black man in pursuit.

Ragen started to take the spot, but Arthur said, "Lee must be taught a lesson."

"I cannot let him be cut," Ragen said.

"If he's not taught proper restraint," Arthur said, "he might be a greater danger in the future."

Ragen accepted the suggestion and made no move to intervene as Lee ran down the hall, terrified, shouting, "Where the hell are you, Ragen?"

When Ragen felt Lee had had enough and the situation had become too dangerous, he bumped Lee off the spot. As the black man came abreast of a gurney, Ragen stopped and spun the hospital bed directly into his pursuer's path. The big man went down with the gurney and fell on the broken flask, cutting his arm.

"*Is finish!*" Ragen roared.

The black man jumped up, shaking with anger. Ragen grabbed him, threw him into the X-ray room and slammed him against the wall.

"Is over," Ragen said. "If you do not stop, I destroy you!"

The man's eyes opened wide at the sudden change. In place of the frightened white boy, he found himself cornered by a nut with a Russian accent and a wild look in his eyes. He was caught in a powerful lock from behind, an arm crushing his neck.

"*Ve stop now,*" Ragen whispered into his ear. "Is necessary to clean this up."

"Yeah, man, that's cool, that's cool . . ."

Ragen let him go. The black man backed away. "I'm goin' now, man. No hard feelin's. Everything's cool . . ." He took off, walking fast.

"That," said Arthur, "was a barbaric way of handling the situation."

"Vat you vould have done?" Ragen asked.

Arthur shrugged. "If I had your physical capabilities, probably the same thing."

Ragen nodded.

"What about Lee?" Arthur asked. "It is your decision."

"He is undesirable."

"Yes. What good is a person whose whole life is made up of practical jokes? He is a useless android."

Lee was banished. But rather than live in the limbo of the darkness around the spot, unable to face an existence without practical jokes and comic behavior, he made himself disappear completely.

For a long time, no one laughed.

(3)

Tommy's letters began to show unpredictable swings of mood. He wrote Marlene, "My knuckles are swollen," and described a fight he'd had with some inmates who had been stealing his postage stamps. On August 6, he swore he was going to commit suicide. Five days later he wrote her to send him acrylics so he could start painting again.

Arthur captured four mice that he kept as pets. He studied their behavior and began to write a long report about the possibility of grafting the skin of mice on human burn victims. One afternoon in the lab, while he was making some notes, three inmates came in. One stood guard and the other two confronted him.

"Gimme the package," one of them said. "We know you got it. Give it over."

Arthur shook his head and went back to writing his notes. The two prisoners came around the desk and grabbed him . . .

Ragen pulled the two men down, kicking one and then the other. When the inmate who had been standing guard outside the lab came at him with a knife, Ragen broke his wrist. The three of them fled, one shouting, "You a dead man, Milligan. I'm contracting your ass."

Ragen asked Arthur if he knew what was going on.

"A package," Arthur said. "From the way they acted, I imagine it would be drugs."

He searched the lab and the dispensary. Finally, behind some books and papers on a top shelf, he found a plastic bag with white powder.

Allen asked, "Is it smack?"

"I'll have to run some tests to be sure," Arthur said, putting it on the scales. "There's half a kilo here."

He discovered it was cocaine.

"What are you gonna do with it?"

Arthur tore open the package and dumped the white powder down the toilet.

"Someone's gonna be awful sore," Allen said.

But Arthur was already back to thinking about his skin-graft report.

Arthur had heard about the state prison blues. Most prisoners went through an anxiety period during the process of becoming institutionalized. As the inmate faced losing his independence and his identity and was forced to accept suppression, the change often led to depression and an emotional breakdown. For Milligan it caused a mix-up time.

The letters to Marlene changed. Philip and Kevin, who had been writing obscenities and drawing pornographic cartoons, stopped. Now the letters showed a fear of insanity. Tommy's letters said he was having strange hallucinations. He also wrote that he was studying medical books day and night. When he got his parole, he wrote, he was going to study medicine, "even if it takes fifteen years." They would marry, he promised, and have a house, and he would do research and be a specialist. "How does that sound?" he wrote. "Dr. and Mrs. Milligan."

On October 4, because of the cocaine episode, Milligan was transferred to C block and kept segregated in protective isolation. His medical books and portable TV set were taken away from him. Ragen ripped the steel bed rails from the wall and jammed them into the door. Workmen had to remove the door to get him out of his cell.

He had difficulty sleeping and complained of frequent vomiting and blurred vision. Dr. Steinberg saw him from time to time and administered mild sedatives and antispasmodics. Though he felt that Milligan's problems were essentially psychological, on October 13 he ordered that Milligan be taken from Lebanon to the Central Medical Center in Columbus for treatment.

While Allen was there, he wrote to the American Civil Liberties Union for help, but nothing came of it. After ten days in Columbus, it was discovered that he had a peptic ulcer. He was put on a Sippy ulcer diet and returned to protective isolation in Lebanon. He learned that he would not be eligible for parole until April 1977—a year and a half away.

(4)

Christmas and New Year's came and went, and on January 27, 1976, Allen took part with the other inmates in a hunger strike. He wrote to his brother:

Dear Jim,

As I lay here in my cell my thoughts are of you and I as children. As my own time goes by my soul gains hatred for life. I am sorry for I'm the fault of your family being broken and which family I was hardly a part of. You have a great life ahead of you with many goals. Don't blow it as I. If you hate me for this I'm sorry. But I still respect you as I do the wind and sun. Jim I swear to God as my witness I didn't do what I am accused of. God says everyone has a place and a destiny. I guess this is mine! I am sorry of the shame I have caused you and everyone around me.

Bill

Tommy wrote to Marlene:

To My Marvene,

OK Marv, there is a hunger strike and big riot starting. I am getting this letter to you in case the inmates take over. No mail will get out if they do. The screaming and glass breaking is getting louder. I would be killed if I try to get food off the cart—
Someone started a fire! but they got it put out. Guards are dragging people out right and left. The movement is slow but the inmates will probably take over by the middle of next week. I told you so!!! They are standing outside with shot guns but that still wont stop these guys. I miss you Marvene! I just want to die. Things are getting bad. In the next few days this thing may get on the 6 oclock news. Right now its just on the Cinci radio. If it becomes a full scale dont come around. I know there will be thousands of people out side, you wouldn't get in the front gate. I love you Marvene and miss you. Do me a favor. The guys around me told me to send this to my Home town radio. They need public support to get what they want. Sent it to W.H.O.K. Thank you from all the guys. Well Marv I love you verry verry verry much take care.

Love Bill

If things are ok bring cocoa.

"Bobby" scratched his name on the steel bunk in solitary confinement. Here he was able to indulge in his fantasies. He saw himself as an actor in a movie or on TV, traveling to far-off places and having heroic adventures.

He hated being called "Robert" by the others and would insist, "I'm *Bobby!*"

He had an inferiority complex, no ambition of his own, and he lived like a sponge, soaking up ideas and thoughts of others, passing them off as his own. But when anyone suggested he do something, he would say, "I can't do it." He alone lacked confidence in his ability to carry out a plan.

When Bobby first heard about the hunger strike, he imagined himself leading it, setting an example for the other prisoners. Like the great Mahatma Gandhi of India, he would bring the repressive authorities to their knees by his fasting. When the strike ended a week later, Bobby decided he wouldn't stop. He lost a great deal of weight.

One evening when a guard opened his cell door to bring his food tray, Bobby pushed it back at him and threw the slop all over his face.

Arthur and Ragen agreed that though Bobby's fantasies helped them survive the long months in prison, his fasting was weakening the body. Ragen declared him undesirable.

Tommy walked out of the visiting room one afternoon after a visit from Billy's mom, who had come to celebrate her son's twenty-first birthday. He looked back through the window and saw something he hadn't noticed before: In different parts of the room, prisoners were sitting beside their women, hands out of sight behind the small square tables, not talking or even looking at each other, but staring straight ahead, nonchalantly, almost glassy-eyed.

When he mentioned it to Jonsie, a prisoner in the cell next to his, Jonsie laughed. "Man, don't you know nothin'? Hell, it's Valentine's Day. They's hand-fuckin'."

"I don't believe it."

"Man, when you got a woman who'll do anythin' for you, she comes up here with a skirt 'steada pants, and she don't got on no underwear. Next time we's visitin' at the same time, I'll show you my honey's ass."

The following week he was coming in to see Billy's mom when Jonsie and his beautiful red-haired girl friend were heading out. Jonsie winked and flipped up the back of her skirt, showing her naked bottom.

Tommy blushed and turned away.

That night, in the middle of Tommy's letter to Marlene, the handwriting changed. Philip wrote: "If you love me, next time you come, wear a skirt, but don't wear no underwear."

(5)

By March 1976, Allen began to hope for parole in June, but when the parole board put the hearing off for two more months, he became worried. He'd heard, through the prison grapevine, that the only way to ensure a parole was to pay off the clerk who filed the application in the central office. Allen wheeled and dealed, sketching in pencil and charcoal, then selling the sketches to inmates and guards for items that could be stockpiled and traded. He wrote to Marlene, begging her once again to bring oranges spiked by hypodermic with hundred-proof vodka. One was for Ragen and the others were to sell.

On June 21, eight months after having first been put in protective isolation, he wrote Marlene that he was certain the parole-hearing delay was some kind of psychological testing, "or else I'm so goddamned stone crazy I don't know what the fuck I'm doing Da-da-da." Still isolated, he was moved to C block's "psych range," a group of ten cells reserved for inmates with mental problems. Danny stabbed himself shortly after, and when he refused treatment, he was taken once again to the Central Medical Center in Columbus. After a brief stay he was returned to Lebanon.

During his stay in C block, Allen kept sending "kites" to Warden Dallman, official messages protesting his protective isolation, which he had been told had to be voluntary. His constitutional rights were being violated, he wrote, and he threatened to sue everybody. After a few weeks, Arthur suggested a change of tactics—silence. Speak to no one, neither inmates nor guards. He knew that would worry them. And the children refused to eat.

In August, after eleven months in protective isolation, being shifted back and forth from the psych range, he was told he could return to the prison population. "We could put you to work where it isn't very dangerous," Warden Dallman said. He indicated the pencil sketches all over the cell wall. "I've heard about your artistic talents. What if we put you to work in Mr. Reinert's art class?"

Allen nodded happily.

The following day Tommy went to the graphic-arts room. It was a busy place, filled with people working on silkscreens, lettering, cameras and a printing press. The thin, wiry man called Mr. Reinert looked at Tommy sidewise through thoughtful eyes as the prisoner sat around for the first few days, not interested in what was going on around him.

"What would you like to do?" Reinert asked him.

"I'd like to paint. I'm good at oils."

Reinert cocked his head and looked up at him. "None of the prisoners do oil painting."

Tommy shrugged. "That's what I do."

"All right, Milligan. Come with me. I think I know where we can get some stuff for you."

Tommy was in luck: The graphic-arts project at the Chillicothe Correctional Facility had recently closed down, and they had sent the oil paints, canvases and stretchers to Lebanon. Reinert helped him set up an easel and told him to go ahead and paint.

Half an hour later, Tommy brought him a landscape and Reinert was stunned. "Milligan, I've never seen someone paint so fast. And it's good."

Tommy nodded. "I had to learn to paint fast if I wanted to be able to finish anything."

Though oil painting was not a part of the program and was generally not done in the graphic-arts classes, Reinert realized that Milligan was most at ease with a brush in his hand; so, Monday through Friday, he allowed him to paint all he wanted. The prisoners, the guards and even some of the administrative staff admired Tommy's landscapes. He painted some fast hackwork for bartering, and these he signed "Milligan"; others he painted for himself, and he was allowed to send them out of the prison when his mother or Marlene came to visit.

Dr. Steinberg began to drop into the graphic-arts unit from time to time to ask Milligan's advice about his own painting. Tommy showed him how to handle perspective, how to paint rocks to make them look as if they were underwater. Steinberg came into the prison on his own time weekends and had Milligan taken out of his cell so that the two of them could paint together. Knowing that Milligan hated prison food, the doctor would always bring along submarine sandwiches or bagels with cream cheese and lox.

"I wish I could paint in my cell," Tommy said to Reinert one weekend.

Reinert shook his head. "Not with two prisoners in a cell. It's against the rules."

But that rule didn't apply for long. Several evenings later, two guards came to shake down Milligan's cell and found marijuana. "Ain't mine," Tommy said, afraid they wouldn't believe him and that he'd be sent to the "hole," a bare, isolated punishment cell. But when they questioned his cell mate, the young man broke down and admitted he'd smoked it because he was upset about his wife leaving him. He was sent to isolation, and Milligan had the cell to himself for a while.

Reinert talked to Lieutenant Moreno, the officer in charge of the cell block, suggesting that Milligan be allowed to paint in his cell until they put another prisoner in with him. Moreno agreed. Thus, every day after the graphic-arts room closed down at three-thirty, Milligan would go back to his cell to paint until it was time to sleep. Days went by quickly. It was easier to do time.

Then one day a guard mentioned that a new prisoner would be put in his cell. Allen stopped by Lieutenant Moreno's office.

"Mr. Moreno, if you put someone else in with me, I won't be able to paint my pictures."

"Well, you'll have to do it elsewhere, then."

"Can I explain something to you?"

"Come back later in the day and we'll talk about it."

After lunch, Allen came back from graphic arts with a painting Tommy had just finished. Moreno stared at it. "You did that?" he asked. The lieutenant held up the painting and looked at the deep-green landscape with the river winding off into the depths. "Hey, I'd sure like to have one of these."

"I'd paint you one," Allen said. "Only I can't paint in my cell anymore."

"Oh . . . well, let's wait a minute here. You'd paint a picture for me?"

"Free of charge."

Moreno called to his assistant: "Casey, take that new man's name out of the slot for Milligan's cell. Put a blank slip in there and put X's on it." Then he turned to Allen. "Don't worry about it. You've got about nine more months, then you go to the board? There won't be anyone else in your cell."

Allen was delighted, and Tommy and Danny and he painted every spare minute, making sure not to finish any single painting.

"You've got to be careful," Arthur suggested. "As soon as Moreno gets his painting, he might back down on his word."

Allen stalled Moreno for nearly two weeks, then walked into his office to present a painting of a wharf with boats tied to it. Moreno was overjoyed.

"You're sure this'll keep anybody else from coming in my cell?" Allen asked.

"I put it right up on the board. You can go in and look at it."

Allen went into the security room, and beneath his name he saw the slip with the notation "Do not put inmate in Milligan's cell." It was covered with transparent tape and it looked permanent.

Milligan painted in a frenzy of productivity. Paintings for the guards, for the administrators, for Mom and Marlene to take home and sell. One day he was asked to do one for the front lobby, and Tommy painted a huge canvas that was to be hung behind the admissions desk. He made the mistake of signing his own name to it, but before he presented it, Allen discovered the error, blacked out the name and signed it "Milligan."

Most of these paintings did not satisfy him. They were for trading or selling quickly. But one day he became involved in a painting that was very important to him, adapted from a painting he saw in an art book.

Allen, Tommy and Danny took turns working on "The Grace of Cathleen." It was originally planned to be a seventeenth-century aristocratic lady holding a mandolin. Allen worked on the face and hands. Tommy worked on the background. Danny painted the details. When the time came to put the mandolin in her hands, Danny realized he didn't know how to paint one, so he painted in a piece of sheet music instead. For forty-eight hours, without stopping, they took turns working on it. And when they were done, Milligan collapsed in his bunk and slept.

"Steve" had not spent much time on the spot before Lebanon. An expert and daring driver, he had been behind the wheel a few times when he was younger, and boasted of being the best driver in the world. Ragen allowed him on the spot in Lebanon after Lee was banished, because Steve, too, had the ability to make people laugh. He was, Steve liked to brag, one of the best mimics alive. He could imitate anyone and send an audience of inmates into spasms of laughter. Imitations were his way of mocking people. Steve was the hell-raiser, the perpetual impostor.

It angered Ragen when Steve imitated his Yugoslavian accent, and it infuriated Arthur when he mocked him by talking in a lower-class British accent. "I do not speak that way," Arthur insisted. "I do not have a cockney accent."

"He's going to get us into trouble," Allen said.

One afternoon Steve was standing in the corridor behind Captain Leach, arms crossed, mimicking Leach's manner of rocking back and forth on his heels. Leach turned and caught him at it. "All right, Milligan, you can practice your performance in the hole. Maybe ten days in isolation will teach you a lesson."

"Allen warned us something would happen," Arthur said to Ragen. "Steve is useless. He has no ambition, no talent. All he does is laugh at people, and while observers may laugh at his antics, the individual who is mocked becomes our enemy. You're in domination, but I put it to you that we hardly need more enemies."

Ragen agreed that Steve was undesirable and told him he was banished. Steve refused to get off the spot, and mocking Ragen's accent, he growled, "Vat you mean? You do not exist. None of you. You are all figments of my imagination. I am only one here. I am only real person. The rest of you are hallucinations."

Ragen slammed him into the wall and bloodied his forehead. Then Steve left the spot.

At Arthur's urging, Allen applied to take courses given at the prison by instructors from the Shaker Valley branch campus of the community college. He enrolled in English, industrial design, basic math and industrial advertising. He got A's in the art classes and B+'s in English and Math. His ratings in graphic arts were all at the highest level—"exceptional," "highly productive," "rapid learner," "highly reliable," "excellent relations," "highly motivated."

On April 5, 1977, Allen appeared before the parole board and was told he would be released within three weeks.

When he finally got the letter of release, Allen was so overjoyed, he couldn't sit still. He paced back and forth in his cell. Finally he took the letter and made it into a paper airplane. The day before his scheduled release, passing Captain Leach's office, he whistled. When Leach looked up, Allen sailed the parole-board-letter airplane past him and walked off with a smile.

The last day in Lebanon, April 25, took forever. Allen had been up the night before until three in the morning, pacing his cell. He told Arthur he felt he should have more say over who was on or off the spot now that they were going to be on the outside again. "I'm the one who has to deal with people," Allen said, "the one who has to talk our way out of situations."

"It will be difficult for Ragen to yield domination as it is," Arthur said, "after two years of absolute control. He would not take kindly to a triumvirate. I believe Ragen has ideas of continuing to rule."

"Well, you'll be the boss as soon as we walk out those doors. I'm the one who's going to have to find a job and readjust to society. I need to have more say in things."

Arthur pursed his lips. "That's not an unreasonable request, Allen. Though I cannot speak for Ragen, you will have my support."

Downstairs, a guard handed him a new suit, and Allen was amazed at the quality and the fit.

"Well, your mother sent it in," the guard said. "It's one of your own."

"Oh yeah," Allen said, pretending to remember.

Another guard came in with a voucher for him to sign. Before he could leave, he had to pay thirty cents for a plastic cup missing from his cell.

"They took that away from me when they moved me out of isolation," Allen said, "and they never gave it back."

"I don't know about that. You got to pay for it."

"Well, I can play that game too!" Allen shouted. "I won't pay!"

They took him down to Mr. Dunn's office, and the administrator asked what the trouble was on his last day there.

"They want to charge me for a plastic cup they took away from me. I didn't have anything to do with that thing coming up missing."

"You've got to pay the thirty cents," Dunn said.

"I'll be damned if I will."

"You can't leave here until you do."

"I can camp right here," Allen said, sitting down. "I'm not paying for something I didn't do. It's the principle of the thing."

Dunn finally let him go, and as he walked to the holding cell where he was to be picked up by his mother, Marlene and Kathy, Arthur asked, "Did you have to do that?"

"Like I said to Dunn, it's the principle."

Bob Reinert came up to see him off, and so did Dr. Steinberg, who slipped him some money as final payment for one of his paintings.

Allen was eager to get out the door, impatient as Billy's mother talked to Dr. Steinberg. "Come on," Allen said to Dorothy. "Let's go."

"Just a minute, Billy," she said. "I'm talking."

He stood there fretting, watching her talk on and on.

"Can we go?"

"All right, just relax a minute."

He paced back and forth, grumbling as his mother kept talking. Finally, he shouted, "Mother, I'm leaving. If you wanna stay, you can."

"Oh well, good-by, Dr. Steinberg. I want to thank you for all you've done for my Billy."

He headed toward the door and she followed him. The steel door whooshed behind them, and Allen realized that on the way in he had never heard that second door close.

By the time Kathy brought the car around, Allen was still angry. When a man is getting out of prison, he thought, what you do is just open the door and let him run. You don't keep him inside by standing around gossiping. It was bad enough when the law kept you in the place, but when your gabby mother was doing it, that was too much. He sulked in the car.

"Pull over to the bank in Lebanon," he said finally. "I'd better cash my prison check here. No sense cashing it in Lancaster, having them all know I just got out of jail."

He went inside, endorsed the paycheck and put it on the counter. When the teller handed him the fifty dollars, he put the bills in his wallet along with the money Dr. Steinberg had given him. Still angry, and now getting angry that he was angry, Allen just didn't want to deal with it . . .

Tommy looked around and wondered what in the world he was doing inside a bank. Was he coming in or going out? He opened his wallet, saw close to two hundred dollars and shoved it back into his pocket. He figured he was going out. Glancing through the big window, he saw his mom and Marlene waiting in the car, Kathy behind the wheel, and he realized what day this had to be. He checked the calendar on the teller's counter. This was the day they set him free.

He ran out the bank door, pretending to be clutching something in his hands. "Quick, let's make our getaway. Hide me. Hide me." He squeezed Marlene and laughed and felt good.

"God, Billy," she said. "As changeable as ever."

They tried to fill him in on all the things that had happened in Lancaster in the past two years, but he didn't really give a damn. All he was looking forward to was spending some time with Marlene. After all those times in the visitors' room at the prison, he longed to be alone with her.

When they reached Lancaster, Marlene told Kathy, "Drop me off at the Plaza Shopping Center. I've got to go to work."

Tommy stared at her. "Work?"

"Yeah. I took the morning off, but I've got to go back."

Tommy was dazed and hurt. He had thought she would want to be with him on his first day out of prison. He said nothing, blinking back the tears, but the hollowness inside was so painful that he left the spot . . .

When he was back in his room, Allen said aloud, "I always knew she was no good for him anyway. If she really gave a damn about Tommy, she'd have taken the rest of the day off. I say we don't have anything more to do with her."

"That," Arthur said, "has been my position from the beginning."

CHAPTER EIGHTEEN

(1)

A few weeks before Billy's parole, Kathy had moved back home to Lancaster, returning to her old job at Anchor Hocking. The only thing that made the job tolerable was her new friend, Bev Thomas. They worked together in the select-and-pack department, examining glassware as it moved along the belt, talking above the roar of glass-firing burners and air blowers. When Kathy quit Anchor Hocking to begin college at Ohio University in Athens, the two girls kept up their friendship.

Bev was an attractive young divorcée about Billy's age, with brownish-blond hair and green eyes. Kathy found Bev independent, tolerant and blunt. Bev was interested in psychology; she said she tried to understand the meanness in people and what in their backgrounds caused them to act the way they did.

Kathy told her how her own family—especially Billy—had suffered from Chalmer's violence. She invited Bev to her mother's house, showed her Billy's paintings and told her about the crimes that had sent him to prison. Bev said she'd like to meet him.

Kathy arranged for Billy to go for a drive with them soon after his return home. In the late afternoon, Bev pulled up in front of the Spring Street house in her white Mercury Montego, and Kathy called to Billy, who was working on his VW. She introduced them, but Billy just nodded and turned back to what he was doing.

"C'mon, Billy," Kathy said. "You promised we'd go for a drive."

He looked at Bev, then at the VW and shook his head. "Oh, I say, I don't really feel confident enough to get behind the wheel. Not quite yet."

Kathy laughed. "He's in his British mood," she told Bev. "Oh, I do say, really."

He glared at the two of them with a haughty look, and Kathy was annoyed. She didn't want Bev to think her brother was a phony.

"C'mon," Kathy insisted. "You can't clown your way out of keeping your promise. Two years without driving isn't that long. It'll come back to you. If you're afraid to drive, I will."

"Or we can take my car," Bev suggested.

"I'll drive," he said finally, and stepped around to the passenger side of the VW, holding the door open for them.

"At least," Kathy said, "you didn't forget your manners in prison."

Kathy got in back and Bev slipped into the front. Billy walked around, got behind the wheel and started the car. He let out the clutch too quickly; the VW lurched forward and pulled out onto the wrong side of the street.

"Maybe I should drive," Kathy said.

He said nothing, but hunched over the wheel as he pulled back to the right and drove very slowly. After several minutes of driving in silence, he pulled into a service station.

"I do believe I need some petrol," he said to the attendant.

"Is he all right?" Bev whispered.

"He'll be okay," Kathy said. "He gets this way every so often. He'll snap out of it."

As they watched, his lips moved silently. Then he looked around, quickly taking in his surroundings. Seeing Kathy in the back of the VW, he nodded and smiled.

"Hi," he said. "Beautiful day for a drive."

"Where are we going?" Kathy asked as he pulled out and drove smoothly and with sudden confidence.

"I want to see Clear Creek," he said. "I dreamed about it so many times during the past two years in . . . in . . ."

"Bev knows," Kathy said. "I explained to her all about what you did."

He looked at Bev thoughtfully. "Not too many people would go around driving with an ex-convict just out on parole."

Kathy saw Bev looking him straight in the eye. "I don't judge people that way," Bev replied, "just as I don't expect to be judged."

In the rear-view mirror, Kathy saw Billy's eyebrows go up and his lips purse. She could tell that Bev's remark impressed him.

He drove to Clear Creek, where he'd gone camping so often, and gazed at it as if taking in the view for the first time. Kathy watched the water glinting in the sunlight through the trees, and she understood why he loved the place.

"I've got to paint this again," he said. "But I'll do it different now. I want to see all the places I knew, and do them over."

"It hasn't changed," Bev said.

"But I have."

After they had driven around the area for two hours, Bev invited them to her mobile home for dinner later that evening. They drove back to Spring Street so that she could pick up her car, and she gave them directions to the Morrison Trailer Court.

Kathy was pleased that Billy wore his new pin-striped suit to dinner. He looked handsome and dignified when he dressed up, trimmed his mustache and brushed his hair back. At the trailer Bev introduced Billy to her children—five-year-old Brian and six-year-old Michelle—and he turned his attention to them immediately, setting one on each knee, telling them jokes, pretending to be a little child himself.

After she fed the children and put them to bed, Bev told him, "You have a way with children. Michelle and Brian took to you right away."

"I love kids," he said. "And yours are particularly delightful."

Kathy smiled, pleased to see that Billy was in his charming mood.

"I've invited another friend for dinner," Bev said. "Steve Love lives in the trailer court, too, but he's separated from his wife. We're best pals. I thought you'd like to meet him. He's a couple of years younger than Billy, half Cherokee, a real nice guy."

When Steve Love came in a short while later, Kathy was struck by his handsome dark complexion, bushy black hair, mustache and the darkest blue eyes she'd ever seen. He was taller than Billy.

During dinner Kathy sensed that Billy liked both Bev and Steve. When Bev asked him about life in Lebanon, he told them about Dr. Steinberg and Mr. Reinert, and how being able to paint had finally made prison endurable. After dinner he told about some of the things that had gotten him into trouble, and Kathy had the feeling he was boasting. Suddenly Billy jumped up and said, "Let's go for a drive."

"At this hour?" Kathy said. "It's after midnight."

"Great idea," Steve said.

"I'll get my neighbor's niece to baby-sit," Bev said. "She sits for me at any hour."

"Where'll we go?" Kathy asked.

"Let's find a playground somewhere," Billy said. "I feel like swinging on a swing."

After the baby-sitter arrived, they crowded into the VW, Kathy and Steve Love in the back, Bev beside Billy in the front.

They drove to a small schoolhouse playground. At two in the morning, they played tag and swung on the swings. Kathy was glad Billy was having such a good time. It was important for him to have new friends so he wouldn't become involved with the people he'd been associating with before he went to prison. That was one of the things his parole officer had tried to impress upon the family.

At four in the morning, after they dropped Bev and Steve back at the trailer court, Kathy asked Billy what he thought of the evening.

"Real nice guys," Billy said. "I feel I've made some friends."

She squeezed his arm.

"And those kids," he said. "I just love those kids."

"You'll make a good father someday, Billy."

He shook his head. "That's physically impossible."

Marlene sensed a change in Billy. He was a different person now, she thought, with a hardened attitude; he seemed to draw away from her, as if wanting to avoid her. That hurt, because all the time he had been in Lebanon, she had never gone out with anyone else, dedicating herself to him alone.

One evening a week after his release, he came by to pick her up after work. He seemed himself again, soft-spoken and polite—the way she liked him—and she was glad. They drove out to Clear Creek, one of their favorite drives, and then back to Spring Street. Dorothy and Del were out, and they went to his room. It was the first time they had been really alone, without arguing, since his return, the first time there had been a chance to hold each other. It had been so long that she was frightened.

He must have felt her fear, because he pulled away.

"What's the matter, Billy?"

"What's the matter with *you*?"

"I'm scared," she said. "That's all."

"What about?"

"It's been over two years since we've been together."

He got out of bed and dressed. "Well," he grumbled, "that really turns me off."

The break came suddenly.

Billy surprised Marlene when he came by the store one afternoon, asking her to drive down to Athens and spend the night there with him. They'd pick up Kathy from school the next morning and drive back to Lancaster.

Marlene said she didn't feel like going.

"I'll call you later," he said, "to see if you've changed your mind."

But he didn't call. And a few days later, she learned that Bev Thomas had made the trip with him.

Furious, Marlene called him and told him she wasn't going to go on like this. "We might as well forget it," she said. "There's nothing there."

He agreed with her. "Something might happen and I'm afraid you might be hurt. I don't want to see you hurt again."

She knew that now she had to take him at his word, and she felt the pain of breaking with someone she'd waited for, more than two years.

"All right," she said. "Let's end it."

What bothered Del Moore most about Billy was the lying. The boy would do stupid or crazy things and then lie to avoid the repercussions. Dr. Steinberg had told him not to let Billy get away with the lies anymore.

Del told Dorothy, "Hey, he's not that dull-witted. He's too bright to pull things that dumb."

All he would get from Dorothy was the same answer: "Well, that's not my Bill. That's the other Bill."

It seemed to Del that Billy had no skills or aptitude of any kind except painting. And he never took advice or listened to instructions. Del said, "Billy would listen to a total stranger before he would listen to someone who had his well-being at heart."

When Del asked him who the people were that gave him information or advice, Billy would always say, "Some guy I know told me." Never a name or explanation who "they" were or where he'd met "them."

It irritated Del that Billy often would not even bother to respond to simple questions, preferring to silently leave the room or turn his back. Del also grew angry with Billy's fears and phobias. He knew, for instance, that Billy was terrified of guns—even though the boy knew nothing at all about them. As far as Del was concerned, Billy knew nothing about anything.

But there was one thing about Billy he could never explain. Del knew he was much stronger than Billy; time and again they would arm-wrestle, and there was just no question in his mind that Billy was no match for him. But one evening when Del challenged him to an arm-wrestling match, he was astonished when Billy put him down.

"Let's do it again," Del insisted. "But this time let'd do it right-handed."

Billy put him down again without saying a word, then got up to leave.

"Big strong guy like you ought to be out working," Del said. "When are you gonna get yourself a job?"

Billy looked at him, confused, and said he *had* been looking for work.

"You're a liar," Del shouted. "If you really was serious about getting work, you would."

The argument went on for over an hour. Finally, Billy grabbed his clothes and most of his stuff and stormed out of the house.

(2)

Bev Thomas was now living with Steve Love, who had been evicted from his own trailer. When Bev heard about Billy's hassles at home, she invited him to move in with them. Billy checked with his parole officer and got the okay.

Bev enjoyed living with two men. No one would believe there was nothing sexual going on, that they were just three best friends who went everywhere together, did everything together and had more fun together than she'd ever had before.

Billy was great with Michelle and Brian. He always took them swimming, or got ice cream for them, or took them to the zoo. He cared about those kids as if they were his own. And Bev was impressed that when she came home from work, he'd have the place cleaned up, all except the dishes. He never did the dishes.

Sometimes he acted so feminine that she and Steve wondered if he was gay. Often Bev and Billy would sleep in the same bed, but he never touched her. When she asked him about it one day, he told her he was impotent.

It didn't matter to her. She cared about him. And she loved the things they all did together, like going to Burr Oak Lodge for three days, camping out and spending fifty dollars on junk food. Or hiking through the woods at Clear Creek in the middle of the night, Billy holding the one flashlight and playing James Bond, trying to find secret caches of marijuana. It was fun the way he would talk with his British accent, giving the Latin names of all the plants. It was all madness, the things they did together, but Bev felt free and happy for the first time in a long time with these two wonderful guys.

One day Bev came home to discover that Billy had painted his green VW black with crazy silver patterns.

"No other VW in the world is like this now," he said.

"But why, Billy?" Bev and Steve both asked.

"Well, the sheriff's office is keeping an eye on me anyway. This'll just make their job easier."

What he didn't tell them was that Allen was sick and tired of panicking when he couldn't remember where someone had parked the car. The distinctive black-and-silver pattern would make it easier to find.

But when Billy met Steve's brother, Bill Love, a few days later and saw the van he owned, Billy traded the VW for it. Then Billy traded the van to a friend of Steve's for a motorcycle that didn't run, but Steve, who had his own bike and who was expert at repairing motorcycles, got it in working order.

Steve discovered that at times Billy rode the motorcycle like a demon and other times he was afraid to ride it at all. One afternoon when they were riding in the countryside, they passed a sharp incline of shale and rock. Steve skirted it and went ahead, but then he heard the roar of an engine above him. When he looked up, he saw Billy at the top of the cliff.

"How'd you get up there?" Steve yelled.

"Rode up!" Billy yelled back.

"That's impossible!" Steve shouted.

Seconds later he could see that Billy had changed and was now trying to get down, acting as if he didn't know the first thing about riding a cycle. Several times the cycle went one way and he went the other. Finally Steve left his own cycle below, climbed up the sheer face of the hill and helped Billy walk the cycle down.

"I can't believe you rode up there," Steve said, glancing back, "but there's no other way."

Billy looked as if he didn't know what Steve was talking about.

Another time, when Steve was alone with Billy, they went walking in the woods. After two hours of climbing hills, they still faced a peak up ahead. Steve knew he was stronger and a better athlete than Billy, but it was too much even for him.

"We'll never make that, Billy. Let's rest and go back."

But when he fell back against a tree, exhausted, he saw Billy suddenly gather incredible energy and run full speed up the steep hillside to the top. Not wanting to be outdone, Steve scrambled his way up. Up ahead, he saw Billy at the top, arms outstretched, shaking his hands and fingers as he looked down at the view below. He was talking in a strange language Steve couldn't make out.

When Steve got up to the top beside him, Billy turned, looked at him as if he were a stranger and then went running down the hillside toward the pond below.

"Oh Jesus, Billy!" Steve shouted. "Where are you getting the energy?"

But Billy kept running, shouting something in that foreign language. He dove fully clothed into the water and swam quickly across the pond.

Steve finally reached Billy, who by now was sitting on a rock on the far bank, shaking his head as if to clear the water from his ears.

He looked up as Steve came toward him, and said accusingly, "Why'd you throw me in the water?"

Steve stared at him. "What are you talking about?"

Billy looked down at his dripping clothes. "You didn't have to push me in."

Steve stared at him and shook his head. He didn't trust himself to argue.

After they went back to their motorcycles and Billy rode as clumsily as a beginner, Steve told himself he had to watch this guy, because he was surely crazy.

"You know what I'd like to do someday?" Billy said when they reached the roadway between the pond and the hillside. "I'd like to stretch a canvas across the road between those two elm trees, high up so cars could pass under it. I'd paint it so it looked like the mountain with shrubs and trees and a tunnel right in the middle."

"Billy, you got some strange ideas."

"I know," Billy said, "but I'd like to do it."

Bev found her money dwindling away on food and repairs for the cycles and cars. (Billy had bought an old Ford Galaxy.) She began to hint that Steve and Billy should start looking for jobs. They applied at several factories around Lancaster, and by the third week in May, Billy was able to fast-talk the people at Reichold Chemical into jobs for both of them.

It was heavy work. As the strings of fiberglass came out of the vat and were rolled into wide mats, their job was to cut the mats when the roll reached a certain size. Then they would lift the hundred-pound roll, place it on the cart and begin the new roll.

On their way home one night, Billy stopped to pick up a hitch-hiker who carried an instamatic camera hanging around his neck.

Driving toward town, Billy offered to trade the young man three hits of speed for the camera. Steve saw Billy dig into his pocket and come up with three white tablets wrapped in a plastic bag.

"I don't do speed," the hitch-hiker said.

"You can sell these for eight bucks apiece, a quick profit."

The hitch-hiker did some quick figuring and handed over the camera in exchange for the plastic bag. When Billy let the man off in Lancaster, Steve turned to him: "I didn't know you did chemicals."

"I don't."

"Where'd you get the speed?"

Billy laughed. "Those were aspirins."

"God," Steve said, slapping his thigh. "I've never seen anything like you."

"I once sold a whole suitcase full of phony pills," Billy said. "I think it's time to do it again. Let's make some blotter acid."

He pulled into a drugstore to buy gelatine and a few other ingredients. Back at the trailer he melted down the gelatine in one of Bev's pans to a patty one sixteenth of an inch thick. When it was hard and dry, he cut it into quarter-inch squares and put it on tape.

"Blotter acid should sell for a few bucks apiece."

"What's it supposed to do?" Steve asked.

"Speed you up. Make you see hallucinations. But the beautiful thing is if you get caught pushing these fake ones, there are no drugs involved. And what's the poor sucker who buys them going to do? Go to the cops?"

Billy took off for Columbus the next day. When he came back, the suitcase was empty. He had sold a batch of aspirin and blotter acid, and he was flashing a roll of money. But Steve noticed that he looked scared.

The following day, while Billy and Steve were working on Billy's motorcycle, a neighbor, Mary Slater, shouted at them to stop making so much noise. Billy threw his screwdriver against the side of her trailer. The sound of the screwdriver against the metal sounded like a gun going off. Mary Slater called the police, who hauled Billy in for criminal trespassing. Del had to post bond. Though the charge was dismissed, Billy's parole officer told him to move back home.

"I'll miss you guys," he said as he packed. "And I'll miss the kids."

"I don't think we're going to be here much longer, either," Steve said. "I've heard that the manager is going to evict all of us."

"What'll you do?" Billy asked.

"Find a place in town," Bev said, "and sell the trailer. Maybe you can come and live with us there."

Billy shook his head. "You don't need me around."

"That's not true, Billy," she said. "You know we're a three-some."

"We'll see. In the meantime, I've go to move back home." When he left, Bev's children cried.

* * *

(3)

Allen was bored with the job at Reichold Chemical, especially now that Steve Love had quit. He grew sick of the foreman, who constantly complained that one day he'd do things right and the next day he couldn't do them at all. Arthur griped to Allen that once again they had taken a job of mindless labor beneath their dignity.

In mid-June he put in a workman's compensation claim and walked off the job.

Del sensed that Billy had lost the job at Reichold Chemical, and he phoned the company to find out. Keeping in mind Dr. Steinberg's advice to confront Billy with his lies, Del asked him, "You lost the job, didn't you?"

"I think that's my business," Tommy said.

"It's my business when you live under my roof and I'm flipping for the bills. Money grows on trees for you. But you can't hold down a simple goddamned job. And you lied about it. You didn't tell us. You can't do anything right."

They arued about it nearly an hour. Tommy kept hearing Del use the same put-down phrases Chalmer always used. He looked to see if Billy's mom would come to his defense, but she never said a word. He knew he couldn't live there anymore.

Tommy went to his room, packed his bags and put them into his car. Then he just sat in the Ford, waiting for someone to drive him away from the goddamned place. Eventually Allen came, saw Tommy was upset and realized what had happened.

"It's okay," Allen said, driving off. "It's time we got out of Lancaster."

They drove around Ohio for six days, job hunting and then pulling off the road into the woods to sleep at night. Ragen insisted on keeping a gun under the seat and another in the glove compartment for protection.

On night, Arthur suggested that Allen try to find a job as a maintenance man. It was the kind of work Tommy could handle easily: repairing electrical appliances, mechanical equipment, heating units and plumbing. As Arthur understood it, a rent-free apartment and free utilities came with the job. He suggested Allen get in touch with a former inmate whom he'd once helped in Lebanon and who now was a maintenance man in a suburb of Columbus called Little Turtle.

"Perhaps he knows of an opening," Arthur said. "Call him. Tell him you're in town and would like to drop by."

Allen grumbled about it but followed Arthur's instructions. Ned Berger was glad to hear from him and invited him over. They weren't hiring at Little Turtle, he said, but Billy Milligan was welcome to spend a couple of nights at his place. Allen dropped by, and they partied and swapped stories about prison life.

On the morning of the third day, Berger came back to the apartment with the news that Channingway Apartments was about to advertise for outdoor maintenance help. "Call 'em," Berger said, "but don't say how you found out they were hiring."

John Wymer, the youthful personnel manager of Kelly and Lemmon Management Company, was impressed with Billy Milligan. Of all the men who answered his help-wanted ad, he found Milligan the most qualified and personable. During the first interview, on August 15, 1977, Milligan assured him he could do grounds-keeping, carpentry, electrical maintenance and plumbing. "If it works electronically or by combustion, I can fix it," he told Wymer. "And if I don't know how, I can figure it out."

Wymer said he would get in touch with him after he interviewed the other applicants for the job.

Checking Milligan's references later that day, Wymer called the most recent employer listed on Milligan's application, Del Moore. Moore gave him a glowing report—a fine worker and a dependable young man. He had left the job because meat-cutting wasn't really in Bill Milligan's line. He would, Del Moore assured Wymer, make an excellent maintenance man.

Unable to check the two personal references—Dr. Steinberg and Mr. Reinert—because Milligan had neglected to give their addresses, Wymer let it go. Since the job was limited to outdoor work, he had enough to go on with the excellent reference from his last employer. But he did instruct his secretary to run the standard police check made on all new employees.

When Milligan came in for a second interview, Wymer's first impressions were confirmed. He hired him for outdoor maintenance at the Williamsburg Square Apartments, adjacent to the Channingway Apartments, both of which were managed by Kelly and Lemmon. He could begin right away.

After Milligan left, Wymer handed his secretary the application and W-2 form to file. He did not notice that on both, Milligan had entered the day and the year—"15-77" and "18-77"—but had left off the month of August.

John Wymer had hired him, but Sharon Roth—a young woman with pale skin and long black hair—was Milligan's supervisor.

She found the new employee an intelligent, handsome fellow. She introduced him to the other "rental girls" and explained the procedure to him. Each day he would come to the office in Williamsburg Square and pick up the work orders filled out by her, Carol or Cathy. When the job was finished, Milligan was to sign the order and return it to Sharon.

Milligan worked well the first week, putting up shutters, repairing fences and walks, and doing lawn work. Everyone agreed that he was an eager, ambitious worker. He slept at the Williamsburg Square apartment of Ned Adkins, one of the other young maintenance men.

One morning during the second week, Milligan dropped by the personnel office to see John Wymer about renting an apartment. Wymer thought about it, and recalling Milligan's description of his strong background and qualifications in electrical, plumbing, and appliance repair, he decided to try him as an inside maintenance man on twenty-four-hour call. He would have to live on the premises to be available for night and emergency calls. A rent-free apartment came with the job.

"You can pick up a set of master keys from Sharon or Carol," Wymer said.

His new apartment was beautiful. It had a fireplace in the living room, a bedroom, dinette and kitchen, and it faced a patio. Tommy took one of the walk-in closets for his electronic equipment, keeping it locked to prevent the children from getting into it. Allen set up a studio in the small dinette area facing the rear. Adalana kept the place clean and did the cooking. Ragen jogged around the neighborhood to keep fit. Life at the apartment and on the job was well-organized.

Arthur approved of the situation, pleased that they were finally settled. Now he could turn his attention to his medical books and research.

Through an oversight on someone's part, the police check was never completed on Billy Milligan.

(4)

Two weeks after the move to Channingway, Ragen was jogging through the nearby poor neighborhood when he saw two black children without shoes playing on the sidewalk. He noticed a sharply dressed white man walking from one of the houses to a white Cadillac. He decided the man had to be a pimp.

Moving quickly, he threw the man against the car.

"What's the matter with you? You crazy?"

Ragen reached into his belt and pulled out a gun. "Give your vallet."

The man handed him his wallet. Ragen emptied it and threw it back at him. "Now drive."

When the car pulled away, Ragen handed the black children more than two hundred dollars. "Here. Buy shoes and food for families."

He smiled as he watched the children run off with the money.

Later Arthur said Ragen had behaved badly that day. "You can't go around the city of Columbus playing Robin Hood, stealing from the rich to give to the poor children."

"It gives pleasure."

"But you know very well that carrying that gun violates the conditions of parole."

Ragen shrugged. "Is not much better out here than prison."

"That's a stupid thing to say. Here we have freedom."

"But vat you do vit freedom?"

Arthur began to suspect Allen's hunch was right. Ragen had come to prefer any environment—even prison—in which he could control the spot.

The more Ragen saw of the working-class district on the east side of Columbus, the angrier he became over the struggle of the people to survive in the shadow of the glass-and-steel office buildings of the wealthy corporations.

One afternoon as he passed a rundown house with a sagging porch, he saw a beautiful bond-haired child with wide blue eyes sitting in a laundry basket, her withered legs bent at awkward angles. An old lady standing in the doorway came onto the porch, and Ragen asked her, "Vy does child not have leg braces? Or veelchair?"

The old lady stared. "Mister, you know what them things cost? I been begging the welfare for two years, and there ain't no way I can get them things for Nancy."

Ragen went on his way, deep in thought.

That evening he told Arthur to find out which medical-supply warehouse would have children's wheelchairs and leg braces. Though he was irritated at being distracted from his reading, as well as at Ragen's demanding tone, Arthur humored him and made several phone calls to medical-supply distributors. He discovered a company in Kentucky that had the size Ragen described. He gave Ragen the model numbers and the warehouse address, but asked, "What do you want this information for?"

Ragen didn't bother to answer.

That night Ragen took the car, his tools and a nylon rope, and drove south to Louisville. He found the hospital-supply warehouse and waited until he was certain everyone had left. It would not be difficult to break into; he would not even need Tommy's help. Strapping on the tools, Ragen climbed over the wire fence, slipped around to the side of the building hidden from the street and examined the brickwork alongside the drainpipe.

In TV shows he had seen, cat burglars always carried grappling hooks to climb up to the roof. Ragen sneered at such devices. He fished a steel shoehorn out of his bag and removed the lace from his left running shoe. With the lace he tied the shoehorn so that its curved end turned downward near the tip of his shoe, creating a hook that served as a crampon. He climbed up to the roof, cut a hole in the skylight, reached in and unlocked it and, using the nylon rope fastened to a bracket, slid down the line into the building. It reminded him of the times he'd gone mountain climbing with Jim years ago.

With the model numbers Arthur had supplied, Ragen searched the warehouse for nearly an hour before he found what he wanted—a pair of leg braces for a four-year-old child, and a small collapsible wheelchair. He unlocked a window, lowered the braces and wheelchair to the ground, and climbed out. Then he put everything into the car and drove back to Columbus.

It was morning when he pulled up to Nancy's house and knocked on the door. "I have something for little Nancy," he said to the old lady, who peered at him through the window. He brought the wheelchair up from the car, opened it and showed them how it worked. Then he showed Nancy how to put on the leg braces.

"It vill take long time to learn use them," he said, "but it is important to valk."

The old lady began to cry. "I won't never get the money to pay you for them things."

"Is not necessary to pay. Is contribution from rich medical-supply company to needy child."

"Can I make you some breakfast?"

"Vould like coffee."

"What's your name?" Nancy asked as her grandmother left for the kitchen.

"Call me Uncle Ragen," he said.

She hugged him. The old lady brought out coffee and the best pie he had ever tasted. Ragen ate the whole thing.

In the evening, Ragen sat up in bed and listened to unfamiliar voices—one with a Brooklyn accent, the other just plain foul-mouthed. Ragen heard something about splitting the money from a bank robbery. He slipped out of bed, got his gun and opened every door, every closet in the place. He put his ear to the walls, but the arguing was coming from right here in the apartment. He spun around and said, "Don't move! I kill you both."

The voices stopped.

Then Ragen heard a voice in his head saying, "Just who d'fuck are you to tell me to shaddup?"

"If you do not show yourself, I vill shoot."

"Shoot what?"

"Vere you are?"

"You wouldn't believe me if I told ya."

"Vat you mean?"

"I can't see where I'm at. I ain't go no idea where I'm at."

"Vy for you are talking?"

"I was arguin' with Kevin."

"Who is Kevin?"

"He's the one I was yellin' at."

Ragen thought a moment. "Give me description of things around you. Vat you see?"

"I see a yella lamp. A red chair near the door. A TV set's on."

"Vat kind is TV? Vat is show?"

"White cabinet. Big color RCA set. *All in the Family*'s on."

Ragen saw his TV set and he knew the strangers were here in the room—invisible. He searched the apartment again. "I look everyvere. Vere you are?"

"I'm right with ya," Philip said.

"Vat you mean?"

"I been here all the time, always have been."

Ragen shook his head. "All right. No more talk." He sat down in the rocking chair and rocked all night, trying to figure it out, amazed that there were others he hadn't known.

The next day Arthur told him about Kevin and Philip. "I believe they are a product of *your* mind," he said.

"Vat you mean?"

"I'll give you the logical side of it first," Arthur said. "As the keeper of hate, you know what a destructive force you possess. Though hate can conquer much through violence, it is unmanageable. Now, if one wants to keep the physical power of hate but remove its evil side, one will still have hatred with some bad traits. Our mind wanted to control your violence, to keep the anger selective and manageable. Getting rid of your evil, so that you could be strong without being angry, led to shaving off some of your evil, and thus to the creation of Philip and Kevin."

"They are same as me?"

"They are criminals. As long as they have your guns, they would not hesitate to put fear into people to achieve their aims. But only with weapons. Their sense of power derives from weapons. This, they feel, brings them to your level. They're very vengeful people and certainly commit crimes against property. I declared them undesirable after Zanesville because they committed unnecessary crimes. But you know what happens during the mix-up times . . . Ragen, though you have shown goodness, you still have an evil aspect to your nature. There is no way to completely cleanse hate. It is the price we pay for maintaining strength and aggressiveness."

"Vould not be mix-up times," Ragen said, "if you controlled spot properly. Vas better in prison."

"There were mix-up times in prison, even when you were dominant, thought you were often not aware of them until afterward. Philip and Kevin and some of the other undesirables stole time in prison. It's most important now that they not get in touch with their old criminal friends from Columbus or Lancaster. They would violate the terms of parole."

"I agree."

"We'll have to make new friends, begin a new life. Working here at Channingway is a splendid opportunity. We must fit into society." Arthur looked around. "To begin with, we should really fix up the flat."

In September, he bought furniture. The bill came to $1,562.21, and the first payment was due the following month.

Things seemed to be going well at first, except that Allen was having problems with Sharon Roth. He didn't know why, but she bothered him. She looked so much like Marlene and she was just as bossy and know-it-all. He sensed she didn't like him.

By mid-September, the mix-up time was worse than ever, confusing everyone. Allen would go to the rental office, pick up the work order, drive to the job location and wait at the apartment for Tommy to come and do the work. But more and more frequently, Tommy wouldn't show up. No one could reach him and no one else could handle the job. Allen knew that he himself could never figure out how to do the plumbing or heating repair. And he was afraid that if he touched something electrical, he might blow his shoes off.

Allen would wait as long as he could for Tommy to show up. When he didn't come, Allen would leave and sign the work order "completed" or write that the apartment door had been "dead-locked," which meant that he couldn't get in. But some tenants would call back three or four times to complain that the work hadn't been done. Once after four callbacks, Sharon decided to drive to the apartment with Billy to see what the problem was.

"For God's sake, Bill," she said, staring down at the dishwasher that wouldn't fill. "Even I can see how to fix that. You're supposed to be a maintenance man. You're supposed to repair appliances."

"I did fix it. I repaired the drain line."

"Well, that's obviously not where the problem is."

When he dropped her off at the rental office, he knew she was angry with him. He suspected she was going to have him fired.

Allen told Tommy it was important for him to get something he could hold over John Wymer and Sharon Roth to keep them from firing him.

Tommy's first idea was to build a telephone blue box for John Wymer's car and bug it.

"It'll be a simple thing to make," Allen told Wymer. "Then you'll have a car telephone you can use without the phone company even knowing about it."

"Wouldn't that be illegal?" Wymer asked.

"Not at all. The airwaves are free."

"You can really do it?"

"Only one way to prove it to you. You pay for the materials and let me make one for you."

Wymer questioned him closely, surprised at Milligan's knowledge of electronics. "I'd like to look into it first," Wymer said. "But it does sound interesting."

A few days later, while Tommy was buying some materials for his own blue box at an electronics supply shop, he discovered a taping bug that could be inserted into a telephone and activated by the phone ringing. All he would have to do was to dial the personnel or rental office, pretend he had called a wrong number and hang up; then the tape recorder would begin. By taping conversations in Roth's or Wymer's office, he might learn if there was something illegal going on, and he could use it to threaten them and get them off his back if they tried to fire him.

Tommy charged the electronic bugs to Kelly and Lemmon, along with other electrical supplies.

That night, he slipped into the rental office and inserted the recording device into Roth's telephone. He did the same in Wymer's office. Then Allen took the spot and went through some of the filing cabinets to see if there might be any useful information. One folder caught his eye—a listing of what the front office called the "blue-chip investors," stockholders in Channingway and Williamsburg Square, normally kept secret. These were the people who employed Kelly and Lemmon to manage the apartment complexes. Allen made copies of the names.

With the bugs in the phones and the list in his pocket, he felt that whatever happened, his job was secure.

Harry Coder first met Billy Milligan when he came to Coder's apartment to replace some broken screens.

"You could use a new water heater," Milligan told him. "I could get one for you."

"How much would it cost?" Coder asked.

"Wouldn't cost you anything. Kelly and Lemmon would never miss it."

Coder looked at him, wondering how Milligan could suggest such a thing, knowing he was a Columbus police officer and a part-time security officer for Channingway.

"I'll think about it," Coder said.

"Just let me know anytime. I'll be glad to install it for you free of charge.

When Milligan left, Coder decided he'd keep a close watch on him. There had been a sharp increase in burglaries in the Channingway and Williamsburg Square apartments. All indications were that whoever was doing it had a master key.

John Wymer got a call from a maintenance man who had been hired about the same time as Milligan was. The man said he felt Wymer should know about Milligan. Wymer asked him to come to the office.

"I feel bad about doing this," the man said, "but that guy's a weirdo."

"What do you mean?"

"He's been bugging the girls at the rental office."

"By 'bugging,' do you mean bothering or—"

"I'm talking about electronic bugging."

"Oh, come on now."

"I mean it."

"Do you have proof?"

The man looked around the room nervously. "Milligan told me himself. And then he repeated, almost word for word, a conversation I had in the rental office with Carol and Sharon. It was just the three of us, talking about how in high school almost everyone did drugs. Stuff like that. He also said when the girls were alone, they used dirtier language than guys in a locker room."

Wymer tapped his fingers on the desk thoughtfully. "Why would Billy do such a thing?"

"He said he had enough on Sharon and Carol that if he got fired, he'd take them with him. If he went down, everyone—including Kelly and Lemmon—would go down with him."

"That's foolish. How could he do that?"

"He told me he offered to make a blue box for your car, free of charge."

"That's true, but I decided against it."

"Well, he also told me he planned to bug that car phone so he could keep tabs on you, too."

When the man was gone, Wymer called Sharon. "I guess you were right about Milligan," he said. "You'd better let him go."

That afternoon Sharon called Billy into the rental office and told him he was fired.

"If I go, then you go too," he said. "I don't think you'll be working here much longer."

At home later that afternoon, Sharon answered her apartment doorbell and was astonished to see Milligan, dressed in a blue business suit and vest, looking like an executive.

"I just dropped by to tell you that you have to be at the district attorney's office tomorrow at one o'clock," he said. "I've also got to see John Wymer. If you can't get to the D.A.'s office on your own, they'll send a car to pick you up." Then he turned and left.

She knew it sounded absurd, but she was frightened. She had no idea what he was talking about or why the district attorney would want to see her. And what did Milligan have to do with it? Who was he and what was he after? One thing she knew for sure—he was no ordinary maintenance man.

Tommy went directly to the closed maintenance office at five-thirty, let himself in and removed the bug from the telephone. Before he left the office, he decided to leave a note for Carol. With the information he was giving Wymer, he knew she, too, would have to be fired. At the desk the two women shared, he flipped the page of the calendar to the next working day, Monday, September 26, 1977. Beneath the date, he printed a note:

A NEW DAY!
Enjoy it while
you CAN!

Then he turned the page back to Friday.

After John Wymer had left his office for the day, Tommy slipped in and removed the bug from his phone, too. On the way out, he ran into Terry Turnock, the district supervisor for Kelly and Lemmon.

"What are you doing here, Milligan?" Turnock asked. "I thought you were fired."

"I came down to see John Wymer. There are some things going on in this company that I'm about to make public. I want to give John a chance to deal with these matters before I notify the authorities and the investors."

"What are you talking about?"

"Well, as John's supervisor, I guess you ought to hear about it first."

A short time after John Wymer got home from the office and settled down for the evening, he got a call from Terry Turnock asking him to come back to the office right away. "Something is strange. Milligan is here, and I think you should come out here and listen to what he's got to say."

When Wymer arrived, Turnock told him Milligan had gone back to his apartment and would return in a few minutes to talk to both of them.

"What did he say?" Wymer asked.

"He's making some accusations. Better let him tell you."

"I've got a funny feeling about this guy," Wymer said, opening his desk drawer. "I'm going to tape this conversation."

He put a fresh cassette into the small tape recorder and left the drawer partly open. When Milligan walked through the door, Wymer stared in astonishment. Until this moment, he'd seen Milligan only in work clothes. Now he looked distinguished in a three-piece suit and tie, and he carried himself with authority.

Milligan sat down and hooked his thumbs through his vest. "There are some things you ought to know about that are going on in your company."

"Like what?" Turnock asked.

"A lot of it is illegal. I want to give you the opportunity to solve these problems before I go to the district attorney."

"Well, Bill, what are you talking about?" asked Wymer.

For the next hour and a half, Allen described how the records in the rental office were manipulated, how the Channingway and Williamsburg Square investors were defrauded.

Units reported as vacant were actually occupied by friends of certain employees, who were collecting and pocketing the rents. Also, he said, he could prove that Kelly and Lemmon was illegally tapping into power lines to defraud the electric company.

He assured them that he did not believe Wymer was involved in this fraud and embezzlement, but that almost everyone else in the company was—especially a certain rental-office supervisor, who was allowing her friends to occupy these apartments.

"I intend to give you time to investigate these charges, John, and to bring the culprits to justice. But if you can't or won't do it, I'll make it public by reporting the matter to the *Columbus Dispatch*."

Wymer was worried. It was always possible that dishonest employees were doing things that might create a scandal. From the way Milligan talked, it was obvious he was alleging that Sharon Roth was behind most of this.

Wymer leaned forward. "Just who are you, Bill?"

"Just an interested party."

"Are you a private investigator?" Turnock asked.

"I see no reason to reveal myself completely at this time. Let's just say I'm working in the interests of certain of the blue-chip investors."

"I always figured you weren't just a maintenance man," Wymer said. "I guess you always struck me as too brilliant. So you're working for the investors. Would you care to tell us which ones?"

Milligan pursed his lips and cocked his head. "I never actually said I was working for the investors."

"If not," Turnock said, "then you've probably been sent by a rival management company to destroy Kelly and Lemmon's credibility."

"Oh?" Milligan, said, tapping his fingertips together. "What makes you think that?"

"Will you tell us who you *are* working for?" Wymer asked.

"All I can tell you now is that you'd better get Sharon Roth in here and ask her some questions about the things I've told you."

"I certainly intend to look into your accusations, Bill, and I'm glad you brought this to my attention first. I can assure you, if there are any dishonest employees working for Kelly and Lemmon, they'll be dealt with."

Milligan stretched out his left arm to show Wymer and Turnock a small microphone wire up his sleeve. "I should point out that this conversation is being recorded. This is the receiver and there is another party, away from this location, taping all this."

"Well, good for you," Wymer said, laughing, and pointed to his open desk drawer. "Because I'm taping it all too."

Milligan laughed. "All right, John. You've got three days, starting Monday, to clear up the situation and fire the guilty parties. Otherwise I make the information public."

A short while after Milligan left, Wymer called Sharon Roth at home and told her of the accusations. She protested that it was a lie, and swore that no one in the rental office was stealing from the company.

Concerned now that Milligan had bugged her office, Sharon went in on Sunday to search it. She found nothing. Either he had sneaked in and removed it, or it was all a hoax. She glanced at her desk calendar and automatically turned the page from Friday to Monday. Then she saw the printed note:

A NEW DAY!
Enjoy it while
you CAN!

Oh my God! she thought. He's going to kill me because I fired him.

Terrified now, she called Terry Turnock and brought him the note. They compared it with samples of Milligan's writing. It matched.

On Monday at two-thirty, Milligan called Sharon and told her she would have to be at the Franklin County district attorney's office at one-thirty on Thursday. If she didn't acknowledge his message, he said, he would have to come for her with the police. Which, he pointed out, wouldn't look real good.

That evening, Harry Coder called Milligan at the apartment to tell him he'd have to back off bothering the girls at the rental office.

"What do you mean 'back off'? I'm not doing anything."

"Look, Bill," Coder said. "If the girls really have to show up at the D.A.'s office, there should be a subpoena."

"What does this have to do with you?" Milligan asked.

"The girls know I'm a police officer. They asked me to look into it."

"Are they scared, Harry?"

"No, Bill. They ain't scared. They just don't want to be hassled."

Allen decided to let the matter drop for the time being, but sooner or later he was going to get Sharon Roth fired. In the meantime, he still had the apartment, but he would have to start looking for another job.

For the next two weeks, Allen job-hunted, but it was impossible to get anything decent. He found himself with nothing to do, no one to talk to. He kept losing time and his depression deepened.

On October 13, 1977, he received John Wymer's eviction notice. He stormed around the apartment. Where was he going to go? What was he going to do?

As he paced up and back, he suddenly noticed Ragen had left his 9-millimeter Smith and Wesson out in plain sight on the mantelpiece. Why was the gun out? What the hell was wrong with him? That and the 25-millimeter Italian gun in the closet could get him sent back to prison on a parole violation.

Allen stopped pacing and took a deep breath. Maybe that was what Ragen wanted deep down, without even knowing it himself—to go back to prison, a place of danger. So he could rule the spot!

"I can't handle this anymore, Arthur," Allen said aloud. "It's just too much."

He closed his eyes and left . . .

Ragen's head snapped up, and he looked around quickly to make sure he was alone. He saw the bills on the table and realized that with no money coming in from the job, they were in great difficulty.

"All right," he said aloud. "Young ones must have clothes for coming vinter and food to eat. I vill commit robbery. "

In the early hours of Friday, October 14, Ragen slipped his Smith and Wesson into a shoulder holster and put on a brown turtleneck sweater, white running shoes, brown jogging jacket, jeans and a windbreaker. He took three hits of Biphetamine 20's, drank some vodka and left before dawn, jogging west toward the Ohio State University campus.

CHAPTER
NINETEEN

(1)

Ragen jogged eleven miles across the city of Columbus and, at seven-thirty Friday morning, reached the Ohio State University East Belmont parking lot. He had no plan; his only thought was to find someone to rob. From the curb between the College of Medicine and the lot, he saw a young woman park a gold Toyota. As she got out of the car, he saw she wore a maroon pants suit under an open buckskin coat. He turned away to look for someone else; he had no intention of robbing a woman.

But Adalana, who had been watching, knew why Ragen was here. She knew he was tired from the cross-city run and the amphetamines and vodka were getting to him. She wished him off the spot . . .

As she approached the young woman, Adalana saw her lean over the seat to pick up some books and papers from the passenger's side. She took Ragen's gun out of the holster and pressed it against the woman's arm.

The woman laughed without turning to look. "C'mon, guys, stop kidding around."

"Would you please get into the car," Adalana said. "We're going for a ride."

Carrie Dryer turned and saw it was not one of her friends, but someone she didn't recognize. She saw the gun in his gloved hand and realized this man wasn't joking. He motioned for her to slide in to the passenger's seat, and she scrambled over the stick shift. He took her car keys and slipped in behind the wheel. At first he had difficulty releasing the emergency brake, but he finally pulled out of the parking lot.

Carrie Dryer observed his appearance carefully: reddish-brown hair, a mustache cut straight and neat, a mole on his right cheek. He was handsome and well-built, about 180 pounds, five feet ten or so.

"Where are we going?" she asked.

"For a ride somewhere," he said softly. "I don't know my way around Columbus very well."

"Look," Carrie said, "I don't know what you want of me, but I've got an optometry exam today."

He pulled into a factory parking lot and stopped the car. Carrie noticed his eyes drifting from side to side, as though he had nystagmus. That was something she would have to remember to tell the police.

He went through her purse, taking out her driver's license and other identification, and his voice turned harsh: "If you go to the cops, I'll get to members of your family." He pulled out a pair of handcuffs and secured her right hand to the Toyota door handle. "You said you're gonna have a test," he murmured. "If you want to go ahead and study for it while I drive, that's fine."

They drove north of the Ohio State University campus. After a while, he stopped on the tracks at a railway crossing. A train was slowly moving down the tracks. He jumped out of the car and went around to the trunk. Carrie was terrified that he was going to leave her stranded there, handcuffed and with a train coming. She wondered if he was crazy.

Outside the car, Kevin, who had taken the spot from Adalana when he heard the tires thudding over the tracks, went to the rear and saw that the tires were okay. If there had been a flat, he would have run off, but everything looked fine, so he got back in and drove away.

"Take your pants off," Kevin said.

"What?"

"Take your fucking pants off!" he shouted.

She did as he said, frightened by the sudden change of mood. She knew he was doing this to keep her from running away. And rightly so. Even if she hadn't been handcuffed, she'd never run without clothes on.

As they drove, she tried to keep her eyes on her optometry book so as not to upset him. But she noticed he was taking King Avenue west, and then he cut onto Olentangy River Road north. He was driving her out into the country, talking at times to himself: "Just escaped this morning . . . beat him up with a baseball bat . . ."

They passed a cornfield, then a barricade in the roadway. He drove around it into a wooded area, past junked cars in a field.

Carrie remembered a pair of sharp scissors she kept between the seat and the shift console, and she thought of grabbing it and stabbing him. But as she glanced at the scissors, he said, "Don't try anything funny," and pulled out a switchblade. He parked the car, unlocked the handcuffs from the door but left them attached to her right wrist, and spread her buckskin coat on the muddy ground.

"Take off your underpants," her whispered, "and lay down."

Carrie Dryer saw his eyes drift from side to side . . .

Adalana lay back beside the woman, looking up at the trees. She didn't understand why she kept losing the spot to Philip and Kevin. Twice they had taken over while she was behind the wheel, and she had to keep wishing them off the spot. Everything was mixed up.

"Do you know what it's like to be lonely?" she asked the woman lying beside her. "Not to be held by anyone for a long time? Not to know the meaning of love?"

Carrie Dryer didn't answer, and Adalana held her as she had Marlene.

But this young woman was very small, and something else was wrong with her as well. Try as Adalana might, each time she attempted to enter, Carrie Dryer's muscles went into spasms and forced her out—rejected her. This was strange and frightening. Confused, Adalan lost the spot . . .

Carrie explained to him tearfully that she had a physical problem, that she was seeing a gynecologist. Anytime she tried to sleep with someone, she got these spasms. Carrie noticed the nystagmus again, and suddenly he turned angry and nasty.

"Of all the damned girls in Columbus," he snarled, "I had to pick on I couldn't do anything with!"

He let her put her slacks back on and told her to get back into the car. Carrie noticed him change again. He reached over and handed her a paper towel. "Here," he said gently, "blow your nose."

Adalana was now nervous. She remembered Ragen's original purpose for this trip—and she realized Ragen might get suspicious if she returned empty-handed.

Carrie watched the rapist's concerned expression, the genuine worry on his face. She almost felt sorry for him as she wondered what was wrong.

"I've got to get some money," he told her, "or someone will be very angry."

"I don't have any money with me," Carrie said, starting to cry again.

"Don't take it so hard." He handed her another paper towel. "I'm not going to hurt you if you do what I tell you."

"Do whatever you want to me," she said, "but don't bother my family. Take all the money I've got, but leave them alone."

He parked the car and went through her purse again until he found her checkbook. Her balance showed four hundred and sixty dollars. "How much do you think you'll need to live for the week?" he asked.

Carrie sniffled through her tears, "About fifty or sixty dollars."

"All right," he said, "leave yourself a balance of sixty dollars and write a check for the four hundred."

Carrie was surprised and pleased, though she knew there was no way she could replace the money she needed for books and tuition.

"We're going to rob a bank," he said suddenly. "You'll come with me."

"No I won't!" she said forcefully. "You can do what you want to me, but I won't help you rob a bank."

"We'll go into a bank and cash your check," he said, but then he seemed to think better of it. "With you crying, they'll know something's wrong. You're not mentally stable enough to go inside a bank and cash a check. You'll foul it up."

"I don't think there's anything wrong with me," Carrie said, still crying. "I think I'm holding up pretty well for someone held at gunpoint all the time."

He just grunted.

They found an Ohio National Bank branch with a drive-in window at 770 West Broad Street. He kept the gun hidden between them but pointed at her as she pulled out her identification. When she turned the check over to endorse it, Carrie thought of writing "Help," but almost as if he'd read her mind, he said, "Don't try anything like putting something on the back."

He passed the check, along with Carrie's identification, to the teller, who cashed it. "You can report to the police that you were robbed, then stop payment on the check," he said as he drove away. "Tell them you were forced to cash it. That way it'll be the bank that gets ripped off."

When they arrived downtown at Broad and High streets, the car got caught in heavy traffic. "Take over and drive," he said. "If you go to the police, don't give them my description. If I see anything in the newspapers, I won't come myself, but someone else will take care of your family or you."

Then he opened the door and walked quickly away, disappearing instantly into the crowd.

Ragen looked around, expecting to find himself in the Ohio State University parking lot, but instead he was walking past Lazarus' Department Store in the middle of the afternoon. Where had the time gone? He reached into his pocket and found a roll of money. Well, he must have done it. He must have robbed someone and not remembered it.

He took an eastbound bus to Reynoldsburg.

Back at Channingway, he put the money and the Master Charge card on the closet shelf and went to sleep.

Half an hour later, Arthur awoke, refreshed, wondering why he had slept so late. He showered, and as he changed into fresh underwear, he noticed the money on the closet shelf. Now, where in the world had that come from? Someone had been busy. Well, as long as it was there, he might as well get some groceries and pay some bills. The car payment was most important.

Arthur pushed the eviction notice aside. Now that the boys had been fired, John Wymer was demanding rent for the apartment. Well, the rent could wait. He had decided how to handle Messrs. Kelly and Lemmon. He would let them keep sending eviction notices. When they took him to court, Allen would tell the judge that these people had made him quit his job, move into their apartment complex as a requirement for the maintenance job, and just as he was settling in with new furniture on credit, they fired him and attempted to put him out on the street.

The judge, he knew, would give him ninety days to move. Even after the final eviction notice, he would still have three days to get out. That should give Allen enough time to get a new job, save a few dollars and find a new apartment.

That night Adalana shaved off the mustache. She'd always hated hair on her face.

Tommy had promised Billy's sister he would spend Saturday, the last day of the Fairfield County Fair, with her in Lancaster. Dorothy and Del were running a restaurant concession, and they might need help closing things down. He took the money he saw on the dresser—there wasn't much—and told Allen to drive him to Lancaster. He spent a wonderful day with Kathy at the fair, going on the rides, playing the games, eating hot dogs and drinking root beer. They talked over old times, speculating how Jim was doing with his new rock group in western Canada and how Challa was doing in the Air Force. Kathy told him she was glad he'd shaved off his mustache.

When they came back to the concession, where Dorothy was working over the grill, Tommy slipped up behind her and handcuffed her to the pipe. "If you're going to slave over a hot stove all day," he said, "you might as well be chained to it." She laughed.

He stayed at the fair with Kathy until it closed; then Allen drove back to Channingway.

Arthur spent a quiet Sunday reading his medical books, and Monday morning Allen set out to look for a new job. He made phone calls and filled out job applications for the rest of the week, but no one was hiring.

(2)

Friday evening, Ragen jumped out of bed, thinking he had just gone to sleep. He went to the dresser. The money—money he didn't even remember stealing—was gone. He ran to the closet, pulled out a .25-caliber automatic and searched the apartment, kicking open doors, looking for the burglar who had broken in while he was asleep. But the apartment was empty. He tried to reach Arthur. When he got no response, he angrily broke open the piggy bank, took out twelve dollars and left to buy a bottle of vodka. He came back, drank and smoked a joint. Still worried about the bills, he realized that whatever he had done to get that money, he had to do it again.

Ragen took a few amphetamines, strapped on his gun, put on his jogging top and a windbreaker. Again he jogged west to

Columbus, reaching the Ohio State University Wiseman parking lot at about seven-thirty in the morning. Off in the distance, he recognized the horeshoe-shaped football stadium of the Buckeyes. Behind him, he noticed the sign on the modern concrete-and-glass building opposite the lot—UPHAM HALL.

A short, chubby nurse stepped through the doorway. She had an olive complexion and high cheekbones and wore her black hair braided in a long ponytail down her back. As she walked toward a white Datsun, he had the odd impression that he recognized her. Someone—Allen, he thought—had seen her a long time ago in a student hangout called the Castle.

Ragen turned away, but before he could leave, Adalana wished him off the spot . . .

Donna West felt exhausted after her eleven-to-seven shift at the university psychaitric hospital. She had told her fiancé she would call him from the hospital to meet him for breakfast, but she'd worked late this morning after a terrible night, and all she wanted was to get out of there. She'd call Sidney when she got back to her apartment. As she walked toward the parking lot, a friend passed, waved and shouted hello. Donna headed for her car, always carefully parked in the first row facing Upham Hall.

"Hey, wait a minute!" someone yelled.

She looked up to see a young man in jeans and a windbreaker waving to her from the other side of the lot. Handsome, she thought, like some actor whose name she couldn't recall. He wore brown-tinted sunglasses. She waited as he came over and asked directions to the main parking lot.

"Listen, it'shard to explain," Donna said. "I'm going around that way. Why don't you get in and I'll drive you around?"

He sat on the passenger's side. While Donna was backing the car out, he pulled a gun from inside his jacket.

"Just drive," he said. "You're gonna help me out." Seconds later, he added, "If you do what I say, you're not gonna get hurt, but believe me, I'm willing to kill."

This is it, Donna thought. I'm going to die. She felt her face burn, her blood vessels constrict, sick deep down. Oh Christ, why hadn't she called Sidney before she left? Well, at least he knew she was supposed to call him. Maybe he'd notify the police.

Her abductor reached behind the seat and picked up her purse. He took out her wallet and looked at her driver's license. "Well, Donna, drive to Interstate 71 north."

He took the ten dollars out of her wallet. She had the impression he was making a big show of taking it, conspicuously folding the bills and slipping them into his shirt pocket. Then he took a cigarette out of her pack and pushed it toward her lips. "I bet you want a smoke," he said, and lit it with her car lighter. She noticed his hands had some kind of stain all over them and under the fingernails, not dirt or grime or oil, but something. Ostentatiously, he wiped his fingerprints off the lighter. That terrified Donna—it meant he was probably a professional with a police record. He noticed her startled reaction.

"I'm a member of a group," he said. "Some of us are involved in political activites."

Her first impression was that he was alluding to the Weathermen, thought he hadn't actually mentioned that name. She assumed, since he was making her take I-71 north, that he was headed for Cleveland to make his escape. He was, she decided, an urban guerrilla.

She was surprised when he told her to get off I-71 at the Delaware County area and made her drive on a back road. She saw him relax, as if he knew the area, and when they were out of sight of all cars, he told her to park.

When Donna West saw how deserted the area was, she realized this abduction had nothing to do with anything political. She was going to be raped or shot or both. He leaned back in the seat, and she knew something really bad was going to happen.

"I want to sit here a minute and get my head together," he said.

Donna sat with her hands on the wheel, staring straight ahead, thinking of Sidney and of her life, wondering what was going to happen. The tears started down her cheeks.

"What's the matter?" he said. "You afraid I'm going to rape you?"

Those words and his sarcastic tone cut through her, and she looked at him. "Yeah," she said. "I am."

"Well, you're so fucking stupid," he said. "Here you are worried about your ass when you ought to be worried about your life."

That was a sobering, shocking thing to hear, and Donna stopped crying immediately. "By God," she said, "you're absolutely right. I *am* worried about my life."

She could barely see his eyes through the sunglasses as his voice softened: "Take your hair out of the ponytail."

She sat gripping the wheel.

"I said take your hair down."

She reached up and pulled a barrette out. Then he undid the braid, caressing her hair, saying how pretty it was.

Then he changed again, becoming loud and mouthy. "You are so fucking stupid," he said. "Jeeze, look how ya got yourself in a situation like this."

"How did I get myself into this situation?"

"Look at your dress. Look at your hair. You oughtta know you would attract attention from someone like me. What were you doin' in the parking lot at seven-thirty in the morning? You're so fucking stupid."

Donna thought he was right in a way. It *was* her fault for offering him a ride. She had herself to blame for what was going to happen. Then she caught herself and realized he was taking her on a guilt trip. She'd heard of rapists doing this before, and she knew better than to fall for it. But still, she thought, when you're helpless and scared to death, it's easy for the guy sitting there with a big gun to make you feel guilty.

She resigned herself to what was going to happen. The thought went through her mind: Well, rape isn't the worst thing that could ever happen to me.

"By the way," he said, shocking her out of her thoughts, "my name is Phil."

She looked straight ahead, not turning to see his face.

He shouted at her: *"I said my name is Phil!"*

She shook her head. "I don't really care what your name is. I don't think I want to know it."

He told her to get out of the car. Then, as he searched her pockets, he said, "As a nurse, I bet you could get a lotta speed."

She didn't answer.

"Get into the back of the car," he ordered.

Donna began to talk quickly as she got into the rear, hoping she could distract him by conversation. "Do you like art?" she asked. "I really like art. I'm a part-time potter. I work with clay." She talked on and on hysterically, but he seemed not to hear what she was saying.

He made her pull down her white pantyhose, and she was almost grateful he didn't make it even more humiliating by forcing her to disrobe completely.

"I don't have any diseases," he said as he unzipped his fly.

It stunned Donna that he would say such a thing. She felt like screaming at him: *I have diseases. I have all kinds of diseases.* But by now she felt he was mentally ill, and she was afraid of agitating him further. Well, diseases were the last thing on her mind right now. She just wanted this over and done with.

She was surprised and relieved at how quickly he finished with her.

"You're fantastic," he said. "You turn me on." He got out of the car, looked around and told her to get back behind the wheel. "This is the first time I've ever raped anybody. I'm more than a guerrilla now. I'm a rapist."

After a short while, Donna said, "May I get out of the car? I have to urinate."

He nodded.

"I can't do it with someone watching me," she said. "Could you walk away out of sight?"

He did as she asked, and when she returned, she noticed his behavior had changed. He was relaxed, joking. But then he suddenly changed again, assuming the same commanding tone and attitude he'd done before the rape, frightening her with violent talk, using foul language.

"Get into the car," he snapped. "Get back on the freeway and go north. I want you to cash checks and get me some money."

Thinking as quickly as she could, wanting desperately to get back to familiar territory, she said, "Look, if it's money you want, let's go back to Columbus. You're not going to get any out-of-town checks cashed on a Saturday."

She waited for his reaction, telling herself that if he insisted on heading north on I-71, it would mean they were headed for Cleveland. She decided then and there that she would crash the car and kill both of them. She hated what he had done to her, and she was going to make sure he would have no use for her money.

"All right," he said. "Take I-71 south."

She hoped he wouldn't see how relieved she was, and she decided to press her luck. "Why don't we take Route 23? There are lots of banks on 23, and we could get to one before they close at noon."

Again he accepted her suggestion, and though she still felt her life was in danger, she hoped that if she could keep talking and keep him off balance, she might get through it alive.

"Are you married?" he asked suddenly.

She nodded, realizing it was important for him to think someone was waiting for her, that someone would know she was missing. "My husband's a doctor."

"How is he?"

"He's an intern."

"That's not what I mean."

"What do you mean?"

"What's he like?"

She was about to describe Sidney when she suddenly understood that he wanted to know how adequate her husband was sexually.

"You're much better than he is," she said, realizing that if she complimented him, he might be nicer to her. "You know, my husband must have a problem. It takes him forever. It's great that you were so fast."

She could see he really got a big kick out of that, and she was more certain than ever that this young man was a schizophrenic, out of touch with reality. If she kept humoring him, perhaps she might get out of this.

He went through her purse again, taking her Master Charge card, her university clinic I.D. and her checkbook. "I have to have two hundred dollars," he said. "Someone needs the money. Write a check for cash, and go to your bank in Westerville. We'll go in together, but if you make one funny move, you try to do anything, I'll be standing right behind you with the gun. I'll shoot."

Walking into the bank, Donna was shaking all over. She found it hard to believe that the tellers she passed didn't catch on—she was grimacing and rolling her eyes frantically, trying to attract attention. But no one noticed a thing. Donna used her Master Charge card to make two withdrawals of fifty dollars each, until the machine receipt indicated she'd reached her limit.

As they drove off, he tore up the bank receipts carefully, then tossed the pieces out the car window. Donna looked through the rear-view mirror and nearly choked—a Westerville police cruiser was right behind them. *O my God*, she thought, clenching a fist to her temple, *we're going to be picked up for littering!*

Reacting to her agitation, he turned and saw the police. "Oh, hot damn! Let the fucking pigs come up here and I'll blow 'em away. Too bad you have to see this, but that's the way it goes. I'll waste 'em, and if you try anything, you'll be next."

Mentally, she crossed her fingers, hoping the police hadn't seen the papers thrown out of the car. She felt certain he would shoot it out with them.

The police cruiser ignored them, and she slumped back, trembling.

"Let's find another bank," he said.

They tried several banks, then Kroger and Big Bear stores, all unsuccessfully. She noticed that he would become agitated and aggressive before they entered each one, but once inside he would be playful, as if it were all a game. At the Kroger store in Raintree Center, he put his arm around her and pretended he was her husband. "We really need the money," he told the clerk. "We're going out of town."

Donna was finally able to cash a hundred dollars using a check-cashing machine.

"I wonder," he said, "if all the computers are connected."

When she told him that he seemed to know a lot about the way banks and bank machines worked, he said, "I need to know all these things because it's useful information for my group to have. We share information. Everyone adds to the group."

Again she assumed he was talking about the Weathermen or some other radical organization, and she decided to divert him with talk about politics and current issues. When he thumbed through a copy of *Time* that had been lying on the floor of the car, she asked his opinion on the voting for the Panama Canal treaty. He looked confused and flustered, and she realized after a few seconds that he knew nothing at all about something that had been in the headlines and on the TV news. He was not the political activist he had led her to believe. She decided he knew very little about what was going on in the world.

"Don't go to the police about this," he said suddenly, "because I or someone else will be watching, and we'll find out. I'll probably be in Algeria, but someone else will be watching you. That's the way we work. We all look out for one another. The brotherhood I belong to will get you."

She wanted to keep him talking to keep him diverted, but decided to keep away from politics. "Do you believe in God?" she asked, figuring that was a topic someone could talk about for hours.

"Well, do *you* think there's a God?" he shouted, pointing the gun right at her face. "Is God helping you right now?"

"No," she gasped. "You know, you're right. God isn't helping me now."

He suddenly calmed down and stared out the window. "I guess I'm really confused about religion. You'll never believe this, but I'm Jewish."

"Gee," she said, without thinking, "that's funny, you don't look Jewish."

"My father was Jewish."

He rambled on, seeming less upset, but finally he said, "All religion is bullshit."

Donna kept silent. Religion had definitely not been the right topic of conversation.

"You know," he said softly, "I really like you, Donna. It's too bad we had to meet under these circumstances."

Donna decided that he was not going to kill her, and she began to think about helping the police catch him.

"It would be wonderful," she said, "if we could meet again. Phone me . . . write me a letter . . . send me a postcard. If you don't want to sign your own name, you could sign it G for 'Guerrilla.'"

"What about your husband?"

She had him, she thought. She had manipulated him and now she had him hooked. "Don't worry about my husband," she said. "I'll take care of him. Write me. Phone me. I'd love to hear from you again."

He pointed out that she was almost out of gas and suggested they pull into a station to fill up.

"No, that's okay. I'll have enough." She was hoping she would run out of gas so that he would have to leave the car.

"How close are we to where I picked you up this morning?"

"Not far."

"Why don't you take me back there?"

She nodded, thinking how appropriate it was to be going back to where it had started. When they were near the College of Dentistry, he told her to pull over. He insisted on leaving her five dollars for gas. She didn't touch it, so he slipped it under the visor. Then he looked at her tenderly. "I'm sorry we had to meet under these circumstances," he whispered again. "I really love you."

He hugged her tightly and ran out of the car.

It was one o'clock Saturday afternoon when Ragen got back to Channingway Apartments, once again remembering nothing of the robbery. He put the money beneath his pillow and the gun on the table beside him. "This money stays vit me," he said, and went to sleep.

Allen woke later that evening, found two hundred dollars under his pillow and wondered where in the world it had come from. When he saw Ragen's gun, he figured it out.

"Well," he said, "might as well go have a good time."

He showered, shaved his three-day growth of beard, dressed and went out for dinner.

(3)

Ragen woke Tuesday evening thinking he had slept for just a few hours. He quickly put his hand under the pillow, only to find the money gone again. Gone. And he still hadn't paid the bills or bought anything for himself. Once again he asked questions inside, and this time he reached Allen and Tommy.

"Yeah," Allen said. "I saw some money laying there. I didn't know I wasn't supposed to spend it."

"I bought some art supplies," Tommy said. "We needed stuff."

"Fools!" Ragen shouted. "I stole it only to pay bills. To buy food. For car. payment."

"Well, where's Arthur?" Allen asked. "He should have told us."

"I cannot find Arthur. He is off somevere vit scientific studies instead of controlling spot. I am one who has to get money to pay bills."

"What are you gonna do now?" Tommy asked.

"I do it once more. Is last time. No one must touch money."

"God," Allen said, "I hate these mix-up times."

* * *

In the early hours of Wednesday, October 26, Ragen put on his leather jacket and made his way, for the third time, across the city of Columbus, toward Ohio State University. He had to get money. He had to rob someone. Anyone. At about seven-thirty, he paused at an intersection where a police cruiser had also stopped. Ragen gripped his gun. The officers might have some money. As he started toward them, the light changed and they drove away.

Walking along East Woodruff Avenue, he saw an attractive blond woman pulling a blue Corvette up the driveway of a brick apartment building. The sign on the wall said GEMINI. He followed her up the driveway around to the back parking area, certain she hadn't seen him. He had never considered robbing a woman, but now he was desperate. It was for the children.

"Get into car."

The woman turned, startled. "What?"

"I have gun. I need you to take me someplace."

Frightened, she followed his instructions. Ragen got in the passenger side and pulled out two guns. Then Adalana wished him off the spot for the third time . . .

Adalana was becoming worried that Arthur might discover she had been stealing Ragen's time. She decided that if Ragen was ever caught, he might as well be blamed for the whole thing. Since he had come out with guns, and certainly had intended to commit robbery, everyone would believe he had been out the whole time. If he couldn't remember what had happened, it would be blamed on the vodka and the drugs.

She admired Ragen, his aggressiveness as well as his tenderness with Christene. There were qualities about Ragen she wished she possessed herself. As the young woman drove her Corvette, Adalana talked about herself as if she *were* Ragen.

"I want you to stop at that office building over there," she said. "There should be a limousine parked in the back lot."

When they saw the limousine, Adalana picked up one of the guns and aimed it at the car. "I'm going to kill the man who owns that car. If he were here now, he'd be dead. That man deals in cocaine, and I happen to know he killed a little girl by giving her cocaine. He does it to children all the time. That's why I'm going to kill him."

Adalana felt something in her jacket pocket. She found Tommy's handcuffs and laid them on the floor of the car.

"What's your name?" Adalana asked.

"Polly Newton."

"Well, Polly, I see you're low on gas. Pull into that service station."

Adalana paid for five gallons of gas, then told Polly to take I-71 north. They drove until they reached Worthington, Ohio, where Adalana insisted they stop at the Friendly ice cream store for a couple of Cokes.

As they drove on, Adalana noticed a river along the right side of the road and some old one-lane bridges crossing it. She knew Polly Newton was studying her face carefully, probably so she could identify her to the police. Adalana talked, pretending to be Ragen, making up stories. It would confuse Arthur and the others, and cover her trail. No one would know she had been on the spot.

"I killed three people, but I killed a lot more than that during the war. I'm a member of the Weathermen's terrorist group, and I was dropped off in Columbus last night to complete a mission. I had to make a man disappear who was going to testify in court against the Weathermen. I should tell you I completed my mission."

Polly Newton listened quietly, nodding.

"I have another identity," Adalana boasted, "where I dress up, and I'm a businessman, and I drive a Maserati."

When they came to a deserted country road, Adalana had Polly drive across a deep ditch and through the high weeds of an overgrown field near a small pond. Adalana got out with her, looked at the water and at the surrounding area, came back and sat on the hood of the car. "I want to wait for about twenty minutes before I have you drop me off."

Polly looked relieved.

Then Adalana added, "And I want to have sex with you."

Polly began to cry.

"I'm not going to hurt you. I'm not the kind who beats women and throws them around. I don't even like to hear about that being done to women."

"Look, you mustn't scream and kick when you're being raped, because that makes a rapist freak out and get violent. The best thing to do is lay back, say 'Go ahead,' and the rapist won't hurt you. I have a soft spot for tears," Adalana said, "but you don't have a choice. I'm going to do it anyway."

She took two bath towels that were in the car and laid them on the ground along with her jacket. "Lie down on them, put your hands on the ground, look up at the sky and try to relax."

Polly did as she was told. Then Adalana lay down beside her, unfastened her blouse and her bra, and kissed her. "You don't have to worry about getting pregnant or anything like that," she said. "I've got Huntington's chorea and I've had a vasectomy. Look."

Adalana pulled down her jogging pants to her knees and showed Polly a scar on the lower abdomen, right above the penis. It wasn't a vasectomy scar at all. It was a diagonal line on the abdomen itself, a hernia scar.

As Adalana lay on top of her, Polly cried, "Please don't rape me!" The girl's cry of "rape" struck deep into Adalana's mind. She remembered the things that had happened to David and Danny and Billy. My God, what a horrible thing rape was.

Adalana stopped, rolled off onto her back and looked at the sky with tears in her eyes. "Bill," she said aloud, "*what's wrong with you*? Get yourself together.:

She got up and put the towels back into the car. Then she took the larger gun from the front seat and threw a beer bottle into the pond, but at first the gun wouldn't go off. She tried again, firing at the beer bottle twice and missing both times. Well, she wasn't a marksman like Ragen.

"We'd better get going," Adalana said.

As they drove off, Adalana rolled down the car window and fired twice at a telephone pole. Then she reached over and searched the young woman's handbag. "I need to get some money for someone," she said. "About two hundred dollars." She held up the check-cashing card. "We'll go into Kroger's and cash a check."

At the Kroger office, Polly was able to cash a check for one hundred and fifty dollars. Then they went to the State Savings Bank on North High Street, which refused to cash her checks. Finally, after a few other futile attempts at drive-in bank windows, Adalana suggested they use her father's Union Company card and try to cash a check with the card as a backup. The Union store at Graceland Shopping Center permitted her to cash a fifty-dollar check. "We could cash another check," Adalana suggested, "and you could keep the money yourself."

In a sudden change of mood, Adalana tore a check out of the checkbook to write Polly a poem, but when she was done, she said, "I can't give it to you because the police might be able to match my handwriting." She destroyed the check and then ripped a page out of Polly's address book.

"I'm going to keep this page," Adalana said. "If you notify the police about me or give them the right description, I'll send the page to the Weathermen group, and they'll come to Columbus and kill your family."

Just then Adalana saw a police car passing on her left. Startled, she slipped away . . .

Philip found himself looking out the window of a moving car. He turned and saw a strange young blond woman at the wheel. "What da fuck am I doin' here?" he said aloud. "Where y'at, Phil?"

"Is that your name, 'Bill'?"

"Nah. Phil." He looked around. "What da fuck is goin' on? Jesus Christ, just a few minutes ago I wuz . . ."

Then Tommy was there, looking at her, wondering why he was here. Maybe someone was out on a date. He looked at his watch. It was almost noon.

"You hungry?" Tommy asked.

She nodded.

"There's a Wendy's over there. Let's go get a couple of hamburgers and some fries."

She placed the order and Tommy paid for the food. She talked about herself as they ate, but he didn't really listen. She wasn't *his* date. He'd just have to wait until whoever was out with her came back and took her wherever they were going.

"Is there anyplace in particular you want me to drop you off?" she asked.

He looked at her. "The campus area's okay."

Whoever's date it was had just jilted him. When they got back to the car, he closed his eyes . . .

Allen looked up quickly at the young woman driving, felt the gun in his pocket and the roll of money. Oh, Jesus Christ, no . . .

"Look," he said. "Whatever I did, I'm sorry. Real sorry. I didn't hurt you, did I? Don't give the police my description, will you?"

She stared at him. He realized he had to confuse the issue in case she went to the police.

"Tell the police I'm Carlos the Jackal from Venezuela."

"Who's Carlos the Jackal?"

"Carlos the Jackal is dead, but the police don't know it yet. You tell them I'm Carlos and they'll probably believe you."

He jumped out of the car and walked quickly away . . .

Back home, Ragen counted the money and made an announcement: "No one is to touch money. I have robbed this for to pay bills."

Arthur said, "Wait a minute. I paid those bills with the money I found on the dresser."

"Vat? Vy don't you tell me? Vy I am going around robbing people?"

"I thought you'd know when you saw the money gone."

"So? And vat about money from second robbery? It vas gone, but not from paying bills."

"The boys explained that to you."

Ragen felt he'd been made a fool of, and he stormed around the apartment in a rage. He demanded to know who had been stealing his time.

Arthur reached Tommy, Kevin and Philip, but all three denied stealing time from Ragen. Philip described the blond girl he had seen in the car: "She looked like a cheerleader type."

"You were not supposed to take the spot," Arthur said.

"Well, shit, I didn't want to. I just found myself sitting with this broad in the goddamned car without knowing why. And I took off as soon as I realized what was goin' down."

Tommy said he'd bought the same girl a hamburger at Wendy's, figuring she was someone's date, "but that was just for about twenty minutes. The money was in my pocket already."

Arthur said, "Everybody stay home for a few days. We've got to figure out what's going on. Nobody's to leave until we find out who's been stealing time from Ragen."

"Well," Tommy said, "tomorrow's Dorothy and Del's fourth anniversary. Kathy called and reminded me. I promised I'd meet her in Lancaster and she'd help me pick out a present."

Arthur nodded. "All right, call her and tell her you'll meet her, but don't take too much money with you. Just what you'll need. And get back here as soon as possible."

The next day Tommy went shopping with Kathy in Lancaster, where they bought a beautiful chenille bedspread for a present. Kathy pointed out that this was just about the date fourteen years ago that their mother had become Mrs. Chalmer Milligan.

After dinner with Dorothy and Del and a quiet, pleasant visit with Kathy, Tommy sat in the car and waited until Allen came to drive him back to Channingway.

As soon as Allen got back to the apartment, he flopped into bed . . .

And David woke up. He didn't know why he was feeling so bad. Something was wrong around here, but he didn't know what. He wandered around the apartment and tried to reach Arthur or Allen or Ragen, but nobody would come. Everybody was mad at everybody else. Then he saw the bullets from Ragen's gun in the plastic bag under the couch, and the gun under the red chair, and he knew that was very bad, because Ragen always kept his guns locked away.

He remembered what Arthur had always told him: "If there's ever any trouble or somebody's doing something bad and you can't reach anyone for help, call the bobbies." He knew "bobbies" was Arthur's way of saying police, because Arthur had written the police number on the paper beside the telephone. He picked the receiver up and dialed the number. When a man answered, David said, "Somebody is doing bad things around here. Something is going on. Everything's wrong."

"Where you at?"

"Old Livingston Avenue, the Channingway Apartments. There's something awfully wrong. But don't tell nobody I called you." Then he hung up. He looked out the window and saw how foggy it was, sort of spooky.

After a while he left the spot. Danny came and started to paint, even though it was getting late. Then he sat down in the living room to watch TV.

When he heard the knock on the door, he was surprised. Through the peephole he saw a man with a Domino's pizza box in his hand. He opened the door and said, "I didn't order pizza."

While Danny was trying to help the man who was looking for Billy, the man slammed him against the wall and put a gun to his head. The police came in through the door with guns, and a pretty lady told him he had the right to remain silent, so he did. Then two men put him into a car and drove very slowly through the thick fog to the police station.

Danny had no idea why he was arrested or what was going on, but he sat in the jail cell until David came to watch cockroaches running in circles. Arthur or Ragen or Allen would come soon and get him out of there. David knew he hadn't been a bad boy. He hadn't done anything bad at all.

BOOK THREE
BEYOND MADNESS

CHAPTER
TWENTY

(1)

In the early weeks of 1979, the writer visited Billy Milligan frequently at the Athens Mental Health Center. As the Teacher spoke to him of the past, describing what the others had seen, thought and done from the beginning, they all—except Shawn, who was deaf—listened and learned their histories.

Now answering to the name of Billy, the Teacher became increasingly confident. Though he still switched from time to time when he wasn't talking to the writer, Billy felt that the longer he could remain fused, and free of the hostility and fear that led to the mix-up times, the sooner he would be able to hold himself together and start a new life. Money from the sale of his paintings would enable him to start a new life after he was cured.

Billy read, studied medical books, exercised in the gym, jogged around the building and painted. He sketched Arthur and painted Danny, Shawn, Adalana and April. He bought molecular models at the university bookstore and studied chemistry, physics and biology on his own. He bought a citizens' band radio and started broadcasting at night from his hospital room—talking to other CBers about combating child abuse.

After reading in the local newspaper that My Sister's Place, the Athens organization for battered women, was having difficulty paying bills and might have to close, he donated a hundred dollars. But when they discovered who the money was from, they refused his contribution.

On January 10, a little more than a month after his transfer to Athens, Billy opened a bank account in the name of the

Foundation Against Child Abuse and deposited a thousand dollars. It was part of the five-figure payment he had received from a woman in Columbus who was planning to open an art gallery and who came to the Athens Mental Health Center to buy the painting of the lady with the sheet music in her hand, "The Grace of Cathleen."

He then had a bumper sticker printed, black letters on a yellow background:

HUG YOUR CHILD TODAY
"IT'S PAINLESS"
PLEASE HELP STOP CHILD ABUSE—BILLY

Billy talked often with the young female patients. The nurses and mental health technicians knew that the young women were playing up to him, competing with each other for his attention. Nurse Pat Perry noticed that Mary, a former anthropology student, came out of her depression when Billy was around and talked to her. Billy admired Mary's intelligence, often asking her advice, as she asked his. He missed her when she was discharged in January, but she promised to come back to visit him.

When he wasn't talking to Mary, Dr. Caul or the writer, the Teacher would find himself bored and irritated by the confinement, and he would drop down to the level of Danny, David or the unfused Billy. It was easier for him to relate to the other patients this way. Some of the staff who had become close to Billy noticed that when he was Danny or David, he had a special empathy for other patients. He knew when they were upset, hurting or feeling fear. When one of the young women would leave the open ward in a state of panic or hysteria, Billy could often tell the staff where to find her.

"David and Danny are the parts of me that have empathy," the Teacher explained to the writer. "They can feel where the hurt is coming from. When someone leaves and is upset, it's like a beacon around where they are, and Danny or David will just point in the right direction."

One evening after dinner, David was sitting in the living room when suddenly he imagined one of the female patients rushing toward the stairway railing outside the ward door—a steep three-floor drop down the center staircase. Ragen, who always thought David was weird for thinking these kinds of things, realized that what David was seeing was probably happening. He took the spot, dashing down the corridor and up the steps, slamming open the door and running out into the hallway.

Katherine Gillott, the mental health technician who had been sitting in the office near the exit, jumped up from her desk and ran after him. She reached the corridor in time to see him grab the girl, who had already gone over the railing. He held on and pulled her up. When Gillott brought her back inside, Ragen slipped away . . .

David felt the pain in his arms.

In addition to the general therapy he had been giving Billy from the beginning to strengthen his control of the consciousness, Dr. Caul used hypnotherapy and taught his patient autosuggestion techniques to help alleviate tension. Weekly group therapy sessions with two other multiple personality patients enabled Billy to understand more about his condition by seeing its effects on other people. His switching was less and less frequent, and Caul felt his patient was improving.

As Billy the Teacher began chafing at his restrictions, Dr. Caul systematically extended his privileges and freedom, first allowing him to leave the building with an attendant, then letting him sign himself out, as other patients did, for short walks—but only on hospital grounds. Billy used this time to test the pollution levels at various points along the Hocking River. He made plans to attend classes at Ohio University in the spring of 1979, to study physics, biology and art. He began to keep a chart of his moods.

In mid-January, Billy pressed Dr. Caul to extend to him the privilege many other patients had—of going into town. He needed to have his hair cut, to go to the bank, to see his lawyer, to buy art supplies and books.

At first Billy was allowed to leave the grounds only when accompanied by two hospital employees. Things went well, and soon Caul decided to allow him to leave with only one attendant. There seemed to be no problem. A few college students, recognizing him from his pictures in the newspapers and on television, waved to him. It made him feel good. Maybe not everyone hated him for what he had done. Maybe society wasn't totally against him, after all.

Finally Billy asked that his therapy take the next step. He had been a good patient, he argued. He had learned to trust others around him. Now his doctor had to show him that he was trusted as well. Other patients, many of them with more severe mental illness than his own, were allowed to go into town unattended. He wanted the same privilege.

Caul agreed that Billy was ready.

To make certain there would be no misunderstandings, Caul checked with Superintendent Sue Foster and concerned law-enforcement officials. Conditions were set: The hospital was to notify the police in Athens and the Adult Parole Authority in Lancaster each time Milligan left the grounds unattended or returned to the hospital. Billy agreed to abide by the rules.

"We've got to plan ahead, Billy," Caul said. "We've got to consider some of the things you might face out on the street alone."

"What do you mean?"

"Let's think of things that might happen and how you might respond. Suppose you were walking down Court Street and a female saw you, recognized you and just walked up to you and slapped the hell out of you right across your face without any warning. Do you understand that's a possibility? People know who you are. What would you do?"

Billy put his hand to his cheek. "I would just step aside and walk around her."

"All right. Suppose a man walked up to you and called you a dirty name, called you a rapist, and then punched you, knocked you down on the street? What would you do?"

"Dr. Caul," Billy said, "I would just lie there rather than go back to prison. I would just lie there and hope that he would go on and leave me alone."

Caul smiled. "Maybe you've learned something. I guess we're just going to have to give you the chance to show you have."

The first time Billy went to town alone, he felt a mixture of headiness and fear. He crossed the streets carefully at corners so that the police wouldn't cite him for jaywalking. He was aware of the people who passed him, praying that no one would come up and attack him. If anyone did, he wouldn't respond. He would do exactly what he'd told Dr. Caul.

He bought art supplies and then went into Your Father's Mustache barbershop. Norma Dishong had called ahead, alerting the manager and staff to the fact that Billy Milligan was coming to have his hair cut. People there greeted him with

"Hi, Billy," "How's it going, Billy?" and "Hey, you're looking good, Billy."

Bobbie, the young woman who cut and styled his hair, spoke to him sympathetically and refused to accept payment. He could come in at any time, she said, without an appointment, and she'd cut his hair free of charge.

Out on the street, several students, recognizing him, waved and smiled. He went back to the hospital feeling terrific. None of the terrible things Dr. Caul had prepared him for had happened. Everything was going to be all right.

On February 19, Dorothy visited her son alone. Billy taped their conversation. He wanted to learn more about his childhood, to understand why his father, Johnny Morrison, had committed suicide.

"You built your own image of your father," Dorothy said. "Sometimes you would ask me questions and I'd answer them to my best ability, but I never tore him down. I never told the sad things. Why hurt you kids? You built your own image, and that was your dad."

"Tell me again," Billy said. "About the time in Florida when you gave him every bit of money you had so he could go on the road, and there was nothing in the house but a can of tuna and a box of macaroni. Did he come back with the money?"

"No. He went on to the borscht circuit. I don't know what happened there. He came back with his—"

"The borscht circuit? Is that a show?"

"It's up in the mountains, the hotels in the Jewish section of the Catskills. He went up there to do his work—his show business. That was when I got the letter from his agent saying, 'I never believed you'd do this thing, Johnny.' I don't know what happened up there. When he came back, he was more despondent than ever, and it went on this way."

"Did you read his suicide note? I heard from Gary Schweickart that it had all the names of the people—"

"There were names of some of the people he owed money to. Not any of the Shylocks; he didn't name them. But I knew they were there, because I'd go with him—I sat in the car when he went to pay them off—and each time it was a different place. He had to pay off gambling debts. At first I thought I was accountable for those gambling debts, but I wasn't gonna pay them. I didn't make the damned debts. I helped out as much as I could, but I couldn't take it away from you kids."

"Well," Billy snickered, "we had a can of tuna and a box of macaroni."

"I went back to work," Dorothy continued, "and then we had a little bit more. I bought the groceries by that time, and I kept on working and supplying the home. That was when I cut off giving him my salary. I'd give him the money for the rent, and he'd go off and pay only half of it."

"And gambled away the other half?"

"That, or paid off the Shylocks. I don't know what he did with it. Confronting him with it, I never got the straight, honest truth. One day the loan company was going to take the furniture. I told 'em, 'Go ahead and take it.' But the guy couldn't do it because I was crying, and here I was pregnant with Kathy."

"It wasn't very nice of Johnny."

"Hey," Dorothy said, "that's it."

After two and a half months in the Athens Mental Health Center, as Billy lost less and less time, he pressed Dr. Caul to take the next promised step in his therapy—a furlough. Other patients—many showing less improvement than he—were allowed to spend weekends at home with relatives. Dr. Caul agreed that his behavior, his insight, the long period of stability, indicated that he was ready. Billy was allowed to take a series of weekends at Kathy's house in Logan, twenty-five miles northwest of Athens. He was overjoyed.

One weekend, Billy pressed Kathy to show him a copy of Johnny Morrison's suicide note, which he knew she had gotten from the public defender's office. She had resisted showing it to him up to this point, afraid it would upset him, but hearing Billy talk of Dorothy's suffering, what a rotten father Johnny Morrison had been, Kathy became annoyed. All her life Kathy had worshiped Johnny's memory. It was time for Billy to know the truth.

"Here," she said, tossing a bulky envelope on the coffee table. Then she left him alone.

The envelope contained a letter to Gary Schweickart from the Office of the Medical Examiner in Dade County, Florida, along with several documents: four separate pages of instruction addressed to four different people, an eight-page letter to

Mr. Herb Rau, reporter for the *Miami News*, and a two-page note, found torn but subsequently pieced together by the police. This appeared to be part of a second note to Rau, which had never been completed.

The instructions concerned payment of outstanding debts and loans, the smallest of which was twenty-seven dollars and the largest one hundred eighty dollars. A note to "Louise" ended with "one last joke. Little Boy: Mama what's a werewolf? Mother: Shut up and comb your face."

The note to "Miss Dorothy Vincent" began with instructions for payment of debts to be made from his insurance, and ended: "My final request is to be cremated—I couldn't stand your dancing over my grave."

The photocopy of the letter to Mr. Herb Rau of the *Miami News* was unreadable in spots, indicated here by asterisks:

Mr. Herb Rau
Miami News

Dear Sir:

Writing this is not an easy task. It might seem the cowardly way out, but as my entire world has collapsed about me there is nothing left. The only hope for temporary security for my 3 children, James, William and Kathy Jo can be derived from what little insurance I have. If it is possible, can you see that their mother, Dorothy Vincent, does *not* get her hands on it! She is mixed up with a crowd that hangs around where she works, Place Pigalle on Miami Beach, that will gladly share it with her! Procurers, Shylocks, etc. These are the people she has broken up the home for, and believe me I did all in my power to hold it together.

The story is sordid enough— The children I love with all my heart, & the fact that they are born without the benefit of marriage, is something she wants to use as a "gimmick" to get some publicity she thinks will further her career! As follows— Since before our first child was born, I tried several times to get her to marry me, (this is after she accused me of making her pregnant when we 1st met,) but she always found one excuse after another to avoid it. (all this and the following can be proven by a deposition given my lawyer M.H. Rosenhaus of Miami) I introduced her to my family as my wife and so that when the baby arrived I had planned to go to some small town, marry her and legitimatize the baby. By this time I was so much in love with the little boy ***

Again she found one excuse after another— "Somebody might read the marriage column that knows us" etc— Well eventually the second boy arrived & for the 1st 2 weeks it was touch & go whether he lived or not, but God was with us & he is now fine & healthy— As if that were a warning I suggested marriage again. By this time she had other excuses, and was getting entirely out of line— Drinking continually, disappearing from the club, & when she was in these conditions the children weren't safe with her. More than once when she hit the children it was with her arm instead of the flat of her hand— I had to threaten her with a beating to get her to stop. Believe me my life was a living hell. It began to show up in my work— I was slipping fast— I knew if this kept up I would eventually kill her— I wanted *** but she begged me to have patience. We put the children in a wonderful nursery in Tampa, Fla. went on the road and agein with me she was able to work decent Night Clubs & Theaters. Then the little girl was on the way.

We came back to Miami, and after the 3rd baby was born she hired a woman to take care of the children and on her oath she wouldn't mix with the customers. I let her go back to the Place Pigalle to sing— It was no time at all before she was back in the same groove drinking and fighting continually ill until she collapsed and was sent to the hospital with the first stages of Hepatitis. She almost didn't make it— she was under constant care of the doctor for several weeks after leaving the hospital when she came back and said the doctor (Saphire of N.M.B.) told her it would be good for her to get back to work to ease her mind as the expenses were mounting up & also a cocktail now and then wouldn't hurt her! I was against the idea so without telling me, she signed a contract, back at the Pigalle. Well, work had slacked off at the hotels so we talked it over & I decided to go up to the Mountains (N.Y.) for a few weeks to work! We had never been separated before and of course at the time I didn't know the type of people she had been cultivating—the pimps, Lesbians, shylocks, etc.— These to her had become a symbol of "sharp" living. When I came home & saw the type clothing she was buying—Mannish looking shirts—the severe suits—certain type toreador pants that seems to be a signal between these type women—Well I blew my top. From then on it was a living hell—

Her continued drinking put her back into the hospital for a hemroid operation & in view of the fact that her liver that by this time was beyond repair they couldn't operate—she was there for weeks— I traveled 150 miles a night so I could be with her during day visiting hours, painting the home etc— she was planning even then to break up our home so she could be with her new type of life. The day of her operation when she started to come out of it, still under the anesthetic, she thought I was somebody else. Her admissions were sickening, it was like a degeneration of an unknown class— I tried to stop her by telling her it was me (she was in a ward) but again it didn't quite penetrate, and she started boasting how she played me for a "sucker" all these years— I never mentioned this to her because of the children, and I begged the ***

Well, when she started to get better, I mentioned the marriage again and she said she had talked to a priest and she claimed he said "you don't have to worry about that." They are "Children of God"— this to me does not sound plausible, but as I have afore-mentioned she wants to build this into a "gimmick." She went so far as to sue me for divorce so it would hit the papers & without warning had a "peace bond" which she tried to have served on Xmas day so I could not be with the children—and on New Year's Eve my little girl was celebrating her second birthday she refused to let me see her & then called me on the phone to tell me what a wonderful time they were having at her party—

Mr. Rau, You can inquire of the show people in M.B. as to my sincerity & loyalty to this woman, but it is more than I can shoulder— You know the Nite Club business down here is a woman's world & she has been instrumental in causing me to lose 2 jobs— You can guess how, she has continually bragged if I fight for the children she can have me run out of Miami— She has disappeared from 1 to 3 days at a time— and I am at the point where I can't face life & see what these children will face— I tried this once before & failed, but this time I hope it will be a success. In order to protect the children I would have to put up with her and I would rather pay for my sin with the Almighty than go through that. As a last request, please have this looked into by the various agencys that can protect my children.

And may God Have Mercy on my Soul

Johnny Morrison

Billy was stunned by his father's suicide letter. He read it over and over, trying to be skeptical about it, but the more he read it, the more he wanted to know. Billy later told the writer of his attempt to check it out.

Before he left his sister's house in Logan, Billy phoned the Florida Bar Association to track down Johnny Morrison's lawyer, only to discover that the lawyer was dead. He called the hall of records and found there was no record of a marriage license for Johnny Morrison or Johnny Sohraner.

He kept making calls until he reached the former owner of a nightclub at which Johnny had worked. The man was retired now but had a boat in Key Biscayne and still brought seafood to the club. He said he had known that someday one of Johnny's kids would be asking about him. He'd fired Billy's mother from the nightclub, he said, because of the caliber of people she was bringing in. Johnny had tried to keep her away from the people she was associating with, but it was an impossible task. He said he had never seen a woman push a man around like that.

Billy said he found somebody else—a man who had worked at the Midget Motel and who remembered his father. He recalled that the phone calls during that Christmas holiday had depressed Johnny. It seemed to fit with Johnny's claim in the note that Dorothy had been calling him, taunting him.

When he returned to the hospital, he began to lose time again. Monday morning he called the writer to ask that their appointment be postponed.

The writer arrived on Wednesday, and knew immediately that the Teacher was gone. He was facing the unfused Billy. They spoke for a while, and the writer, hoping to recapture the Teacher's interest, asked Billy to explain the radiotelephone he had been working on. As Billy fumbled for words, slowly, almost imperceptibly, the voice strengthened, the language became more articulate, and the discussion became more technical. The Teacher had come back.

"Why are you so upset and depressed?" the writer asked.

"I've been tired. I'm not getting any sleep."

The writer gestured toward the book from the Cody Electronics and Radio School. "Who's been working on that equipment?"

"That's the reason this thing was built, because Tommy's been here most of the day. Dr. Caul's been talking to him."

"Who are you right now?"

"The Teacher, but in a very depressed state."

"Why did you leave? Why did Tommy come?"

"My mom, and her husband now. And her past. I'm at a point where not a whole lot matters to me. I'm so tense. I took a Valium yesterday and slept the whole day. I was up all last night, until six o'clock this morning. I wanted to get away . . . I was upset about the parole board. They want me back in Lebanon. Sometimes I feel I'd rather let them take me back and get it over with. Somehow I've got to get them to leave me alone."

"But unfusing isn't the answer, Billy."

"I know. I've seen myself struggling day to day, trying to achieve more and more and more. I try to do all the things every one of my personalities did, and it's very tiring. I'll be here painting a picture, and as soon as I finish it and put it away and wipe my hands off, I'll pull down a book, turn my chair around and take notes, read for a few hours. Then I'll stop and get up and start working on this radiotelephone thing."

"You're pushing yourself too hard. It doesn't have to be done all at once."

"But I've got such a drive to do it. I've got so many years to make up for, and so little time. I just feel I've got to push."

He got up and looked out the window. "Another thing: I've got to confront my mother eventually. I don't know what I'm going to say to her. I can't act the same as I did before. Everything's different now. The parole board, my upcoming sanity hearing, and now reading my father's suicide letter—it's very hard to stay in one piece. It tore me apart."

On February 28, Billy called his attorney and told him he didn't want his mother present at his commitment review hearing the next morning.

CHAPTER
TWENTY-ONE

(1)

After his March 1, 1979, review hearing, Billy Milligan was recommitted to the Athens Mental Health Center for another six months. All those working with him were aware of the threat hanging over him. He knew that as soon as he was cured and discharged, he would be arrested by the Adult Parole Authority of Fairfield County as a parole violator and returned to prison to serve the remaining three years of his two- to five-year term for the Gray Drug Store robbery. He might also be declared a probation violator and then be forced to serve a consecutive six- to twenty-five-year sentence on the roadside-rest assaults.

L. Alan Goldsberry and Steve Thompson, his Athens attorneys, filed motions in Fairfield County court to have his pleas of guilty dismissed. They argued that in 1975, unknown to the court, he had been a multiple personality, and because he had been insane and unable to assist in his own defense at that time, there had been "manifest justice."

Goldsberry and Thompson held out the hope that if the judge in Lancaster would vacate the guilty plea, Billy would be a free man after he was cured.

He lived on that hope.

At about the same time, Billy was delighted to learn that Kathy and her longtime sweetheart, Rob Baumgardt, had decided to marry in the fall. Billy liked Rob, and he began to plan for the wedding.

As he walked the hospital grounds and saw the signs of spring, he began to feel the bad times had passed. He was getting better. On weekend leave, staying at Kathy's house, he started painting a mural on her wall.

Dorothy Moore denied the allegations in the suicide note and agreed to its publication. Johnny Morrison had been mentally ill before he died, she said. He'd been involved with another woman—a stripper—and he had probably confused this woman with her when he wrote about the people she'd been hanging around with.

Billy made his peace with his mother.

On Friday afternoon, March 30, back in the ward, Billy noticed unusual glances, hushed talking and a general sense of uneasiness.

"Did ja see the afternoon paper?" one of the female patients asked, handing it to him. "You're in the news again."

He stared at the bold banner headline across the top of the front page of the March 30 *Columbus Dispatch:*

DOCTOR SAYS RAPIST ALLOWED TO ROAM FROM CENTER
By John Switzer

William Milligan, the multipersonality rapist who was sent to the Athens Mental Health Center last December, is allowed to roam free and unsupervised daily, The Dispatch has learned . . . Milligan's doctor, David Caul, told *The Dispatch* that Milligan is allowed to leave the hospital grounds to roam Athens and is even given weekend leaves to visit relatives . . .

Athens Police Chief Ted Jones was quoted as saying that he'd had numerous expressions of concern from the community, and that he was "concerned about the mental patient roaming around the university community." The reporter also quoted Judge Flowers, who had found Milligan not guilty, as saying he was "not in favor of Milligan being free to roam at will." The article ended with reference to "the man who spread terror among women in the OSU area during late 1977."

The *Columbus Dispatch* began a series of almost daily follow-up articles deploring that Milligan was allowed to "roam free." An editorial on April 5, referring to Milligan, was headlined: LEGISLATION NEEDED TO PROTECT SOCIETY.

Frightened readers from Columbus and anxious parents of students at Ohio University in Athens began to call the university president Charles Ping, who then called the hospital requesting clarification.

Two state legislators, Claire "Buzz" Ball, Jr., of Athens, and Mike Stinziano, of Columbus, criticized the hospital and Dr. Caul, and began to press for hearings to reconsider the statute under which Milligan had been sent to Athens in the first place. They also demanded a change in the "not guilty by reason of insanity" laws.

Some of Billy's enemies on the hospital staff, outraged that he was making money by selling his paintings, leaked stories to the *Columbus Dispatch,* the *Columbus Citizen-Journal* and the *Dayton Daily News* about the large sums of money he had at his disposal. When he used some of the money from the sale of "The Grace of Cathleen" to buy a compact Mazda to help carry his paintings, it hit the headlines.

Representatives Stinziano and Ball demanded an investigative hearing at the Athens hospital. Mounting attacks and criticism stirred up by almost daily articles and front-page headlines forced Dr. Caul and Superintendent Sue Foster to ask Milligan to give up his furloughs and his privilege of leaving the grounds unattended until the furor died down.

Billy was unprepared for this. He had obeyed the hospital rules, kept his word and broken no laws since his illness had been diagnosed and treated. Yet now his privileges had been taken away.

Saddened, the Teacher gave up and left the spot.

When Mike Rupe came on duty at eleven o'clock, Milligan was sitting in a brown vinyl chair, huddled and rubbing his hands as if frightened. Mike wondered if he should approach him. He had been warned of Milligan's fear of males, he knew about Ragen, and he had seen Dr. Caul's training tapes about multiple personalities. Up to now, he had just laid back and let the patient be. Unlike a lot of others on the staff who thought Milligan was faking, Mike Rupe believed the diagnosis. After reading the history and nursing notes, he just couldn't imagine that all those professional psychologists and psychiatrists could be taken in by a young man without even a high school education.

Milligan usually seemed stable to him, and that was all he really cared about. But for the past week, ever since the *Dispatch* headlines, he had gotten more and more depressed. Rupe felt bad about those lousy headlines and the fact that Milligan had been shafted by the politicians.

Rupe came around from behind the counter and sat on a chair near the terrified boy. He had no idea how Milligan would react, so he had to be as easy and as subtle as possible.

"How're you feeling?" he asked. "Anything I can do for you?"

Milligan looked at him with frightened eyes.

"I can see you're upset. I just want to know if you need someone to talk to, that's what I'm here for."

"I'm scared."

"I can see that. Do you want to talk to me about it?"

"It's the younger ones. They don't know what's happening. They're frightened too."

"Would you tell me your name?" Rupe asked.

"Danny."

"Do you know me?"

Danny shook his head.

"I'm Mike Rupe. I'm the mental health technician on night duty. I'm here to help you if you need it."

Danny kept rubbing his wrists and looked around. Then he stopped, listened to an inner voice and nodded. "Arthur says we can trust you."

"I've heard about Arthur," Rupe said. "You can tell him I appreciate that. I sure wouldn't do anything to hurt you."

Danny told him he thought Ragen was very angry about what was happening with the newspapers and all, and wanted to end it by killing himself. That frightened the younger ones. Rupe could tell by the fluttering lids, the drifting glazed eyes, that Milligan was switching again, and then a little boy cringed and sobbed and looked as if he was in pain.

The switching went back and forth, and they spoke until two in the morning, when Rupe led Danny back to his room.

From that time on, Rupe found he could relate to several of Milligan's personalities. Though the male RN was pretty strict about bedtime (eleven-thirty weekdays and two o'clock in the morning on weekends), Rupe knew that Milligan slept very little, and he spent long night hours talking with him. He was pleased that Danny and the unfused Billy would seek him out to talk, and he began to understand why Billy was so difficult to deal with. Billy, he realized, felt that once again he was being punished for someone else's crimes.

* * *

On Thursday, April 5, at three-thirty in the afternoon, Danny found himself walking the hospital grounds. He looked around, trying to figure out where he was and why. Behind him he saw the old Victorian red-brick mansion with the white columns, and in front of him the river and the town. Strolling along the grass, he realized that before Rosalie Drake helped him at Harding Hospital, he could not walk outside like this— without terror.

Suddenly, he noticed some pretty little white flowers. He picked a few, but saw that on the higher ground the blossoms were larger. Following the flowers up the hill and around the gate, he found himself near a small cemetery. The markers had no names—only numbers—and he wondered why. The memory of being buried alive when he was nine years old made him tremble, and he backed away. There would have been neither a name nor a number on *his* grave.

Danny saw that the blossoms were largest at the top of the hill, so he kept climbing until he reached a cliff that dropped off sharply. He moved to the edge and braced himself against a tree as he looked at the road below, the river and the houses.

Suddenly he heard cars screeching and saw flashing lights in the curved road beneath him. Looking down made him dizzy. Very dizzy. He started to sway forward when he heard a voice behind him say, "Billy, come down."

He looked around. Why were all these people surrounding him? Why wasn't Arthur or Ragen here to protect him? His foot slipped and pebbles under his feet bounced down the cliffside. Then a man reached for his hand. Danny took it and held on as the man pulled him back to safety. The nice man walked back with him to the big building with the pillars on it.

"Were you going to jump, Billy?" someone asked him.

He looked up at a strange lady. Arthur had told him never to talk to strangers. But he could tell there was a lot of excitement in the ward, and people were looking at him and talking about him, and he decided to go to sleep and let someone else have the spot . . .

Allen walked the ward that evening, wondering what had happened. His digital watch said ten forty-five. He hadn't been out for a long time, satisfied, along with the others, to listen and learn from the Teacher's story of their lives. It was as if each of them had possessed just a few pieces in the giant puzzle of consciousness, but now the Teacher, in trying to make the writer see it clearly by putting it all together, had made all of them aware of the lives they had lived. There were still gaps because the Teacher hadn't told *everything*, just the memories that would answer the writer's questions.

But now the Teacher was gone, and the lines of communication between the Teacher and the writer, and between himself and the others, were broken. Allen felt confused and alone.

"What's the matter, Billy?" one of the female patients asked.

He looked at her. "I'm kinda groggy. Guess I took too many pills," he said. "I think I'll go to sleep early."

A few minutes later Danny woke to see several people rushing into his room, pulling him out of bed.

"What'd I do?" he begged.

Someone held up a pill bottle, and he saw some had spilled on the floor.

"I didn't take any," Danny said.

"You've got to go to the hospital," he heard, and someone yelled for a wheeled cot to take Milligan away. Danny left and David came . . .

When Mike Rupe approached him, Ragen, thinking he was going to hurt David, took the spot. As Rupe tried to help him to his feet, Ragen grappled with him, and they fell back onto the bed.

"I vill break your neck!" Ragen roared.

"No you won't either," Rupe said.

They had each other by the arms and rolled over onto the floor.

"Let go! I break your bones!"

"In that case, I sure as hell ain't lettin' go."

"I hurt you if you don't release me."

"I ain't lettin' go as long as you're tellin' me that shit," Rupe said.

They wrestled back and forth, neither able to subdue the other. Finally, Rupe said, "I'll let go of you if you let go of me and promise not to break my bones."

Seeing it was a stalemate, Ragen agreed: "I vill let go if you let go and you move back avay."

"We both let go at the same time," Rupe said, "and everything's cool."

They looked into each other's eyes; then each released the other and moved away.

Dr. Caul, who had appeared in the doorway, gave instructions for the other attendants to move the wheeled cot in.

"I do not need that," Ragen said. "No one took overdose."

"You're going to the hospital to be checked out," Dr. Caul said. "We have no way of knowing how much of his leave medication Billy saved up. Someone said something about taking too much medication. We've got to be sure."

Caul spoke to Ragen until he finally slipped away. Then Danny's knees buckled, and as his eyes rolled back, Rupe caught him and helped him onto the stretcher.

They went out to the waiting ambulance. Rupe sat inside with Milligan as they drove to the O'Bleness Memorial Hospital.

Rupe felt that the emergency room doctor didn't much like the idea of having Billy Milligan there to treat. He tried to explain to the doctor, as well as he could, that Milligan had to be handled carefully: "If he starts to talk in that Slavic accent, the best thing is to back away from him and let a female nurse deal with him."

The doctor ignored him and watched as Danny's eyes rolled back. Rupe could see he was switching from David to Danny.

"He's faking," the doctor said.

"He's just switching and—"

"Listen, Milligan, I'm going to pump your stomach. I'm going to put some tubes down your nose and pump your stomach."

"No," Danny moaned. "No tubes . . . no hose."

Rupe guessed what Danny was thinking. He had told Rupe of an incident with a hosepipe being shoved up his rear end.

"Well, I'm going to do it," the doctor said. "Whether you like it or not, it's going to be done."

Rupe saw the switch.

Ragen sat up quickly, completely alert. "Listen," he said. "I do not allow two-bit doctor vorking his vay through medical school practice on me."

The doctor took a step back, his face suddenly pale. He turned and walked out of the room. "Fuck him," he said. "I don't care if the sonofabitch dies."

Rupe heard him phone Dr. Caul a few minutes later, explaining what had happened. Then the doctor came back, less nasty and mouthy, and had one of the nurses bring a double dose of ipecac to make Milligan vomit. Ragen left, and Danny came back.

When Danny threw up, the doctor had the vomit checked. No signs of medication.

Rupe rode back with Danny in the ambulance. It was two o'clock in the morning, and Danny was quiet and confused. All he wanted to do was sleep.

The next day the therapy team informed Billy that they had decided to transfer him to Ward 5—the men's locked ward. He didn't understand why. He knew nothing about the alleged overdose or the trip with Mike Rupe to the hospital. As several strange male attendants started through his door, Ragen jumped up on the bed, smashed a drinking glass against the wall and held up the sharp edge. "Do not approach!" he warned them.

Norma Dishong ran to the phone and called for help. Seconds later, the words "Code Green" reverberated over the loudspeaker.

Dr. Caul came to the doorway and saw the tense expression, heard the voice of an angry Ragen: "I have not broken bones in long time. Come, Dr. Caul. You are first."

"Why are you doing this, Ragen?"

"You have betrayed Billy. Everyone here has betrayed him."

"That's not true. You know all these problems are because of the *Dispatch* articles."

"I vill not go to Vard Five."

"You'll have to go, Ragen. It's out of my hands. It's now a security matter." He shook his head sadly and walked away.

Three guards, holding a mattress in front of them, rushed Ragen, pinning him to the wall. Three others pushed him, face down, on the bed, holding his arms and legs. Arthur stopped Ragen. Nurse Pat Perry heard Danny scream, "Don't rape me!"

Arthur saw another nurse with a hypo and heard her say, "A shot of Thorazine will stop him."

"Not Thorazine!" Arthur shouted, but it was too late. He had heard Dr. Wilbur say that antipsychotic drugs were bad for multiple personalities and caused worse splitting. He tried slowing the flow of blood to keep the Thorazine from going to his brain. Then he felt himself being lifted by six pairs of hands and dragged out of his room, down into the elevator, out onto the second floor and Ward 5. He saw curious faces peering into his. Someone stuck out his tongue. Someone talked to a wall. Someone urinated on the floor. The smell of vomit and feces was overwhelming.

They threw him into a small bare room with a plastic-covered mattress, and locked the door. When Ragen heard the door slam, he got up to break it down, but Arthur froze him. Samuel took the spot, dropping to his knees, wailing, "*Oy vey!* God, why have you forsaken me?" Philip cursed and threw himself to the floor; David felt the pain. Lying on the mattress, Christene wept; Adalana felt her face wet in the pool of tears. Christopher sat up and played with his shoes. Tommy started to check the door to see if he could unlock it, but Arthur yanked him off the spot. Allen started calling for his lawyer. April, filled with desire for revenge, saw the place burning. Kevin cursed. Steve mocked him. Lee laughed. Bobby fantasized that he could fly out the window. Jason threw a tantrum. Mark, Walter, Martin and Timothy raved wildly in the locked room. Shawn made a buzzing sound. Arthur no longer controlled the undesirables.

Through the observation window, the young Ward 5 attendants watched Milligan bang into walls, spin around, babble in different voices and accents, laugh, cry, fall to the ground and get up again. They agreed that they were witnessing a raving lunatic.

Dr. Caul came in the next day and gave Milligan a shot of Amytal, the one drug that had a calming and restorative effect. Billy felt himself coming together into partial fusion, but something was missing: Without Arthur and Ragen, who stood apart, as they had before the trial, he was the unfused Billy, empty, frightened and lost.

"Let me go back upstairs to AIT, Dr. Caul," he begged.

"The staff on the open ward is afraid of you now, Billy."

"I wouldn't hurt anyone."

"Ragen almost did. He had a broken glass. He was going to cut the security guards. He was going to break my bones. The hospital staff has threatened to go out on strike if you're brought back to an open ward. They're talking about sending you away from Athens."

"Where to?"

"Lima."

The name frightened him. In prison he had heard stories of the place. He remembered Schweickart and Stevenson fighting to keep him from being sent to that hellhole.

"Don't send me away, Dr. Caul. I'll be good. I'll do whatever they say."

Caul nodded thoughtfully. "I'll see what I can do."

(2)

Continuous information leaks from somewhere in the Athens Mental Health Center kept the headlines sizzling. On April 7, the *Columbus Dispatch* proclaimed: MILLIGAN IN SECURITY WARD AFTER FAKED DRUG OVERDOSE.

The *Dispatch*'s attacks on Milligan were now also directed against the Athens Mental Health Center and Dr. Caul. Caul began to receive abusive telephone calls and threats. One caller shouted, "How could you stand up for that rapist, you jive no-good dope-fiend motherfucker? I'm gonna kill you!" After that, Dr. Caul always looked around carefully before getting into his car, and he slept with a loaded revolver on the bedside table.

The following week, the *Dispatch* reported Stinziano's protests against the attempt by the Athens Mental Health Center and hospital superintendent Sue Foster to find a new hospital for Milligan.

STINZIANO DOUBTS ATHENS AIDES ON MILLIGAN TRANSFER

State Rep. Mike Stinziano, D–Columbus, is skeptical about efforts by Athens Mental Health Center officials to down play the possibility that William S. Milligan could be transferred to another institution.

The Columbus Democrat is convinced that newspaper publicity early last week stopped state officials from quietly transferring the 24-year-old mentally ill rapist and robber.

"Frankly, without the publicity, I feel certain he (Milligan) would have been transferred out of state or to Lima (State Hospital)," Stinziano said . . .

During the Wednesday press conference in Athens, Mrs. Foster said, "Treatment of Billy Milligan has been compromised by the press and his reaction to the press."

The superintendent referred to the numerous reports which followed The *Dispatch*'s revelation that Milligan had been allowed on unsupervised leaves from the Athens Hospital.

Mrs. Foster's comment brought a rebuff from Stinziano. "Blaming the press for reporting the facts is irresponsible," he said . . .

When Stinziano and Ball demanded that the Ohio Mental Health Department call in outside experts to evaluate Milligan's treatment, Dr. Cornelia Wilbur agreed to come to Athens. Her report praised Dr. Caul's treatment program. Setbacks like this, she explained, occurred often with multiple personalities.

The *Columbus Dispatch* reported on April 28, 1979:

SYBIL'S PSYCHIATRIST APPROVES OF LEAVES IN MILLIGAN THERAPY
By Melissa Widner

The psychiatrist asked by the Ohio Department of Mental Health . . . to consult on the case of mental patient William Milligan has recommended that no major changes be made in his treatment.

In her report to the department, made public Friday, Dr. Cornelia Wilbur supported Milligan's therapy, which until recently included frequent furloughs from the Athens Mental Health Center, where he is a patient. . . . Dr. Wilbur said he is no longer dangerous after 13 months of therapy in state and private mental institutions. She suggested his treatment at the Athens facility be continued.

She said the unchaperoned leaves as part of his treatment were well conceived, but publicity about those leaves had had a negative effect . . .

The following article appeared in the *Columbus Citizen-Journal* on May 3, 1979:

MILLIGAN DOCTOR'S OBJECTIVITY QUESTIONED

State Rep. Mike Stinziano, D–Columbus, is questioning the objectivity of a psychiatrist who recommended treatments for William Milligan . . . In a letter to Myers Kurtz [sic], acting director of the Ohio Department of Mental Health and Mental Retardation, Stinziano said Dr. Cornelia Wilbur should not give advice on the Milligan case "since she was originally responsible for the placement of William Milligan in Athens."

Stinziano said the selection of Dr. Wilbur as an outside physician "makes about as much sense as asking Miss Lillian what kind of job Jimmy Carter is doing in the White House."

On May 11, the Columbus chapter of the National Organization for Women wrote a three-page letter to Dr. Caul and sent copies to Meyers Kurtz, Mike Stinziano, Phil Donahue, Dinah Shore, Johnny Carson, Dr. Cornelia Wilbur and the *Columbus Dispatch*. It opened with the following:

Dr. Caul,
   The treatment program you have prescribed for William Milligan, which according to newspaper accounts, includes unsupervised furloughs, unrestricted use of an automobile, and assistance in financial arrangements for books and movie rights, displays a deliberate and flagrant disregard for the safety of women in the surrounding communities. It cannot be tolerated under any circumstances . . .

The letter went on to say that not only did Dr. Caul's treatment program not teach Milligan that violence and rape are unconscionable, but he was in fact getting positive reinforcement "for his reprehensible actions." It charged that with Caul's collusion, Milligan had learned "the culture's subliminal but actual message—that violence against women is an accepted occurance [*sic*], a commercialized and eroticized commodity . . ."

The letter argued that Caul's "lack of clinical insight is as misogynist as it is predictable. The claim that the rapist personality was a lesbian is a transparent ruse to excuse the patriarchal culture . . . The fictionalized, lesbian character is a convenient but fallacious, stereotypic scapegoat who can be blamed for Milligan's own retaliative violent/aggressive [*sic*] sexuality. Once again the male is relieved from responsibility for his actions and the woman gets victimized."

As a result of Dr. Wilbur's recommendation, the decision was made to keep Billy in Athens.

The staff on the Admissions and Intensive Treatment ward, upset by the publicity and Billy's reaction to it, demanded changes in his treatment plan or, they warned, they would strike. Because some of them felt he was spending too much time with Billy, they insisted that Dr. Caul turn over authority for day-to-day management to the staff team and limit his own involvement to medical and therapeutic concerns. To keep Billy from being sent to Lima, Caul reluctantly agreed.

Social worker Donna Hudnell drew up a "contract" for Billy to sign in which he promised to abide by a series of restrictions, the first of which was that there would be "no threats of alienation nor depravation of character and position made toward any staff member." The penalty for the first violation of this clause would be the restriction of the writer's visits.

Milligan was not to have glass or sharp objects in his room. No general privileges without prior agreement by the morning treatment team. No incoming phone calls. Outgoing calls were limited to once a week to his attorney, and twice a week to either his mother or his sister. Visitors were to be limited to his sister and her fiancé, his mother, his attorney and the writer. He was forbidden "to give advice of any nature whether it be medical, social, legal, economical, or psychological to any other patient on AIT." He would not be allowed to withdraw more than $8.75 per week from his account at the business office, and he was not to have more than that in his possession at any time. His paint supplies could be given to him for limited amounts of time, but he had to be supervised while painting. The finished paintings had to be removed weekly. Only if he complied with the rules for two weeks would his privileges be restored in stages.

Billy agreed to their terms.

The unfused Billy followed the rules, feeling that the staff had turned the hospital into a prison. He felt he was again being punished for something he hadn't done. With Arthur and Ragen still gone, the unfused Billy spent most of his time watching television with the other patients.

The first of his privileges to be restored after two weeks was visits by the writer.

The Teacher had not reappeared since the beginning of the *Dispatch* attacks. Unable to provide memories or details of what had been happening to him, Billy was embarrassed. To avoid confusion, he and the writer decided to refer to the unfused Billy as "Billy-U" when the writer asked who he was talking to.

"I'll be all right," Billy-U said to the writer. "I'm sorry I can't be more helpful. But I'll be all right when my Arthur and Ragen come back."

(3)

When the writer arrived the following Friday, May 22, he was still facing the unfused Billy. The halting speech, the distracted gaze, the general air of depression, saddened the writer.

"For the record," he asked, "who am I talking to?"

"It's me, Billy-U. Still unfused. I'm sorry, but Arthur and Ragen are still gone."

"No need to apologize, Billy."

"I won't be much help."

"That's okay. We can talk."

Billy nodded, but he looked listless and drained.

After a while the writer suggested they ask if he would be permitted to take Billy out for a walk. They found Norma Dishong, who agreed, as long as they stayed on hospital grounds.

It was a bright afternoon, and as they strolled along, the writer urged Billy to walk the route Danny had taken the day he went to the cliff.

Uncertain of the path, but with a general sense of the direction, Billy tried to reenact what had happened that day, but it was no use. His memory was vague.

"There's a place I like to go when I want to be alone," he said. "Let's go over there."

As they walked, the writer asked, "What's happening to the other people in your head when you're only partially fused? What's it like?"

"I think it's changing," Billy said. "What they call 'co-consciousness.' It's like I'm piercing co-consciousness with some of the other people. I think it's happening gradually. I don't think everybody has co-consciousness with everybody else, but things are opening up. Every so often, So-and-so knows what's going on with So-and-so, and I don't know why or how.

"Like last week there was a big argument in one of the meetings upstairs with Dr. Caul, another psychiatrist, and that clients' rights advocate. Allen was there, arguing with them. But then he got up and said, 'The hell with ya. I'll see ya in

Lima,' and walked out. I was out in the lobby sitting in a chair, and all of a sudden I heard exactly what he'd just said.

"And I shouted, 'What? Hey, wait a minute here! Whaddya mean "Lima?"' I'm sittin' on the edge of my chair, getting scared, because I'm hearing the conversation that just happened seconds ago, like an instant replay, and it was somebody else saying that. I saw the other psychiatrist, who came out of the room, standing there, and I said, 'Look, you guys, you gotta help me.'

"He says, 'What do you mean?' And I started shaking and told him what I just heard in my head. And I asked him if it was true: 'Did I just say to send me to Lima?' He said yes. Then I started crying, 'Don't listen to me. Don't listen to what I'm saying.'"

"Is this a new development?"

Billy looked at the writer thoughtfully. "I guess it's the first sign of co-consciousness without complete fusion."

"That's very important."

"But it's scary. I was crying and yelling. Everybody in the room turned and looked at me. I didn't know what I'd just said, and I'm wondering, 'Why is everybody looking at me?' Then I heard it over again in my head."

"You're still the unfused Billy?"

"Yes. I'm Billy-U."

"Are you the only one who gets this instant replay?"

He nodded. "Because I'm the host, the core, I'm the one developing the co-consciousness."

"How do you feel about it?"

"It means I'm getting well, but it's scary. Sometimes I wonder: Do I want to get well? Is all this fear, all this shit I'm going through now worth it? Or should I bury myself back here in the brain and forget about it?"

"What's your answer?"

"I don't know."

Billy became quieter when they reached the small cemetery near the Beacon School for the Mentally Retarded. "This is where I come sometimes to try and sort things out. It's the saddest place you can imagine."

The writer looked at the little headstones, many of which had fallen over and were overgrown with weeds. "I wonder why they just have numbers," he said.

"Well, when you don't have family or a friend in the world," Billy said, "and nobody really gives a damn and you die here, all your records are destroyed. But there's a list of who's buried where in case anybody shows up again. Most of these people died during the fever of . . . 1950, I think it was. But there's markers over there from 1909 and earlier."

Billy began to wander among the graves.

"I'd come up here and sit on the bank over there near those pine trees, to be alone. It's depressing to be in this graveyard and know what it's about, but it's also got a kind of peace to it. You notice how that dead tree hovers over it? There's a kind of grace and dignity about it."

The writer nodded, not wanting to interrupt.

"What they did when they started to build this graveyard was to make it in a circle. You see how they go around like a big spiral? Then when that big fever came and they started running out of space. They had to start burying them in rows."

"Do they still use this graveyard?"

"If someone dies and they have no family. It's painful. How would you like to come up here looking for a long-lost relative and find out he or she's number 41? And there are so many of these stones lying over there on the bank, just thrown in piles. That's really depressing. No respect for the dead. The good markers haven't been put up by the state. They're set up by people who discovered their relatives. They have names on them. People like to chase back and want to know where they're from. When they find their ancestors and relatives have been planted out here with a number over their heads, it kind of pisses them off. They'll say, 'That's my family. There's got to be a little more respect than that.' It doesn't matter if they were the black sheep or sick or whatever. It's sad that there are only a few nice stones out there. I spent a lot of time around here when I was able to roam around—" He stopped, chuckled and said, "When I could 'roam' around."

The writer knew he was referring to the word used in the *Dispatch* headline. "I'm glad you can laugh at it. I hope you don't let it get you anymore."

"It doesn't. I got over that hump. I realize there's going to be a lot more, but I don't think they'll be sprung on me, and I'll be able to handle them easier."

During their conversation, the writer realized he had been sensing a barely perceptible change in Billy's expression. His gait was quicker. His speech had become more articulate. And now the mocking reference to the headline.

"Let me ask you something," the writer said. "In talking to you now, if you hadn't told me you were Billy-U, you could have fooled me, because you sound like the Teacher . . ."

His eyes brightened and he smiled. "Well, why don't you ask me?"

"Who are you?"

"I'm the Teacher."

"You sonofabitch. You like to spring things on me."

He smiled. "That's the way it goes. When I become relaxed, it happens. It's got to take an inner peace. That's what I've found out here . . . talking with you, being able to see these things again and relive and remember."

"Why did you wait for me to ask you? Why didn't you say, 'Hey, I'm the Teacher'?"

He shrugged. "It's not as if I'm re-meeting you. The unfused Billy has been talking to you. And then all of a sudden Ragen joins the conversation, and then Arthur, because they have something to contribute. And in a way it's also very embarrassing to say, 'Oh, hey, hi, how are you?' as if I haven't been talking to you all the while."

They walked on, and the Teacher said, "Arthur and Ragen really want to help Billy explain to you what happened during the last mix-up time."

"Go ahead," the writer said. "Tell me."

"Danny was never going to jump off that cliff. He was only following the flowers up the hill to where the bigger ones were growing."

The Teacher walked ahead, showing the writer the path Danny had taken and the tree behind which he had braced himself. The writer looked down. Had Danny jumped, he would surely have killed himself.

"And Ragen never intended to hurt those guards," the Teacher said. "The broken glass was for him. He knew Billy had been betrayed, and he was going to ice himself." He held his hand up to show that what had been seen by outsiders as a threat to them was actually the glass at his own neck level. "Ragen was going to cut his own throat and end it all."

"But why did you tell Dr. Caul you were going to break his bones?"

"What Ragen actually intended to say was, 'Come, Dr. Caul. You first vatch me break some bones.' I wasn't going to hurt that little man."

"Stay fused, Billy," the writer said. "The Teacher is needed. We have work to do. Your story is important."

Billy nodded. "That's what I want now," he said. "For the world to know."

As therapy went forward, outside pressure on the hospital administration continued. Billy's two-week contract with the staff was renewed. Privileges were slowly restored. The *Columbus Dispatch* continued to run hostile Milligan stories.

The state legislators, in response to the newspaper reports, pressed on with hearings. When Stinziano and Ball learned that a book on Milligan was being written, they introduced House Bill 557 to prevent offenders—including those found not guilty by reason of insanity—from keeping any of the money they might make from the stories of their lives or from revelations about the crimes they commited. The hearings on this bill before the state Judiciary Committee were to begin in two months.

(4)

By June, despite the ongoing newspaper attacks and upheavals they caused in his living conditions and treatment, Billy remained stable. He was once again allowed to sign himself out to exercise on the hospital grounds (but not to go to town unattended). His therapy sessions with Dr. Caul continued. He started painting again. But now both the writer and Dr. Caul agreed that there was a noticeable change in the Teacher. His memory was less accurate. He was becoming as manipulative as Allen and as antisocial as Tommy, Kevin and Phillip.

The Teacher told the writer that one day, when he'd been working with Tommy's CB equipment, he'd heard himself say aloud, "Hey, what am I doing? Broadcasting without a license is illegal." Then without switching to Tommy, he said, "What the hell do I care?"

He was shocked and worried at his own attitude. He had come to believe that these personalities—as the Teacher he now accepted the term "personalities" rather than "people"—had been part of him. Suddenly, for the first time, without switching, he *felt* like them. This, then, was the real fusion.

He was becoming the common denominator of all twenty-four personalities, and that made him not a Robin Hood or a Superman, but a very ordinary, antisocial, impatient, manipulative, bright, talented young man.

As Dr. George Harding had earlier suggested, the fused Billy Milligan would probably be less than the sum of his parts.

At about this time Norma Dishong, his morning case manager, felt she no longer wanted to handle Billy's case. The pressure had gotten to her. None of the other mental health technicians wanted the case, either. Finally, Dishong's "case buddy," Wanda Pancake, new to the AIT unit, although she had been at the hospital for ten years, agreed to be his case manager.

A young divorcée, with a square-shaped face and a short, stocky figure, Wanda Pancake approached her new patient with trepidation. "When I first heard he was coming here," she later admitted, "I thought to myself: That's all we need. I was scared to death of him because of what I'd read in the papers. I mean, he was a rapist. And he'd been violent."

She recalled the first time she saw him, a few days after he'd been admitted to AIT the previous December. He was in the recreation room, painting. She went in to talk to him, and found herself trembling so hard that she could see a lock of her hair that had fallen across her forehead was vibrating.

She had been one of those who didn't believe in multiple personalities. But after he had been there a few months, she lost her fear of him. He made it a point to tell her what he'd told all the women on the unit—that they should not worry if he ever switched to Ragen, because Ragen would never harm a woman or a child.

She got along well with him now. She would check on him in his room from time to time, and they would have long talks. She found herself starting to like him and to believe he was a tormented multiple personality. She and Nurse Pat Perry defended him to those of the staff who were still hostile.

Wanda Pancake met Danny for the first time when she saw him lying on the couch trying to pull the buttons off the tufted vinyl back. She asked him why he was doing that.

"Just tryin' to pull them off," he said in a boyish voice.

"Well, stop it. Who are you, anyway?"

He laughed and pulled harder. "I'm Danny."

"Well, if you don't stop, Danny, I'm gonna slap your hands."

He looked up at her and gave a few extra tugs to have the last lick, but when she came closer, he stopped.

The next time she met Danny, he was throwing clothes and some of his personal possessions into the trash can.

"What are you doing?"

"Throwing stuff away."

"Why?"

"Ain't mine. I don't want 'em."

"Now, you've got to stop it. Take that stuff back into your room, Danny."

He walked away, leaving the things in the trash, and Wanda had to pull them out and put them back in his room.

Several times she caught him throwing away clothes and cigarettes. Other times people would bring back things he had thrown out the window. Later, Billy would always ask who had been taking his things.

One day she brought her eighteen-month-old niece, Misty, back to the recreation room, where Billy was painting. When he leaned over and smiled, the baby drew back and cried. Billy looked at her ruefully and said, "You're kind of young to be reading the newspapers, aren't you?"

Wanda looked at the landscape he was working on. "That's really good, Billy," she said. "You know, I'd like to own one of your paintings. I don't have much money, but if you'd paint me a deer, just a small picture, I'd be glad to pay for it."

"I'll work on something," he said. "But first I'd like to do a portrait of Misty."

He began painting Misty, pleased that Wanda liked his work. She was down-to-earth, easier to talk to than most of the others. He knew she was divorced, had no children, and that she lived in a trailer near her family in the small Appalachian town where she'd been born. She was rugged, a tough young woman with a dimpled smile and probing eyes.

He was thinking about her one afternoon while he jogged around the building when she pulled up in her pickup truck, a sharp new four-wheel drive.

"You've got to let me drive that someday," he said, jogging in place as she got out of the truck.

"No way, Billy."

He saw the CB antenna and the call number on the back window. "I didn't know you were a CBer."

"Yep," she said, locking up and turning to walk into the hospital.

"What's your handle?" he asked, following her inside.

"Deerslayer."

"That's a strange handle for a woman. Why'd you choose that?"

"Because I like to hunt deer."

He stopped and stared at her.

"What's the matter?"

"You hunt deer? You kill animals?"

She looked him in the eye. "I shot my first buck when I was twelve years old, and I've hunted every year since. I didn't have much luck last season, but I can tell you I'm lookin' forward to goin' out next fall. I hunt for the meat. I think it's right. So don't start arguing about it."

They rode up together in the elevator. Billy went to his room and tore up the sketches for her deer painting.

On July 7, 1979, boxed in red on the front page, the *Columbus Dispatch* ran a banner-headlined story by Robert Ruth:

RAPIST MILLIGAN COULD BE FREE WITHIN FEW MONTHS

Describing the possibility that Milligan might be found sane in three or four months, and that he might be released under U.S. Supreme Court interpretations of federal law, the article concluded:

"He [Rep. Mike Stinziano] predicted Milligan's life might be in danger if some Columbus residents found him wandering in the city."

After reading the story, Dr. Caul said, "I'm afraid that newspaper article is going to put ideas into some people's heads."

Kathy's fiancé, Rob Baumgardt, and his brother Boyce, wearing Army fatigues from work as extras in Robert Redford's movie *Brubaker*, came to pick Billy up a week later for his chaperoned weekend leave. As he walked down the steps with the uniformed men Billy saw the officers staring through the window of the security office. He tried to keep from smiling while he was driven off by what must have looked like a military escort.

* * *

Billy told the writer of disturbing changes he was noticing in himself. Without switching to Tommy, he opened locked doors without keys. He rode his new motorcycle without switching to Ragen, yet he rode it as Ragen would have, up steep hills. He felt the pulsating adrenaline, as Ragen had felt it, physically aware of himself, every muscle working well to do the things he was now able to do, though he himself had never been on a bike before.

He also found himself becoming antisocial, annoyed at the other inmates, impatient with the staff. He had the strange sense of wanting desperately to get a six-foot metal rod with a hook at the end and go down to the electric terminal. He knew where the U-80 current transformer was. By pulling it down, he could turn the juice off.

He argued with himself that it was wrong. If the pole lights went off in the street, someone might have a wreck. But why did he *want* to do it? Then he remembered one night when his mother and Chalmer had been arguing. Unable to stand it, Tommy had gone off on his bicycle down Spring Street. He'd ridden to the terminal, crawled in and knocked the electricity out. Tommy knew that when the lights went out, people got calmer. They'd have to stop fighting. Three streets had lost power—Hubert Avenue, Methoff Drive and Spring Street. When he got back it was dark, but the argument was over, and Dorothy and Chalmer were sitting in the kitchen, drinking coffee by candlelight.

That's what had made him want to do it again now. He'd heard from Kathy that Dorothy had been having some bad arguments with Del. Billy smiled as he looked up at the power transformer. Just a case of sociopathic déjà vu.

He also suspected there was something else wrong with him now, because he had little interest in sex. He'd had opportunities. Twice when he was supposed to be on leave at his sister's house, he had checked into motels in Athens with young women who had shown interest in him, but both times, seeing the police cars watching him from the road, he had given it up. He felt like a guilty kid anyway.

He intensified his study of himself, watching the phases of the others inside him, and he knew their influence was getting milder. He had bought a drum set during the weekend, after playing on it in the store and being amazed at his skill. Allen used to play the drums, but the ability now belonged to the Teacher and even the unfused Billy. He also played the tenor sax and the piano, but the drums gave him a more powerful emotional release than any of the other instruments. They stirred him.

When the news reached Columbus that Milligan's treatment plan once again included furloughs, the attacks against Dr. David Caul were renewed. The Ohio Ethics Commission was instructed to begin an investigation with a view to pressing charges against Caul for improper conduct in the performance of his duties. It was alleged that Milligan was receiving special privileges because Caul was secretly writing a book about him. Since the law required that a complaint be lodged before such an investigation could take place, the Ohio Ethics Commission had one of its own attorneys file the complaint.

Finding himself now attacked from another quarter, his efforts to treat his patient compromised and his reputation and medical career threatened, Dr. Caul filed an affidavit on July 17, 1979:

> Events of the past several months concerning the Billy Milligan case have created issues and upheavals that reach proportions beyond appropriateness and beyond what I believe to be within the bounds of logic, reason and even the law . . .

> My clinical decision as to how the patient was treated is the thing that generated most if not all of the controversy. My clinical decision was supported by all the professionals who are knowledgeable on this subject . . .

> It is my belief that I have been abused and attacked for some very base motives, the least of which is publicity for a legislator and material for some very questionable journalism . . .

Later, after many months of complex and expensive legal manuevering, including subpoenas, depositions and counter-suits, Dr. Caul was unanimously cleared of any wrongdoing. But during this period, he found that more and more of his time and energy had to go into protecting himself, his reputation and his family. He knew what everyone wanted, and that he could stop the threats by keeping Billy locked away, but he refused to give in to the emotional demands of the legislators and the newspapers when he knew Billy's therapy demanded that he treat him as he would any other patient.

* * *

(5)

On Friday, July 3, Billy was given permission to carry some of his paintings to the Athens National Bank, which had agreed to display his art in the lobby for the month of August. Billy worked happily, preparing new work, mounting canvases, painting and framing. He also spent time making arrangements for Kathy's wedding, now set for September 28. He used some of his money from the painting sales to hire a wedding hall and had himself fitted for a tuxedo. He looked forward to the celebration.

The news of his art exhibit brought reporters and TV cameras from Columbus. With his attorney's approval, Billy granted interviews for the evening news to Jan Ryan, of WTVN-TV, and Kevyn Burger, of WBNS-TV.

To Jan Ryan, he talked of his artwork and of his feeling that therapy at the Athens Mental Health Center was helping him. When she asked how much of the artwork was done by his other personalities, Billy said, "Basically it's a touch of all. They're all part of me, and I have to learn to accept that. Their abilities are my abilities. But I am the one responsible for my own actions now, and I want to keep it that way."

He told her that the proceeds from his artwork would go to pay his state hospital bill and his lawyer and to contribute to work against child abuse.

He also told her he felt his personalities were joining into one whole and he was now able to turn his attention to his future work—the prevention of child abuse. "I would like to see more foster homes adequately investigated," he said, "to make sure that they're safe and a comfortable environment. A child's needs must be taken care of emotionally as well as custodially."

The biggest change Jan Ryan found in Billy from the previous December, when she had filmed a half-hour documentary on him, was in his attitude toward society. Despite the severe abuse he had suffered as a child, he now faced the future with hope.

"I have put a little bit more faith in our judicial system as it stands. I don't feel that everyone in the world is against me now."

On the six o'clock news, Kevyn Burger pointed out that Milligan's therapy program at the Athens Mental Health Center had been controversial and harshly criticized, but that Billy felt a sense of belonging in the community now.

"I feel a lot better about the people in Athens," he told her. "They are not as hostile, because they're getting to know me. They're not afraid of me, as they were when I first came here. That was stirred up by . . . other means . . ."

He pointed out that he had selected, very carefully, the paintings he was putting on public view. He was holding others back because he feared people would try to analyze him through his artwork. He was worried, he admitted, about how people would judge his work. "If they come to see my work," he said, "I hope it's not because they're thrill-seeking, but because they're interested in art."

He wanted to go to school, he said, to improve his techniques, but because his reputation had preceded him, he felt he wouldn't be accepted in a college classroom. Perhaps that would change someday. He would wait.

"I'm facing reality now," he told her, "and that's what's important."

Billy felt the staff at the hospital reacted well to the evening newscasts, which showed him hanging his paintings and talking to the newscasters. Most of the staff had become warm toward him; few were openly critical. He'd even gotten word that some people who had been openly hostile before had recently written positive statements about him in the progress notes. It amazed him that some would tell him what went on in team meetings and what had been reported in his charts.

He knew he'd made a lot of progress since Ward 5.

On Saturday, August 4, he was heading out the door of AIT when he heard the elevator alarm. The elevator was stuck between the third and fourth floors. A mentally retarded young girl was trapped inside. Billy could see the sparking and hear the crackling and sputtering and humming of the outer electrical box, and he realized there must have been a short circuit. As several of the patients gathered in the hallway, the girl began screaming inside the elevator and banging on the panels. Billy shouted for help, and with the assistance of one of the workmen, he pried the outer door open.

Katherine Gillott and Pat Perry came out to see what the commotion was about. They watched as Billy went down into the elevator shaft, squeezing through the overhead trap door. Billy dropped down beside the girl and began talking to keep her calm. They waited while an elevator serviceman was called. Billy worked on the electrical box from the inside.

"Do you know any poems?" he asked her.

"I know the Bible."

"Recite some psalms for me," he said.

They talked about the Bible for nearly half an hour.

When the elevator maintenance man finally got it moving, and they came out on the third floor, the girl looked up at Billy and said, "Can I have a can of pop now?"

The following Saturday, Billy rose early. Though he felt good about his art exhibit, he was upset about the *Dispatch* article that described the exhibit, rehashing—as they always did—the *ten* personalities and calling him a "multi-personality rapist." He had to get used to handling mixed emotions. It was a new kind of feeling—confusing but necessary to his mental stability.

This morning he decided to jog to the Ohio University Inn, adjacent to the hospital grounds, and get a pack of cigarettes. He knew he shouldn't be smoking. In the old days only Allen had smoked cigarettes. But he needed it. There would be time enough to give up the habit when he was cured.

He walked down the front steps of the hospital and noticed two men in a car parked opposite the entrance. He assumed they were visiting someone. But when he crossed the road, the car passed him. Coming around the building to a secondary road, he saw it again.

He cut across the freshly mowed field, walked toward the footbridge over the creek that bordered the hospital property, and saw the car for the fourth time, turning up Dairy Lane, the road between the creek and the inn, the road he would have to pass after he crossed the footbridge.

As he stepped on the bridge, the car window rolled down. A hand held a gun. Someone yelled, "Milligan!"

He froze.

He defused.

The shot missed Ragen as he turned and jumped into the creek. The second shot also missed. Then another. Ragen grabbed a broken branch from the creek bed, scrambled up the bank and, using the branch as a club, shattered the rear window of the car before it sped off.

He stood there for a long time, trembling with rage. The Teacher had frozen on that bridge—weak and indecisive. If not for his own quick action on the spot, they would all have been dead.

Ragen walked back slowly to the hospital, discussing with Allen and Arthur what to do. Dr. Caul had to be told. Here in the hospital, they were an easy target. They could be found and killed anytime.

Allen told Dr. Caul about it. Furloughs from the hospital were now more important than ever, he argued, because he had to find a place that would be safe until his hearing in Lancaster to vacate his guilty plea. Then he could arrange to leave Ohio and go to Kentucky to be treated by Dr. Cornelia Wilbur.

"It is important," Arthur told Allen, "not to release word of this attack. If those men read nothing about it in the newspapers, they will be off balance. They will fear that Billy is doing something."

"Do we tell the writer?" Allen asked.

"No one but Dr. Caul must know," Ragen insisted.

"Well, the Teacher has his regular one o'clock appointment with the writer. Will the Teacher be there?"

"I don't know," Arthur said. "The Teacher is gone. I believe he's ashamed of freezing on the bridge."

"So what do I tell the writer?"

"You are good talker," Ragen said. "Pretend you are Teacher."

"He'll know."

"Not if you tell him you're the Teacher," Arthur said. "He'll believe you."

"You mean *lie*?"

"It will upset the man if he knows the Teacher has unfused and disappeared. They've become friends. We cannot take a chance of jeopardizing the book. Everything must go forward just as before this attempt on Billy's life."

Allen shook his head. "I never thought you'd tell me to lie."

"If it's done in a good cause," Arthur said, "to keep someone from being hurt, it's not really a lie."

* * *

But during the meeting, the writer found himself uncomfortable with Billy's attitudes and actions. He seemed too arrogant, too manipulative and demanding. He had always been taught to look for the worst, Billy said, and hope for the best. Now his hopes had been turned around. He was sure he'd be sent back to prison.

The writer felt this was not the Teacher, but he couldn't be sure. Billy's lawyer Alan Goldsberry arrived, and the writer sensed it was Allen explaining why he wanted to make out his will, leaving everything to his sister: "At school there was a bully who always picked on me. One day he was going to punch me, but then he didn't. I discovered later that Kathy gave him her last twenty-five cents not to hit me. That's something I'll never forget."

That weekend at Kathy's, Danny and Tommy painted a mural while Allen worried about the upcoming court hearing in Lancaster. If he won, and Dr. Caul sent him to Kentucky, he knew Dr. Wilbur could help him. But what if Judge Jackson ruled against him? What if he were destined to spend the rest of his life in mental hospitals and prisons? The state was sending him hospital bills now at the rate of over a hundred dollars a day. They wanted all his money. They wanted him broke.

He couldn't sleep Saturday night. At about three in the morning, Ragen went outside, wheeling his motorcycle silently from the house. A fog was drifting into the valley, and he felt like riding until early light. He started down the road toward Logan Dam.

He loved the fog best in the dark of night, and often he would wander out into the densest, deepest fog, whether in the middle of the forest or the center of a lake, watching the foreground blend into nothing. Three in the morning was his favorite hour.

As he approached the top ledge of Logan Dam, a narrow ridge just wide enough for his cycle wheel, he turned his headlight off; its reflection in the fog would blind him. With the headlight out, he could see black on two sides and the light strip of the ridge down the middle. He kept his wheel centered. It was dangerous, but he needed the danger. He needed, once again, to conquer something. It didn't have to be something illegal, but every now and then he had to do something dangerous, had to feel the adrenaline pumping. He needed to be a victor.

He had never ridden the dam ridge before. He didn't know how long it was. He couldn't see that far ahead. But he knew he had to go across it fast enough, with high enough torque, to keep from falling to either side. He was terrified, but he had to give it one hell of a try.

He kicked off and roared down the center of the narrow ledge. When he was safely across, the turned and came back again. Then he screamed and cried and the tears rolled down his cheeks, chilled by the wind in his face.

He went home exhausted and dreamed he was shot and dying on the footbridge because the Teacher had frozen and let them all down.

CHAPTER TWENTY-TWO

(1)

On Monday, September 17, the day of the hearing, as the writer walked down the corridor of AIT and saw Billy waiting for him, he could tell by the knowing smile, the clear-eyed look and nod, that it was the Teacher. They gripped each other's hands.

"Good to see you," the writer said. "It's been a long while."

"A lot's been going on."

"Let's talk privately before Goldsberry and Thompson get here."

They stepped into a small conference room, and the Teacher told the writer of the shooting, of unfusing, of Allen leasing a new sports car so that he could take off for Lexington to be treated by Dr. Wilbur as soon as the judge reversed the guilty plea.

"Who's been talking to me, pretending to be you in the last month while you were gone?"

"It was Allen," he said. "I'm sorry. Arthur knew you'd be hurt to find out that I'd unfused. Normally he would not have concerned himself with a person's emotions. I can only assume he reacted like that because his judgment was impaired by the shock of the shooting."

They talked until Goldsberry and Thompson arrived, and then they all drove to the Fairfield County courthouse in Lancaster.

Goldsberry and Thompson had provided the court with depositions from Drs. George Harding, Cornelia Wilbur, Stella Karolin and David Caul, and Psychologist Dorothy Turner, all agreeing that there was "a reasonable medical certainty" that

Billy Milligan had been a mentally ill multiple personality when the roadside-rest assaults and the Gray Drug Store robbery were committed in December 1974 and January 1975. They agreed that he had probably not been able, at that time, to assist his attorney, George Kellner, in his own defense.

The Fairfield County prosecutor, Mr. Luse, called only Dr. Harold T. Brown, who stated on the witness stand that he had treated Billy at the age of fifteen and had him sent to the Columbus State Hospital for three months. He would, he said, in the light of current knowledge, have changed his diagnosis from hysterical neurosis with passive-aggressive features to a new diagnosis of dissociative disorder with possible multiple personality. However, Brown told the court, he had been sent by the prosecuting attorney to interview Billy in Athens, and during that visit, Billy Milligan seemed to have knowledge of the acts he had committed. Brown said Milligan was probably not really a multiple personality, since multiple personalities were not supposed to have knowledge of the actions of the alter egos.

. When they left the courtroom, Goldsberry and Thompson were optimistic and Billy was elated. He was sure Judge Jackson would take the testimony of four highly regarded psychiatrists and a psychologist over the testimony of Dr. Brown.

The judge told a reporter he would make his decision within two weeks.

On September 18, seeing Billy's agitation after his return from Lancaster and aware of his fear of being shot at again, Dr. Caul allowed him a furlough. Since Billy realized he would be a target at his sister's house as well as at the hospital, it was understood he would stay at the Hocking Valley Motor Lodge in nearby Nelsonville. He would take his easel, paints and canvas to work undisturbed.

He checked in on Tuesday under a false name and tried to relax, but the tension was too strong. He heard noises while he painted. After searching the room and the hall, he decided it was in his head—his own voices. He tried not to listen, concentrating on his brush strokes, but they were still talking. It wasn't Ragen or Arthur; he'd have recognized their accents immediately. It had to be the undesirables. Now what was wrong with him? He couldn't work, he couldn't sleep, he was afraid to go back to Kathy's or to Athens.

He phoned Mike Rupe on Wednesday and asked him to come out. When Rupe got there and saw how nervous Billy was, he phoned Dr. Caul.

"You're on night duty anyway," Caul said. "Stay with him tonight and bring him back tomorrow."

With Mike Rupe there, Billy relaxed. They had a drink at the bar, and Billy talked of his hope of being treated by Sybil's physician.

"I'll check myself into a hospital for a couple of weeks until Dr. Wilbur thinks I can stay in an apartment by myself. I think I can, because even while I'm having trouble, I'm still able to function. Then I'll start my treatment and follow her guidelines."

Rupe listened as he spoke about his plans for the future, about the new life ahead of him if Judge Jackson wiped the slate clean in Lancaster.

They talked through the night, fell asleep in the early hours and, after a late breakfast, drove back to the hospital Thursday morning.

Back on the ward, Billy sat in the lobby and thought about how he couldn't do anything right anymore. He felt like a dunce because he was losing all the things his other personalities had given him: Arthur's intelligence, Ragen's strength, Allen's smooth talking, Tommy's electronics knowledge. He was feeling more and more stupid, pressures were building and building. The stress and the fear were getting to him. Noises were amplified, colors became unbearably intense. He wanted to go into his room, slam the door, and scream and scream and scream . . .

The following day, Wanda Pancake was finishing her lunch in the coffee room when a friend jumped out of his chair and ran to the window. Wanda turned and peered through the rain to see what he was staring at.

"I saw somebody," he said, pointing. "A guy in a tan trench coat ran across the Richland Avenue bridge and then went under it."

"Where?" She stood on tiptoe, stretching her short, stocky frame, but all she could see through the rain-streaked window was a car parked on the bridge. The driver got out, looked over the side of the bridge wall, went back to his car and then to the wall, looking down as if watching something or someone below.

Wanda had an odd sinking feeling. "I'd better go check where Billy is."

She went up and down the ward, asking staff and patients, but no one had seen him. She checked his room. His tan trench coat was gone from his closet.

Charlotte Johnson, the unit supervisor, came to the nurses' station to say she'd been told on the phone that another employee, who'd been uptown, had seen Billy on Richland Avenue. Dr. Caul emerged from his office; he'd gotten a call about Billy being on the bridge.

Everyone began shouting at once. They didn't want Security to go after him because they knew the uniforms would upset him.

"I'll go," Wanda said, grabbing her coat.

Clyde Barnhart of Security drove her out to the Richland Bridge. She climbed down and looked under the bridge among the pipes. Then she walked along the riverbank, peering in all directions. Nothing. When she came back, she saw the driver of the parked car and was surprised he was still there.

"Did you see a guy in a tan trench coat?" she asked.

He pointed to the nearby university Convocation Center.

The security cruiser picked her up and drove her to the modern brick-and-glass building shaped like a birthday cake with a dome.

"There he is," Security Officer Barnhart said, pointing to the third-level concrete walkway that circled the building.

"Wait here," she told him. "I'd better handle him myself."

"Don't go inside the building with him. Don't be alone with him," Barnhart said.

She ran up one of the ramps and saw him trying door after door to get into the building.

"Billy!" she shouted, running from the ramp to the walkway. "Wait for me!"

He didn't answer.

She tried other names: "Danny! Allen! Tommy!"

He ignored her, moving quickly around the walkway, trying one door after another until finally he found an open one and disappeared inside. She'd never been inside the Convocation

Center. Frightened, not knowing what to expect of him or why he was here, she raced in and caught up to him as he started up a steep staircase. She stayed at the foot of the stairs.

"Come on down, Billy."

"The hell with you. I ain't Billy."

She'd never seen him chew gum before, but now he was chomping away hard and fast.

"Who are you?" she asked.

"Steve."

"What are you doing here?"

"Shit, what the hell does it look like? I want to get to the top of the building."

"Why?"

"To jump."

"Come on down, Steve, and let's talk about it."

He refused to come down, though she tried to reason with him. It was no use. She believed he was determined to kill himself. She noticed how different he was: cocky now, his voice higher, speech faster, macho arrogance in his expression and tone.

"I'm gonna go to the bathroom," he said, and went through the lavatory door.

She ran quickly to the exit and stepped out on the circular walk to see if Clyde was still there with the security cruiser. He wasn't. He'd gone. When she got back inside, Steve came out of the men's room and disappeared through another door. She tried to follow, but he locked it from the inside.

She found a wall phone, dialed the hospital and asked for Dr. Caul.

"I don't know what to do," she said. "He's Steve and talking about killing himself."

"Calm him down," Caul said. "Tell him everything's going to be okay. Tell him it's not going to be as bad as he thinks. He'll be able to go to Kentucky for treatment with Dr. Wilbur. Tell him to come on back."

She hung up and went back to the door, banging and calling, "Steve! Open this door! Dr. Caul says you'll be able to go to Kentucky!"

Seconds later, a student coming through unlocked the door. Wanda discovered it led to a narrow circular corridor. She stuck her head into offices and lounges as she ran, feeling like someone on a nightmare merry-go-round. Can't find him. Keep looking. Keep going.

When she passed two students talking, she shouted, "Did you see a guy go by here? Six feet tall. Tan trench coat. Dripping wet."

One of them pointed ahead. "He went thataway . . ."

She kept running along the circular corridor, checking exit doors to the outer walk from time to time, in case he'd gone back outside. Finally, through one exit, she saw him on the outside walkway.

"Steve!" she shouted. "Wait a minute! I've gotta talk to you!"

"Ain't nothin' to talk about."

She circled him, wedging herself between him and the concrete balustrade, to keep him from jumping. "Dr. Caul says to come back."

"Fuck that fat-bellied sonofabitch!"

"He says things aren't as bad as you think they are."

"Shit they ain't."

He was pacing back and forth, chewing his gum furiously.

"Dr. Caul says you'll be able to go to Kentucky and Dr. Wilbur can help you."

"I don't trust any of them shrinks. They're trying to tell me that bullshit about I got multiple personality. That's goddamn crazy. They're the ones that's nuts."

He stripped off his wet trench coat, plastered it against a large windowpane and drew his fist back to smash it. She dove for him, caught his arm and hung on to keep him from swinging. She knew he wanted the glass to cut himself with, though it was too thick to smash. He'd probably just break his fist. But she clung to him and he fought to shake her off.

As they grappled, she tried to talk him into going back, but there was no reasoning with him. Drenching wet and freezing, she finally said, "I'm tired of it. I'm giving you a choice: Either you come back with me right now, or I'll kick you in the fucking balls."

"You wouldn't," he said.

"I will," she said, still holding his arm. "I'm going to count to three. If you don't quit and start walking with me back to the hospital, I'm going to kick you."

"Well," he said, "I don't hit females."

"One . . . two . . ." She drew her knee back.

He crossed his legs to protect himself. "You would, wouldn't you?"

"Yeah."

"Well, I'm gonna do it," he said. "I'm going to the top."

"No, you're not. I'm not letting you."

He struggled against her, then broke loose and ran to the concrete balustrade. It was three flights to the ground. When he reached the edge, she rushed him, got one arm around his neck and the other through his belt, and pulled him back against the concrete, tearing his shirt as they wrestled.

Then she saw something snap in him. He wilted and dropped to the floor, his eyes glazed, and she knew it was someone else. He began to cry, shivering and shaking. Scared, she thought. She knew who he was.

Wanda hugged him and told him there was nothing to worry about. "Everything's going to be okay, Danny."

"I'm gonna get a whipping," he whined. "My shoes is untied and all muddy, my pants and my hair is wet. My clothes is muddy and all messed up."

"You want to go for a walk with me?"

"Yeah," he said.

She picked his coat up from the floor, put it on him and guided him around the walkway toward the front of the building. Through the trees, she could see the hospital up on the hill. He must have seen this round building often from up there. The security cruiser had returned. It was parked in the lot below, doors open, no one inside.

"You want to go sit in the car with me? Let's get out of the rain."

He hung back.

"It's okay. It's Security. Clyde Barnhart is driving. You get along okay with him. You like him, don't you?"

Danny nodded and started into the back seat, but when he saw the wire protection frame that made the back look like a cage, he drew away, trembling.

"Okay," Wanda said, understanding what was bothering him. "We can both sit up front and wait for Clyde to come and drive us."

He slipped inside and sat quietly beside her, looking dazed at his wet trousers and muddy shoes.

Wanda left the doors open, but reached over to turn the headlights on as a signal. A short while later Clyde came down the ramp of the Convocation Center with Norma Dishong.

"I went back to the hospital and got her," Clyde Barnhart explained. "We were inside looking for you and Bill."

Wanda said, "This is Danny. He's all right now."

(2)

On Tuesday, September 25, Nurse Pat Perry watched Billy talk to Gus Holston in the lounge. Holston had been admitted a few weeks earlier; he and Billy knew each other from Lebanon. Lori and Marsha walked by, flirting with the two young men. Lori, who had never made any attempt to hide her attraction for Billy, now pretended to be interested in Holston to make Billy jealous. Nurse Perry, who was Lori's case manager, knew the girl had been all over Billy from the time he'd come to Athens. A pretty, not too bright young woman, she followed him around, leaving him notes and telling the staff of the things she and Billy were going to do someday. She had even spread the rumor that she and Billy were eventually going to be married.

Billy, for his part, never really paid much attention to her. His grandest gesture had been to give both Lori and Marsha fifty dollars earlier in the week when they told him they were broke. In exchange for the money, they picked up his HUG YOUR CHILD TODAY bumper stickers from the printer and passed them out downtown.

Eileen McClellan, Billy's afternoon case manager, was off that day, and her case buddy, Katherine Gillott, looked after him. Shortly after the grandmotherly Gillott came on duty, Billy asked her if he could go for a walk.

"We'll have to include Dr. Caul on this decision," she said, "because I'm not going to make it."

Billy waited in the TV room while she consulted with Dr. Caul, who decided to talk to Billy. After a few questions about his mood, they both agreed he could go out for a walk with Gus Holston.

Billy and Gus came back within half an hour, then went out for a second walk. When Billy returned the second time, about six o'clock, Gillott was busy with a new admission, but she heard him say, "That girl was screaming."

She knew it wasn't Billy talking. She recognized David's voice.

"What did you say?"

"She's gonna get hurt."

Gillott followed him down the hall. "What are you talking about?"

"There was a girl. I could hear a girl screaming somewhere when I was outside."

"What girl?"

"I don't know. There were two of them. One of the girls told Gus to bring me back because I was in the way."

Gillott smelled his breath to see if he'd been drinking, but there was no indication that he had.

A few minutes later the downstairs switchboard called for her. Mrs. Gillott went down to see a security officer bring Marsha in. She could smell the liquor on Marsha's breath as she brought her upstairs and took her to her room.

"Where's Lori?" Gillott asked.

"I don't know."

"Where've you been?"

"I don't know."

"You have been drinking, haven't you?"

Marsha hung her head. She was sent to Ward 1, the women's maximum-security ward.

In the meantime Billy switched from David to Danny. He seemed disturbed when he saw Marsha alone, without Lori, and suddenly he took off out of the building to go find the missing Lori. Gillott went puffing after him. By the time she had caught up to him behind the Beacon School cottage, Security Officer Glenn was bringing Lori in. She'd been throwing up and had been lying on the grass, her face in the vomit, Glen told Gillott. "She could have strangled," he said.

Gillott could see that Danny was worried about the women. She heard people in the corridor whispering the word "rape," but she felt that neither of the young men had been out long enough to do anything to either Lori or Marsha. She just didn't believe it. When she left at eleven that night, everything seemed calm, both women in Ward 1 and Milligan and Holston off in their rooms asleep.

When Pat Perry came on duty at seven the next morning, rumors had spread over the ward and the hospital. The two young women had been found drunk and unconscious out on the hill. Lori's clothes had been ripped. Some said she'd complained of having been raped; others said there had been no mention of rape. Billy and Gus Holston had been out for a walk at the same time, and suspicion pointed to them. But almost everyone on the Admissions and Intensive Treatment ward agreed that there could not have been a rape.

The state highway patrol was called to investigate, and they requested that AIT be locked temporarily to ensure that all the males on the ward be available for questioning. Dr. Caul spoke to several of the staff; Billy and Holston weren't awake yet. The question was, Who would tell Billy about the accusations being made against him and Holston? Pat Perry could see he didn't want to do it himself. Everyone else refused. Perry hadn't been on duty the day last spring when Ragen exploded, threatening the attendants with the broken drinking glass, but others who had been feared the same violence might happen when Billy heard the news.

Dr. Caul had the ward door locked before he talked to either of them. Holston was the first one up, and Dr. Caul told him what he was being accused of. Then he went into Billy's room and told him the same thing.

Both young men seemed confused at first and hurt at the accusations, but as the morning wore on, they became more agitated, more frightened. They spoke of people coming after them to take them to Lima, of the FBI out to get them, of being sent back to Lebanon.

Throughout the day, the staff tried to keep them calm. The staff was angry too. They didn't believe it at all. Wanda Pancake and Pat Perry kept assuring Holston and Billy that no one was coming to take them away. But they both knew they weren't talking to Billy. It was one of the others. Wanda felt sure it was Steve.

Pat Perry gave Billy a lot of Amytal that day, trying to keep him under control; at one point he took a nap and seemed all right. But by two in the afternoon, both young men were agitated again. Billy was switching from Steve to David, whining and crying; then he'd be tough again, and he and Holston would pace up and back, edgy about anyone walking near them. Every time the phone rang, Billy jumped and said, "They're coming after me."

Billy and Holston moved to the back of the lobby near the locked rear door leading to the fire escape. They pulled the tables and chairs around them to form a barricade, then took off their belts, wrapping them around their fists.

"I don't want any men coming towards us," Steve said, "or we'll bust out the back door." He picked up a chair in his left hand, holding it like a lion tamer. The staff realized they could no longer handle the situation. They called for a "Code Green."

Pat Perry heard it over the loudspeaker system. She expected the usual wait and then to see eight or ten guards and attendants from other wards come throught the door of the ward to help out.

"My God!" she gasped as the door burst open. There was a mob of men—security guards, attendants, aides, supervisors, men from health care and from psychology who had no business there, men from geriatrics who would never come on a regular Code Green. There were at least thirty of them. It was, she thought, like trapping an animal. As if everyone had just been waiting for the signal.

She and Wanda stood close to Billy and Holston, who made no attempt to touch or harm them. But as the wave of men approached, the two patients brandished chairs and gestured menacingly with their belt-wrapped fists.

"I'm not going to Lima!" Steve shouted. "Just when everything was going all right, I get blamed for something I didn't do! Now I'll never get my chance. Now I've got no more hopes."

"Billy, listen to me," Caul said. "This isn't the way to handle it. You've got to settle down."

"If you come after us, we'll bust the door and get the car and leave."

"You're wrong, Billy. This behavior isn't going to help you. You've been accused of this thing and it might come out bad. But this isn't the way to behave. We're not going to put up with it."

Billy refused to listen.

Dave Malawista, a senior psychologist, tried to reason with him: "Come on, Billy. Have we ever let anything happen to you before? We've invested so much time in you, do you think we're going to let them take you away from us over this? We want to help you, not make things worse for you. The staff doesn't believe all that stuff. We've documented your charts and the girls' charts as well. The time is accounted for. The investigation should go in your favor."

Billy put the chair down and came out of the corner. He calmed down and the men left the ward. But Billy soon began whining and crying again. And Holston was still acting out his hostility. He ranted and raved about being taken away, and that was upsetting Billy even more.

"We won't get our chance," Holston said. "I've been accused unjustly before. You just wait, they'll sneak up here without tellin' us. We'll be whisked off and never seen again."

The staff was more on edge than Pat had ever seen before. They sensed that something was going to happen.

The three o'clock shift took over, and the younger women were replaced by the elderly Eileen McClellan and Katherine Gillott. Mrs. Gillott had been surprised to hear about the rape investigation. Forewarned by the morning shift, she tried to keep the two young men calm. But as the afternoon wore on, their nervous glances and movements began again, the talk of being interrogated and taken off to prison, the threats of ripping out phones if anyone tried to call security, of busting out the fire-escape door if anyone came after them.

"I don't want to have it end this way," Billy said. "I'd rather be dead than have it end this way."

Gillott was sitting talking to Billy when he asked for some Amytal. She consented. He went to the nurses' station to get his medication, and Gillott turned her attention to another patient.

Then she heard the back door being smashed open. Gillott saw Gus Holston and Billy Milligan running down the fire escape. The nurse on duty called the second Code Green of the day.

A short while later one of the nursing staff phoned for Katherine Gillott. Would she come down to the second floor? They had Billy and he was asking for her. When she got there, she saw that four men had Billy pinned to the floor in front of the elevator.

"Katherine," he said, "help me. Don't let them hurt me. If they tie me up, Chalmer'll come."

"No, Danny. Chalmer isn't going to be here. You may have to be in a room by yourself. You left the hospital. You busted out and you left, and now we've got to do this to you."

He sobbed, "Would you ask them to let me up?"

"You can let go of him," she told the men.

The officers hesitated, not knowing what to expect.

"He'll be all right," Gillott said. "He'll go with me. Won't you, Danny?"

"Yes."

She led him to Ward 5, into the seclusion room, staying to take his personal effects. He wouldn't give her his necklace with an arrowhead on it.

"Better empty your pockets now. Give me your wallet so I can put it away." She saw he was carrying a lot of money.

One of the Ward 5 attendants, impatient to shut Milligan in, shouted, "Come on outta there, Katherine, or I'll lock you in with him."

She understood that they were scared of the boy.

A short while after she returned to AIT, a nurse called to say something was going on with Milligan in the seclusion room. He had put his mattress over the observation window, preventing the staff from looking in, and they were afraid to unlock the door to see what he was doing. Would she come down again?

She took a male attendant with her—someone Billy knew—and called through the seclusion-room door: "This is Katherine. I'm coming in to check on you. Don't be afraid."

They went in. Billy was making a gurgling, choking sound. The arrowhead was gone from his necklace; the chain lay broken on the floor.

Dr. Sammi Michaels ordered Billy transferred to a room with a bed, but when the staff went in to get him, he fought. It took several men to move him.

Mrs. Gillott stayed with him in the new room. She gave Billy several cups of water, and in a few minutes he spit out the arrowhead. The nurse gave him an injection, and Gillott talked with him for a while longer, assuring him she'd be back, telling him to get some rest. Then she went back to her ward, thinking about how very frightened he was.

The following morning, when Wanda, Pat Perry and Mike Rupe came on duty, they learned that Billy and Holston had been taken to Ward 5. Though Rupe, now on the morning shift, wanted to visit Billy, word was sent up by Ward 5 that the staff of AIT was not to visit him. He was theirs now.

When Billy's sister, Kathy, called, she was told there had been trouble and that Billy had been placed on the male maximum-security ward. Billy would not be allowed to leave to attend her wedding the next day.

The story was leaked to the newspapers, and the following appeared in the *Columbus Citizen-Journal* on October 3, 1979:

MILLIGAN FINANCED RUM PARTY, PATROL WILL REVEAL—STINZIANO
By Eric Rosenman

William S. Milligan, the alleged multiple personality rapist, was one of four patients who engaged in a "rum and Coke party" on the grounds of the Athens Mental Health Center last week, a state legislator claimed Wednesday.

Rep. Mike Stinziano of Columbus said a secret Ohio Highway Patrol investigation will conclude Milligan provided two women patients with money to buy rum and then the women, Milligan and a second male patient held a "rum and Coke" party. . . .

The representative said the story indicates that "there appears to be little control over activities at the center."

"As I understand it, the report will not be able to prove the women were raped," Stinziano said Wednesday. "But it will say the two women were given money by Milligan to buy liquor, went off the grounds to make the purchase and then returned with rum . . ."

Last Friday, Lt. Richard Wilcox, head of the patrol's investigation section, said tests to determine whether the women had been raped or had been intoxicated were incomplete and would not be made public until the investigation was over.

Stinziano said he was certain of his sources who supplied the tale of the party.

The same day, the writer was permitted to visit Ward 5. Milligan did not recognize him until the writer prompted him.

"Oh, yeah," he said with a dazed expression, "you're the guy who's been talking to Billy."

"Who are you?" the writer asked.

"I don't know."

"What's your name?"

"I don't think I have one."

They spoke for a while, though Milligan had no awareness of what had happened to him. There were long silences as the writer waited for one of the personalities to come forward with information. After a while the nameless one said, "They won't let him paint anymore. There's two paintings, and somebody'll destroy them if they're here. You oughtta take them in case you need them for the book."

Milligan left the conference room, then returned with two canvases, one an unfinished, unsigned gloomy night scene with black trees silhouetted against a dark-blue sky, a black barn and a curving path. The other was a richly colored landscape, signed "Tommy."

"Are you Tommy?" the writer asked.

"I don't know who I am."

(3)

The next morning, Alan Goldsberry was notified to appear in Athens County Common Pleas Court before Judge Roger J. Jones. Assistant Attorney General David Belinky had filed a motion on behalf of the state of Ohio to transfer Milligan to the Lima State Hospital for the Criminally Insane. Gus Holston was being sent back to Lebanon.

Goldsberry appealed to Judge Jones to allow him time to confer with his client. "It's my belief that Mr. Milligan has a right to know about this motion and has a right under the second paragraph of 5122.20 to at least be advised that he can request a hearing immediately. Since he hasn't been given this notice, I want to request for him that he have a right to a hearing with him being present. I don't think these proceedings give him that opportunity."

The judge disagreed, and Belinky called as his only witness Russell Cremeans, chief of Security and Safety at the Athens Mental Health Center.

"Mr. Cremeans, are you aware of any physical assaults that have occurred between Mr. Milligan and any of the personnel at the hospital within the most recent events?"

"Yes. I have reports from . . . from an individual, M. Wilson, who is an aide at the hospital, and also the officer on duty that night, Officer Clyde Barnhart. The date of this incident was September 26, 1979. . . . I'm concerned about being able to contain Mr. Milligan on the locked unit where he is right now."

"Would you, as a security officer and chief of Security, have severe reservations whether . . . the facility could adequately hold Mr. Milligan if he had intentions of leaving the grounds?"

"I have serious reservations whether the institution would be able to hold him if he actually wanted to leave, yes."

"Do you have firsthand knowledge as to what happened on the night of the escape attempt?" Belinky asked.

"Yes, I do. Mr. Milligan and another patient, Mr. Gus Holston, proceeded to break the door down on our AIT, which is a receiving hospital unit where they were being housed. A chair was used to break the lock off the fire escape door, and the two proceeded down the fire escape . . . in an A.W.O.L. attempt. . . . The two, Milligan and Holston, proceeded to the parking lot, where Milligan had a vehicle which was brought back from an A.W.L., proceeded to unlock the car and enter the car . . ."

Milligan, he said, was prevented from entering the car, and Milligan and Holston then ran over the hill. Three men were able to subdue Milligan and take him back to Ward 5.

After hearing Chief Cremeans' evidence, Judge Jones granted the motion of the attorney general's office that Milligan be sent to Lima.

At two o'clock, on October 4, 1979, Billy was handcuffed and belt-shackled, and with no time to say good-by to anyone but Dr. Caul, he was driven 180 miles away to Lima State Hospital for the Criminally Insane.

CHAPTER
TWENTY-THREE

(1)

Columbus Dispatch, October 5, 1979:

TOP OFFICIALS SEEN SPURRING MILLIGAN TRANSFER
By Robert Ruth

Direct intervention by top state mental health officials prompted the transfer Thursday of multi-personality rapist William S. Milligan to Lima State Hospital, a maximum security facility, a reliable source reports.

The transfer order came after top officials in the Ohio Mental Health and Mental Retardation's Columbus headquarters made several phone calls Wednesday to the Athens Mental Health Center where Milligan had been confined for 10 months, the source said.

Mental Health Director Timothy Moritz made at least one of the calls, the source added. . . . Two state legislators—Reps. Mike Stinziano D-Columbus, and Claire Mr. Ball, Jr., R-Athens—repeatedly have complained about what they charged was lenient treatment given the rapist.

Thursday both Stinziano and Ball praised the decision to transfer Milligan to the Lima facility, but Ball added, "I only wonder what took so long?"

Stinziano said he will continue to keep a close watch on Milligan's case to ensure Milligan is not released from a maximum security facility until he is no longer a threat to society.

The day after Milligan's transfer, Judge S. Farrell Jackson of the common pleas court in Lancaster filed his ruling on Milligan's motion to vacate his guilty plea for the Gray Drug Store robbery:

This court is of the opinion that the burden of proof as to the matter of the insanity of William S. Milligan on March 27, 1975, is upon the defendant, William S. Milligan . . . After a careful analysis of all the evidence, this court is not convinced by a preponderance of the evidence that on March 27, 1975 that William Stanley Milligan was insane, was unable to counsel in his own defense or was unable to understandingly enter a plea of guilty to the charges and, therefore, there has been no showing of a manifest injustice and the motion of William Stanley Milligan to withdraw his pleas of guilty is denied.

Goldsberry filed an appeal with the Ohio Fourth Circuit Court of Appeals on the grounds that Judge Jackson had improperly considered the weight of the evidence—balancing the opinions of four eminently qualified psychiatrists and a psychologist against the solitary opinion of Dr. Brown.

He also filed a motion in the city of Lima, Ohio, at the Allen County Courthouse, charging that his client had not been given an opportunity to confer with his attorney and that he had been transferred to a more restrictive facility without due process.

(2)

A week later, at the Allen County Courthouse, where the referee would hear Goldsberry's motion to return Milligan to Athens, the writer saw Billy in handcuffs for the first time. It was the Teacher, and he smiled sheepishly.

Alone in the room with Goldsberry and the writer, the Teacher spoke of his treatment at Lima during the past week. Dr. Lindner, the clinical director, had diagnosed him as a pseudo-psychopathic schizophrenic, and he prescribed Stelazine, one of the psychotropic drugs in the same family as Thorazine, the drug that made the splitting so much worse.

They talked until the bailiff informed them the referee was ready to begin. Goldsberry and Billy asked that the writer be allowed to sit at the table with them, across from Assistant Attorney General David Belinky and his witness for the state of Ohio, Dr. Lewis Lindner, a thin man with a pinched face, metal-rimmed glasses and a Vandyke beard. He looked across the room at Milligan with an undisguised sneer.

After several more minutes of conferences between the attorneys and the referee, the referee made the decision—on the basis of law only, with no testimony—that since Judge Jones had ruled the appropriate place for hospitalization was Lima State Hospital, and since by the end of November Milligan would have the right to present evidence at his ninety-day review, the hearing was moot. The court would decide in six weeks whether or not Milligan was still mentally ill, and whether or not to keep him at Lima.

The Teacher addressed the court: "I know I have to wait before I can resume my treatment, and my doctors have told me for the past two years, 'You have to *want* help from the people who can give it to you. You have to be able to totally trust your physician, your psychiatrist, your treatment team.' I just want the speediness of the court to help me resume my treatment properly."

"Mr. Milligan," the referee said. "Let me make a statement to you on that. I think you're assuming an incorrect fact, that you can't receive treatment at Lima State Hospital."

"Well," said Billy, looking directly at Dr. Lindner, "you have to be able to want treatment, want help from a person before you can receive it. You have to be trusting of that person. I don't know these doctors. I don't trust them by what they've told me already. My physicians have stated they don't believe in my illness, and that scares me to go back and wait where I'm not going to be treated. Well, I'll receive a treatment, but for another mental illness. My doctors have made it clear they do not believe in multiple personality."

"That is a medical issue," said the referee, "that we're not ready to argue today, although your counsel may present that at a review hearing and it will be properly considered as to whether or not Lima is the appropriate place."

After the hearing, the writer and Goldsberry visited Billy at Lima. They passed through metal detectors, had their briefcases searched, went through two sets of barred doors and were escorted by an attendant to the visitors' room. A short while later, a guard brought Billy in. He was still the Teacher. During the two-hour visit he told the writer about the events at Athens leading up to the investigation of the alleged rape, and he described his transfer to Lima.

"The two girls were sitting in the hall one night, talking about how they didn't have jobs or money. I felt sorry for them. I'm a sucker, I guess. So I told them if they would pass out some bumper stickers for me, I would pay them a salary. They got half of the bumper stickers passed out. I paid them.

"Four days later, they disappeared in the afternoon. They wanted to get smashed. They went over to the state liquor store and bought a bottle of rum.

"I was restricted to the unit. I could leave only if I was escorted by a staff member or by another patient who signed out for a walk, if he'd let me go with him. Okay, Gus Holston and I went outside. Katherine timed it. She said we weren't outside more than nine or ten minutes. We went out and walked around the building. When we went out there, I was uncomfortable because I was outside. I was defused at the time."

"Who walked out?" the writer asked.

"It was Danny. Holston was kind of apprehensive at this point—he didn't know what to make of me. He didn't know what my problem was. As we were walking around the building, we heard the girls back there scream out to Gus and, well, they called me 'Billy.' When they got up to us, they were very, very intoxicated. One had—I think it was—a bottle of Pepsi. It looked clearer than usual, so it must have been cut. We could smell booze all over them."

The Teacher described how one of the girls, realizing he was Danny and not Billy, leaned close to Gus and said, "Take *the nuisance* back up and come join us."

Gus told them he couldn't, but before he and Danny could pull away, one of the girls threw up all over Gus's shirt, and some of it got on Danny's trouser leg.

Danny jumped back, nauseated, and covered his face with his hands. Gus shouted at the girls, cursing them. He and Danny turned and headed back toward the building. The girls followed behind them a short way, giggling and cursing them, then headed up the brick road toward the cemetery.

That was all there was to it, the Teacher said. He couldn't be sure about Holston, but he, himself, had never touched either of the girls.

The eight days in Lima had been hell, he said. "I'll write down some of the things that happened to me here. I'll send them to you."

When the visit was over, the Teacher went through the metal detector to be checked for contraband or anything the visitors might have brought in. He turned to the writer and waved good-by. "I'll see you at the end of November, at my next review hearing. But in the meantime, I'll write to you."

The writer tried to make an appointment to speak with Dr. Lindner, but the response on the phone was hostile: "I believe it's not therapeutically desirable for him to have all this publicity."

"We're not the ones seeking the publicity," the writer said.

"I don't wish to discuss it any further," Lindner said, and hung up.

When the writer asked to join a group tour of the Lima State Hospital facility the day before the November hearing, it was granted at first by the public relations department. The day before the tour, however, he received a call telling him that his visit had been canceled by Dr. Lindner and Superintendent Hubbard, and that the Security Department had been told the writer was to be barred from the hospital grounds permanently.

When the writer inquired as to the reason, Assistant Attorney General David Belinky said he had been advised by hospital officials that the writer was suspected of having smuggled drugs to Milligan. Later the reason was changed to "not therapeutically advisable."

(3)

November 30 was cold; the first snow lay on the ground. The Allen County Courthouse in Lima, Ohio, was an old building, and though Courtroom 3 was large enough to seat about fifty people, most of the chairs were empty. The Milligan review hearing had been closed to the public and the media, but the TV cameras were waiting outside.

The Teacher sat, in handcuffs, between his attorneys. In addition to the attorneys, only Dorothy, Del Moore and the writer were admitted as observers by the court. Also present were James O'Grady, assistant prosecutor for Franklin County, William Jan Hans, a representative of the Ohio Adult Parole Authority, and Ann Henkiner, an attorney observer for Southwest Community Mental Health Center in Columbus.

Judge David R. Kinworthy, a clean-shaven, handsome young man with sharply chiseled features, reviewed the history of commitment hearings from December 4, 1978, when Milligan had been found not guilty by reason of insanity, through the various re-commitments, to the present day, almost one year later. The hearing, Kinworthy said, was being held in accordance with the statutes of the Ohio Revised Code, paragraph 5122, section 15.

Assistant Attorney General Belinky's motion for separation of witnesses was granted. Attorney Steve Thompson's motion for the court to return Billy Milligan to Athens, considering the procedural defects in the transfer to Lima, was denied.

With preliminary motions over, the commitment review hearings began.

The first witness for the state was sixty-five-year-old Dr. Frederick Milkie, a short, fat psychiatrist with baggy pants and a baggy sweater. His dark hair was slicked down, and he waddled from the table beside Belinky (from which he would later serve as the state's technical consultant) to the witness stand.

Dr. Milkie testified that he had seen Milligan twice, once briefly on October 24, 1979, when the patient had been transferred to his care at Lima, and then again on October 30, for review of his treatment plan. He had also been allowed to observe Milligan this morning for a half-hour before the hearing, to see if he had changed since a month ago. Referring to hospital records, Dr. Milkie stated that he had diagnosed Milligan as having a personality disorder, that he was antisocial and suffered from psychoneurotic anxiety with depressive and dissociative features.

David Belinky, a boyish-faced attorney with frizzy hair, asked his witness, "Is he exactly the same today?"

"Yes," said Milkie. "He is mentally ill."

"What are his symptoms?"

"His behavior is unacceptable," Dr. Milkie said, looking directly at Milligan. "He is a criminal with rape and robbery charges. He's at odds with his environment, the kind of individual who doesn't profit from punishment."

Milkie said he had considered the multiple personality diagnosis, but had seen no symptoms of it. In answer to Belinky's questions, Milkie said he considered Milligan a high suicide risk and a danger to others.

"There is no improvement in this patient," Milkie said. "He's arrogant, uncooperative. He has an expansive ego. He doesn't accept his milieu." When asked by Belinky how he treated the patient, Milkie answered, "With skillful neglect."

Milkie testified that he had prescribed five milligrams of Stelazine. He had seen no ill effects, but since there were also no beneficial effcts, he discontinued the antipsychotic drug. He told the court that in his opinion, Milligan needed a maximum-security facility, and Lima was the only place for him in Ohio.

Under cross-examination by Steve Thompson, Goldsberry's lanky young associate, Milkie said he rejected the diagnosis of multiple personality because he had not seen the symptoms. He did not, himself, accept the definition of multiple personality in DSM-II, the second edition of the *Diagnostic and Statistical Manual*. Milkie said, "I ruled out multiple personality just as I ruled out syphilis when I saw his blood test. It wasn't there."

"What symptoms did you observe?" Thompson asked.

"Anger, panic. Things weren't going Milligan's way. His anger takes over and he acts under impulse."

Thompson frowned. "Are you saying that a person is mentally ill when he's angry or depressed?"

"That's right."

"Don't we all have periods of anger and depression?"

Milkie looked around the courtroom and shrugged. "Everybody is mentally ill."

Thompson stared at the witness and then made some notes. "Does Billy trust you?"

"No."

"Would he make better progress with someone he trusted?"

"Yes."

"Your Honor, I have no further questions of this witness."

Before the hearing went into luncheon recess, Alan Goldsberry introduced into evidence a deposition of Dr. Caul's testimony taken three days earlier. Goldsberry wanted it on the record before he called his other witnesses, Dr. George Harding, Jr., Dr. Stella Karolin and Psychologist Dorothy Turner.

In the deposition, Steve Thompson, questioning Caul about the proper treatment of multiple personality patients, had asked, "I wonder if you could tell me, Doctor, what you consider to be the essential requirements for a treatment program for an individual who is diagnosed as being a multiple personality."

Dr. Caul, reading from notes, including a letter he had sent to Goldsberry on November 19, answered at length:

The treatment of any patient with the diagnosis of multiple personality should be undertaken only by a mental health professional, preferably a psychiatrist who meets the following criteria:

One—He (or she) must accept the condition. It should not be undertaken by someone who "doesn't believe" in this phenomenon.

Two—If the psychiatrist is not experienced but is willing to undertake such treatment and accept the conditions, he should be supervised by, or at least have ongoing consultation with, a colleague who has such experience and expertise.

Three—He should have available the techniques of hypnosis as an adjunct in therapy if it is needed. This is not a necessity but is highly desirable.

Four—He should have read significant literature on the subject and personally should have attended some form of continuing education in this regard.

Five—He should possess the quality of almost infinite patience as well as tolerance and perseverance. Treatment of such a case requires an ongoing commitment to what will surely be long, laborious, and difficult theraphy.

Some general principles of therapy that are now accepted by those who have treated multiples are as follows:

One—All of the personalities must be identified and recognized.

Two—The therapist must ascertain the reason for the existence of such personalities.

Three—The therapist must then be willing to do therapy with all of the personalities in an attempt to effect change.

Four—The therapist should focus on whatever positive qualities may be identified and attempt to bring about some sort of compromise among the alter personalities, especially those which may pose a threat to the self or others.

Five—The patient must become fully aware of the nature and extent of the problems and must be helped through therapy, to contribute to positive resolution. In other words, Counselor, the patient must become aware of the treatment process and not just be a passive recipient of the therapy.

Six—Antipsychotic medication should be avoided, since it has become fairly well known that it may produce fragmentation as well as other side effects detrimental to treatment.

These are but some of the issues involved in doing therapy with such cases. By no means is this a complete description of how one does such therapy.

The deposition went on to explore these criteria in depth.

When Belinky suggested in cross-examination that Caul had referred to the conditions for treating multiple personality as optimal, Caul responded sharply: "No sir, I didn't say that these were basically the optimal. I would even say that those are *minimal*. Counselor, I believe that should be the scene for openers in treating a multiple. Otherwise a person should leave them alone and not treat them."

When Milligan was brought back from the hospital after lunch, he had changed his shirt. The writer suspected the Teacher was gone.

Goldsberry and Thompson called Dr. George Harding, Jr., to the stand. After he summarized his involvement in the Milligan case, Dr. Harding said he still felt Athens was the proper place for Billy's treatment.

"Dr. Harding," asked Belinky, in cross-examination, isn't multiple personality very rare?"

"It is."

"Aren't we all different people inside?"

"The difference," said Dr. Harding, "is the amnesia."

"How do you prove amnesia? Couldn't it be faked?"

"We were very careful," Harding said. "We made repeated explorations. We approached it skeptically. His amnesia was legitimate. He was not feigning."

"Dr. Harding," Goldsberry asked, in redirect examination, "did *you* use case histories and other hospital records to come to *your* diagnosis?"

"I did. We used everything we could find."

"Do you think it is *necessary* for a psychiatrist to use past records and the opinions of other treating physicians in arriving at a diagnosis?"

"I believe it's absolutely essential."

When Harding was shown the letter by Dr. Caul setting forth the criteria for treating multiple personality, he told the court he felt it was an excellent statement, and agreed that those conditions were the minimum requirements.

Harding was followed to the witness stand by Psychologist Dorothy Turner, who testified that she had seen Billy on almost a daily basis before his trial and had given several of the personalities intelligence tests.

"What were the results?" Goldsberry asked.

"Two had IQ's of 68 to 70. One was average. Another was cleary superior—an IQ of 130."

"Is it possible," Belinsky asked, "that these IQ differences could have been faked?"

"Absolutely not," Turner said with anger in her voice. "I have no doubt that there was no way to fake these differences."

Dr. Stella Karolin testified that she had arrived independently at the same diagnosis as Dorothy Turner, Dr. Cornelia Wilbur and Dr. George Harding. Karolin had seen Milligan in April, June and July of this year and felt he was still split.

"What if there are other problems?" Belinky asked.

"The multiple personality should be treated first," Karolin said. "He may have other mental problems—different personalities might have different illnesses—but the overall problem should be treated first."

"Do you think he was receiving correct treatment in Athens?"

"I do."

Goldsberry showed her the Caul letter. She nodded and agreed that these were the minimum basic requirements.

After Harding, Karolin and Turner were dismissed as witnesses, they were permitted to remain in the courtroom as observers.

For the first time in his life, at three-fifty that afternoon, Billy Milligan was allowed to testify in his own behalf.

With the handcuffs on, it was difficult for him to place his left hand on the Bible and raise his right hand. He bent over and smiled as he tried to do it. Then, after swearing to tell the whole truth and nothing but the truth, he took his seat and looked up at the judge.

"Mr. Milligan," Judge Kinworthy said, "I am going to advise you that although you have the right to participate in these proceedings, you cannot be compelled to testify. You may remain silent."

Billy nodded.

Alan Goldsberry began direct examination in his soft, precise manner. "Billy, do you recall speaking in this courtroom on October 12?"

"Yes, I do."

"I'd like to ask you about the treatment you're receiving at Lima State Hospital. Are you getting hypnotherapy?"

"No."

"Group therapy?"

"No."

"Music therapy?"

Billy looked at the judge. "They took a bunch of us into a room where there was a piano and told us to sit there. There was no therapist. We just sat around for hours."

"Do you have any confidence in Dr. Milkie?" Goldsberry asked.

"No. He ordered Stelazine. It messed me up."

"How would you describe your treatment?"

"When I got here, I was on Ward 22. A psychologist was very rude to me. I went to sleep."

"When did you first learn you were a multiple personality, Billy?"

"At the Harding Hospital. I kind of believed it, but I really *knew* it when I saw the videotapes at the Athens Mental Health Center."

"Why do you think it happened, Billy?"

"Because of the things my stepfather did to me. I didn't want to be me anymore. I didn't want to be Billy Milligan."

"Could you give us an example of what happens to you when you're a multiple personality?"

"Well, it's like this. One day I was standing in front of a mirror in my apartment shaving. I'd had problems. I'd just moved to Columbus and I felt bad because I didn't leave home on good terms. I was standing there shaving, and it was as if the lights went out. It was real peaceful. When I opened my eyes, I was on a jet plane. I got real scared. I didn't know where I was going until we landed and I found out it was San Diego."

The courtroom was silent. The judge listened attentively. The woman at the taping equipment looked up at Billy Milligan, her mouth open, eyes staring in amazement.

David Belinky rose to cross-examine the witness.

"Billy, why did you trust Dr. Caul and not the doctors at Lima?"

"I had a strange trust in Dr. Caul from the day I met him. The policeman who brought me there from Columbus a year ago had put the handcuffs on me real tight." He held his handcuffs up to show how loose they were now. "Dr. Caul started yelling at the policeman for having them so tight, and he made him take them off. It didn't take me long to know he was on my side."

"Wouldn't it be better for you to cooperate with the treatment at Lima?" asked Belinky.

"I can't give *myself* therapy," Billy said. "Ward A is run like a sheep-dip—in and out. At Athens, I had my regressions, but I had to learn to correct them. They knew how to handle it—not with punishment but with treatment, with therapy."

During his closing remarks, Belinky argued that it was the burden of the state to prove only that the respondent was mentally ill and subject to hospitalization. The diagnosis didn't have to be proven. The only *current* testimony, he said, was from Dr. Caul and Dr. Milkie. Dr. Caul had said emphatically that Billy Milligan was still mentally ill. And Dr. Milkie had said that Lima State Hospital was the least restrictive environment in which to treat this patient.

"I urge the court," Belinky said, "to commit him to Lima."

Steve Thompson, in his summation, pointed out that an awesome array of psychiatric talent had been presented to the court on behalf of his client, and all agreed with the diagnosis of multiple personality.

"Once this is done, the question now is, How do we treat him?" Thompson said. "Taking into account Billy Milligan's mental status, these experts agree that he should be sent to Athens as the most appropriate place for treatment. All these expert witnesses agree that he needs long-term treatment. On October 4 he was transferred to Lima and examined by a physician who claims he made no reference to his prior medical history or treatment, and he concludes that Billy Milligan is a threat to himself and others. And how does he come to the conclusion he is a threat? Based on prior convictions, Your

Honor. Based on the stale evidence introduced into these hearings. Dr. Milkie says he displays antisocial behavior. Dr. Milkie says Billy Milligan showed no improvement. Your Honor, it is clear that Dr. Milkie is not an expert in multiple personality. It is the position of the respondent that the quality of experts are on Billy Milligan's side."

Judge Kinworthy announced he would take the matter under advisement and render a decision in not more than ten days. Until then, Milligan would remain at Lima.

On December 10, 1979, the court made the following findings:

1. The respondent is a mentally ill person in that his condition represents a substantial disorder of thought, mood, perception, orientation and memory that grossly impairs his judgment, behavior and capacity to recognize reality.

2. That respondent's mental illness is a condition diagnosed as multiple personality.

3. That respondent is a mentally ill person subject to hospitalization by Court order in that, because of his illness, he represents a substantial risk of physical harm to himself as manifested by evidence of threats of suicide; represents a substantial risk of physical harm to others as manifested by evidence of recent violent behavior; and further that he would benefit from treatment in a hospital for his mental illness and is in need of such treatment as manifested by evidence of behavior that creates a grave and imminent risk to the substantial rights of others and to himself.

4. That respondent, due to his mental illness, is dangerous to himself and to others and therefore requires hospitalization in a maximum security facility.

5. That by reason of respondent having been diagnosed as a multiple personality, his treatment should be consistent with such diagnosis.

It is ordered therefore that the said respondent be committed to the Lima State Hospital, Lima, Ohio, for treatment consistent with the diagnosis of said respondent as a multiple personality and that copies under seal of the findings in this case be transmitted to the Lima State Hospital, Lima, Ohio.

David R. Kinworthy, Judge
Allen County Common Pleas Court
Probate Division

(4)

Billy called the writer from the Lima State Hospital male infirmary on December 18. He had been badly beaten by a hospital employee. A Lima attorney who had been appointed guardian ad litem at the hearing had taken Polaroids of welts across his back from being whipped with an extension cord. Billy's eyes and face were blackened, and he had two cracked ribs.

The hospital administrators released a statement to the press saying that following an "altercation with an attendant," Milligan was found to have no injuries other than those that had been apparently self-inflicted.

The next day, after a visit by Attorney Steve Thompson, the Lima administration reversed itself, issuing a statement confirming that Milligan had "subsequently been severely injured." Both the FBI and the Ohio State Highway Patrol were called in to make investigations for possible submission to the grand jury.

Thompson was outraged by the reports from Billy as well as from the Lima attorney, and he released a statement reported only on the radio. "Ultimately, anyone who is incarcerated still has the protection of his civil rights," he told the newscaster, "and in Ohio statutory law, patients have rights that were granted by the recent amendments to the mental health bill—patients' civil rights. Under the United States statutes, they have the protection of the federal civil rights bills, too. And those ultimately can be enforced in court. It would be too early to say what's going to happen here."

The Lima State Hospital "Third Monthly Treatment Plan Review" of January 2, 1980, made the determination that:

> The Patient's treatment plan is both valid and proper for his condition.
>
> Patient's diagnosis is: (1) Psuedopsychopathic Schizophrenia (DSM II, 295.5) with dissociative episodes; (2) R/O Anti-Social Personality, hostile subtype (DSM II, 301.7); (3) Alcohol Addiction (DSM II, 303-2) by history; and (4) Drug Dependence, stimulants (304.6) by history.
>
> The patient was referred to the ITU Unit a couple of weeks ago due to the patient's acting out, violently, at the male hospital

. . . The patient, I believe, has been adversely affected by the notoriety which he has received in the paper, and as such, is carrying around this "star status" attitude . . . Mr. Milligan shows marked characteristics of the true psychopath, and as such is [as] hard to deal with as any other psychopathic patient. . . . In addition, the patient displays many of the characteristics of Hysteric Personality. Even though this disorder is usually seen in females, there are numerous cases of male hysterical personality. This condition should not be ruled out.

[signed] Lewis A. Linder, M.D.
Staff psychiatrist 1/4/80
[signed] J. William McIntosh, Ph.D.
Psychologist 1/4/80
[signed] John Doran, M.A.
Psychology Assistant 1/7/80

Angered at the Lima State Hospital officials for not adhering to Judge Kinworthy's court order to treat Milligan as a multiple personality, Alan Goldsberry and Steve Thompson filed a contempt-of-court motion against the Lima authorities and the Ohio State Department of Mental Health. They pressed the Office of the State Director of Mental Health to transfer Billy Milligan to a less restrictive hospital.

(5)

Locked in the strong ward of the Lima State Hospital for the Criminally Insane, the unfused Billy Milligan checked out a pencil from one of the attendants and began to write the first of a series of letters to the writer:

Suddenly an attendant, stepping through the doorway, belched a threatening command to the patients of ward 22.

"All right you stupid mother fuckers lets clear out this God Damn day hall. Move it. NOW!" Pausing for another gasp and to adjust the juicy cigar stub he mumbled, "When the glass is cleaned up we'll call *yous* ass holes, but until then get the fuck in your rooms."

Glaring coldly at us, the small crowd got out of their hard back chairs and zombied down the hall until the closing clanks of the big iron doors began. The expressionless men that wore drooling towels like bibs walked even slower but the burly attendants hurried them with a stinging crack of the wide leather belts, allowing them no dignity whatsoever. Thorazine, Prolixion, Haldol and any other psychotropic drug on the market maintained and assured obedience of the strictest kind, so it was fed like candy. No humanity, but I almost forgot. We are not human. *Clank!*

Every joint in my body seemed to stiffen and freeze as I stepped in claustrophobically ridden 8 by 10 room and pulled the door. *Clank.* Edging over to sit on my bed is becoming more of a chore but I did adjust myself on the plastic mattress. With the mass of nothingness I decided to use my imagination on the chipping paint on the opposite wall. I could conjure up silhouette images for my own amusement and try to identify them. Today, only faces, old, ugly and ravaged demonic faces seemed to hallucinate from the chips of an aging institution. It was scary but I allowed it. The wall was laughing at me. I hate that wall. Damn that wall! It wants to come closer and closer and laugh harder. The sweat from my brow was stinging my eyes but I fought to keep them open. I have to guard that wall, or that loud laughing wall will move in on me, invade me, crush me. I will stay frozen and guard the damn loud laughing wall. 410 men declared criminally insane shadow the endless halls of this God forgotten pit. I grow angry at the fact that the State had the gall to call this place a hospital. Lima State Hospital. *Clank!*

Silence fell over Ward 22 except the tinkling and sweeping of the broken window. Someone smashed a small window in the day hall where we sit against the wall in hard, thick wooden chairs. You sit, you may smoke. You do not talk, you have both feet on the floor, or life will get very hard on you. Who broke a window? Now the attendants will be in a bitchy mood because their card game was interrupted and one will be ordered to stay in the dayroom if they will let us out of our little boxes.

—I could hear nothing, dazed in my trance-like stupor. My body was numb and hollow. The damn loud laughing wall stopped laughing. The wall was a wall and the chips were chips. My hands were cold but clammy and the thumping of my heart echoes inside my hollow body. The waitful anxiety began to choke me, waiting to come out of my little box, but I remain frozen on my bed staring at the silent, motionless wall. Me, a nothingness zombie in a nothingness box in a nothingness hell. Saliva trying to spill over my dry parched lips was a sure sign that the psychotropic medication was fighting for control of my mind, soul and body. Should I fight it? Declare it the winner?

Succumb to the third world to escape the tragic realities that lie beyond my steel door? Is life worth living in the jaws of society's trash can for misfit minds? What can I possibly achieve or contribute to mankind in this steel and concrete box with a damn loud laughing wall that moves? Just give up? More questions raced through my mind like a 33 record set on 78, growing more and more intense. Suddenly a horrifying shock volted through my body that threw my slumped shoulders back and set me even more upright. Reality forcing itself upon me like a vicious slap in the face broke my trance and cracked my frozen joints. Something was crawling up my spine. My imagination? After gathering what few senses I had left I knew it was not. There was something crawling up my spine. I reacted by jerking my shirt over my head ignoring the fact it had buttons. Blind fear has no mercy for material items. 3 buttons popped. Flinging the shirt to the floor the feeling left my back. Peering down at the shirt I saw the invader. A cockroach about 3 centimeters long and black had been tap dancing on my lumbars. The gross insect was harmless but shocking. The rodent did make up my mind for me. I came back to this side of reality but was still thinking about my inner-debate. I did let the hideous little thing go. Secretly I was content with the awareness I had of myself, proud of the mental and physical victory. I am not a mental basket case. I still had some fight in me. I have not lost but I have not won. I broke a window and I don't even know why.

The writer received a letter, dated January 30, from another patient at Lima:

Dear Sir,

Let me get to the main point. Within twenty four hours of Bill's visit by his attorney, Bill was transferred from I.T.U. 5 to I.T.U. 9. Nine is a stronger ward than five.

The decision for the transfer was made by the "team personnel" in the daily team meeting. It came as a surprise and shock for Bill, yet he handled it well . . .

The only time Bill and I can converse now is at recreation. This is where I found out that the pressure on him was on full. He says his visits, mail, phone calls are all cut off until he fires his attorneys. He has been told to stop the book, and is harassed by attendants. (I too have been accused of aiding Bill on the

book and have realized that these people don't want the book
out.)

I was told Bill will be staying the remainder of his time here
on a strong ward . . .

[name withheld]

On March 12 the writer received a letter written in Serbo-
Croatian, postmarked Lima. The handwriting was unfamiliar.

Subata Mart Osmi 1980

Kako ste? Kazma nadamo. Zaluta Vreme. Ne lečenje Billy je
spavanje. On je U redu ne brinite. I dem na pega. Učinicu sve
šta mogu za gaň možete ra čunati na mene "Nužda ne poznaje
zakona."

Nemojete se
Ragen

Saturday March 8, 1980

How are you? I hope splendid. I lost time. There is no cure for
Billy in sleep. He is fine. Do not worry. I am going to rule. I will
do everything I can for him. You can count on me. "Necessity
knows no laws."

Ragen

EPILOGUE

In the months that followed, I kept in touch with Billy by mail and telephone. He continued to hope that the court of appeals would overturn the decision that had sent him to Lima, and that he would be able to return to Athens to continue his treatment with Dr. Caul.

On April 14, 1980, at a second review hearing, Judge Kinworthy threw out contempt-of-court charges filed by Billy's lawyer against Superintendent Ronald Hubbard and Clinical Director Lewis Lindner for not treating Billy as a multiple personality. The judge ordered that Billy remain at Lima.

During most of 1979, the Ohio legislature had been considering changes in the existing laws regarding persons found not guilty by reason of insanity. Before such an individual could be transferred to a less restrictive environment (as the law required), the county prosecutor would have the right to demand a hearing in the jurisdiction in which the crime had been committed. The patient's right to a review would be changed from every 90 days to every 180 days, and would also be open to the public, the press and TV. This soon came to be called by many, "the *Columbus Dispatch* law" or "the Milligan law."

Bernie Yavitch, who had been the prosecutor on the Milligan case, later told me he had worked on the subcommittee of the Ohio Prosecuting Attorneys Association that drafted the new law. Yavitch said: "The group was meeting, I guess, in response to the outcry that was going on over the Milligan situation . . ."

The new law, Senate Bill 297, was passed, effective May 20, 1980. Judge Flowers told me that the new law had been passed because of Billy.

413

* * *

On July 1, 1980, I received a letter postmarked Lima, with the word *Urgent* printed on the back of the envelope. When I opened it, I discovered a three-page letter written in flowing Arabic script. According to the translator, it was in perfect, fluent Arabic. It read, in part:

> Sometimes I do not know who I am or what I am. And sometimes I do not even know the other people surrounding me. The echo of the voices are still in my mind, but they have no meaning at all. Several faces appear to me, as if from a darkness, but I am feeling very fearful because my mind is totally divided.

> My [internal] family, in fact, is not in continuous contact with me at all, and have not been for a long time. . . . The events here in the last weeks were not very good. I am not responsible for it at all. I hate everything that transpires around me, but I can't stop it, and I can't alter it. . . .

It was signed "Billy Milligan." A few days later I received another letter, explaining who had written the first one.

> Again I am sorry for the non English letters. It really embarrasses me to do everything wrong. Arthur knows you don't speak Arabic but he sends you a dumb letter like that.

> Arthur has never tried to impress anyone so he must be getting mixed up and just forgot. Samuel was taught by Arthur about Arabic, but he never writes letters. Arthur says it is bad to boast. I wish he would talk to me. Bad things are happening and I don't know why.

> Arthur also speaks Swahili. Arthur read many books in Lebanon [prison] about the fundamentals of Arabic. He wanted to explore the pyramids and the Egyptian culture. He had to learn their language and to know what they wrote on the wall. I asked Arthur one day why he was interested in that big pile of triangled rocks. He told me that he was not as interested in what was in the tomb, but it might give a key to how the tomb got there. He said something about how it defies a law of physics and he was looking for the answer. He even made little cardboard pyramids, but David smashed them.

> [signed] Billy U.

During this period at the hospital, according to Billy, there was much harassment and beatings of patients by attendants, but besides Ragen, only Kevin, of all the personalities, stood up to the attendants. In recognition of this, Arthur removed him from the list of undesirables.

Kevin wrote to me on March 28, 1980:

Something very bad has happened but I don't know what. I did know it would be only a matter of time before total unfusion and Billy would go to sleep for good. Arthur said Billy had only a small taste of conscious life but unfortunately the taste was a bitter one. Day by day he grew weaker in this place. He could not understand the hate and jealousy displayed by the authority figures of this institution. They also provoked the patients to hurt him and make Ragen fight, but Billy could hold Ragen back . . . but not anymore. The doctors say bad things about us, and what hurts the most is they are right.

We, I, am a freak, a misfit, a biological error. We all hate this place but it is where we belong. We weren't accepted very well, were we?

Ragen is stopping everything for good. He has to. He said if you do not speak, you do no damage to anyone on the outside or inside. No one can blame us for anything. Ragen stopped the hearing. The span of attention will be turned inward and it will enforce the total block.

By shutting out the real world we can live peacefully in ours.

We know that a world without pain is a world without feeling . . . but a world without feeling is a world without pain.

Kevin

In October 1980, the State Department of Mental Health released the news that Lima was to be phased out as a state hospital for the criminally insane and would become a prison under the Department of Correction.

Once again the issue of where Milligan might be transferred made headlines. The possibility that he might be sent back to Athens or to another minimum-security hospital led Prosecutor Jim O'Grady to demand that under the new law, Billy be sent back to Columbus for his sanity review hearing. Judge Flowers agreed to hear his case.

Originally scheduled to take place on October 31, 1980, the hearing was postponed by mutual agreement to November 7, *after* election day. To avoid having the politicians and the press make the Milligan hearing a political issue, a delay was desirable.

But officials of the state Department of Mental Health used this delay to take action on their own. They informed Prosecutor O'Grady that the decision had been made to send Milligan to the new Dayton Forensic Center, which had opened in April. This new maximum-security facility was surrounded by double fences, topped by rolls of razor-ribbon concertina wire wrapped around barbed wire, and had a security system more stringent than most prisons. The prosecutor's office dropped its demand for a hearing.

On November 19, 1980, Billy Milligan was moved to the Dayton Forensic Center. Arthur and Ragen, sensing Billy-U's despair and afraid he might try to kill himself, put him to sleep again.

When he wasn't in the visiting room, he spent his time reading, writing and sketching. He was not allowed to paint. He had visits from Mary, a young outpatient he had met during his first months in Athens. She moved to Dayton so that she could see him daily. Billy was well behaved, and he told me he looked forward to his 180-day hearing, hoping that Judge Flowers would decide he didn't need a maximum-security institution and would send him back to Athens. He knew that Dr. Caul could treat him, fuse him again and bring back the Teacher. With Billy-U asleep, he said, things were now as they had been before Dr. Cornelia Wilbur wakened him.

I could see that he was deteriorating. Several times during my visits, he would tell me he didn't know who he was. When there was a partial fusion, he became a person with no name. Ragen, he reported, had lost the ability to speak English. People had stopped communicating with each other. I suggested he keep a daily log so whoever was on the spot could write messages. It worked for a while, but interest flagged and the entries were fewer and fewer.

On April 3, 1981, Billy had his 180-day hearing. Of the four psychiatrists and two mental health professionals who testified, only Dr. Lewis Lindner of Lima, who had not seen him in five months, testified that he should be kept in maximum security.

A letter was introduced by the prosecutor into evidence. In it Milligan was apparently responding to news that another patient at Lima had planned to have Dr. Lindner killed. "Your tactic is completely wrong . . . Have you considered the fact that not many doctors would consider taking your case, knowing they may be hit for saying the wrong thing? But in fact, if Lindner has damaged you and your case beyond repair and if you feel your life is over because you're going to spend eternity behind bars, you have my blessing."

When Milligan was called to the witness stand and asked his name under oath, he said, "Tommy." Tommy explained that Allen had written the letter in an attempt to talk the other patient out of killing Dr. Lindner. "It's wrong to go around shooting people just because they testify against you in court. Dr. Lindner testified against me today, but I certainly wouldn't shoot him for it."

Judge Flowers deferred his decision. The newspapers ran front-page stories, feature articles and editorials opposing any move to Athens.

While waiting to hear his fate, Allen spent most of his time at Dayton working on a painting for the cover of this book. He planned to send the editor several sketches to choose from, but one morning he awoke to discover that one of the children had come out while he was asleep and scribbled over the sketches with orange crayon. On the morning of the assigned deadline, Allen worked furiously and finished the desired oil painting on time.

On April 21, 1981, the Fourth District Court of Appeals of Ohio ruled on the judgment of the court that had sent Billy to Lima. It found that removing him from a less restrictive setting to the maximum-security mental health facility in Ohio, the Lima State Hospital, "without notice to that person or his family, without allowing the patient to be present, to consult with counsel, to call witnesses, or to in general advise him of or allow him the rights of a full hearing . . . is a fatal violation . . . and must result in the reversal of the transfer order and the replacement of the patient in his position prior to the unlawful transfer proceeding."

Although the appeals court found this judicial error, they decided that the error was not prejudicial, since Milligan had

had a hearing in Allen County that "found upon what we must presume to be sufficient and adequate evidence that appellant, due to his mental illness, was a danger to himself and others . . ."

The appeals court, therefore, disagreed with Judge Jones' actions, but would not return Billy to Athens. Goldsberry and Thompson have since appealed this decision to the supreme court of Ohio.

On May 20, 1981, six and a half weeks after the 180-day hearing, Judge Flowers handed down his decision. His court entry gives two explanations: First, "the Court in its decision weighs heavily upon State's Exhibit #1 [the letter] and its interpretation by Dr. Lewis Lindner's testimony. The Court finds this persuasive by a clear and convincing standard that William S. Milligan presently lacks accepted moral restraints, shows familiarity with the criminal sub-culture, and shows a disregard for human life." Second, the judge found that Dr. David Caul's testimony, given in a deposition, "that he would be unwilling to accept Court imposed limitations" made the Athens Mental Health Center "less than adequate."

Making no references to the other psychologists and psychiatrists who had testified that Milligan was *not* dangerous, Judge Flowers ordered continued treatment at the Dayton Forensic Hospital "as the least restrictive alternative available consistent with the treatment goals of the defendant and with the public safety." Judge Flowers further *authorized* Milligan to submit to treatment by a Dayton psychologist (who had informed the judge earlier that she had no experience in the treatment of multiple personality)—"at his [Milligan's] own expense." This decision was handed down three and a half years from the time Billy Milligan had been arrested and brought before Judge Flowers; two years and five months after Judge Flowers had found him not guilty by reason of insanity.

Alan Goldsberry immediately filed an appeal and brief with the 10th Appellate District in Franklin County, Ohio, challenging Senate Bill 297 (the Milligan law) as a denial of equal protection of the law and a denial of due process, and therefore unconstitutional. He also argued that its application to Billy Milligan "retroactively" was a violation of the Ohio constitution's protection against retroactive laws.

* * *

Billy did not seem bitter at the appeals court ruling against him, or at Judge Flowers' decision. I had the impression he was weary of it all.

Billy and I still talk frequently by phone, and I visit him at Dayton from time to time. Sometimes it's Tommy, or Allen, or Kevin. At other times he's the one with no name.

On one of my visits, when I asked who he was, he said, "I don't know who I am. I feel hollow."

I asked him to tell me about it.

"When I'm not asleep and not on the spot," he said, "it's like I'm lying face down on a sheet of glass that stretches out forever, and I can look down through it. Beyond that, in the farthest ground, it seems like stars of outer space, but then there's a circle, a beam of light. It's almost as if it's coming out of my eyes because it's always in front of me. Around it, some of my people are lying in coffins. The lids aren't on them because they're not dead yet. They're asleep, waiting for something. There are some empty coffins because not everyone has come there. David and the other young ones want a chance at life. The older ones have given up hope."

"What is this place?" I asked him.

"David named it," he said, "because he made it. David calls it 'the Dying Place.'"

AFTERWORD

Since first publication of this book, I have received letters from readers all over the country asking what happened to Billy Milligan after Judge Flowers turned down his request to be transferred to Athens.

To sum it up briefly:

In his notes to me, "Allen" described the Lima State Hospital for the Criminally Insane as "a chamber of horrors." He later referred to the Dayton Forensic Center as an "ultra-clean germ-tank jail." Dayton's superintendent, Allen Vogel, was sympathetic and understanding of Milligan's needs, but he was increasingly hampered by his security staff. Though Vogel gave Milligan permission to paint in oils, and "Tommy" and "Allen" ordered art supplies brought in, Vogel was overruled by his security office on the grounds that the linseed oil used in painting could be dangerous. The art supplies were removed from the hospital.

Increasingy depressed, Allen insisted that Mary, his friend and constant visitor, return to graduate school and make a life of her own. "I just can't keep her in prison with me," he said.

Several weeks after Mary left Dayton, another young woman entered Milligan's life. Tanda, a resident of Dayton, who regularly visited her brother at the Dayton Forensic Center, became aware of Milligan in the visitors' room. Her brother introduced them. Soon she began to do for Milligan some of the things Mary had done for him: typing, bringing in outside food, buying him clothing.

On July 22, 1981, Tanda called me and said she was worried about Billy. He wasn't changing his clothes, or shaving, or eating. He was withdrawing from all outside contacts. He had, she felt, lost interest in living.

When I went to visit him at the hospital, Tommy told me that Arthur, having given up hope of treatment and cure, had decided to commit suicide.

I argued that there had to be an alternative to suicide—a transfer from Dayton. I had learned that Dr. Judyth Box, a psychiatrist who had testified on his behalf at the last court hearing, had recently been appointed clinical director at the newly opened Central Ohio Regional Forensic Unit (CORFU), in Columbus.

At first, Tommy refused to consider a transfer from one maximum security hospital to another. CORFU was part of the Central Ohio Psychiatric Hospital (COPH), where Milligan had spent three months when he was fifteen years old. If he couldn't get back to Athens and Dr. David Caul, Tommy insisted, he might as well be dead. I pointed out that since Dr. Box had treated other multiple personality patients, knew Dr. Caul very well, and had already shown interest in Billy's case, she might be able to help him. Tommy finally agreed to be transferred.

The Department of Mental Health, the prosecutor, and the judge agreed that since this would be an internal transfer from one maximum security hospital to another, no court hearing would be required. But the wheels turned slowly.

One day, before the transfer, I received a call from another patient who said that Milligan—afraid he might hurt someone and jeopardize the transfer to Columbus—had volunteered to be put into seclusion. After four security guards got him into the seclusion room and strapped down his arms and legs, they jumped on him and beat him.

When I next saw Allen, on August 27, his left arm, now black and blue, was swollen, his left hand paralyzed. His left leg was bandaged. On September 22, 1981, he was transferred to the Central Ohio Regional Forensic Unit—in a wheelchair.

Shortly after his transfer, the Department of Mental Health filed a lawsuit against Billy Milligan for fifty thousand dollars to pay for his involuntary hospitalization and treatment at Athens, Lima, and Dayton. Billy's attorneys later filed a countersuit, charging for murals he painted on the walls of Lima State Hospital and asking damages for physical abuse and malpractice. The countersuit was denied. The state's suit is still pending.

Tanda, eager to be close to him, got a job in Columbus and moved in with his sister, Kathy. She loved him, she said, and wanted to be able to visit him often.

Dr. Box began the intensive therapy methods that had earlier been successful in fusing the personalities at the Athens Mental Health Center. She worked with David, Ragen, Arthur, Allen, Kevin, and, finally, was able to reach the Teacher. Each time I visited, Allen or Tommy would tell me I had just missed seeing the Teacher. Finally, I left them instructions to post a message in the room. The next time the Teacher was there, he was to phone me. About a week later, I got a call from him, saying "Hi, I hear you've been wanting to talk to me."

It was the first time I had spoken to the Teacher since we had gone over the manuscript of the book together, in Lima. Now we talked for a long time, and he was able to fill in some of the gaps that the others had no knowledge of.

One day the Teacher called and said, "I've got to tell someone. I'm in love with Tanda, and she's in love with me. We want to get married." They planned the wedding for December 15th so that Dr. Box could attend before she went on her month long vacation to her native Australia.

As part of the treatment plan, Dr. Box moved Milligan onto a new ward, along with three other patients she had tentatively diagnosed as multiples. Since multiple personalities required specialized treatment and attention, she felt it might be best to have them together. Dr. Box was not prepared for the criticism by Columbus politicians which followed, two weeks before election day.

The *Columbus Dispatch* reported on October 17, 1981, that State Representative Don Gilmore, R-Columbus, had charged that Billy Milligan was receiving preferential treatment at the Columbus hospital, including: "Allowing Milligan to choose the patients who will live with him on the ward." Though hospital administrators denied that Milligan was getting any preferential treatment, Gilmore continued to press his accusations.

The Columbus *Citizen-Journal* of November 19, reported:

GILMORE CALLS FOR NEW MILLIGAN PROBE

Despite assurances that William Milligan is receiving no extra privileges at the Central Ohio Psychiatric Hospital, a state representative has asked for another investigation into the possibility. . . .

One of Gilmore's concerns centered around an incident several weeks ago when Milligan . . . reportedly ordered a bologna sandwich at 2:30 A.M. He said the hospital staff then had to prepare sandwiches for everyone in Milligan's ward . . .

Tanda tried for weeks to find a preacher, minister, priest, or judge who would perform the ceremony. Finally, she found a young Methodist minister, director of the city's new transient "open shelter," who agreed to marry them. Gary Witte had hoped to remain anonymous, fearing that the publicity might harm his work at the shelter. However, a *Columbus Dispatch* reporter recognized and identified him. "My personal philosophy," the young minister told him, "is that I've always been for the underdog. . . . I did the ceremony because nobody else would do it . . ."

The marriage took place on December 22, 1981, with only the minister, an officer of the probate court who had brought the marriage license, and myself present. Dr. Box had already left for Australia. It was the Teacher who placed the ring on Tanda's finger, and kissed her. Since Ohio does not have conjugal visits, there would be no possibility for them to be alone together unless he was transferred to a minimum security or a civil-mental hospital.

After the wedding, Tanda faced the dozens of waiting reporters, photographers, and TV cameramen at a brief press conference. She told them she had met most of the personalities and they had accepted her. She said a day would come when they would live a normal life.

Soon afterward, the Teacher and Tanda began to notice ominous changes. The Teacher was taken off all medication. Security began a pattern of shaking down his room, and strip-searching him before and after each visitor. Even Tanda was strip-searched on occasion when she came to visit. Both of them found it humiliating and felt it was calculated harassment.

When Dr. Box returned from Australia, she learned that her contract would not be renewed by the Department of Mental Health. "I was squeezed out," she told me.

The *Columbus Dispatch* reported the story on January 17, 1982:

MILLIGAN'S PSYCHIATRIST QUITS STATE JOB

Dr. Judyth M. Box, psychiatrist of convicted [*sic*] multiple personality rapist William S. Milligan, has resigned her state job in a dispute with officials at the Central Ohio Forensic Hospital.

State Rep. Don E. Gilmore, R-Columbus, lauded the resignation . . .

The Teacher fragmented.

Milligan's new therapist, Dr. John ("Jay") Davis, a young, ex-Navy psychiatrist, was skeptical when he took over the case, but he found himself drawn into a study of Milligan's background. He won the confidence of most of the personalities and was able to work with them.

On February 12th, Kathy discovered her sister-in-law's clothing and possessions were missing, and Billy's car was gone. Tanda had left a note addressed to "Billy" saying she had taken all his money out of their joint bank account, but that she would pay it back some day. The note also said she knew it was wrong to steal away in the night, but she couldn't handle the pressure from all sides.

"I was in love, and I was gullible," Allen told me. "I felt broken. For a while I felt cold. Then I told myself I have to get over her and forget what she did to me. I have no right to judge all women by Tanda just as I have no right to judge all men by Daddy Chal."

Dr. Jay Davis was impressed by the way his patient handled the news. Although the personalities felt cheated and betrayed, they took it quite well.

On March 26, 1982, the commitment hearing was held in Judge Flowers' court to determine if Milligan was dangerous to himself or others, or if he could now be transferred to a minimum security hospital like the Athens Mental Health Center. The testimony of the psychiatrists and psychologists was contradictory.

The position of the prosecutor's office had been made clear in an interview given by the assistant Franklin County prosecutor, Thomas D. Beal, to a reporter of the Columbus *Citizen-Journal*, published on January 14: ". . . I'm kind of hoping there is [evidence Milligan is violent] so we can have more ammunition to keep him in a maximum security facility."

At the hearing, Dr. Mijo Zakman, clinical director of COPH, testified that he and two other psychiatrists had examined Milligan for about two hours, in preparation for the hearing, and reported they saw no personalities. Milligan, he said, was not mentally ill at all but was an antisocial personality.

This was a startling and threatening development. If the Department of Mental Health could convince Judge Flowers that Milligan was not mentally ill, he could be discharged from the hospital, be picked up immediately by the Ohio Adult Parole Authority, and sent to prison as a parole violator.

But Dr. Jay Davis testified, "He's at the baseline level . . . He is fragmented. I could name the personality sitting there right now, and it's not Billy."

He pointed out to Judge Flowers why Columbus was not the place for Milligan. "Maximum security facilities obstruct the therapy of multiple personality patients." If he stayed at the Columbus facility, Davis explained, the treatment was likely to be nonproductive.

Dr. Harry Eisel, a clinical psychologist, testified that he had administered the "Hand" test to several of the aggressive personalities to determine whether or not they might be dangerous. The "Hand" test, a series of pictures of hands in different positions, about which the patient makes judgments, is a projective technique to evaluate the individual's potential for violent behavior. Eisel testified that none of the personalities he had tested (I later learned they were Philip, Kevin, and Ragen) were dangerous to any significant degree.

Although a social worker testified for the prosecutor that Milligan had threatened him and his family, under cross-examination he admitted he was threatened often by mental patients, but that nothing had ever come of them.

Dr. Caul testified that he would accept Milligan for treatment and would abide by any restrictions imposed by the court.

On April 8, 1982, Judge Jay Flowers ordered the Department of Mental Health to transfer Billy Milligan back to the Athens Mental Health Center. He ordered that the patient be allowed to paint and do woodworking, but he also suggested close supervision off the ward. Before Milligan could be permitted to leave the hospital grounds, the court must be notified. "People say he deserves another chance," Judge Flowers said. "Let's give him another chance."

At eleven o'clock, on the morning of April 15, 1982, after two and a half years in three Ohio maximum security hospitals, Billy Milligan was returned to Athens.

I visit him regularly, and speak with Tommy or Allen. According to both of them, there has been no co-consciousness among the "people" for a long time. Allen hears the voices in his head—the British and Yugoslav accents—but neither he nor Tommy can get through to them, or to each other. There is no communication inside. There is much lost time. The Teacher has not, at this writing, returned.

Tommy is painting landscapes. Danny is painting still lifes. Allen is painting portraits, and making notes of the incredible experiences at Lima, Dayton, and Columbus, and how his people coped and survived.

Dr. David Caul has begun the difficult task of undoing the damage of the past two and a half years, and of trying to put pieces back together again. No one knows how long it will take.

Although Billy Milligan's return to Athens stirred up controversy in Columbus that upset him, he was pleased when he read a copy of the Ohio University student newspaper. *The Post* had published an editorial on April 12th, anticipating the transfer:

". . . Milligan, who has certainly not been given a fair shake in life, has come to Athens to be treated by the experts here. And this community, if it does anything at all, should help to give him the supportive atmosphere he needs . . . We're not asking you to welcome Milligan with open arms. But we are asking you to understand. It's the least he deserves."

Athens, Ohio
May 7, 1982

AUTHOR'S NOTE

Among the many documents I examined for background before writing this book, I found two puzzling reports of electroencephalograms taken of Billy Milligan's brain. These were done two weeks apart in May, 1978, by different physicians, while he was being examined under court order at Harding Hospital. Current research has shed new light on the meaning of Milligan's EEG's.

Dr. Frank W. Putnam, Jr., a psychiatrist at the National Institute of Mental Health, has discovered that the alter personalities of multiple personality subjects have measurably different physiological characteristics from each other and from the "core personality," including different galvanic skin response and different patterns of brain wave activity.

In a recent telephone interview, I discussed with Dr. Putnam the EEG brain wave research he had presented at the May, 1982, Toronto meeting of the American Psychiatric Association. He had made a series of controlled tests on ten subjects who had previously been diagnosed as having the multiple personality disorder, testing, in each case, the core personality and two or three alter personalities. As controls, he used ten other individuals, matched with the subjects for age and sex, who had been instructed to invent alter personalities of their own choosing, with detailed histories and traits, and to practice switching to these personalities.

The tests were repeated in random order, for each core and alter personality, on five different days—a total of fifteen or twenty tests for each body. While the control subjects and their pretended personalities showed no significant change in brain wave patterns, *the personalities of the diagnosed multiples showed marked differences from their core and from each other.*

According to *Science News* (May 29, 1982), Dr. Putnam's findings are supported by research at the Institute for Living, in Hartford, Connecticut, in which psychologist Collin Pitblado reported similar results with one multiple-personality patient's four personalities.

After learning of this new research, I went back to my files and looked at the Milligan EEG's made four years before the presentation of Putnam's results.

On May 9, 1978, Dr. P. R. Hyman, M.D., reported that the tracing made that day was "an abnormal electroencephalogram." Because of the activity of theta and delta waves [slow waves not normally seen in the brain of an awake adult, though seen in children] in the right rear hemisphere, Dr. Hyman wrote that the abnormality was probably due to a technical problem. He pointed out, "However, the technologist did not prove this one way or the other despite changing the electrode." He suggested a repeat EEG.

Dr. James Parker, M.D., wrote on May 22, 1978, that the localized area of abnormality that had appeared in the first EEG was not present in this second one. The second tracing revealed background intermittent alpha activity. Parker described this EEG as having "Abnormal bilateral theta and delta [and] bilateral temporal sharp waves." The sharp waves, he wrote, could be epileptiform.

Dr. Frank Putnam told me that ten to fifteen percent of the EEG's of multiple personality patients he had tested showed abnormal brain waves, and that these patients also had a history of having been diagnosed previously as epileptics. Similar case reports, he said, had been made at Harvard, of abnormal EEG's and multiple personality.

When I showed the descriptions of the Milligan EEG's to a registered EEG technologist, he assured me that they seemed to be describing two different people. I believe it is consistent with the results of the research done in this area to suggest that the EEG's done at Harding Hospital were actually administered to different personalities—probably the children.

In discussing the significance of the new research Dr. Putnam said, "The study of multiple personalities has something to offer the rest of us in terms of control of the mind and the body. I think multiples may, in fact, be one of those experiments of nature that will tell us a whole lot more about ourselves . . ."

July 20, 1982
Athens, Ohio

ABOUT THE AUTHOR

DANIEL KEYES, born in New York City, is a graduate
of Brooklyn College. His award-winning first novel,
Flowers for Algernon (filmed as *CHARLY*), is studied
in high schools and colleges across the country. Keyes
is married, has two grown daughters and is, at
present, professor of English at Ohio University in
Athens, Ohio.

We Deliver!
And So Do These Bestsellers.